# Scaling Networks
## Companion Guide

**Cisco Networking Academy**

**Cisco Press**

800 East 96th Street

Indianapolis, Indiana 46240 USA

# Scaling Networks Companion Guide

Cisco Networking Academy

Published by:
Cisco Press
800 East 96th Street
Indianapolis, IN 46240 USA

Printed in the United States of America

Second Printing July 2014

Library of Congress Control Number: 2014932475

ISBN-13: 978-1-58713-328-2
ISBN-10: 1-58713-328-8

## Warning and Disclaimer

This book is designed to provide information about the Cisco Networking Academy Scaling Networks course. Every effort has been made to make this book as complete and as accurate as possible, but no warranty or fitness is implied.

The information is provided on an "as is" basis. The authors, Cisco Press, and Cisco Systems, Inc. shall have neither liability nor responsibility to any person or entity with respect to any loss or damages arising from the information contained in this book or from the use of the discs or programs that may accompany it.

The opinions expressed in this book belong to the author and are not necessarily those of Cisco Systems, Inc.

**Publisher**
Paul Boger

**Associate Publisher**
Dave Dusthimer

**Business Operation Manager, Cisco Press**
Jan Cornelssen

**Executive Editor**
Mary Beth Ray

**Managing Editor**
Sandra Schroeder

**Development Editor**
Ellie C. Bru

**Project Editor**
Mandie Frank

**Copy Editor**
John Edwards

**Technical Editor**
Aubrey Adams

**Editorial Assistant**
Vanessa Evans

**Designer**
Mark Shirar

**Composition**
Bumpy Design

**Indexer**
Ken Johnson

**Proofreader**
Debbie Williams

# Trademark Acknowledgments

All terms mentioned in this book that are known to be trademarks or service marks have been appropriately capitalized. Cisco Press or Cisco Systems, Inc., cannot attest to the accuracy of this information. Use of a term in this book should not be regarded as affecting the validity of any trademark or service mark.

# Special Sales

For information about buying this title in bulk quantities, or for special sales opportunities (which may include electronic versions; custom cover designs; and content particular to your business, training goals, marketing focus, or branding interests), please contact our corporate sales department at corpsales@pearsoned.com or (800) 382-3419.

For government sales inquiries, please contact governmentsales@pearsoned.com.

For questions about sales outside the U.S., please contact international@pearsoned.com.

At Cisco Press, our goal is to create in-depth technical books of the highest quality and value. Each book is crafted with care and precision, undergoing rigorous development that involves the unique expertise of members from the professional technical community.

Readers' feedback is a natural continuation of this process. If you have any comments regarding how we could improve the quality of this book, or otherwise alter it to better suit your needs, you can contact us through email at feedback@ciscopress.com. Please make sure to include the book title and ISBN in your message.

We greatly appreciate your assistance.

| Americas Headquarters | Asia Pacific Headquarters | Europe Headquarters |
| --- | --- | --- |
| Cisco Systems, Inc. | Cisco Systems, Inc. | Cisco Systems International BV |
| 170 West Tasman Drive | 168 Robinson Road | Haarlerbergpark |
| San Jose, CA 95134-1706 | #28-01 Capital Tower | Haarlerbergweg 13-19 |
| USA | Singapore 068912 | 1101 CH Amsterdam |
| www.cisco.com | www.cisco.com | The Netherlands |
| Tel: 408 526-4000 | Tel: +65 6317 7777 | www-europe.cisco.com |
| 800 553-NETS (6387) | Fax: +65 6317 7799 | Tel: +31 0 800 020 0791 |
| Fax: 408 527-0883 | | Fax: +31 0 20 357 1100 |

Cisco has more than 200 offices worldwide. Addresses, phone numbers, and fax numbers are listed on the Cisco Website at **www.cisco.com/go/offices.**

©2007 Cisco Systems, Inc. All rights reserved. CCVP, the Cisco logo, and the Cisco Square Bridge logo are trademarks of Cisco Systems, Inc.; Changing the Way We Work, Live, Play, and Learn is a service mark of Cisco Systems, Inc.; and Access Registrar, Aironet, BPX, Catalyst, CCDA, CCDP, CCIE, CCIP, CCNA, CCNP, CCSP, Cisco, the Cisco Certified Internetwork Expert logo, Cisco IOS, Cisco Press, Cisco Systems, Cisco Systems Capital, the Cisco Systems logo, Cisco Unity, Enterprise/Solver, EtherChannel, EtherFast, EtherSwitch, Fast Step, Follow Me Browsing, FormShare, GigaDrive, GigaStack, HomeLink, Internet Quotient, IOS, IP/TV, iQ Expertise, the iQ logo, iQ Net Readiness Scorecard, iQuick Study, LightStream, Linksys, MeetingPlace, MGX, Networking Academy, Network Registrar, Packet, PIX, ProConnect, RateMUX, ScriptShare, SlideCast, SMARTnet, StackWise, The Fastest Way to Increase Your Internet Quotient, and TransPath are registered trademarks of Cisco Systems, Inc. and/or its affiliates in the United States and certain other countries.

All other trademarks mentioned in this document or Website are the property of their respective owners. The use of the word partner does not imply a partnership relationship between Cisco and any other company. (0609R)

## About the Contributing Author

**Allan Johnson** entered the academic world in 1999 after ten years as a business owner/operator to dedicate his efforts to his passion for teaching. He holds both an MBA and an M.Ed. in Occupational Training and Development. He is an information technology instructor at Del Mar College in Corpus Christi, Texas. In 2003, Allan began to commit much of his time and energy to the CCNA Instructional Support Team, providing services to Networking Academy instructors worldwide and creating training materials. He now works full-time for Cisco Networking Academy as a learning systems developer.

# Contents at a Glance

# Contents

# Icons Used in This Book

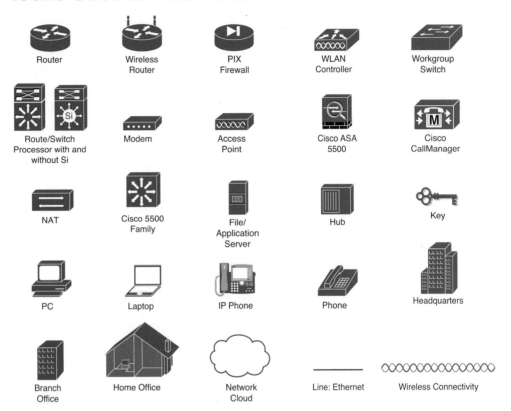

# Syntax Conventions

The conventions used to present command syntax in this book are the same conventions used in the IOS Command Reference. The Command Reference describes these conventions as follows:

- **Boldface** indicates commands and keywords that are entered literally as shown. In actual configuration examples and output (not general command syntax), boldface indicates commands that are manually input by the user (such as a **show** command).

- *Italics* indicate arguments for which you supply actual values.

- Vertical bars (|) separate alternative, mutually exclusive elements.

- Square brackets ([ ]) indicate an optional element.

- Braces ({ }) indicate a required choice.

- Braces within brackets ([{ }]) indicate a required choice within an optional element.

# Introduction

*Scaling Networks Companion Guide* is the official supplemental textbook for the Cisco Networking Academy Scaling Networks course. Cisco Networking Academy is a comprehensive program that delivers information technology skills to students around the world. The curriculum emphasizes real-world practical application, while providing opportunities for you to gain the skills and hands-on experience needed to design, install, operate, and maintain networks in small- to medium-sized businesses, as well as enterprise and service provider environments.

As a textbook, this book provides a ready reference to explain the same networking concepts, technologies, protocols, and devices as the online curriculum. This book emphasizes key topics, terms, and activities and provides some alternate explanations and examples as compared with the course. You can use the online curriculum as directed by your instructor and then use this Companion Guide's study tools to help solidify your understanding of all the topics.

## Who Should Read This Book

This book is intended for students enrolled in the Cisco Networking Academy Scaling Networks course. The book, as well as the course, is designed as an introduction to data network technology for those pursuing careers as network professionals as well as those who need only an introduction to network technology for professional growth. Topics are presented concisely, starting with the most fundamental concepts and progressing to a comprehensive understanding of network communication. The content of this text provides the foundation for additional Cisco Networking Academy courses, and preparation for the CCNA Routing and Switching certification.

## Book Features

The educational features of this book focus on supporting topic coverage, readability, and practice of the course material to facilitate your full understanding of the course material.

### Topic Coverage

The following features give you a thorough overview of the topics covered in each chapter so that you can make constructive use of your study time:

- **Objectives:** Listed at the beginning of each chapter, the objectives reference the core concepts covered in the chapter. The objectives match the objectives stated in the corresponding chapters of the online curriculum. However, the question format in the Companion Guide encourages you to think about finding the answers as you read the chapter.

- **Notes:** These are short sidebars that point out interesting facts, timesaving methods, and important safety issues.

- **Chapter summaries:** At the end of each chapter is a summary of the chapter's key concepts. It provides a synopsis of the chapter and serves as a study aid.

- **Practice:** At the end of each chapter, there is a full list of all the Labs, Class Activities, and Packet Tracer Activities to refer back to for study time.

## Readability

The following features have been updated to assist your understanding of the networking vocabulary:

- **Key terms:** Each chapter begins with a list of key terms, along with a page-number reference from inside the chapter. The terms are listed in the order in which they are explained in the chapter. This handy reference allows you to find a term, flip to the page where the term appears, and see the term used in context. The Glossary defines all the key terms.

- **Glossary:** This book contains an all-new Glossary with almost 200 terms.

## Practice

Practice makes perfect. This new Companion Guide offers you ample opportunities to put what you learn into practice. You will find the following features valuable and effective in reinforcing the instruction that you receive:

- **Check Your Understanding questions and answer key:** Updated review questions are presented at the end of each chapter as a self-assessment tool. These questions match the style of questions that you see in the online course. Appendix A, "Answers to 'Check Your Understanding' Questions," provides an answer key to all the questions and includes an explanation of each answer.

- **Labs and activities:** Throughout each chapter, you will be directed back to the online course to take advantage of the activities created to reinforce concepts. In addition, at the end of each chapter, there is a Practice section that collects a list of all the labs and activities to provide practice with the topics introduced in this chapter. The labs and class activities are available in the companion *Scaling Networks Lab Manual* (ISBN 978-1-58713-325-1). The Packet Tracer Activities PKA files are found in the online course.

- **Page references to online course:** After headings, you will see, for example, (1.1.2.3). This number refers to the page number in the online course so that you can easily jump to that spot online to view a video, practice an activity, perform a lab, or review a topic.

## Lab Manual

The supplementary book *Scaling Networks Lab Manual*, by Cisco Press (ISBN 978-1-58713-325-1), contains all the labs and class activities from the course.

## Practice and Study Guide

Additional Study Guide exercises, activities, and scenarios are available in the *CCNA Routing and Switching Practice and Study Guide* (ISBN 978-1-58713-344-2), by Allan Johnson. The Practice and Study Guide coordinates with the recommended curriculum sequence and follows the course outlines for *Scaling Networks and Connecting Networks*.

## About Packet Tracer Software and Activities

Interspersed throughout the chapters you'll find many activities to work with the Cisco Packet Tracer tool. Packet Tracer allows you to create networks, visualize how packets flow in the network, and use basic testing tools to determine whether the network would work. When you see this icon, you can use Packet Tracer with the listed file to perform a task suggested in this book. The activity files are available in the course. Packet Tracer software is available only through the Cisco Networking Academy website. Ask your instructor for access to Packet Tracer.

## How This Book Is Organized

This book corresponds closely to the Cisco Networking Academy Scaling Networks course and is divided into nine chapters, one appendix, and a glossary of key terms:

- **Chapter 1, "Introduction to Scaling Networks":** Introduces strategies that can be used to systematically design a highly functional network, such as the hierarchical network design model, the Cisco Enterprise Architecture, and appropriate device selections.

- **Chapter 2, "LAN Redundancy":** Focuses on the protocols used to manage redundancy (STP and FHRP) as well as some of the potential redundancy problems and their symptoms.

- **Chapter 3, "LAN Aggregation":** Describes EtherChannel, the methods used to create an EtherChannel, and the EtherChannel protocols PAgP and LACP. The configuration, verification, and troubleshooting of EtherChannel are discussed.

- **Chapter 4, "Wireless LANs":** Covers WLAN technology, components, security, planning, implementation, and troubleshooting. The types of network attacks to which wireless networks are particularly susceptible are discussed.

- **Chapter 5, "Adjust and Troubleshoot Single-Area OSPF":** Examines the methods for modifying the default operation of OSPF, including manipulating the DR/BDR election process, propagating default routes, fine-tuning the OSPFv2 and OSPFv3 interfaces, and enabling authentication. In addition, techniques for troubleshooting OSPFv2 and OSPFv3 are discussed.

- **Chapter 6, "Multiarea OSPF":** Multiarea OSPF is introduced as the method to effectively partition a large single area into multiple areas. Discussion is focused on the LSAs exchanged between areas. In addition, activities for configuring OSPFv2 and OSPFv3 are provided. The chapter concludes with the **show** commands used to verify OSPF configurations.

- **Chapter 7, "EIGRP":** Introduces EIGRP and provides basic configuration commands to enable it on a Cisco IOS router. It also explores the operation of the routing protocol and provides more detail on how EIGRP determines best path.

- **Chapter 8, "EIGRP Advanced Configurations and Troubleshooting":** Discusses methods for modifying the EIGRP for IPv4 and EIGRP for IPv6 implementations, including propagating a default, fine-tuning timers, and configuring authentication between EIGRP neighbors. In addition, techniques for troubleshooting EIGRP are discussed.

- **Chapter 9, "IOS Images and Licensing":** Explains the naming conventions and packaging of IOS Releases 12.4 and 15. Beginning with IOS Release 15, Cisco implemented a new packaging format and licensing process for IOS. This chapter discusses the process of obtaining, installing, and managing Cisco IOS Release 15 software licenses.

- **Appendix A, "Answers to 'Check Your Understanding' Questions":** This appendix lists the answers to the "Check Your Understanding" review questions that are included at the end of each chapter.

- **Glossary:** The glossary provides you with definitions for all the key terms identified in each chapter.

# CHAPTER 1

# Introduction to Scaling Networks

## Objectives

Upon completion of this chapter, you will be able to answer the following questions:

- How is the hierarchical network used in small business?

- What are the recommendations for designing a network that is scalable?

- What features in switch hardware are necessary to support small- to medium-sized business network requirements?

- What types of routers are available for small- to medium-sized business networks?

- What are the basic configuration settings for a Cisco IOS device?

## Key Terms

This chapter uses the following key terms. You can find the definitions in the Glossary.

# Introduction (1.0.1.1)

As a business grows, so do its networking requirements. Businesses rely on the network infrastructure to provide mission-critical services. Network outages can result in lost revenue and lost customers. Network designers must design and build an enterprise network that is scalable and highly available.

This chapter introduces strategies that can be used to systematically design a highly functional network, such as the *hierarchical network* design model, the *Cisco Enterprise Architecture*, and appropriate device selections. The goals of network design are to limit the number of devices impacted by the failure of a single network device, provide a plan and path for growth, and create a reliable network.

**Class Activity 1.0.1.2: Network by Design**

Your employer is opening a new branch office.

You have been reassigned to the site as the network administrator, where your job will be to design and maintain the new branch network.

The network administrators at the other branches used the Cisco three-layer hierarchical model when designing their networks. You decide to use the same approach.

To get an idea of what using the hierarchical model can do to enhance the design process, you research the topic.

# Implementing a Network Design (1.1)

Effective network design implementation requires a solid understanding of the current state of recommended network models and their ability to scale as the network grows.

## Hierarchical Network Design (1.1.1)

The hierarchical network model and the Cisco Enterprise Architecture are models to consider when designing a network. This section reviews the importance of scalability and how these models can effectively address that need.

### The Need to Scale the Network (1.1.1.1)

Businesses increasingly rely on their network infrastructure to provide mission-critical services. As businesses grow and evolve, they hire more employees, open branch offices, and expand into global markets. These changes directly affect the requirements of a network. A large business environment with many users, locations, and systems is referred to as an *enterprise*. The network that is used to support the business enterprise is called an *enterprise network*.

In Figure 1-1, the following steps occur as the network grows from a small company to a global enterprise:

1. The company begins as a small, single-location company.

2. The company increases its number of employees.

3. The company grows to multiple locations in the same city.

4. The enterprise grows to multiple cities.

5. The enterprise hires teleworkers.

6. The enterprise expands to other countries (not all enterprises are international).

7. The enterprise centralizes network management in a Network Operations Center (NOC).

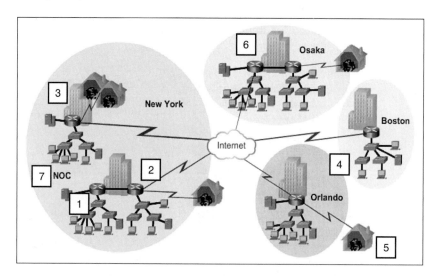

**Figure 1-1**   Scaling the Network as the Business Grows

An enterprise network must support the exchange of various types of network traffic, including data files, email, IP telephony, and video applications for multiple business units. All enterprise networks must

- Support critical applications
- Support converged network traffic

- Support diverse business needs

- Provide centralized administrative control

## Enterprise Business Devices (1.1.1.2)

Users expect enterprise networks, such as the example shown in Figure 1-2, to be up 99.999 percent of the time. Outages in the enterprise network prevent the business from performing normal activities, which can result in a loss of revenue, customers, data, and opportunities.

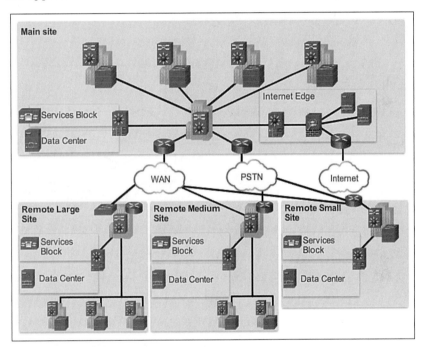

**Figure 1-2**  Large Enterprise Network Design

To obtain this level of *reliability*, high-end, enterprise-class equipment is commonly installed in the enterprise network. Designed and manufactured to more stringent standards than lower-end devices, enterprise equipment moves large volumes of network traffic.

Enterprise-class equipment is designed for reliability, with features such as redundant power supplies and failover capabilities. *Failover capability* refers to the ability of a device to switch from a nonfunctioning module, service, or device to a functioning one with little or no break in service.

Purchasing and installing enterprise-class equipment does not eliminate the need for proper network design.

## Hierarchical Network Design (1.1.1.3)

To optimize bandwidth on an enterprise network, the network must be organized so that traffic stays local and is not propagated unnecessarily onto other portions of the network. Using the three-layer hierarchical design model helps organize the network.

This model divides the network functionality into three distinct layers, as shown in Figure 1-3:

- Access layer

- Distribution layer

- Core layer

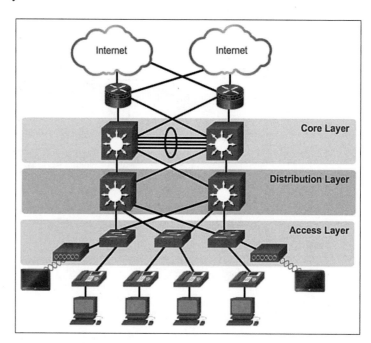

**Figure 1-3**   Hierarchical Design Model

Each layer is designed to meet specific functions.

The *access layer* provides connectivity for the users. The *distribution layer* is used to forward traffic from one local network to another. Finally, the *core layer* represents a high-speed backbone layer between dispersed networks. User traffic is initiated at the access layer and passes through the other layers if the functionality of those layers is required.

Even though the hierarchical model has three layers, some smaller enterprise networks might implement a two-tier hierarchical design. In a two-tier hierarchical design, the core and distribution layers are collapsed into one layer, reducing cost and complexity, as shown in Figure 1-4.

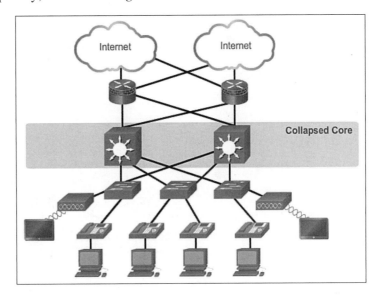

**Figure 1-4**   Collapsed Core

## Cisco Enterprise Architecture (1.1.1.4)

The Cisco Enterprise Architecture divides the network into functional components while still maintaining the core, distribution, and access layers. As Figure 1-5 shows, the primary Cisco Enterprise Architecture modules include

- Enterprise Campus
- Enterprise Edge
- Service Provider Edge
- Remote

**Figure 1-5**   Enterprise Architecture

## Enterprise Campus

The *Enterprise Campus* consists of the entire campus infrastructure, to include the access, distribution, and core layers. The access layer module contains Layer 2 or Layer 3 switches to provide the required *port density*. Implementation of VLANs and trunk links to the building distribution layer occurs here. *Redundancy* to the building distribution switches is important. The distribution layer module aggregates building access using Layer 3 devices. Routing, access control, and QoS are performed at this distribution layer module. The core layer module provides high-speed interconnectivity between the distribution layer modules, data center server farms, and the enterprise edge. Redundancy, fast convergence, and fault tolerance are the focus of the design in this module.

In addition to these modules, the Enterprise Campus can include other submodules such as

- *Server Farm and Data Center Module*: This area provides high-speed connectivity and protection for servers. It is critical to provide security, redundancy, and fault tolerance. The network management systems monitor performance by monitoring device and network availability.

- *Services Module*: This area provides access to all services, such as IP Telephony services, wireless controller services, and unified services.

## Enterprise Edge

The *Enterprise Edge* consists of the Internet, VPN, and WAN modules connecting the enterprise with the service provider's network. This module extends the enterprise services to remote sites and enables the enterprise to use Internet and partner resources. It provides QoS, policy reinforcement, service levels, and security.

## Service Provider Edge

The *Service Provider Edge* provides Internet, Public Switched Telephone Network (PSTN), and WAN services.

All data that enters or exits the Enterprise Composite Network Model (ECNM) passes through an edge device. This is the point where all packets can be examined and a decision made whether the packet should be allowed on the enterprise network. Intrusion detection systems (IDS) and intrusion prevention systems (IPS) can also be configured at the enterprise edge to protect against malicious activity.

## Failure Domains (1.1.1.5)

A well-designed network not only controls traffic but also limits the size of failure domains. A *failure domain* is the area of a network that is impacted when a critical device or network service experiences problems.

The function of the device that initially fails determines the impact of a failure domain. For example, a malfunctioning switch on a network segment normally affects only the hosts on that segment. However, if the router that connects this segment to others fails, the impact is much greater.

The use of redundant links and reliable enterprise-class equipment minimizes the chance of disruption in a network. Smaller failure domains reduce the impact of a failure on company productivity. They also simplify the troubleshooting process, thereby shortening the downtime for all users.

Failure domains often include other, smaller failure domains. For example, Figure 1-6 shows the following failure domains:

1. If the Edge Router fails, it will impact every device connected to it.

2. If S1 fails, it will impact H1, H2, H3, and AP1.

3. If S2 fails, it will impact S3, H4, H5, and H6.

4. If AP1 fails, it will impact H1.

5. If S3 fails, it will impact H5 and H6.

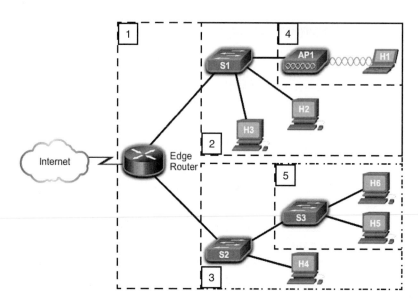

**Figure 1-6**   Failure Domain Examples

## Limiting the Size of Failure Domains

Because a failure at the core layer of a network can have a potentially large impact, the network designer often concentrates on efforts to prevent failures. These efforts can greatly increase the cost of implementing the network. In the hierarchical design model, it is easiest and usually least expensive to control the size of a failure domain in the distribution layer. In the distribution layer, network errors can be contained to a smaller area, thus affecting fewer users. When using Layer 3 devices at the distribution layer, every router functions as a gateway for a limited number of access layer users.

## Switch Block Deployment

Routers, or *multilayer switches*, are usually deployed in pairs, with access layer switches evenly divided between them. This configuration is referred to as a building, or departmental, switch block. Each switch block acts independently of the others. As a result, the failure of a single device does not cause the network to go down. Even the failure of an entire switch block does not affect a significant number of end users.

Interactive
Graphic

**Activity 1.1.1.6: Identify Cisco Enterprise Architecture Modules**

Go to the course online to perform this practice activity.

# Expanding the Network (1.1.2)

A solid network design is not all that is needed for network expansion. This section reviews the features necessary to ensure that the network scales well as the company grows.

## Design for Scalability (1.1.2.1)

To support an enterprise network, the network designer must develop a strategy to enable the network to be available and to scale effectively and easily. Included in a basic network design strategy are the following recommendations:

- Use expandable, modular equipment or clustered devices that can be easily upgraded to increase capabilities. Device modules can be added to the existing equipment to support new features and devices without requiring major equipment upgrades. Some devices can be integrated in a *cluster* to act as one device to simplify management and configuration.

- Design a hierarchical network to include modules that can be added, upgraded, and modified, as necessary, without affecting the design of the other functional areas of the network. For example, you can create a separate access layer that can be expanded without affecting the distribution and core layers of the campus network.

- Create an IPv4 or IPv6 address strategy that is hierarchical. Careful address planning eliminates the need to re-address the network to support additional users and services.

- Choose routers or multilayer switches to limit broadcasts and filter other undesirable traffic from the network. Use Layer 3 devices to filter and reduce traffic to the network core.

Figure 1-7 shows examples of some more advanced network requirements.

Advanced network design requirements shown in Figure 1-7 include

- Implementing redundant links in the network between critical devices and between access layer and core layer devices.

- Implementing multiple links between equipment, with either link aggregation (*EtherChannel*) or equal-cost load balancing, to increase bandwidth. Combining multiple Ethernet links into a single, load-balanced EtherChannel configuration increases available bandwidth. EtherChannel implementations can be used when budget restrictions prohibit purchasing high-speed interfaces and fiber runs.

- Implementing wireless connectivity to allow for mobility and expansion.

- Using a scalable routing protocol and implementing features within that routing protocol to isolate routing updates and minimize the size of the routing table.

**Figure 1-7**   Design for Scalability

## Planning for Redundancy (1.1.2.2)

Redundancy is a critical design feature for most company networks.

### Implementing Redundancy

For many organizations, the availability of the network is essential to supporting business needs. Redundancy is an important part of network design for preventing disruption of network services by minimizing the possibility of a single point of failure. One method of implementing redundancy is by installing duplicate equipment and providing failover services for critical devices.

Another method of implementing redundancy is using redundant paths, as shown in Figure 1-8.

Redundant paths offer alternate physical paths for data to traverse the network. Redundant paths in a switched network support high availability. However, because of the operation of switches, redundant paths in a switched Ethernet network can cause logical Layer 2 loops. For this reason, *Spanning Tree Protocol (STP)* is required.

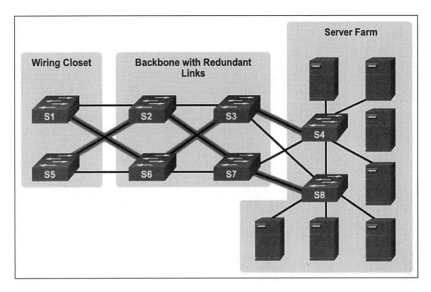

**Figure 1-8**   LAN Redundancy

STP allows for the redundancy required for reliability but eliminates the switching loops. It does this by providing a mechanism for disabling redundant paths in a switched network until the path is necessary, such as when failures occur. STP is an open standard protocol, used in a switched environment to create a loop-free logical topology.

More details about LAN redundancy and the operation of STP are covered in Chapter 2, "LAN Redundancy."

## Increasing Bandwidth (1.1.2.3)

Bandwidth demand continues to grow as users increasingly access video content and migrate to IP phones. EtherChannel can quickly add more bandwidth.

### Implementing EtherChannel

In hierarchical network design, some links between access and distribution switches might need to process a greater amount of traffic than other links. As traffic from multiple links converges onto a single, outgoing link, it is possible for that link to become a bottleneck. *Link aggregation* allows an administrator to increase the amount of bandwidth between devices by creating one logical link made up of several physical links. EtherChannel is a form of link aggregation used in switched networks, as shown in Figure 1-9.

**Figure 1-9**   Advantages of EtherChannel

EtherChannel uses the existing switch ports; therefore, additional costs to upgrade the link to a faster and more expensive connection are not necessary. The Ether-Channel is seen as one logical link using an EtherChannel interface. Most configuration tasks are done on the EtherChannel interface, instead of on each individual port, ensuring configuration consistency throughout the links. Finally, the Ether-Channel configuration takes advantage of load balancing between links that are part of the same EtherChannel, and depending on the hardware platform, one or more *load-balancing* methods can be implemented.

EtherChannel operation and configuration will be covered in more detail in Chapter 3, "LAN Aggregation."

## Expanding the Access Layer (1.1.2.4)

Except in the most secure setting, today's users expect wireless access to the networks.

### Implementing Wireless Connectivity

The network must be designed to be able to expand network access to individuals and devices, as needed. An increasingly important aspect of extending access layer connectivity is through wireless connectivity. Providing wireless connectivity offers many advantages, such as increased flexibility, reduced costs, and the ability to grow and adapt to changing network and business requirements.

To communicate wirelessly, end devices require a wireless NIC that incorporates a radio transmitter/receiver and the required software driver to make it operational.

Additionally, a wireless router or a *wireless access point* (AP) is required for users to connect, as shown in Figure 1-10.

**Figure 1-10**    Wireless LANs

There are many considerations when implementing a wireless network, such as the types of wireless devices to use, wireless coverage requirements, interference considerations, and security considerations.

Wireless operation and implementation will be covered in more detail in Chapter 4, "Wireless LANs."

## Fine-tuning Routing Protocols (1.1.2.5)

Routing protocol configuration is usually rather straightforward. However, to take full advantage of a protocol's feature set, it is often necessary to modify the configuration.

### Managing the Routed Network

Enterprise networks and ISPs often use more advanced protocols, such as link-state protocols, because of their hierarchical design and ability to scale for large networks.

*Link-state routing protocols* such as *Open Shortest Path First (OSPF)*, as shown in Figure 1-11, work well for larger hierarchical networks, where fast convergence is important.

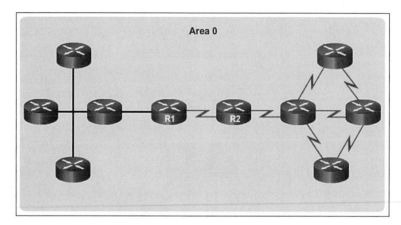

**Figure 1-11**   Single-Area OSPF

OSPF routers establish and maintain neighbor adjacency or adjacencies with other connected OSPF routers. When routers initiate an adjacency with neighbors, an exchange of link-state updates begins. Routers reach a FULL state of adjacency when they have synchronized views on their link-state database. With OSPF, link-state updates are sent when network changes occur.

OSPF is a popular link-state routing protocol that can be fine-tuned in many ways. Chapter 5, "Adjust and Troubleshoot *Single-Area OSPF*," will cover some of the more advanced features of OSPF configuration and troubleshooting.

Additionally, OSPF supports a two-layer hierarchical design, or *multiarea OSPF*, as shown in Figure 1-12.

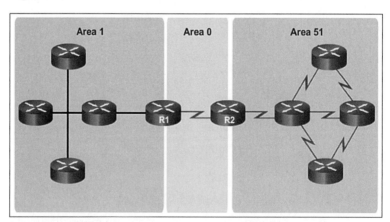

**Figure 1-12**   Multiarea OSPF

All OSPF networks begin with Area 0, also called the backbone area. As the network is expanded, other nonbackbone areas can be created. All nonbackbone areas must directly connect to area 0. Chapter 6, "Multiarea OSPF," introduces the benefits, operation, and configuration of multiarea OSPF.

Another popular routing protocol for larger networks is *Enhanced Interior Gateway Routing Protocol (EIGRP)*. Cisco developed EIGRP as a proprietary *distance vector routing protocol* with enhanced capabilities. Although configuring EIGRP is relatively simple, the underlying features and options of EIGRP are extensive and robust. For example, EIGRP uses multiple tables to manage the routing process using *Protocol Dependent Modules (PDM)*, as shown in Figure 1-13.

**Figure 1-13**    EIGRP Protocol Dependent Modules (PDM)

EIGRP contains many features that are not found in any other routing protocols. It is an excellent choice for large, multiprotocol networks that employ primarily Cisco devices.

Chapter 7, "EIGRP," introduces the operation and configuration of the EIGRP routing protocol, while Chapter 8, "EIGRP Advanced Configurations and Troubleshooting," covers some of the more advanced configuration options of EIGRP.

**Interactive Graphic**

**Activity 1.1.2.6: Identify Scalability Terminology**

Go to the course online to perform this practice activity.

# Selecting Network Devices (1.2)

A basic understanding of switch and router hardware is essential to implementing network designs that scale.

## Switch Hardware (1.2.1)

Cisco switches address the needs at the access, distribution, and core layers. Many models scale well with the network as it grows.

### Switch Platforms (1.2.1.1)

When designing a network, it is important to select the proper hardware to meet current network requirements, as well as to allow for network growth. Within an enterprise network, both switches and routers play a critical role in network communication.

There are five categories of switches for enterprise networks, as shown in Figure 1-14:

- **Campus LAN Switches:** To scale network performance in an enterprise LAN, there are core, distribution, access, and compact switches. These switch platforms vary from fanless switches with eight fixed ports to 13-blade switches supporting hundreds of ports. Campus LAN switch platforms include the Cisco 2960, 3560, 3750, 3850, 4500, 6500, and 6800 Series.

- **Cloud-Managed Switches:** The Cisco Meraki cloud-managed access switches enable virtual stacking of switches. They monitor and configure thousands of switch ports over the web, without the intervention of onsite IT staff.

- **Data Center Switches:** A data center should be built based on switches that promote infrastructure scalability, operational continuity, and transport flexibility. The data center switch platforms include the Cisco Nexus Series switches and the Cisco Catalyst 6500 Series switches.

- **Service Provider Switches:** Service provider switches fall under two categories: aggregation switches and Ethernet access switches. Aggregation switches are carrier-grade Ethernet switches that aggregate traffic at the edge of a network. Service provider Ethernet access switches feature application intelligence, unified services, virtualization, integrated security, and simplified management.

- **Virtual Networking:** Networks are becoming increasingly virtualized. Cisco Nexus virtual networking switch platforms provide secure multitenant services by adding virtualization intelligence technology to the data center network.

**Figure 1-14**   Switch Platforms

When selecting switches, network administrators must determine the switch form factors. This includes the *fixed configuration* shown in Figure 1-15, the *modular configuration* shown in Figure 1-16, the *stackable configuration* shown in Figure 1-17, or the nonstackable configuration.

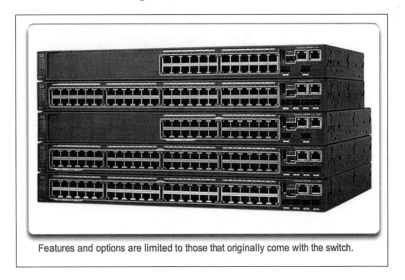

Features and options are limited to those that originally come with the switch.

**Figure 1-15**   Fixed Configuration Switches

The chassis accepts line cards that contain the ports.

**Figure 1-16**  Modular Configuration Switches

Stackable switches, connected by a special cable, effectively operate as one large switch.

**Figure 1-17**  Stackable Configuration Switches

The height of the switch, which is expressed in the number of rack units, is also important for switches that are mounted in a rack. For example, the fixed configuration switches shown in Figure 1-15 are all one rack unit (1U) high.

In addition to these considerations, the following list highlights other common business considerations when selecting switch equipment:

- **Cost:** The cost of a switch will depend on the number and speed of the interfaces, supported features, and expansion capability.

- **Port Density:** Network switches must support the appropriate number of devices on the network.

- **Power:** It is now common to power access points, IP phones, and even compact switches using Power over Ethernet (PoE). In addition to PoE considerations, some chassis-based switches support redundant power supplies.

- **Reliability:** The switch should provide continuous access to the network.

- **Port Speed:** The speed of the network connection is of primary concern to end users.

- **Frame Buffers:** The ability of the switch to store frames is important in a network where there might be congested ports to servers or other areas of the network.

- **Scalability:** The number of users on a network typically grows over time; therefore, the switch should provide the opportunity for growth.

## Port Density (1.2.1.2)

The port density of a switch refers to the number of ports available on a single switch. Figure 1-18 shows the port density of three different switches.

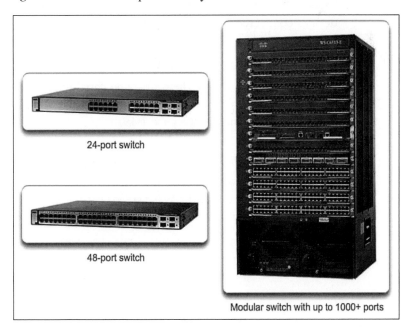

24-port switch

48-port switch

Modular switch with up to 1000+ ports

**Figure 1-18**   Port Densities

Fixed configuration switches typically support up to 48 ports on a single device. They have options for up to four additional ports for small form-factor pluggable (SFP) devices. High-port densities allow for better use of limited space and power. If there are two switches that each contain 24 ports, they would be able to support up to 46 devices, because at least one port per switch is lost with the connection of each switch to the rest of the network. In addition, two power outlets are required. Alternatively, if there is a single 48-port switch, 47 devices can be supported, with only one port used to connect the switch to the rest of the network, and only one power outlet needed to accommodate the single switch.

Modular switches can support very high-port densities through the addition of multiple switch port line cards. For example, some Catalyst 6500 switches can support in excess of 1000 switch ports.

Large enterprise networks that support many thousands of network devices require high-density, modular switches to make the best use of space and power. Without using a high-density modular switch, the network would need many fixed configuration switches to accommodate the number of devices that need network access. This approach can consume many power outlets and a lot of closet space.

The network designer must also consider the issue of uplink bottlenecks: A series of fixed configuration switches can consume many additional ports for bandwidth aggregation between switches, for the purpose of achieving target performance. With a single modular switch, bandwidth aggregation is less of an issue, because the backplane of the chassis can provide the necessary bandwidth to accommodate the devices connected to the switch port line cards.

## Forwarding Rates (1.2.1.3)

*Forwarding rates* define the processing capabilities of a switch by rating how much data the switch can process per second. Switch product lines are classified by forwarding rates, as shown in Figure 1-19.

Entry-level switches have lower forwarding rates than enterprise-level switches. Forwarding rates are important to consider when selecting a switch. If the switch forwarding rate is too low, it cannot accommodate full wire-speed communication across all of its switch ports. *Wire speed* is the data rate that each Ethernet port on the switch is capable of attaining. Data rates can be 100 Mb/s, 1 Gb/s, 10 Gb/s, or 100 Gb/s.

**Figure 1-19**  Forwarding Rate

For example, a typical 48-port gigabit switch operating at full wire speed generates 48 Gb/s of traffic. If the switch only supports a forwarding rate of 32 Gb/s, it cannot run at full wire speed across all ports simultaneously. Fortunately, access layer switches typically do not need to operate at full wire speed, because they are physically limited by their uplinks to the distribution layer. This means that less expensive, lower-performing switches can be used at the access layer, and more expensive, higher-performing switches can be used at the distribution and core layers, where the forwarding rate has a greater impact on network performance.

## Power over Ethernet (1.2.1.4)

*Power over Ethernet (PoE)* allows the switch to deliver power to a device over the existing Ethernet cabling. This feature can be used by IP phones and some wireless access points, as shown in Figure 1-20.

PoE allows more flexibility when installing wireless access points and IP phones, allowing them to be installed anywhere that there is an Ethernet cable. A network administrator should ensure that the PoE features are required, because switches that support PoE are expensive.

The relatively new Cisco Catalyst 2960-C and 3560-C Series compact switches support PoE pass-through, as shown in Figure 1-21.

**Figure 1-20**   Power over Ethernet

**Figure 1-21**   PoE Pass-Through

PoE pass-through allows a network administrator to power PoE devices connected to the switch, as well as the switch itself, by drawing power from certain upstream switches.

## Multilayer Switching (1.2.1.5)

Multilayer switches are typically deployed in the core and distribution layers of an organization's switched network. Multilayer switches are characterized by their ability to build a routing table, support a few routing protocols, and forward IP packets at a rate close to that of Layer 2 forwarding. Multilayer switches often support specialized hardware, such as *application-specific integrated circuits (ASIC)*. ASICs, along with dedicated software data structures, can streamline the forwarding of IP packets independent of the CPU.

There is a trend in networking toward a pure Layer 3 switched environment. When switches were first used in networks, none of them supported routing; now, almost all switches support routing. It is likely that soon all switches will incorporate a route processor because the cost of doing so is decreasing relative to other constraints. Eventually the term *multilayer switch* will be redundant.

As shown in Figure 1-22, the Catalyst 2960 switches illustrate the migration to a pure Layer 3 environment.

**Figure 1-22**   Cisco Catalyst 2960 Series Switches

With IOS versions prior to 15.x, these switches supported only one active switched virtual interface (SVI). The Catalyst 2960 also supports multiple active SVIs. This means that the switch can be remotely accessed through multiple IP addresses on distinct networks.

**Activity 1.2.1.6: Selecting Switch Hardware**

Go to the course online to perform this practice activity.

**Packet Tracer Activity 1.2.1.7: Comparing 2960 and 3560 Switches**

In this activity, you will use various commands to examine three different switching topologies and compare the similarities and differences between the 2960 and 3560 switches. You will also compare the routing table of a 1941 router with a 3560 switch.

**Lab 1.2.1.8: Selecting Switching Hardware**

In this lab, you will complete the following objectives:

- Part 1: Explore Cisco Switch Products
- Part 2: Select an Access Layer Switch
- Part 3: Select a Distribution/Core Layer Switch

# Router Hardware (1.2.2)

Like switches, routers can play a role in the access, distribution, and core layers of the network. In many small networks like branch offices and a teleworker's home network, all three layers are implemented within a router.

## Router Requirements (1.2.2.1)

In the distribution layer of an enterprise network, routing is required. Without the routing process, packets cannot leave the local network.

Routers play a critical role in networking by interconnecting multiple sites within an enterprise network, providing redundant paths, and connecting ISPs on the Internet. Routers can also act as a translator between different media types and protocols. For example, a router can accept packets from an Ethernet network and reencapsulate them for transport over a serial network.

Routers use the network portion of the destination IP address to route packets to the proper destination. They select an alternate path if a link goes down or traffic is congested. All hosts on a local network specify the IP address of the local router interface in their IP configuration. This router interface is the default gateway.

Routers also serve the following beneficial functions, as shown in Figure 1-23:

- Provide broadcast containment

- Connect remote locations

- Group users logically by application or department

- Provide enhanced security

Routers limit broadcasts to the local network.

Routers can be configured with access control lists to filter unwanted traffic.

Routers can be used to interconnect geographically separated locations.

Routers logically group users who require access to the same resources.

**Figure 1-23**    Router Functions

With the enterprise and the ISP, the ability to route efficiently and recover from network link failures is critical to delivering packets to their destination.

## Cisco Routers (1.2.2.2)

As the network grows, it is important to select the proper routers to meet its requirements. As shown in Figure 1-24, there are three categories of routers:

**Figure 1-24**   Router Platforms

- *Branch Routers*: Branch routers optimize branch services on a single platform while delivering an optimal application experience across branch and WAN infrastructures. Maximizing service availability at the branch requires networks designed for 24x7x365 uptime. Highly available branch networks must ensure fast recovery from typical faults, while minimizing or eliminating the impact on service, and provide simple network configuration and management.

- *Network Edge Routers*: Network edge routers enable the network edge to deliver high-performance, highly secure, and reliable services that unite campus, data center, and branch networks. Customers expect a high-quality media experience and more types of content than ever before. Customers want interactivity, personalization, mobility, and control for all content. Customers also want to access content anytime and anyplace they choose, over any device, whether at home, at work, or on the go. Network edge routers must deliver enhanced quality of service and nonstop video and mobile capabilities.

■ *Service Provider Routers*: Service provider routers differentiate the service portfolio and increase revenues by delivering end-to-end scalable solutions and subscriber-aware services. Operators must optimize operations, reduce expenses, and improve scalability and flexibility to deliver next-generation Internet experiences across all devices and locations. These systems are designed to simplify and enhance the operation and deployment of service-delivery networks.

## Router Hardware (1.2.2.3)

Routers also come in many form factors, as shown in Figure 1-25. Network administrators in an enterprise environment should be able to support a variety of routers, from a small desktop router to a rack-mounted or blade model.

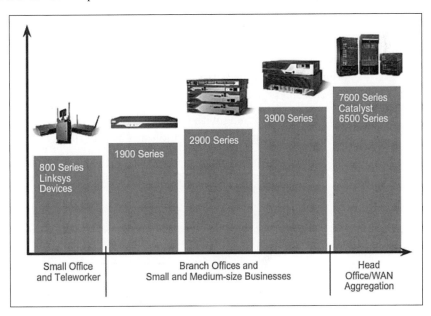

**Figure 1-25**  Routing Devices

Routers can also be categorized as fixed configuration or modular. With the fixed configuration, the desired router interfaces are built in. Modular routers come with multiple slots that allow a network administrator to change the interfaces on the router. As an example, a Cisco 1841 router comes with two Fast Ethernet RJ-45 interfaces built in and two slots that can accommodate many different network interface modules. Routers come with a variety of different interfaces, such as Fast Ethernet, Gigabit Ethernet, Serial, and Fiber-Optic.

**Activity 1.2.2.4: Identify the Router Category**

Go to the course online to perform this practice activity.

## Managing Devices (1.2.3)

Routers and switches all come with Cisco IOS Software. Network administrators are responsible for managing these devices. This includes initial configuration, verification, and troubleshooting tasks as well as maintaining up-to-date images and backing up the configuration files.

### Managing IOS Files and Licensing (1.2.3.1)

With such a wide selection of network devices to choose from in the Cisco product line, an organization can carefully determine the ideal combination to meet the needs of the employees and the customers.

When selecting or upgrading a *Cisco IOS* device, it is important to choose the proper IOS image with the correct feature set and version. IOS refers to the package of routing, switching, security, and other internetworking technologies integrated into a single multitasking operating system. When a new device is shipped, it comes preinstalled with the software image and the corresponding permanent licenses for the customer-specified packages and features.

For routers, beginning with Cisco IOS Software Release 15.0, Cisco modified the process to enable new technologies within the IOS feature sets, as shown in Figure 1-26.

**Figure 1-26**   Cisco IOS Software 15 Release Family

Chapter 9, "IOS Images and Licensing," covers more information on managing and maintaining the Cisco IOS licenses.

### In-Band Versus Out-of-Band Management (1.2.3.2)

Regardless of the Cisco IOS network device being implemented, there are two methods for connecting a PC to that network device for configuration and monitoring tasks. These methods include out-of-band and *in-band management*, as shown in Figure 1-27.

**Figure 1-27**    In-Band Versus Out-of-Band Configuration Options

*Out-of-band management* is used for initial configuration or when a network connection is unavailable. Configuration using out-of-band management requires

- Direct connection to console or AUX port

- Terminal emulation client

In-band management is used to monitor and make configuration changes to a network device over a network connection. Configuration using in-band management requires

- At least one network interface on the device to be connected and operational

- Telnet, SSH, or HTTP to access a Cisco device

## Basic Router CLI Commands (1.2.3.3)

A basic router configuration includes the host name for identification, passwords for security, assignment of IP addresses to interfaces for connectivity, and basic routing. Assuming that the physical interfaces are connected to the network, Example 1-1 shows the commands entered to enable a router with OSPF. Verify and save configuration changes using the **copy running-config startup-config** command.

**Example 1-1**   Enabling a Router with OSPF

```
Router# configure terminal
Router(config)# hostname R1
R1(config)# enable secret class
R1(config)# line con 0
R1(config-line)# password cisco
R1(config-line)# login
R1(config-line)# exec-timeout 0 0
R1(config-line)# line vty 0 4
R1(config-line)# password cisco
R1(config-line)# login
R1(config-line)# exit
R1(config)# service password-encryption
R1(config)# banner motd $ Authorized Access Only! $
R1(config)# interface GigabitEthernet0/0
R1(config-if)# description Link to LAN 1
R1(config-if)# ip address 172.16.1.1 255.255.255.0
R1(config-if)# no shutdown
R1(config-if)# interface Serial0/0/0
R1(config-if)# description Link to R2
R1(config-if)# ip address 172.16.3.1 255.255.255.252
R1(config-if)# clock rate 128000
R1(config-if)# no shutdown
R1(config-if)# interface Serial0/0/1
R1(config-if)# description Link to R3
R1(config-if)# ip address 192.168.10.5 255.255.255.252
R1(config-if)# no shutdown
R1(config-if)# router ospf 10
R1(config-router)# router-id 1.1.1.1
R1(config-router)# network 172.16.1.0 0.0.0.255 area 0
R1(config-router)# network 172.16.3.0 0.0.0.3 area 0
R1(config-router)# network 192.168.10.4 0.0.0.3 area 0
R1(config-router)# end
R1# copy running-config startup-config
```

Example 1-2 shows the results of the configuration commands that were entered in Example 1-1. To clear the router configuration, use the **erase startup-config** command and then the **reload** command.

**Example 1-2**   Router Running Configuration

```
R1# show running-config
Building configuration...
```

```
Current configuration : 1242 bytes
!
Version 15.1
Service timestamps debug datetime msec
Service timestamps log datetime msec
Service password-encryption
!
hostname R1
!
enable secret class
!
<output omitted>
!
interface GigabitEthernet0/0
 description Link to LAN 1
 ip address 172.16.1.1 255.255.255.0
 no shutdown
!
interface Serial0/0/0
 description Link to R2
 ip address 172.16.3.1 255.255.255.252
 clock rate 128000
 no shutdown
!
interface Serial0/0/1
 description Link to R3
 ip address 192.168.10.5 255.255.255.252
 no shutdown
!
router ospf 10
 router-id 1.1.1.1
 network 172.16.1.0 0.0.0.255 area 0
 network 172.16.3.0 0.0.0.3 area 0
 network 192.168.10.4 0.0.0.3 area 0
!
banner motd ^C Authorized Access Only! ^C
!
line console 0
 password cisco
 login
 exec-timeout 0 0
Line aux 0
line vty 0 4
 password cisco
 login
```

## Basic Router show Commands (1.2.3.4)

Here are some of the most commonly used IOS commands to display and verify the operational status of the router and related network functionality. These commands are divided into several categories.

The following show commands are related to routing:

- **show ip protocols:** As shown in Example 1-3, this command displays information about the routing protocols configured. If OSPF is configured, this includes the OSPF process ID, the router ID, networks the router is advertising, the neighbors the router is receiving updates from, and the default administrative distance, which is 110 for OSPF.

**Example 1-3   show ip protocols Command**

```
R1# show ip protocols

Routing Protocol is "ospf 10"
  Outgoing update filter list for all interfaces is not set
  Incoming update filter list for all interfaces is not set
  Router ID 1.1.1.1
  Number of areas in this router is 1. 1 normal 0 stub 0 nssa
  Maximum path: 4
  Routing for Networks:
    172.16.1.0 0.0.0.255 area 0
    172.16.3.0 0.0.0.3 area 0
    192.168.10.4 0.0.0.3 area 0
  Passive Interface(s):
    GigabitEthernet0/0
  Routing Information Sources:
    Gateway         Distance      Last Update
    1.1.1.1              110       00:11:48
    2.2.2.2              110       00:11:50
    3.3.3.3              110       00:11:50
  Distance: (default is 110)
```

- **show ip route:** As shown in Example 1-4, this command displays routing table information, including routing codes, known networks, administrative distance and metrics, how routes were learned, next hop, static routes, and default routes.

Chapter 1: Introduction to Scaling Networks 35

**Example 1-4  show ip route** Command

```
R1# show ip route
Codes: L - local, C - connected, S - static, R - RIP, M - mobile, B - BGP
       D - EIGRP, EX - EIGRP external, O - OSPF, IA - OSPF inter area
       N1 - OSPF NSSA external type 1, N2 - OSPF NSSA external type 2
       E1 - OSPF external type 1, E2 - OSPF external type 2, E - EGP
       i - IS-IS, L1 - IS-IS level-1, L2 - IS-IS level-2, ia - IS-IS inter area
       * - candidate default, U - per-user static route, o - ODR
       P - periodic downloaded static route

Gateway of last resort is not set

     172.16.0.0/16 is variably subnetted, 5 subnets, 3 masks
C       172.16.1.0/24 is directly connected, GigabitEthernet0/0
L       172.16.1.1/32 is directly connected, GigabitEthernet0/0
O       172.16.2.0/24 [110/65] via 172.16.3.2, 01:43:03, Serial0/0/0
C       172.16.3.0/30 is directly connected, Serial0/0/0
L       172.16.3.1/32 is directly connected, Serial0/0/0
O    192.168.1.0/24 [110/65] via 192.168.10.6, 01:43:03, Serial0/0/1
     192.168.10.0/24 is variably subnetted, 3 subnets, 2 masks
C       192.168.10.4/30 is directly connected, Serial0/0/1
L       192.168.10.5/32 is directly connected, Serial0/0/1
O       192.168.10.8/30 [110/128] via 172.16.3.2, 01:43:03, Serial0/0/0
                        [110/128] via 192.168.10.6, 01:43:03, Serial0/0/1
```

- **show ip ospf neighbor:** As shown in Example 1-5, this command displays information about OSPF neighbors that have been learned, including the Router ID of the neighbor, the priority, the state (Full = adjacency has been formed), the IP address, and the local interface that learned of the neighbor.

**Example 1-5  show ip ospf neighbor** Command

```
R1# show ip ospf neighbor

Neighbor ID     Pri    State       Dead Time    Address         Interface
2.2.2.2           0    FULL/   -    00:00:34     172.16.3.2      Serial0/0/0
3.3.3.3           0    FULL/   -    00:00:34     192.168.10.6    Serial0/0/1
```

The following show commands are related to interfaces:

- **show interfaces:** As shown in Example 1-6, this command displays interfaces with line (protocol) status, bandwidth, delay, reliability, encapsulation, duplex, and I/O statistics. If specified without a specific interface designation, all interfaces will be displayed. If a specific interface is specified after the command, information about that interface only will be displayed.

**Example 1-6    show interfaces Command**

```
R1# show interfaces
GigabitEthernet0/0 is up, line protocol is up (connected)
  Hardware is CN Gigabit Ethernet, address is 00e0.8fb2.de01 (bia 00e0.8fb2.de01)
  Description: Link to LAN 1
  Internet address is 172.16.1.1/24
  MTU 1500 bytes, BW 1000000 Kbit, DLY 10 usec,
      reliability 255/255, txload 1/255, rxload 1/255
<output omitted>
Serial0/0/0 is up, line protocol is up (connected)
  Hardware is HD64570
  Description: Link to R2
  Internet address is 172.16.3.1/30
  MTU 1500 bytes, BW 1544 Kbit, DLY 20000 usec,
      reliability 255/255, txload 1/255, rxload 1/255
  Encapsulation HDLC, loopback not set, keepalive set (10 sec)
  Last input never, output never, output hang never
  Last clearing of "show interface" counters never
<output omitted>
Serial0/0/1 is up, line protocol is up (connected)
  Hardware is HD64570
  Description: Link to R3
  Internet address is 192.168.10.5/30
  MTU 1500 bytes, BW 1544 Kbit, DLY 20000 usec,
      reliability 255/255, txload 1/255, rxload 1/255
  Encapsulation HDLC, loopback not set, keepalive set (10 sec)
  Last input never, output never, output hang never
  Last clearing of "show interface" counters never
```

- **show ip interfaces:** As shown in Example 1-7, this command displays interface information, including protocol status, IP address, whether a helper address is configured, and whether an ACL is enabled on the interface. If specified without a specific interface designation, all interfaces will be displayed. If a specific interface is specified after the command as shown in Example 1-7, information about that interface only will be displayed.

**Example 1-7   show ip interface** Command

```
R1# show ip interface gigabitEthernet 0/0
GigabitEthernet0/0 is up, line protocol is up
  Internet address is 172.16.1.1/24
  Broadcast address is 255.255.255.255
  Address determined by setup command
  MTU is 1500 bytes
  Helper address is not set
  Directed broadcast forwarding is disabled
  Multicast reserved groups joined: 224.0.0.5 224.0.0.6
  Outgoing access list is not set
  Inbound  access list is not set
  Proxy ARP is enabled
  Local Proxy ARP is disabled
  Security level is default
  Split horizon is enabled
  ICMP redirects are always sent
  ICMP unreachables are always sent
  ICMP mask replies are never sent
  IP fast switching is enabled
  IP fast switching on the same interface is disabled
  IP Flow switching is disabled
  IP CEF switching is enabled
  IP CEF switching turbo vector
  IP multicast fast switching is enabled
  IP multicast distributed fast switching is disabled
  IP route-cache flags are Fast, CEF
  Router Discovery is disabled
  IP output packet accounting is disabled
  IP access violation accounting is disabled
  TCP/IP header compression is disabled
  RTP/IP header compression is disabled
  Policy routing is disabled
  Network address translation is disabled
  BGP Policy Mapping is disabled
  Input features: MCI Check
  IPv4 WCCP Redirect outbound is disabled
  IPv4 WCCP Redirect inbound is disabled
  IPv4 WCCP Redirect exclude is disabled
```

■ **show ip interface brief:** As shown in Example 1-8, this command displays all interfaces with IP addressing information and interface and line protocol status.

**Example 1-8    show ip interface brief Command**

```
R1# show ip interface brief
Interface              IP-Address     OK?  Method  Status                  Protocol
GigabitEthernet0/0     172.16.1.1     YES  manual  up                      up
GigabitEthernet0/1     unassigned     YES  unset   administratively down   down
Serial0/0/0            172.16.3.1     YES  manual  up                      up
Serial0/0/1            192.168.10.5   YES  manual  up                      up
Vlan1                  unassigned     YES  unset   administratively down   down
```

■ **show protocols:** As shown in Example 1-9, this command displays information about the routed protocol that is enabled and the protocol status of interfaces.

**Example 1-9    show protocols Command**

```
R1# show protocols
Global values:
  Internet Protocol routing is enabled
GigabitEthernet0/0 is up, line protocol is up
  Internet address is 172.16.1.1/24
GigabitEthernet0/1 is administratively down, line protocol is down
Serial0/0/0 is up, line protocol is up
  Internet address is 172.16.3.1/30
Serial0/0/1 is up, line protocol is up
  Internet address is 192.168.10.5/30
Vlan1 is administratively down, line protocol is down
```

Other connectivity-related commands include the **show cdp neighbors** command shown in Example 1-10.

**Example 1-10    show cdp neighbors Command**

```
R1# show cdp neighbors
Capability Codes: R - Router, T - Trans Bridge, B - Source Route Bridge
                  S - Switch, H - Host, I - IGMP, r - Repeater, P - Phone
Device ID  Local Intrfce   HoldtmeCapability     Platform    Port ID
S1         Gig 0/0         126       S           2960        Gig 1/1
R2         Ser 0/0/0       136       R           C1900       Ser 0/0/0
R3         Ser 0/0/1       133       R           C1900       Ser 0/0/0
```

This command displays information on directly connected devices, including Device ID, local interface that the device is connected to, capability (R = router, S = switch), platform, and Port ID of the remote device. The details option includes IP addressing information and the IOS version.

## Basic Switch CLI Commands (1.2.3.5)

Basic switch configuration includes the host name for identification, passwords for security, and assignment of IP addresses for connectivity. In-band access requires the switch to have an IP address. Example 1-11 shows the commands entered to enable a switch.

**Example 1-11**   Enable a Switch with a Basic Configuration

```
Switch# enable
Switch# configure terminal
Switch(config)# hostname S1
S1(config)# enable secret class
S1(config)# line con 0
S1(config-line)# password cisco
S1(config-line)# login
S1(config-line)# line vty 0 4
S1(config-line)# password cisco
S1(config-line)# login
S1(config-line)# service password-encryption
S1(config)# banner motd $ Authorized Access Only! $
S1(config)# interface vlan 1
S1(config-if)# ip address 192.168.1.5 255.255.255.0
S1(config-if)# no shutdown
S1(config-if)# ip default-gateway 192.168.1.1
S1(config)# interface fa0/2
S1(config-if)# switchport mode access
S1(config-if)# switchport port-security
S1(config-if)# end
S1# copy running-config startup-config
```

Example 1-12 shows the results of the configuration commands that were entered in Example 1-11.

**Example 1-12**   Switch Running Configuration

```
S1# show running-config
<some output omitted>
version 15.0
```

```
service password-encryption
!
hostname S1
!
enable secret 4 06YFDUHH61wAE/kLkDq9BGho1QM5EnRtoyr8cHAUg.2
!
interface FastEthernet0/2
 switchport mode access
 switchport port-security
!
interface Vlan1
 ip address 192.168.1.5 255.255.255.0
!
ip default-gateway 192.168.1.1
!
banner motd ^C Authorized Access Only ^C
!
line con 0
 exec-timeout 0 0
 password 7 1511021F0725
 login
line vty 0 4
 password 7 1511021F0725
 login
line vty 5 15
 login
!
end
```

Verify and save the switch configuration using the **copy running-config startup-config** command. To clear the switch configuration, use the **erase startup-config** command and then the **reload** command. It might also be necessary to erase any VLAN information using the **delete flash:vlan.dat** command. When switch configurations are in place, view the configurations using the **show running-config** command.

## Basic Switch show Commands (1.2.3.6)

Switches make use of common IOS commands for configuration, to check for connectivity, and to display current switch status. For example, the following commands are useful for gathering some important information:

- **show port-security interface:** Displays any ports with security activated. To examine a specific interface, include the interface ID, as shown in Example 1-13. Information included in the output: the maximum addresses allowed, current count, security violation count, and action to be taken.

**Example 1-13   show port-security interface** Command

```
S1# show port-security interface fa0/2
Port Security              : Enabled
Port Status                : Secure-up
Violation Mode             : Shutdown
Aging Time                 : 0 mins
Aging Type                 : Absolute
SecureStatic Address Aging : Disabled
Maximum MAC Addresses      : 1
Total MAC Addresses        : 1
Configured MAC Addresses   : 0
Sticky MAC Addresses       : 0
Last Source Address:Vlan   : 0024.50d1.9902:1
Security Violation Count   : 0
```

- **show port-security address:** As shown in Example 1-14, this command displays all secure MAC addresses configured on all switch interfaces.

**Example 1-14   show port-security address** Command

```
S1# show port-security address
              Secure Mac Address Table
-------------------------------------------------------------------
Vlan    Mac Address     Type                  Ports   Remaining Age
                                                      (mins)
----    -----------     ----                  -----   -------------
  1     0024.50d1.9902  SecureDynamic         Fa0/2        -
-------------------------------------------------------------------
Total Addresses in System (excluding one mac per port)    : 0
Max Addresses limit in System (excluding one mac per port) : 1536
```

- **show interfaces:** As shown in Example 1-15, this command displays one or all interfaces with line (protocol) status, bandwidth, delay, reliability, encapsulation, duplex, and I/O statistics.

**Example 1-15   show interfaces** Command

```
S1# show interfaces fa0/2
FastEthernet0/2 is up, line protocol is up (connected)
  Hardware is Fast Ethernet, address is 001e.14cf.eb04 (bia 001e.14cf.eb04)
  MTU 1500 bytes, BW 100000 Kbit/sec, DLY 100 usec,
      reliability 255/255, txload 1/255, rxload 1/255
  Encapsulation ARPA, loopback not set
  Keepalive set (10 sec)
  Full-duplex, 100Mb/s, media type is 10/100BaseTX
  input flow-control is off, output flow-control is unsupported
  ARP type: ARPA, ARP Timeout 04:00:00
  Last input 00:00:08, output 00:00:00, output hang never
  Last clearing of "show interface" counters never
  Input queue: 0/75/0/0 (size/max/drops/flushes); Total output drops: 0
  Queueing strategy: fifo
  Output queue: 0/40 (size/max)
  5 minute input rate 0 bits/sec, 0 packets/sec
  5 minute output rate 2000 bits/sec, 3 packets/sec
     59 packets input, 11108 bytes, 0 no buffer
     Received 59 broadcasts (59 multicasts)
     0 runts, 0 giants, 0 throttles
     0 input errors, 0 CRC, 0 frame, 0 overrun, 0 ignored
     0 watchdog, 59 multicast, 0 pause input
     0 input packets with dribble condition detected
     886 packets output, 162982 bytes, 0 underruns
     0 output errors, 0 collisions, 1 interface resets
     0 unknown protocol drops
     0 babbles, 0 late collision, 0 deferred
     0 lost carrier, 0 no carrier, 0 pause output
     0 output buffer failures, 0 output buffers swapped out
```

■ **show mac-address-table:** As shown in Example 1-16, this command displays all MAC addresses that the switch has learned, how those addresses were learned (dynamic/static), the port number, and the VLAN assigned to the port.

**Example 1-16    show mac address-table** Command

```
S1# show mac address-table
          Mac Address Table
-------------------------------------------

Vlan    Mac Address      Type       Ports
----    -----------      --------   -----
All     0100.0ccc.cccc   STATIC     CPU
All     0100.0ccc.cccd   STATIC     CPU
All     0180.c200.0000   STATIC     CPU
All     0180.c200.0001   STATIC     CPU
All     0180.c200.0002   STATIC     CPU
All     0180.c200.0003   STATIC     CPU
All     0180.c200.0004   STATIC     CPU
All     0180.c200.0005   STATIC     CPU
All     0180.c200.0006   STATIC     CPU
All     0180.c200.0007   STATIC     CPU
All     0180.c200.0008   STATIC     CPU
All     0180.c200.0009   STATIC     CPU
All     0180.c200.000a   STATIC     CPU
All     0180.c200.000b   STATIC     CPU
All     0180.c200.000c   STATIC     CPU
All     0180.c200.000d   STATIC     CPU
All     0180.c200.000e   STATIC     CPU
All     0180.c200.000f   STATIC     CPU
All     0180.c200.0010   STATIC     CPU
All     ffff.ffff.ffff   STATIC     CPU
  1     001e.4915.5405   DYNAMIC    Fa0/3
  1     001e.4915.5406   DYNAMIC    Fa0/4
  1     0024.50d1.9901   DYNAMIC    Fa0/1
  1     0024.50d1.9902   STATIC     Fa0/2
  1     0050.56be.0e67   DYNAMIC    Fa0/1
  1     0050.56be.c23d   DYNAMIC    Fa0/6
  1     0050.56be.df70   DYNAMIC    Fa0/3
Total Mac Addresses for this criterion: 27
```

Like the router, the switch also supports the **show cdp neighbors** command.

The same in-band and out-of-band management techniques that apply to routers also apply to switch configuration.

# Summary (1.3)

### Class Activity 1.3.1.1: Layered Network Design Simulation

As the network administrator for a very small network, you want to prepare a sim-ulated-network presentation for your branch manager to explain how the network currently operates.

The small network includes the following equipment:

- One 2911 Series router
- One 3560 switch
- One 2960 switch
- Four user workstations (PCs or laptops)
- One printer

### Activity 1.3.1.2: Basic Switch Configurations

Go to the course online to perform this practice activity.

### Packet Tracer Activity 1.3.1.3: Skills Integration Challenge

As a recently hired LAN technician, your network manager has asked you to dem-onstrate your ability to configure a small LAN. Your tasks include configuring initial settings on two switches using the Cisco IOS and configuring IP address parameters on host devices to provide end-to-end connectivity. You are to use two switches and two hosts/PCs on a cabled and powered network.

The hierarchical network design model divides network functionality into the access layer, the distribution layer, and the core layer. The Cisco Enterprise Architecture further divides the network into functional components.

A well-designed network controls traffic and limits the size of failure domains. Rout-ers and multilayer switches can be deployed in pairs so that the failure of a single device does not cause service disruptions.

A network design should include an IP addressing strategy, scalable and fast-converging routing protocols, appropriate Layer 2 protocols, and modular or clus-tered devices that can be easily upgraded to increase capacity.

A mission-critical server should have a connection to two different access layer switches. It should have redundant modules when possible and a power backup source. It might be appropriate to provide multiple connections to one or more ISPs.

Security monitoring systems and IP telephony systems must have high availability and often have special design considerations.

The network designer should specify a router from the appropriate category: branch router, network edge router, or service provider router. It is important to also deploy the appropriate type of switches for a given set of requirements, switch features and specifications, and expected traffic flow.

# Practice

The following activities provide practice with the topics introduced in this chapter. The Labs and Class Activities are available in the companion *Introduction to Scaling Networks Lab Manual* (ISBN 978-1-58713-325-1). The Packet Tracer Activities PKA files are found in the online course.

## Class Activities

- Class Activity 1.0.1.2: Network by Design
- Class Activity 1.3.1.1: Layered Network Design Simulation

## Labs

- Lab 1.2.1.8: Selecting Switching Hardware

## Packet Tracer Activities

- Packet Tracer 1.2.1.7: Comparing 2960 and 3560 Switches
- Packet Tracer 1.3.1.3: Skills Integration Challenge

# Check Your Understanding Questions

Complete all the review questions listed here to test your understanding of the topics and concepts in this chapter. The appendix "Answers to 'Check Your Understanding' Questions" lists the answers.

1. What are the expected features of modern enterprise networks? (Choose two.)

    A. Support for 90 percent reliability

    B. Support for limited growth

    C. Support for converged network traffic

    D. Support for distributed administrative control

    E. Support for critical applications

2. Which of the following methods help to prevent the disruption of network services? (Choose two.)

    A. Changing the routing protocols at regular intervals

    B. Using redundant connections to provide alternate physical paths

    C. Installing duplicate equipment to provide failover services

    D. Removing switches that cause loops

    E. Using VLANs to segment network traffic

3. Which feature could be used in a network design to increase the bandwidth by combining multiple physical links into a single logical link?

    A. VLANs

    B. Trunk ports

    C. EtherChannel

    D. Subinterfaces

4. Which network design solution will best extend access layer connectivity to host devices?

    A. Implementing EtherChannel

    B. Implementing redundancy

    C. Implementing routing protocols

    D. Implementing wireless connectivity

5. How much traffic is a 48-port gigabit switch capable of generating when operating at full wire speed?

   A. 44 Gb/s, because of overhead requirements

   B. 48 Gb/s, by providing full bandwidth to each port

   C. 24 Gb/s, because this is the maximum forwarding rate on Cisco switches

   D. 1 Gb/s, because data can only be forwarded from one port at a time

6. Which type of router would an enterprise use to allow customers to access content anytime and anyplace, regardless of whether they are at home or work?

   A. Service provider routers

   B. Network edge routers

   C. Branch routers

   D. Modular routers

7. What is a characteristic of out-of-band device management?

   A. It requires a terminal emulation client.

   B. It requires Telnet, SSH, or HTTP to access a Cisco device.

   C. It requires at least one network interface on the device to be connected and operational.

   D. Out-of-band device management requires a direct connection to a network interface.

8. The number of ports available on a single switch is referred to as _____.

9. Among the beneficial functions of a router are enhanced network security and containment of _____ traffic.

10. Indicate the design model layer described by the following network functions:

   The _____ layer provides connectivity for the users.

   The _____ layer forwards traffic from one local network to another.

   The _____ layer provides a high-speed backbone link between dispersed networks.

## Objectives

Upon completion of this chapter, you will be able to answer the following questions:

- What are the issues that you should be concerned with when implementing a redundant network?

- How does IEEE 802.1D STP operate?

- What are the different varieties of spanning tree?

- How does PVST+ operate in a switched LAN environment?

- How does Rapid PVST+ operate in a switched LAN environment?

- What are the commands to configure PVST+ in a switched LAN environment?

- What are the commands to configure Rapid PVST+ in a switched LAN environment?

- What are the common STP configuration issues?

- What are the purpose and operation of First Hop Redundancy Protocols?

- What are the different varieties of First Hop Redundancy Protocols?

- What are the commands to verify HSRP and GLBP implementations?

## Key Terms

This chapter uses the following key terms. You can find the definitions in the Glossary.

*First Hop Redundancy Protocols (FHRP)*    page 51

*broadcast storm*    page 54

*time to live (TTL)*    page 54

*root bridge*    page 59

*bridge protocol data unit (BPDU)*    page 59

*blocking state*    page 60

*Rapid Spanning Tree Protocol (RSTP)*    page 61

*Multiple Spanning Tree Protocol (MSTP)*    page 61

*IEEE-802.1D-2004*    page 61

*bridge ID (BID)*    page 61

*extended system ID*    page 62

*root port*    page 62

*designated port*    page 63

*alternate and backup port*    page 63

*disabled port*    page 63

*default port cost*    page 64

*bridge priority*    page 74

*Common Spanning Tree (CST)*    page 78

*PVST+   page 78*

*PortFast   page 78*

*BPDU guard   page 78*

*IEEE 802.1w (RSTP)   page 78*

*Rapid PVST+   page 78*

*listening state   page 82*

*learning state   page 82*

*forwarding state   page 82*

*disabled state   page 82*

*edge port   page 87*

*point-to-point link   page 89*

*shared link   page 89*

*Hot Standby Router Protocol (HSRP) page 109*

*Virtual Router Redundancy Protocol (VRRP)   page 110*

*Gateway Load Balancing Protocol (GLBP)   page 110*

*ICMP Router Discovery Protocol (IRDP) page 110*

# Introduction (2.0.1.1)

Network redundancy is a key to maintaining network reliability. Multiple physical links between devices provide redundant paths. The network can then continue to operate when a single link or port has failed. Redundant links can also share the traffic load and increase capacity.

Multiple paths need to be managed so that Layer 2 loops are not created. The best paths are chosen, and an alternate path is immediately available should a primary path fail. The Spanning Tree Protocols are used to manage Layer 2 redundancy.

Redundant devices, such as multilayer switches or routers, provide the capability for a client to use an alternate default gateway should the primary default gateway fail. A client can now have multiple paths to more than one possible default gateway. *First Hop Redundancy Protocols* are used to manage how a client is assigned a default gateway, and to be able to use an alternate default gateway should the primary default gateway fail.

This chapter focuses on the protocols used to manage these forms of redundancy. It also covers some of the potential redundancy problems and their symptoms.

### Class Activity 2.0.1.2: Stormy Traffic

It is your first day on the job as a network administrator for a small- to medium-sized business. The previous network administrator left suddenly after a network upgrade took place for the business.

During the upgrade, a new switch was added. Since the upgrade, many employees complain that they are having trouble accessing the Internet and servers on your network. In fact, most of them cannot access the network at all. Your corporate manager asks you to immediately research what could be causing these connectivity problems and delays.

So you take a look at the equipment operating on your network at your main distribution facility in the building. You notice that the network topology seems to be visually correct and that cables have been connected correctly, routers and switches are powered on and operational, and switches are connected together to provide backup or redundancy.

However, one thing you do notice is that all of your switches' status lights are constantly blinking at a very fast pace to the point that they almost appear solid. You think you have found the problem with the connectivity issues your employees are experiencing.

Use the Internet to research STP. As you research, take notes and describe

- Broadcast storm
- Switching loops
- The purpose of STP
- Variations of STP

Complete the reflection questions that accompany the PDF file for this activity. Save your work and be prepared to share your answers with the class.

# Spanning Tree Concepts (2.1)

This section focuses on the purpose and operation of the Spanning Tree Protocol.

## Purpose of Spanning Tree (2.1.1)

STP provides the mechanism to have redundant links at Layer 2 while avoiding the potential for loops and MAC address database instability.

### Redundancy at OSI Layers 1 and 2 (2.1.1.1)

The three-tier hierarchical network design that uses core, distribution, and access layers with redundancy attempts to eliminate a single point of failure on the network. Multiple cabled paths between switches provide physical redundancy in a switched network. This improves the reliability and availability of the network. Having alternate physical paths for data to traverse the network makes it possible for users to access network resources, despite path disruption.

The following steps explain how redundancy works in the topology shown in Figure 2-1.

1. PC1 is communicating with PC4 over a redundant network topology.

2. When the network link between S1 and S2 is disrupted, the path between PC1 and PC4 is automatically adjusted to compensate for the disruption (shown in Figure 2-1).

3. When the network connection between S1 and S2 is restored, the path is then readjusted to route traffic directly from S2 to S1 to get to PC4.

**Note**

To view an animation of these steps, refer to the online course.

**Figure 2-1**   Redundancy in a Hierarchical Network

For many organizations, the availability of the network is essential to supporting business needs; therefore, the network infrastructure design is a critical business element. Path redundancy is a solution for providing the necessary availability of multiple network services by eliminating the possibility of a single point of failure.

Redundancy is an important part of hierarchical design for preventing disruption of network services to users. Redundant networks require adding physical paths, but logical redundancy must also be part of the design. However, redundant paths in a switched Ethernet network can cause both physical and logical Layer 2 loops.

Logical Layer 2 loops can occur because of the natural operation of switches, specifically, the learning and forwarding process. When multiple paths exist between two devices on a network, and there is no spanning tree implementation on the switches, a Layer 2 loop occurs. A Layer 2 loop can result in three primary issues:

- **MAC database instability:** Instability in the content of the MAC address table results from copies of the same frame being received on different ports of the switch. Data forwarding can be impaired when the switch consumes the resources that are coping with instability in the MAC address table.

■ **Broadcast storms:** Without some loop-avoidance process, each switch can flood broadcasts endlessly. This situation is commonly called a *broadcast storm*.

■ **Multiple frame transmission:** Multiple copies of unicast frames can be delivered to destination stations. Many protocols expect to receive only a single copy of each transmission. Multiple copies of the same frame can cause unrecoverable errors.

## Issues with Layer 1 Redundancy: MAC Database Instability (2.1.1.2)

Ethernet frames do not have a *time to live* (TTL) attribute, like IP packets. As a result, if there is no mechanism enabled to block continued propagation of these frames on a switched network, they continue to propagate between switches endlessly, or until a link is disrupted and breaks the loop. This continued propagation between switches can result in MAC database instability. This can occur because of broadcast frames forwarding.

Broadcast frames are forwarded out all switch ports, except the original ingress port. This ensures that all devices in a broadcast domain are able to receive the frame. If there is more than one path for the frame to be forwarded out, an endless loop can result. When a loop occurs, it is possible for the MAC address table on a switch to constantly change with the updates from the broadcast frames, resulting in MAC database instability.

The following steps demonstrate the MAC database instability issue. Figure 2-2 shows a snapshot during Step 4.

1. PC1 sends out a broadcast frame to S2. S2 receives the broadcast frame on F0/11. When S2 receives the broadcast frame, it updates its MAC address table to record that PC1 is available on port F0/11.

2. Because it is a broadcast frame, S2 forwards the frame out all ports, including Trunk1 and Trunk2. When the broadcast frame arrives at S3 and S1, they update their MAC address tables to indicate that PC1 is available out port F0/1 on S1 and out port F0/2 on S3.

3. Because it is a broadcast frame, S3 and S1 forward the frame out all ports, except the ingress port. S3 sends the broadcast frame from PC1 to S1. S1 sends the broadcast frame from PC1 to S3. Each switch updates its MAC address table with the incorrect port for PC1.

4. Each switch again forwards the broadcast frame out all of its ports, except the ingress port, resulting in both switches forwarding the frame to S2 (shown in Figure 2-2).

**Figure 2-2**   MAC Database Instability Example

**5.** When S2 receives the broadcast frames from S3 and S1, the MAC address table is updated again, this time with the last entry received from the other two switches.

This process repeats over and over again until the loop is broken by physically disconnecting the connections causing the loop or powering down one of the switches in the loop. This creates a high CPU load on all switches caught in the loop. Because the same frames are constantly being forwarded back and forth between all switches in the loop, the CPU of the switch must process a lot of data. This slows down performance on the switch when legitimate traffic arrives.

A host caught in a network loop is not accessible to other hosts on the network. Additionally, because of the constant changes in the MAC address table, the switch does not know out of which port to forward unicast frames. In the previous example, the switches will have the incorrect ports listed for PC1. Any unicast frame destined for PC1 loops around the network, just as the broadcast frames do. More and more frames looping around the network eventually create a broadcast storm.

## Issues with Layer 1 Redundancy: Broadcast Storms (2.1.1.3)

A broadcast storm occurs when there are so many broadcast frames caught in a Layer 2 loop that all available bandwidth is consumed. Consequently, no bandwidth is available for legitimate traffic and the network becomes unavailable for data communication. This is an effective denial of service.

A broadcast storm is inevitable on a looped network. As more devices send broadcasts over the network, more traffic is caught within the loop, consuming resources. This eventually creates a broadcast storm that causes the network to fail.

There are other consequences of broadcast storms. Because broadcast traffic is forwarded out every port on a switch, all connected devices have to process all broadcast traffic that is being flooded endlessly around the looped network. This can cause the end device to malfunction because of the high processing requirements for sustaining such a high traffic load on the NIC.

The following steps demonstrate the broadcast storm issue. Figure 2-3 shows the final result during Step 6.

1. PC1 sends a broadcast frame out onto the looped network.

2. The broadcast frame loops between all the interconnected switches on the network.

3. PC4 also sends a broadcast frame out on to the looped network.

4. The PC4 broadcast frame also gets caught in the loop between all the interconnected switches, just like the PC1 broadcast frame.

5. As more devices send broadcasts over the network, more traffic is caught within the loop, consuming resources. This eventually creates a broadcast storm that causes the network to fail.

6. When the network is fully saturated with broadcast traffic that is looping between the switches, new traffic is discarded by the switch because it is unable to process it. In Figure 2-3, S2 is now discarding additional frames.

**Note**

To view an animation of these steps, refer to the online course.

Because devices connected to a network are regularly sending out broadcast frames, such as ARP requests, a broadcast storm can develop in seconds. As a result, when a loop is created, the switched network is quickly brought down.

**Figure 2-3**   Broadcast Storms

### Issues with Layer 1 Redundancy: Duplicate Unicast Frames (2.1.1.4)

Broadcast frames are not the only type of frames that are affected by loops. Unicast frames sent onto a looped network can result in duplicate frames arriving at the destination device.

The following steps demonstrate the duplicate unicast frames issue. Figure 2-4 shows a snapshot during Step 5 and Step 6.

1. PC1 sends a unicast frame destined for PC4.

2. S2 does not have an entry for PC4 in its MAC table, so it floods the unicast frame out all switch ports in an attempt to find PC4.

3. The frame arrives at switches S1 and S3.

4. S1 does have a MAC address entry for PC4, so it forwards the frame out to PC4.

5. S3 also has an entry in its MAC address table for PC4, so it forwards the unicast frame out Trunk3 to S1.

6. S1 receives the duplicate frame and forwards the frame out to PC4.

7. PC4 has now received the same frame twice.

**Figure 2-4**   S1 and S3 Send Duplicate Frame to PC4

Most upper-layer protocols are not designed to recognize, or cope with, duplicate transmissions. In general, protocols that make use of a sequence-numbering mechanism assume that the transmission has failed and that the sequence number has recycled for another communication session. Other protocols attempt to hand the duplicate transmission to the appropriate upper-layer protocol to be processed and possibly discarded.

Layer 2 LAN protocols, such as Ethernet, lack a mechanism to recognize and eliminate endlessly looping frames. Some Layer 3 protocols implement a TTL mechanism that limits the number of times a Layer 3 networking device can retransmit a packet. Lacking such a mechanism, Layer 2 devices continue to retransmit looping traffic indefinitely. A Layer 2 loop-avoidance mechanism, STP, was developed to address these problems.

To prevent these issues from occurring in a redundant network, some type of spanning tree must be enabled on the switches. Spanning tree is enabled, by default, on Cisco switches to prevent Layer 2 loops from occurring.

**Packet Tracer**
**☐ Activity**

**Packet Tracer Activity 2.1.1.5: Examining a Redundant Design**

In this activity, you will observe how STP operates, by default, and how it reacts when faults occur. Switches have been added to the network "out of the box." Cisco switches can be connected to a network without any additional action required by the network administrator. For the purpose of this activity, the bridge priority was modified.

## STP Operation (2.1.2)

STP uses the concepts of a *root bridge*, port roles, and path costs to calculate which links to use in a redundant topology.

### Spanning Tree Algorithm: Introduction (2.1.2.1)

Redundancy increases the availability of the network topology by protecting the network from a single point of failure, such as a failed network cable or switch. When physical redundancy is introduced into a design, loops and duplicate frames occur. Loops and duplicate frames have severe consequences for a switched network. The Spanning Tree Protocol (STP) was developed to address these issues.

STP ensures that there is only one logical path between all destinations on the network by intentionally blocking redundant paths that could cause a loop. A port is considered blocked when user data is prevented from entering or leaving that port. This does not include *bridge protocol data unit* (BPDU) frames that are used by STP to prevent loops. Blocking the redundant paths is critical to preventing loops on the network. The physical paths still exist to provide redundancy, but these paths are disabled to prevent the loops from occurring. If the path is ever needed to compensate for a network cable or switch failure, STP recalculates the paths and unblocks the necessary ports to allow the redundant path to become active.

In Figure 2-5, all switches have STP enabled:

**Figure 2-5**  Normal STP Operation

1. PC1 sends a broadcast out onto the network.

2. S2 is configured with STP and has set the port for Trunk2 to a *blocking state*, as shown in Figure 2-5. The blocking state prevents ports from being used to forward user data, thus preventing a loop from occurring. S2 forwards a broadcast frame out all switch ports, except the originating port from PC1 and the port for Trunk2.

3. S1 receives the broadcast frame and forwards it out all of its switch ports, where it reaches PC4 and S3. S3 forwards the frame out the port for Trunk2 and S2 drops the frame. The Layer 2 loop is prevented.

### Note

To view an animation of these steps, refer to the online course.

In Figure 2-6, STP recalculates the path when a failure occurs.

**Figure 2-6**   STP Compensates for Network Failure

1. PC1 sends a broadcast out onto the network.

2. The broadcast is then forwarded around the network, just as in the previous animation.

3. The trunk link between S2 and S1 fails, resulting in the previous path being disrupted.

4. S2 unblocks the previously blocked port for Trunk2 and allows the broadcast traffic to traverse the alternate path around the network, permitting communication to continue. If this link comes back up, STP reconverges and the port on S2 is again blocked.

> **Note**
>
> To view an animation of these steps, refer to the online course.

STP prevents loops from occurring by configuring a loop-free path through the network using strategically placed "blocking-state" ports. The switches running STP are able to compensate for failures by dynamically unblocking the previously blocked ports and permitting traffic to traverse the alternate paths.

Up to now, we have used the term Spanning Tree Protocol and the acronym STP. The usage of the Spanning Tree Protocol term and the STP acronym can be misleading. Many professionals generically use these to refer to various implementations of spanning tree, such as *Rapid Spanning Tree Protocol (RSTP)* and *Multiple Spanning Tree Protocol (MSTP)*. In order to communicate spanning tree concepts correctly, it is important to refer to the particular implementation or standard in context. The latest IEEE documentation on spanning tree, IEEE-802-1D-2004, says "STP has now been superseded by the Rapid Spanning Tree Protocol (RSTP)." So one sees that the IEEE uses "STP" to refer to the original implementation of spanning tree and "RSTP" to describe the version of spanning tree specified in *IEEE-802.1D-2004*. In this book, when the original Spanning Tree Protocol is the context of a discussion, the phrase "original 802.1D spanning tree" is used to avoid confusion.

> **Note**
>
> STP is based on an algorithm invented by Radia Perlman while working for Digital Equipment Corporation, and published in the 1985 paper "An Algorithm for Distributed Computation of a Spanning Tree in an Extended LAN."

## Spanning Tree Algorithm: Port Roles (2.1.2.2)

IEEE 802.1D STP uses the Spanning Tree Algorithm (STA) to determine which switch ports on a network must be put in blocking state to prevent loops from occurring. The STA designates a single switch as the root bridge and uses it as the reference point for all path calculations. In Figure 2-7, the root bridge (switch S1) is chosen through an election process. All switches participating in STP exchange BPDU frames to determine which switch has the lowest *bridge ID* (BID) on the network. The switch with the lowest BID automatically becomes the root bridge for the STA calculations.

> **Note**
>
> For simplicity, assume until otherwise indicated that all ports on all switches are assigned to VLAN 1. Each switch has a unique MAC address associated with VLAN 1.

**Figure 2-7**   STP Algorithm

A BPDU is a messaging frame exchanged by switches for STP. Each BPDU contains a BID that identifies the switch that sent the BPDU. The BID contains a priority value, the MAC address of the sending switch, and an optional *extended system ID*. The lowest BID value is determined by the combination of these three fields.

After the root bridge has been determined, the STA calculates the shortest path to it. Each switch uses the STA to determine which ports to block. While the STA determines the best paths to the root bridge for all switch ports in the broadcast domain, traffic is prevented from being forwarded through the network. The STA considers both path and port costs when determining which ports to block. The path costs are calculated using port cost values associated with port speeds for each switch port along a given path. The sum of the port cost values determines the overall path cost to the root bridge. If there is more than one path to choose from, STA chooses the path with the lowest path cost.

When the STA has determined which paths are most desirable relative to each switch, it assigns port roles to the participating switch ports. The port roles describe their relation in the network to the root bridge and whether they are allowed to forward traffic:

- *Root ports*: Switch ports closest to the root bridge. In Figure 2-7, the root port on S2 is F0/1 configured for the trunk link between S2 and S1. The root port on S3 is F0/1, configured for the trunk link between S3 and S1. Root ports are selected on a per-switch basis.

- *Designated ports*: All nonroot ports that are still permitted to forward traffic on the network. In Figure 2-7, switch ports (F0/1 and F0/2) on S1 are designated ports. S2 also has its port F0/2 configured as a designated port. Designated ports are selected on a per-trunk basis. If one end of a trunk is a root port, the other end is a designated port. All ports on the root bridge are designated ports.

- *Alternate and backup ports*: Alternate ports and backup ports are configured to be in a blocking state to prevent loops. In the figure, the STA configured port F0/2 on S3 in the alternate role. Port F0/2 on S3 is in the blocking state. Alternate ports are selected only on trunk links where neither end is a root port. Notice in Figure 2-7 that only one end of the trunk is blocked. This allows for faster transition to a forwarding state, when necessary. (Blocking ports only come into play when two ports on the same switch are connected to each other through a hub or single cable.)

- *Disabled ports*: A disabled port is a switch port that is shut down.

### Spanning Tree Algorithm: Root Bridge (2.1.2.3)

As shown in Figure 2-8, every spanning tree instance (switched LAN or broadcast domain) has a switch designated as the root bridge. The root bridge serves as a reference point for all spanning tree calculations to determine which redundant paths to block.

**Figure 2-8** Root Bridge

An election process determines which switch becomes the root bridge.

Figure 2-9 shows the BID fields. The BID is made up of a priority value, an extended system ID, and the MAC address of the switch.

**Figure 2-9**   BID Fields

All switches in the broadcast domain participate in the election process. After a switch boots, it begins to send out BPDU frames every two seconds. These BPDUs contain the switch BID and the root ID.

As the switches forward their BPDU frames, adjacent switches in the broadcast domain read the root ID information from the BPDU frames. If the root ID from a BPDU received is lower than the root ID on the receiving switch, the receiving switch updates its root ID, identifying the adjacent switch as the root bridge. Actually, it might not be an adjacent switch, but could be any other switch in the broadcast domain. The switch then forwards new BPDU frames with the lower root ID to the other adjacent switches. Eventually, the switch with the lowest BID ends up being identified as the root bridge for the spanning tree instance.

There is a root bridge elected for each spanning tree instance. It is possible to have multiple distinct root bridges. If all ports on all switches are members of VLAN 1, there is only one spanning tree instance. The extended system ID plays a role in how spanning tree instances are determined.

## Spanning Tree Algorithm: Path Cost (2.1.2.4)

When the root bridge has been elected for the spanning tree instance, the STA starts the process of determining the best paths to the root bridge from all destinations in the broadcast domain. The path information is determined by summing up the individual port costs along the path from the destination to the root bridge. Each "destination" is actually a switch port.

The *default port costs* are defined by the speed at which the port operates. As shown in Table 2-1, 10-Gb/s Ethernet ports have a port cost of 2, 1-Gb/s Ethernet ports have a port cost of 4, 100-Mb/s Fast Ethernet ports have a port cost of 19, and 10-Mb/s Ethernet ports have a port cost of 100.

**Table 2-1**   Best Paths to the Root Bridge

| Link Speed | Cost (Revised IEEE Specification) | Cost (Previous IEEE Specification) |
|---|---|---|
| 10 Gbps | 2 | 1 |
| 1 Gbps | 4 | 1 |
| 100 Mbps | 19 | 10 |
| 10 Mbps | 100 | 100 |

**Note**

As newer, faster Ethernet technologies enter the marketplace, the path cost values can change to accommodate the different speeds available. The nonlinear numbers in Table 2-1 accommodate some improvements to the older Ethernet standard. The values have already been changed to accommodate the 10-Gb/s Ethernet standard. To illustrate the continued change associated with high-speed networking, Catalyst 4500 and 6500 switches support a longer path cost method. For example, 10 Gb/s has a 2000 path cost, 100 Gb/s has a 200 path cost, and 1 Tb/s has a 20 path cost.

Although switch ports have a default port cost associated with them, the port cost is configurable. The ability to configure individual port costs gives the administrator the flexibility to manually control the spanning tree paths to the root bridge.

To configure the port cost of an interface, enter the **spanning-tree cost** *value* command in interface configuration mode. The value can be between 1 and 200,000,000.

In Example 2-1, switch port F0/1 has been configured with a port cost of 25 using the **spanning-tree cost 25** interface configuration mode command on the F0/1 interface.

**Example 2-1**   Configure Port Cost

```
S2# configure terminal
Enter configuration commands, one per line. End with CNTL/Z.
S2(config)# interface f0/1
S2(config-if)# spanning-tree cost 25
S2(config-if)# end
S2#
```

To restore the port cost to the default value of 19, enter the **no spanning-tree cost** interface configuration mode command.

The path cost is equal to the sum of all the port costs along the path to the root bridge, as shown in Figure 2-10.

**Figure 2-10**  Path Cost

Paths with the lowest cost become preferred, and all other redundant paths are blocked. In the example, the path cost from S2 to the root bridge S1, over path 1 is 19 (based on the IEEE-specified individual port cost), while the path cost over path 2 is 38. Because path 1 has a lower overall path cost to the root bridge, it is the preferred path. STP then configures the redundant path to be blocked, preventing a loop from occurring.

To verify the port and path cost to the root bridge, enter the **show spanning-tree** command, as shown in Example 2-2.

**Example 2-2  show spanning-tree** Command

```
S1# show spanning-tree
VLAN0001
  Spanning tree enabled protocol ieee
  Root ID    Priority    27577
             Address     000A.0033.0033
             Cost        19
             Port        1
             Hello Time   2 sec  Max Age 20 sec  Forward Delay 15 sec

  Bridge ID  Priority    32769  (priority 32768 sys-id-ext 1)
             Address     000A.0011.1111
```

```
            Hello Time   2 sec  Max Age 20 sec  Forward Delay 15 sec
            Aging Time  15  sec
Interface           Role Sts Cost      Prio.Nbr Type
------------------- ---- --- --------- -------- -----------------------
Fa0/1               Root FWD 19          128.1   Edge P2p
Fa0/2               Desg FWD 19          128.2   Edge P2p
```

The Cost field near the top of the output is the total path cost to the root bridge.
This value changes depending on how many switch ports must be traversed to get
to the root bridge. In the output, each interface is also identified with an individual
port cost of 19.

## 802.1D BPDU Frame Format (2.1.2.5)

The spanning tree algorithm depends on the exchange of BPDUs to determine a root
bridge. As shown in Table 2-2, a BPDU frame contains 12 distinct fields that convey
path and priority information used to determine the root bridge and paths to the
root bridge.

**Table 2-2**   BPDU Fields

| Field Number | Bytes | Field |
|---|---|---|
| 1–4 | 2 | Protocol ID |
|  | 1 | Version |
|  | 1 | Message type |
|  | 1 | Flags |
| 5–8 | 8 | Root ID |
|  | 4 | Cost of path |
|  | 8 | Bridge ID |
|  | 2 | Port ID |
| 9–12 | 2 | Message age |
|  | 2 | Max age |
|  | 2 | Hello time |
|  | 2 | Forward delay |

The first four fields identify the protocol, version, message type, and status flags.

- The next four fields are used to identify the root bridge and the cost of the path to the root bridge.

- The last four fields are all timer fields that determine how frequently BPDU messages are sent and how long the information received through the BPDU process (next topic) is retained.

Figure 2-11 shows a BPDU frame that was captured using Wireshark.

```
⊞ Frame 1 (60 bytes on wire, 60 bytes captured)
⊟ IEEE 802.3 Ethernet
  ⊞ Destination: Spanning-tree-(for-bridges)_00 (01:80:c2:00:00:00)
  ⊞ Source: Cisco_9e:93:03 (00:19:aa:9e:93:03)
    Length: 38
    Trailer: 0000000000000000
⊞ Logical-Link Control
⊟ Spanning Tree Protocol
    Protocol Identifier: Spanning Tree Protocol (0x0000)
    Protocol Version Identifier: Spanning Tree (0)
    BPDU Type: Configuration (0x00)
  ⊞ BPDU flags: 0x01 (Topology Change)
    Root Identifier: 24577 / 00:19:aa:9e:93:00
    Root Path Cost: 0
    Bridge Identifier: 24577 / 00:19:aa:9e:93:00
    Port identifier: 0x8003
    Message Age: 0
    Max Age: 20
    Hello Time: 2
    Forward Delay: 15
```

**Figure 2-11**   Captured BPDU Frame

In the capture, the BPDU frame contains more fields than previously described. The BPDU message is encapsulated in an Ethernet frame when it is transmitted across the network. The 802.3 header indicates the source and destination addresses of the BPDU frame. This frame has a destination MAC address of 01:80:C2:00:00:00, which is a multicast address for the spanning tree group. When a frame is addressed with this MAC address, each switch that is configured for spanning tree accepts and reads the information from the frame; all other devices on the network disregard the frame.

Also note in the capture, the root ID and the BID are the same in the captured BPDU frame. This indicates that the frame was captured from a root bridge. The timers are all set to the default values.

## BPDU Propagation and Process (2.1.2.6)

Each switch in the broadcast domain initially assumes that it is the root bridge for a spanning tree instance, so the BPDU frames sent contain the BID of the local switch as the root ID. By default, BPDU frames are sent every two seconds after a switch is booted; that is, the default value of the Hello timer specified in the BPDU frame is two seconds. Each switch maintains local information about its own BID, the root ID, and the path cost to the root.

When adjacent switches receive a BPDU frame, they compare the root ID from the BPDU frame with the local root ID. If the root ID in the BPDU is lower than the local root ID, the switch updates the local root ID and the ID in its BPDU messages. These messages indicate the new root bridge on the network. The distance to the root bridge is also indicated by the path cost update. For example, if the BPDU was received on a Fast Ethernet switch port, the path cost would increment by 19. If the local root ID is lower than the root ID received in the BPDU frame, the BPDU frame is discarded.

After a root ID has been updated to identify a new root bridge, all subsequent BPDU frames sent from that switch contain the new root ID and updated path cost. That way, all other adjacent switches are able to see the lowest root ID identified at all times. As the BPDU frames pass between other adjacent switches, the path cost is continually updated to indicate the total path cost to the root bridge. Each switch in the spanning tree uses its path costs to identify the best possible path to the root bridge.

The following summarizes the BPDU process:

**Note**

Priority is the initial deciding factor when electing a root bridge. If the priorities of all the switches are the same, the device with the lowest MAC address becomes the root bridge.

1. Initially, each switch identifies itself as the root bridge. S2 forwards BPDU frames out all switch ports. (See Figure 2-12.)

**Figure 2-12**    BPDU Process: Step 1

2. When S3 receives a BPDU from switch S2, S3 compares its root ID with the BPDU frame it received. The priorities are equal, so the switch is forced to examine the MAC address portion to determine which MAC address has a lower value. Because S2 has a lower MAC address value, S3 updates its root ID with the S2 root ID. At that point, S3 considers S2 as the root bridge. (See Figure 2-13.)

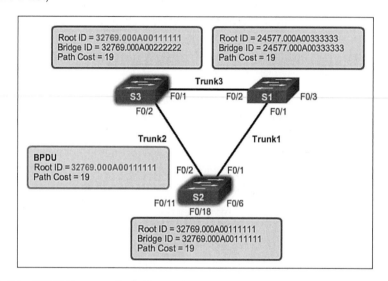

**Figure 2-13** BPDU Process: Step 2

3. When S1 compares its root ID with the one in the received BPDU frame, it identifies its local root ID as the lower value and discards the BPDU from S2. (See Figure 2-14.)

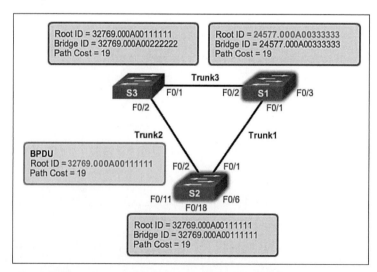

**Figure 2-14** BPDU Process: Step 3

4. When S3 sends out its BPDU frames, the root ID contained in the BPDU frame is that of S2. (See Figure 2-15.)

**Figure 2-15**    BPDU Process: Step 4

5. When S2 receives the BPDU frame, it discards it after verifying that the root ID in the BPDU matched its local root ID. (See Figure 2-16.)

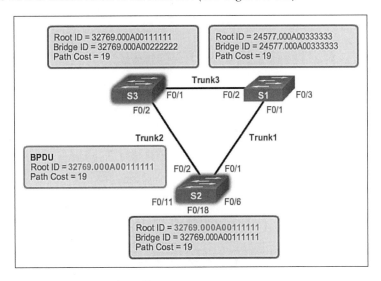

**Figure 2-16**    BPDU Process: Step 5

6. Because S1 has a lower priority value in its root ID, it discards the BPDU frame received from S3. (See Figure 2-17.)

**Figure 2-17**    BPDU Process: Step 6

7. S1 sends out its BPDU frames. (See Figure 2-18.)

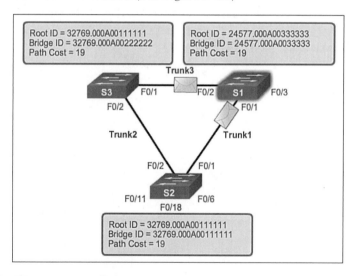

**Figure 2-18**    BPDU Process: Step 7

8. S3 identifies the root ID in the BPDU frame as having a lower value and, therefore, updates its root ID values to indicate that S1 is now the root bridge. (See Figure 2-19.)

**Figure 2-19** BPDU Process: Step 8

9. S2 identifies the root ID in the BPDU frame as having a lower value and, therefore, updates its root ID values to indicate that S1 is now the root bridge. (See Figure 2-20.)

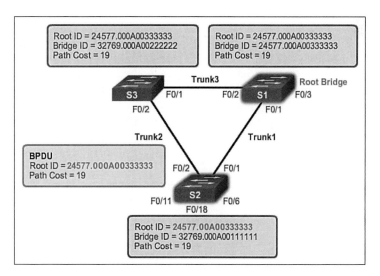

**Figure 2-20** BPDU Process: Step 9

## Extended System ID (2.1.2.7)

The bridge ID (BID) is used to determine the root bridge on a network. The BID field of a BPDU frame contains three separate fields:

- Bridge priority

- Extended system ID

- MAC address

Each field is used during the root bridge election.

### Bridge Priority

The *bridge priority* is a configurable value that can be used to influence which switch becomes the root bridge. The switch with the lowest priority, which implies the lowest BID, becomes the root bridge because a lower-priority value takes precedence. For example, to ensure that a specific switch is always the root bridge, set the priority to a lower value than the rest of the switches on the network. The default priority value for all Cisco switches is 32768. The range is 0 to 61440 in increments of 4096. Valid priority values are 0, 4096, 8192, 12288, 16384, 20480, 24576, 28672, 32768, 36864, 40960, 45056, 49152, 53248, 57344, and 61440. All other values are rejected. A bridge priority of 0 takes precedence over all other bridge priorities.

### Extended System ID

Early implementations of IEEE 802.1D were designed for networks that did not use VLANs. There was a single common spanning tree across all switches. For this reason, in older Cisco switches, the extended system ID could be omitted in BPDU frames. As VLANs became common for network infrastructure segmentation, 802.1D was enhanced to include support for VLANs, requiring the VLAN ID to be included in the BPDU frame. VLAN information is included in the BPDU frame through the use of the extended system ID. All newer switches include the use of the extended system ID by default.

As shown in Figure 2-21, the bridge priority field is 2 bytes or 16 bits in length; 4 bits are used for the bridge priority and 12 bits for the extended system ID, which identifies the VLAN participating in this particular STP process.

Using these 12 bits for the extended system ID reduces the bridge priority to 4 bits. This process reserves the rightmost 12 bits for the VLAN ID and the far left 4 bits for the bridge priority. This explains why the bridge priority value can only be configured in multiples of 4096, or $2^{12}$. If the far left bits are 0001, the bridge priority is 4096; if the far left bits are 1111, the bridge priority is 61440 (= 15 x 4096). The Catalyst 2960 and 3560 Series switches do not allow the configuration of a bridge priority of 65536 (= 16 x 4096) because it assumes the use of a fifth bit that is unavailable because of the use of the extended system ID.

**Figure 2-21**  BID Fields

The extended system ID value is added to the bridge priority value in the BID to identify the priority and VLAN of the BPDU frame.

When two switches are configured with the same priority and have the same extended system ID, the switch having the MAC address with the lowest hexadecimal value will have the lower BID. Initially, all switches are configured with the same default priority value. The MAC address is then the deciding factor on which switch is going to become the root bridge. To ensure that the root bridge decision best meets network requirements, it is recommended that the administrator configure the desired root bridge switch with a lower priority. This also ensures that the addition of new switches to the network does not trigger a new spanning tree election, which can disrupt network communication while a new root bridge is being selected.

In Figure 2-22, S1 has a lower priority than the other switches; therefore, it is preferred as the root bridge for that spanning tree instance.

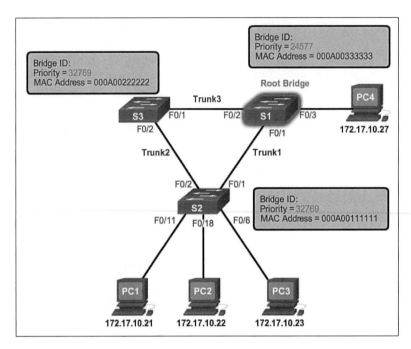

**Figure 2-22**   Priority-Based Decision

When all switches are configured with the same priority, as is the case with all switches kept in the default configuration with a priority of 32768, the MAC address becomes the deciding factor for which switch becomes the root bridge, as shown in Figure 2-23.

> **Note**
>
> In the example, the priority of all the switches is 32769. The value is based on the 32768 default priority and the VLAN 1 assignment associated with each switch (32768+1).

The MAC address with the lowest hexadecimal value is considered to be the pre-ferred root bridge. In the example, S2 has the lowest value for its MAC address and is, therefore, designated as the root bridge for that spanning tree instance.

**Interactive Graphic**

**Activity 2.1.2.8: Identify 802.1D Port Roles**

Go to the course online to perform this practice activity.

**Video**

**Video Demonstration 2.1.2.9: Observing Spanning Tree Protocol Operation**

View the video in the online course for an understanding of STP operation.

**Figure 2-23**    MAC-Based Decision

 **Lab 2.1.2.10: Building a Switched Network with Redundant Links**

In this lab, you will complete the following objectives:

- Part 1: Build the Network and Configure Basic Device Settings
- Part 2: Determine the Root Bridge
- Part 3: Observe STP Port Selection Based on Port Cost
- Part 4: Observe STP Port Selection Based on Port Priority

# Varieties of Spanning Tree Protocols (2.2)

STP has evolved into several different versions since the original specification. Some versions are IEEE standards, while others are proprietary. This section reviews the features unique to each of the more popular STP versions.

## Overview (2.2.1)

To begin to understand the scope of STP versions available, let's briefly look at a list of all of them.

## List of Spanning Tree Protocols (2.2.1.1)

Several varieties of spanning tree protocols have emerged since the original IEEE 802.1D.

The varieties of spanning tree protocols include

- **STP:** This is the original IEEE 802.1D version (802.1D-1998 and earlier) that provides a loop-free topology in a network with redundant links. *Common Spanning Tree (CST)* assumes one spanning tree instance for the entire bridged network, regardless of the number of VLANs.

- *PVST+:* This is a Cisco enhancement of STP that provides a separate 802.1D spanning tree instance for each VLAN configured in the network. The separate instance supports *PortFast*, UplinkFast, BackboneFast, *BPDU guard*, BPDU filter, root guard, and loop guard.

- **802.1D-2004:** This is an updated version of the STP standard, incorporating *IEEE 802.1w*.

- **Rapid Spanning Tree Protocol (RSTP) or IEEE 802.1w:** This is an evolution of STP that provides faster convergence than STP.

- *Rapid PVST+:* This is a Cisco enhancement of RSTP that uses PVST+. Rapid PVST+ provides a separate instance of 802.1w per VLAN. The separate instance supports PortFast, BPDU guard, BPDU filter, root guard, and loop guard.

- **Multiple Spanning Tree Protocol (MSTP):** This is an IEEE standard inspired by the earlier Cisco proprietary Multiple Instance STP (MISTP) implementation. MSTP maps multiple VLANs into the same spanning tree instance. The Cisco implementation of MSTP is MST, which provides up to 16 instances of RSTP and combines many VLANs with the same physical and logical topology into a common RSTP instance. Each instance supports PortFast, BPDU guard, BPDU filter, root guard, and loop guard.

A network professional, whose duties include switch administration, might be required to decide which type of spanning tree protocol to implement.

---

**Note**

The legacy Cisco-proprietary features UplinkFast and BackboneFast are not described in this course. These features are superseded by the implementation of Rapid PVST+, which incorporates these features as part of the implementation of the RSTP standard.

---

## Characteristics of the Spanning Tree Protocols (2.2.1.2)

These are characteristics of the various spanning tree protocols:

- **STP:** Assumes one *IEEE 802.1D* spanning tree instance for the entire bridged network, regardless of the number of VLANs. Because there is only one instance, the CPU and memory requirements for this version are lower than for the other protocols. However, because there is only one instance, there is only one root bridge and one tree. Traffic for all VLANs flows over the same path, which can lead to suboptimal traffic flows. Because of the limitations of 802.1D, this version is slow to converge.

- **PVST+:** A Cisco enhancement of STP that provides a separate instance of the Cisco implementation of 802.1D for each VLAN that is configured in the network. The separate instance supports PortFast, UplinkFast, BackboneFast, BPDU guard, BPDU filter, root guard, and loop guard. Creating an instance for each VLAN increases the CPU and memory requirements, but allows for per-VLAN root bridges. This design allows the spanning tree to be optimized for the traffic of each VLAN. Convergence of this version is similar to the convergence of 802.1D. However, convergence is per-VLAN.

- **RSTP** (or *IEEE 802.1w*): An evolution of spanning tree that provides faster convergence than the original 802.1D implementation. This version addresses many convergence issues, but because it still provides a single instance of STP, it does not address the suboptimal traffic flow issues. To support that faster convergence, the CPU usage and memory requirements of this version are slightly higher than those of CST, but less than those of RSTP+.

- **Rapid PVST+:** A Cisco enhancement of RSTP that uses PVST+. It provides a separate instance of 802.1w per VLAN. The separate instance supports PortFast, BPDU guard, BPDU filter, root guard, and loop guard. This version addresses both the convergence issues and the suboptimal traffic flow issues. However, this version has the largest CPU and memory requirements.

- **MSTP:** The *IEEE 802.1s* standard, inspired by the earlier Cisco-proprietary MISTP implementation. To reduce the number of required STP instances, MSTP maps multiple VLANs that have the same traffic flow requirements into the same spanning tree instance.

- **MST:** The Cisco implementation of MSTP, which provides up to 16 instances of RSTP (802.1w) and combines many VLANs with the same physical and logical topology into a common RSTP instance. Each instance supports PortFast, BPDU guard, BPDU filter, root guard, and loop guard. The CPU and memory requirements of this version are less than those of Rapid PVST+, but more than those of RSTP.

Table 2-3 summarizes these STP characteristics.

**Table 2-3**    Spanning Tree Protocol Characteristics

| Protocol | Standard | Resources Needed | Convergence | Tree Calculation |
|----------|----------|------------------|-------------|------------------|
| STP | 802.1D | Low | Slow | All VLANs |
| PVST+ | Cisco | High | Slow | Per VLAN |
| RSTP | 802.1w | Medium | Fast | All VLANs |
| Rapid PVST+ | Cisco | Very high | Fast | Per VLAN |
| MSTP | 802.1s, Cisco | Medium or high | Fast | Per Instance |

The default spanning tree mode for Cisco Catalyst switches is PVST+, which is enabled on all ports. PVST+ has much slower convergence after a topology change than Rapid PVST+.

**Note**

It is important to distinguish between the legacy IEEE 802.1D-1998 (and earlier) standard and the IEEE 802.1D-2004 standard. IEEE 802.1D-2004 incorporates RSTP functionality, while IEEE 802.1D-1998 refers to the original implementation of the spanning tree algorithm. Newer Cisco switches running newer versions of the IOS, such as Catalyst 2960 switches with IOS 15.0, run PVST+ by default, but incorporate many of the specifications of IEEE 802.1D-1998 in this mode (such as alternate ports in place of the former nondesignated ports). But to run rapid spanning tree on such a switch, it still must be explicitly configured for rapid spanning tree mode.

**Interactive Graphic**

**Activity 2.2.1.3: Identify Types of Spanning Tree Protocols**

Go to the course online to perform this practice activity.

# PVST+ (2.2.2)

PVST+ is a Cisco implementation of STP and is the default STP mode on Cisco Catalyst switches.

## Overview of PVST+ (2.2.2.1)

The original IEEE 802.1D standard defines a Common Spanning Tree (CST) that assumes only one spanning tree instance for the entire switched network, regardless of the number of VLANs. A network running CST has these characteristics:

- No load sharing is possible. One uplink must block for all VLANs.

- The CPU is spared. Only one instance of spanning tree must be computed.

Cisco developed PVST+ so that a network can run an independent instance of the Cisco implementation of IEEE 802.1D for each VLAN in the network. With PVST+, it is possible for one trunk port on a switch to be blocking for a VLAN while not blocking for other VLANs. PVST+ can be used to implement Layer 2 load balancing. Because each VLAN runs a separate instance of STP, the switches in a PVST+ environment require greater CPU process and BPDU bandwidth consumption than a traditional CST implementation of STP.

In a PVST+ environment, spanning tree parameters can be tuned so that half of the VLANs forward on each uplink trunk. In Figure 2-24, port F0/3 on S2 is the forwarding port for VLAN 20, and F0/2 on S2 is the forwarding port for VLAN 10.

**Figure 2-24**   PVST+ Example

This is accomplished by configuring one switch to be elected the root bridge for half of the VLANs in the network, and a second switch to be elected the root bridge for the other half of the VLANs. In the figure, S3 is the root bridge for VLAN 20, and S1 is the root bridge for VLAN 10. Multiple STP root bridges per VLAN increase redundancy in the network.

Networks running PVST+ have these characteristics:

- Optimum load balancing can result.

- One spanning tree instance for each VLAN maintained can mean a considerable waste of CPU cycles for all the switches in the network (in addition to the bandwidth that is used for each instance to send its own BPDU). This would only be problematic if a large number of VLANs are configured.

## Port States and PVST+ Operation (2.2.2.2)

STP facilitates the logical loop-free path throughout the broadcast domain. The spanning tree is determined through the information learned by the exchange of the BPDU frames between the interconnected switches. To facilitate the learning of the logical spanning tree, each switch port transitions through five possible port states and three BPDU timers.

The spanning tree is determined immediately after a switch is finished booting up. If a switch port transitions directly from the blocking to the forwarding state without information about the full topology during the transition, the port can temporarily create a data loop. For this reason, STP introduces the following five port states that ensure that no loops are created during the creation of the logical spanning tree:

- **Blocking:** The port is an alternate port and does not participate in frame forwarding. The port receives BPDU frames to determine the location and root ID of the root bridge switch and what port roles each switch port should assume in the final active STP topology.

- *Listening*: Listens for the path to the root. STP has determined that the port can participate in frame forwarding according to the BPDU frames that the switch has received thus far. At this point, the switch port not only receives BPDU frames, but it also transmits its own BPDU frames and informs adjacent switches that the switch port is preparing to participate in the active topology.

- *Learning*: Learns the MAC addresses. The port prepares to participate in frame forwarding and begins to populate the MAC address table.

- *Forwarding*: The port is considered part of the active topology. It forwards data frames and sends and receives BPDU frames.

- *Disabled*: The Layer 2 port does not participate in spanning tree and does not forward frames. The disabled state is set when the switch port is administratively disabled.

Table 2-4 summarizes the operations that are allowed during each port state.

**Table 2-4**  Port States

| Operation Allowed | Port State | | | | |
| --- | --- | --- | --- | --- | --- |
| | Blocking | Listening | Learning | Forwarding | Disabled |
| Can receive and process BPDUs | yes | yes | yes | no | — |
| Can forward data frames received on interface | no | no | no | yes | no |

| Operation Allowed | Port State | | | | |
|---|---|---|---|---|---|
| | Blocking | Listening | Learning | Forwarding | Disabled |
| Can forward data frames switched from another interface | no | no | no | yes | no |
| Can learn MAC addresses | no | no | yes | yes | no |

Note that the number of ports in each of the various states (blocking, listening, learning, or forwarding) can be displayed with the **show spanning-tree summary** command.

For each VLAN in a switched network, PVST+ performs four steps to provide a loop-free logical network topology:

1. **Elects one root bridge:** Only one switch can act as the root bridge (for a given VLAN). The root bridge is the switch with the lowest bridge ID. On the root bridge, all ports are designated ports (in particular, no root ports).

2. **Selects the root port on each nonroot bridge:** STP establishes one root port on each nonroot bridge. The root port is the lowest-cost path from the nonroot bridge to the root bridge, indicating the direction of the best path to the root bridge. Root ports are normally in the forwarding state.

3. **Selects the designated port on each segment:** On each link, STP establishes one designated port. The designated port is selected on the switch that has the lowest-cost path to the root bridge. Designated ports are normally in the forwarding state, forwarding traffic for the segment.

4. **The remaining ports in the switched network are alternate ports:** Alternate ports normally remain in the blocking state, to logically break the loop topology. When a port is in the blocking state, it does not forward traffic, but can still process received BPDU messages.

## Extended System ID and PVST+ Operation (2.2.2.3)

In a PVST+ environment, the extended switch ID, shown in Figure 2-25, ensures that each switch has a unique BID for each VLAN.

For example, the VLAN 2 default BID would be 32770 (priority 32768, plus the extended system ID of 2). If no priority has been configured, every switch has the same default priority, and the election of the root for each VLAN is based on the MAC address. This method is a random means of selecting the root bridge.

**Figure 2-25**  PVST+ and the Extended System ID

There are situations where the administrator might want a specific switch to be selected as the root bridge. This can be for a variety of reasons, including the switch is more centrally located within the LAN design, the switch has higher processing power, or the switch is simply easier to access and manage remotely. To manipulate the root bridge election, simply assign a lower priority to the switch that should be selected as the root bridge.

**Interactive Graphic**

**Activity 2.2.2.4: Identifying PVST+ Operation**

Go to the course online to perform this practice activity.

# Rapid PVST+ (2.2.3)

Rapid PVST+ is the Cisco-proprietary implementation of RSTP.

## Overview of Rapid PVST+ (2.2.3.1)

RSTP (IEEE 802.1w) is an evolution of the original 802.1D standard and is incorporated into the IEEE 802.1D-2004 standard. The 802.1w STP terminology remains primarily the same as the original IEEE 802.1D STP terminology. Most parameters have been left unchanged, so users familiar with STP can easily configure the new protocol. Rapid PVST+ is simply the Cisco implementation of RSTP on a per-VLAN basis. With Rapid PVST+, an independent instance of RSTP runs for each VLAN.

Figure 2-26 shows a network running RSTP.

**Figure 2-26**   RSTP Port Roles

S1 is the root bridge with two designated ports in a forwarding state. RSTP supports a new port type: Port F0/3 on S2 is an alternate port in discarding state. Notice that there are no blocking ports. RSTP does not have a blocking port state. RSTP defines port states as discarding, learning, or forwarding.

RSTP speeds the recalculation of the spanning tree when the Layer 2 network topology changes. RSTP can achieve much faster convergence in a properly configured network, sometimes in as little as a few hundred milliseconds. RSTP redefines the type of ports and their state. If a port is configured to be an alternate port or a backup port, it can immediately change to forwarding state without waiting for the network to converge. The following briefly describes RSTP characteristics:

- RSTP is the preferred protocol for preventing Layer 2 loops in a switched network environment. Many of the differences were established by Cisco-proprietary enhancements to the original 802.1D. These enhancements, such as BPDUs carrying and sending information about port roles only to neighboring switches, require no additional configuration and generally perform better than the earlier Cisco-proprietary versions. They are now transparent and integrated in the protocol's operation.

- Cisco-proprietary enhancements to the original 802.1D, such as UplinkFast and BackboneFast, are not compatible with RSTP.

- RSTP (802.1w) supersedes the original 802.1D while retaining backward compatibility. Much of the original 802.1D terminology remains and most parameters are unchanged. In addition, 802.1w is capable of reverting to legacy 802.1D to interoperate with legacy switches on a per-port basis. For example, the RSTP spanning tree algorithm elects a root bridge in exactly the same way as the original 802.1D.

- RSTP keeps the same BPDU format as the original IEEE 802.1D, except that the version field is set to 2 to indicate RSTP, and the flags field uses all 8 bits.

- RSTP is able to actively confirm that a port can safely transition to the forwarding state without having to rely on any timer configuration.

## RSTP BPDU (2.2.3.2)

RSTP uses type 2, version 2 BPDUs. The original 802.1D STP uses type 0, version 0 BPDUs. However, a switch running RSTP can communicate directly with a switch running the original 802.1D STP. RSTP sends BPDUs and populates the flag byte in a slightly different manner than in the original 802.1D:

- Protocol information can be immediately aged on a port if Hello packets are not received for three consecutive Hello times, six seconds by default, or if the max age timer expires.

- Because BPDUs are used as a keepalive mechanism, three consecutively missed BPDUs indicate lost connectivity between a bridge and its neighboring root or designated bridge. The fast aging of the information allows failures to be detected quickly.

> **Note**
>
> Like STP, an RSTP switch sends a BPDU with its current information every Hello time period (two seconds, by default), even if the RSTP bridge does not receive any BPDUs from the root bridge.

As shown in Figure 2-27, RSTP uses the flag byte of version 2 BPDU:

- Bits 0 and 7 are used for topology change and acknowledgment as they are in the original 802.1D.

- Bits 1 and 6 are used for the Proposal Agreement process (used for rapid convergence).

- Bits from 2 to 5 encode the role and state of the port.

- Bits 4 and 5 are used to encode the port role using a 2-bit code.

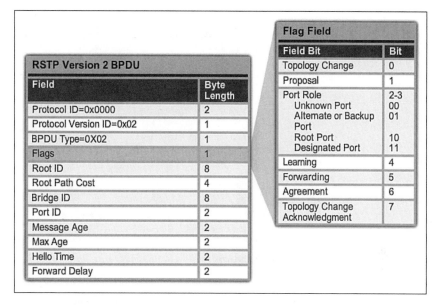

**Figure 2-27**   RSTP BPDU

## Edge Ports (2.2.3.3)

An RSTP *edge port* is a switch port that is never intended to be connected to another switch device. It immediately transitions to the forwarding state when enabled.

The RSTP edge port concept corresponds to the PVST+ PortFast feature; an edge port is directly connected to an end station and assumes that no switch device is connected to it. RSTP edge ports should immediately transition to the forwarding state, thereby skipping the time-consuming original 802.1D listening and learning port states.

The Cisco RSTP implementation, Rapid PVST+, maintains the PortFast keyword, using the **spanning-tree portfast** command for edge port configuration. This makes the transition from STP to RSTP seamless.

Figure 2-28 shows examples of ports that can be configured as edge ports.

Figure 2-29 shows examples of ports that are nonedge ports.

**Figure 2-28**   Edge Ports

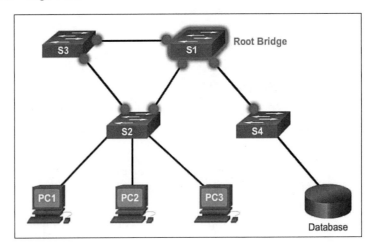

**Figure 2-29**   Nonedge Ports

## Link Types (2.2.3.4)

The link type provides a categorization for each port participating in RSTP by using the duplex mode on the port. Depending on what is attached to each port, two different link types can be identified, as shown in Figure 2-30:

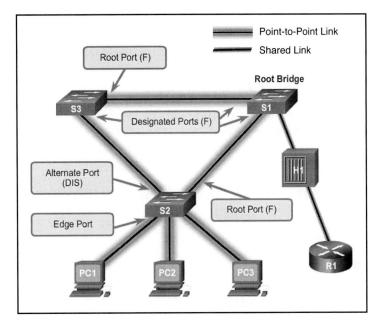

**Figure 2-30**   RSTP Link Types

- *Point-to-Point Link*: A port operating in full-duplex mode typically connects a switch to a switch and is a candidate for rapid transition to a forwarding state.

- *Shared Link*: A port operating in half-duplex mode connects a switch to a hub that attaches multiple devices.

The link type can determine whether the port can immediately transition to a forwarding state, assuming that certain conditions are met. These conditions are different for edge ports and nonedge ports. Nonedge ports are categorized into two link types, point-to-point and shared. The link type is automatically determined, but can be overridden with an explicit port configuration using the **spanning-tree link-type** *parameter* command.

Edge port connections and point-to-point connections are candidates for rapid transition to the forwarding state. However, before the link-type parameter is considered, RSTP must determine the port role. Characteristics of port roles with regard to link types include the following:

- Root ports do not use the link-type parameter. Root ports are able to make a rapid transition to the forwarding state as soon as the port is in sync.

- Alternate and backup ports do not use the link-type parameter in most cases.

- Designated ports make the most use of the link-type parameter. Rapid transition to the forwarding state for the designated port occurs only if the link-type parameter is set to *point-to-point*.

**Interactive Graphic**

**Activity 2.2.3.5: Identify Port Roles in Rapid PVST+**

Go to the course online to perform this practice activity.

**Interactive Graphic**

**Activity 2.2.3.6: Compare PVST+ and Rapid PVST+**

Go to the course online to perform this practice activity.

# Spanning Tree Configuration (2.3)

Although STP runs by default, there are some configurations that allow the network administrator to modify the version and behavior of STP, including root bridge election, speeding up convergence, and load balancing.

## PVST+ Configuration (2.3.1)

In this topic, we review the commands to modify the default PVST+ configuration.

### Catalyst 2960 Default Configuration (2.3.1.1)

Table 2-5 shows the default spanning tree configuration for a Cisco Catalyst 2960 Series switch. Notice that the default spanning tree mode is PVST+.

**Table 2-5**   Default Switch Configuration

| Feature | Default Setting |
|---|---|
| Enable state | Enabled on VLAN 1 |
| Spanning-tree mode | PVST+ |
| Switch priority | 32768 |
| Spanning-tree port priority (configurable on a per-interface basis) | 128 |
| Spanning-tree port cost (configurable on a per-interface basis) | 1000 Mbps: 4<br>100 Mbps: 19<br>10 Mbps: 100 |
| Spanning-tree VLAN port priority (configurable on a per-VLAN basis) | 128 |

| Feature | Default Setting |
|---------|-----------------|
| Spanning-tree VLAN port cost (configurable on a per-VLAN basis) | 1000 Mbps: 4 |
| | 100 Mbps: 19 |
| | 10 Mbps: 100 |
| Spanning-tree timers | Hello time: 2 seconds |
| | Forward-delay time: 15 seconds |
| | Maximum-aging time: 20 seconds |
| | Transmit hold count: 6 BPDUs |

### Configuring and Verifying the Bridge ID (2.3.1.2)

When an administrator wants a specific switch to become a root bridge, the bridge priority value must be adjusted to ensure that it is lower than the bridge priority values of all the other switches on the network. There are two different methods to configure the bridge priority value on a Cisco Catalyst switch, as shown in Figure 2-31.

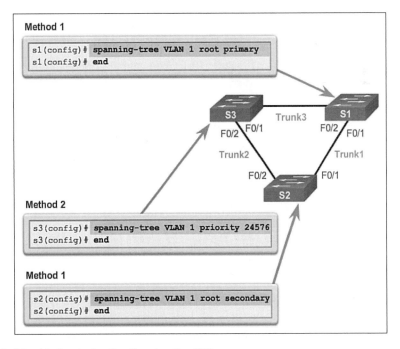

**Figure 2-31**   Methods for Configuring the BID

## Method 1

To ensure that the switch has the lowest bridge priority value, use the **spanning-tree vlan** *vlan-id* **root primary** command in global configuration mode. The priority for the switch is set to the predefined value of 24,576 or to the highest multiple of 4,096, less than the lowest bridge priority detected on the network.

If an alternate root bridge is desired, use the **spanning-tree vlan** *vlan-id* **root secondary** global configuration mode command. This command sets the priority for the switch to the predefined value of 28,672. This ensures that the alternate switch becomes the root bridge if the primary root bridge fails. This assumes that the rest of the switches in the network have the default 32,768 priority value defined.

In Figure 2-31, S1 has been assigned as the primary root bridge using the **spanning-tree vlan 1 root primary** command, and S2 has been configured as the secondary root bridge using the **spanning-tree vlan 1 root secondary** command.

## Method 2

Another method for configuring the bridge priority value is using the **spanning-tree vlan** *vlan-id* **priority** *value* global configuration mode command. This command gives more granular control over the bridge priority value. The priority value is configured in increments of 4,096 between 0 and 61,440.

In Figure 2-31, S3 has been assigned a bridge priority value of 24,576 using the **spanning-tree vlan 1 priority 24576** command.

To verify the bridge priority of a switch, use the **show spanning-tree** command. In Example 2-3, the priority of the switch has been set to 24,576. Also notice that the switch is designated as the root bridge for the spanning tree instance.

**Example 2-3**   Verifying That S3 Is the Root Bridge

```
S3# show spanning-tree
VLAN0001
  Spanning tree enabled protocol ieee
  Root ID    Priority    24577
             Address     000A.0033.0033
             This bridge is the root
             Hello Time   2 sec  Max Age 20 sec  Forward Delay 15 sec

  Bridge ID  Priority    24577  (priority 24576 sys-id-ext 1)
             Address     000A.0033.3333
             Hello Time   2 sec  Max Age 20 sec  Forward Delay 15 sec
             Aging Time   300
```

```
Interface           Role Sts Cost     Prio.Nbr Type
------------------- ---- --- --------- -------- ------------------------
Fa0/1               Desg FWD 4         128.1    P2p
Fa0/2               Desg FWD 4         128.2    P2p
```

## PortFast and BPDU Guard (2.3.1.3)

PortFast is a Cisco feature for PVST+ environments. When a switch port is configured with PortFast, that port transitions from blocking to forwarding state immediately, bypassing the usual 802.1D STP transition states (the listening and learning states). You can use PortFast on access ports to allow these devices to connect to the network immediately, rather than waiting for IEEE 802.1D STP to converge on each VLAN. Access ports are ports that are connected to a single workstation or to a server, as shown in Figure 2-32.

**Figure 2-32**   PortFast and BPDU Guard

In a valid PortFast configuration, BPDUs should never be received, because that would indicate that another bridge or switch is connected to the port, potentially causing a spanning tree loop. Cisco switches support a feature called BPDU guard. When it is enabled, BPDU guard puts the port in an *error-disabled* state on receipt of a BPDU. This will effectively shut down the port. The BPDU guard feature provides a secure response to invalid configurations because you must manually put the interface back into service.

Cisco PortFast technology is useful for DHCP. Without PortFast, a PC can send a DHCP request before the port is in forwarding state, denying the host from getting a usable IP address and other information. Because PortFast immediately changes the state to forwarding, the PC always gets a usable IP address.

> **Note**
>
> Because the purpose of PortFast is to minimize the time that access ports must wait for spanning tree to converge, it should only be used on access ports. If you enable PortFast on a port connecting to another switch, you risk creating a spanning tree loop.

To configure PortFast on a switch port, enter the **spanning-tree portfast** interface configuration mode command on each interface that PortFast is to be enabled. The **spanning-tree portfast default** global configuration mode command enables PortFast on all nontrunking interfaces.

To configure BPDU guard on a Layer 2 access port, use the **spanning-tree bpduguard enable** interface configuration mode command. The **spanning-tree portfast bpduguard default** global configuration command enables BPDU guard on all PortFast-enabled ports.

To verify that PortFast and BPDU guard have been enabled for a switch port, use the **show running-config** command. PortFast and BPDU guard are disabled, by default, on all interfaces.

In Example 2-4, the FastEthernet 0/11 interface is configured with PortFast and BPDU guard.

**Example 2-4**   Configuring and Verifying PortFast and BPDU Guard

```
S2(config)# interface FastEthernet 0/11
S2(config-if)# spanning-tree portfast
%Warning: portfast should only be enabled on ports connected to a single
 host. Connecting hubs, concentrators, switches, bridges, etc... to this
 interface  when portfast is enabled, can cause temporary bridging loops.
 Use with CAUTION


%Portfast has been configured on FastEthernet0/11 but will only
 have effect when the interface is in a non-trunking mode.

S2(config-if)# spanning-tree bpduguard enable
S2(config-if)# end
S2# show running-config interface f0/11
Building configuration...


Current configuration : 90 bytes
```

```
!
interface FastEthernet0/11
 spanning-tree portfast
 spanning-tree bpduguard enable
end
```

## PVST+ Load Balancing (2.3.1.4)

The topology in Figure 2-33 shows three switches with 802.1Q trunks connecting them.

**Figure 2-33** Configure PVST+

There are two VLANs, 10 and 20, that are being trunked across these links. The goal is to configure S3 as the root bridge for VLAN 20 and S1 as the root bridge for VLAN 10. Port F0/3 on S2 is the forwarding port for VLAN 20 and the blocking port for VLAN 10. Port F0/2 on S2 is the forwarding port for VLAN 10 and the blocking port for VLAN 20.

In addition to establishing a root bridge, it is also possible to establish a secondary root bridge. A secondary root bridge is a switch that can become the root bridge for a VLAN if the primary root bridge fails. Assuming that the other bridges in the VLAN retain their default STP priority, this switch becomes the root bridge if the primary root bridge fails.

The steps to configure PVST+ on this example topology are

**Step 1.**   Select the switches that you want for the primary and secondary root bridges for each VLAN. For example, in Figure 2-33, S3 is the primary bridge for VLAN 20 and S1 is the secondary bridge for VLAN 20.

**Step 2.**   Configure the switch to be a primary bridge for the VLAN by using the **spanning-tree vlan** *number* **root primary** command, as shown in Example 2-5.

**Step 3.**   Configure the switch to be a secondary bridge for the VLAN by using the **spanning-tree vlan** *number* **root secondary** command.

Another way to specify the root bridge is to set the spanning tree priority on each switch to the lowest value so that the switch is selected as the primary bridge for its associated VLAN.

Notice that in Example 2-5, S3 is configured as the primary root bridge for VLAN 20 and S1 is configured as the primary root bridge for VLAN 10. S2 retained its default STP priority.

**Example 2-5**   Configuring Primary and Secondary Root Bridge for Each VLAN

```
S3(config)# spanning-tree vlan 20 root primary
S3(config)# spanning-tree vlan 10 root secondary

S1(config)# spanning-tree vlan 10 root primary
S1(config)# spanning-tree vlan 20 root secondary
```

Example 2-5 also shows that S3 is configured as the secondary root bridge for VLAN 10, and S1 is configured as the secondary root bridge for VLAN 20. This configuration enables spanning tree load balancing, with VLAN 10 traffic passing through S1 and VLAN 20 traffic passing through S3.

Another way to specify the root bridge is to set the spanning tree priority on each switch to the lowest value so that the switch is selected as the primary bridge for its associated VLAN, as shown in Example 2-6.

**Example 2-6**   Configuring the Lowest Possible Priority to Ensure That the Switch Is Root

```
S3(config)# spanning-tree vlan 20 priority 4096

S3(config)# spanning-tree vlan 20 priority 4096
```

The switch priority can be set for any spanning tree instance. This setting affects the likelihood that a switch is selected as the root bridge. A lower value increases the probability that the switch is selected. The range is 0 to 61,440 in increments of 4,096; all other values are rejected. For example, a valid priority value is 4,096 x 2 = 8,192.

As shown in Example 2-7, the **show spanning-tree active** command displays spanning tree configuration details for the active interfaces only.

**Example 2-7**  Verifying STP Active Interfaces

```
S1# show spanning-tree active
<output omitted>
VLAN0010
  Spanning tree enabled protocol ieee
  Root ID    Priority    4106
             Address     ec44.7631.3880
             This bridge is the root
             Hello Time   2 sec  Max Age 20 sec  Forward Delay 15 sec

  Bridge ID  Priority    4106    (priority 4096 sys-id-ext 10)
             Address     ec44.7631.3880
             Hello Time   2 sec  Max Age 20 sec  Forward Delay 15 sec
             Aging Time   300 sec


Interface          Role Sts Cost      Prio.Nbr Type
------------------ ---- --- --------- -------- --------------------------------
Fa0/3              Desg FWD 19        128.5    P2p
Fa0/4              Desg FWD 19        128.6    P2p
```

The output shown is for S1 configured with PVST+. There are a number of Cisco IOS command parameters associated with the **show spanning-tree** command.

In Example 2-8, the output shows that the priority for VLAN 10 is 4,096, the lowest of the three respective VLAN priorities.

**Example 2-8**  Verifying the S1 STP Configuration

```
S1# show running-config | include span
spanning-tree mode pvst
spanning-tree extend system-id
spanning-tree vlan 1 priority 24576
spanning-tree vlan 10 priority 4096
spanning-tree vlan 20 priority 28672
```

**Packet Tracer 2.3.1.5: Configuring PVST+**

In this activity, you will configure VLANs and trunks, and examine and configure the Spanning Tree Protocol primary and secondary root bridges. You will also optimize the switched topology using PVST+, PortFast, and BPDU guard.

# Rapid PVST+ Configuration (2.3.2)

Because PVST+ is the default STP mode, Rapid PVST+ must be explicitly configured.

## Spanning Tree Mode (2.3.2.1)

Rapid PVST+ is the Cisco implementation of RSTP. It supports RSTP on a per-VLAN basis. The topology in Figure 2-34 has two VLANs: 10 and 20.

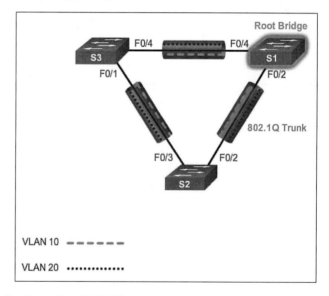

**Figure 2-34**   Configure Rapid PVST+

> **Note**
>
> The default spanning tree configuration on a Catalyst 2960 Series switch is PVST+. A Catalyst 2960 switch supports PVST+, Rapid PVST+, and MST, but only one version can be active for all VLANs at any time.

Rapid PVST+ commands control the configuration of VLAN spanning tree instances. A spanning tree instance is created when an interface is assigned to a VLAN and is removed when the last interface is moved to another VLAN. As well, you can configure STP switch and port parameters before a spanning tree instance is created. These parameters are applied when a spanning tree instance is created.

Table 2-6 displays the Cisco IOS command syntax needed to configure Rapid PVST+ on a Cisco switch.

**Table 2-6**   Rapid PVST+ Configuration Commands

| Description | Command Syntax |
|---|---|
| Enter global configuration mode. | **configure terminal** |
| Configure Rapid PVST+ spanning-tree mode. | **spanning-tree mode rapid-pvst** |
| Enter interface configuration mode. | **interface** *interface-id* |
| Specify that the link type for this port is point-to-point. | **spanning-tree link-type point-to-point** |
| Return to privileged EXEC mode. | **end** |
| Clear all detected STP. | **clear spanning-tree detected-protocols** |

The **spanning-tree mode rapid-pvst** global configuration mode command is the one required command for the Rapid PVST+ configuration. When specifying an interface to configure, valid interfaces include physical ports, VLANs, and port channels. The VLAN ID range is 1 to 4094 when the enhanced software image (EI) is installed and 1 to 1005 when the standard software image (SI) is installed. The port-channel range is 1 to 6.

Example 2-9 shows Rapid PVST+ commands configured on S1.

**Example 2-9**   Configuring Rapid PVST+ on S1

```
S1# configure terminal
S1(config)# spanning-tree mode rapid-pvst
S1(config)# interface f0/2
S1(config-if)# spanning-tree link-type point-to-point
S1(config-if)# end
S1# clear spanning-tree detected-protocols
```

In Example 2-10, the **show spanning-tree vlan 10** command shows the spanning tree configuration for VLAN 10 on switch S1.

**Example 2-10** Verifying That VLAN 10 Is Using RSTP

```
S1# show spanning-tree vlan 10


VLAN0010
  Spanning tree enabled protocol rstp
  Root ID    Priority    4106
             Address     ec44.7631.3880
             This bridge is the root
             Hello Time   2 sec  Max Age 20 sec  Forward Delay 15 sec

  Bridge ID  Priority    4106   (priority 4096 sys-id-ext 10)
             Address     ec44.7631.3880
             Hello Time   2 sec  Max Age 20 sec  Forward Delay 15 sec
             Aging Time  300 sec


Interface          Role Sts Cost      Prio.Nbr Type
------------------ ---- --- --------- -------- --------------------------------
Fa0/3              Desg FWD 19        128.5    P2p Peer(STP)
Fa0/4              Desg FWD 19        128.6    P2p Peer(STP)
```

Notice that the BID priority is set to 4,096. In the output, the statement "Spanning tree enabled protocol rstp" indicates that S1 is running Rapid PVST+. Because S1 is the root bridge for VLAN 10, all of its interfaces are designated ports.

In Example 2-11, the **show running-config** command is used to verify the Rapid PVST+ configuration on S1.

**Example 2-11** Verifying the Rapid PVST+ Configuration

```
S1# show running-config | include span
spanning-tree mode rapid-pvst
spanning-tree extend system-id
spanning-tree vlan 1 priority 24576
spanning-tree vlan 10 priority 4096
spanning-tree vlan 20 priority 28672
spanning-tree link-type point-to-point
```

**Note**

Generally, it is unnecessary to configure the point-to-point *link-type* parameter for Rapid PVST+, because it is unusual to have a shared *link-type*. In most cases, the only difference between configuring PVST+ and Rapid PVST+ is the **spanning-tree mode rapid-pvst** command.

**Packet Tracer 2.3.2.2: Configuring Rapid PVST+**

In this activity, you will configure VLANs and trunks, and examine and configure the Spanning Tree primary and secondary root bridges. You will also optimize them by using rapid PVST+, PortFast, and BPDU guard.

**Lab 2.3.2.3: Configuring Rapid PVST+, PortFast, and BPDU Guard**

In this lab, you will complete the following objectives:

- Part 1: Build the Network and Configure Basic Device Settings

- Part 2: Configure VLANs, Native VLAN, and Trunks

- Part 3: Configure the Root Bridge and Examine PVST+ Convergence

- Part 4: Configure Rapid PVST+, PortFast, BPDU Guard, and Examine Convergence

# STP Configuration Issues (2.3.3)

If STP configuration is left unchanged, the algorithm might not choose the best root bridge. So it is usually desirable to change the configuration. This topic reviews some of the common issues that can occur when the STP configuration is modified.

## Analyzing the STP Topology (2.3.3.1)

To analyze the STP topology, follow these steps as shown in Figure 2-35:

Step 1.    Discover the Layer 2 topology. Use network documentation if it exists or use the **show cdp neighbors** command to discover the Layer 2 topology.

Step 2.    After discovering the Layer 2 topology, use STP knowledge to determine the expected Layer 2 path. It is necessary to know which switch is the root bridge.

Step 3.    Use the **show spanning-tree vlan** command to determine which switch is the root bridge.

Step 4.    Use the **show spanning-tree vlan** command on all switches to find out which ports are in the blocking or forwarding state and confirm your expected Layer 2 path.

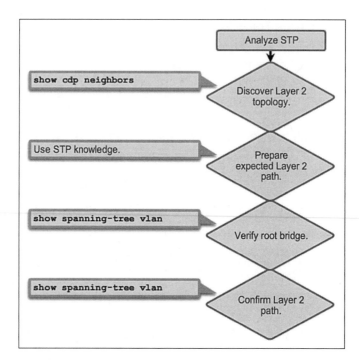

**Figure 2-35**   Analyzing the STP Topology

## Expected Topology Versus Actual Topology (2.3.3.2)

In many networks, the optimal STP topology is determined as part of the network design and then implemented through manipulation of STP priority and cost values. Situations can occur where STP was not considered in the network design and implementation, or where it was considered or implemented before the network underwent significant growth and change. In such situations, it is important to know how to analyze the actual STP topology in the operational network.

A big part of troubleshooting consists of comparing the actual state of the network against the expected state of the network and spotting the differences to gather clues about the troubleshooting problem. A network professional should be able to examine the switches and determine the actual topology, and be able to understand what the underlying spanning tree topology should be.

## Overview of Spanning Tree Status (2.3.3.3)

Using the **show spanning-tree** command without specifying any additional options provides a quick overview of the status of STP for all VLANs that are defined on a switch. If interested only in a particular VLAN, limit the scope of this command by specifying that VLAN as an option.

Use the **show spanning-tree vlan** *vlan_id* command to get STP information for a particular VLAN. Use this command to get information about the role and status of each port on the switch. In Figure 2-36, the example output on switch S1 shows all three ports in the forwarding (FWD) state and the role of the three ports as either designated ports or root ports. Any ports being blocked display the output status as "BLK."

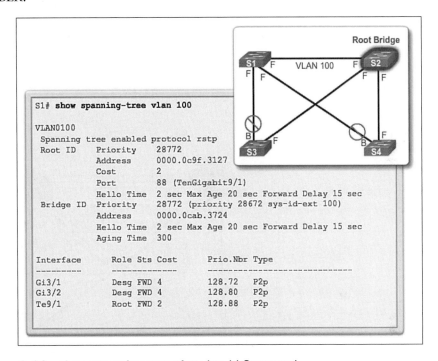

**Figure 2-36   show spanning-tree vlan** vlan_id Command

The output also gives information about the BID of the local switch and the root ID, which is the BID of the root bridge.

## Spanning Tree Failure Consequences (2.3.3.4)

With many protocols, a malfunction means that you lose the functionality that the protocol was providing. For example, if OSPF malfunctions on a router, connectivity to networks that are reachable through that router might be lost. This would generally not affect the rest of the OSPF network. If connectivity to the router is still available, it is possible to troubleshoot to diagnose and fix the problem.

With STP, there are two types of failure. The first is similar to the OSPF problem; STP might erroneously block ports that should have gone into the forwarding state. Connectivity might be lost for traffic that would normally pass through this switch, but the rest of the network remains unaffected. The second type of failure is much more disruptive. It happens when STP erroneously moves one or more ports into the forwarding state.

Remember that an Ethernet frame header does not include a TTL field, which means that any frame that enters a bridging loop continues to be forwarded by the switches indefinitely. The only exceptions are frames that have their destination address recorded in the MAC address table of the switches. These frames are simply forwarded to the port that is associated with the MAC address and do not enter a loop. However, any frame that is flooded by a switch enters the loop. This can include broadcasts, multicasts, and unicasts with a globally unknown destination MAC address.

Figure 2-37 graphically displays the consequences and corresponding symptoms of STP failure.

**Figure 2-37**    STP Failure

The load on all links in the switched LAN quickly starts increasing as more and more frames enter the loop. This problem is not limited to the links that form the loop, but also affects any other links in the switched domain because the frames are flooded on all links. When the spanning tree failure is limited to a single VLAN, only links in that VLAN are affected. Switches and trunks that do not carry that VLAN operate normally.

If the spanning tree failure has created a bridging loop, traffic increases exponentially. The switches will then flood the broadcasts out multiple ports. This creates copies of the frames every time the switches forward them.

When control plane traffic starts entering the loop (for example, OSPF Hellos or EIGRP Hellos), the devices that are running these protocols quickly start getting overloaded. Their CPUs approach 100 percent utilization while they are trying to process an ever-increasing load of control plane traffic. In many cases, the earliest indication of this broadcast storm in progress is that routers or Layer 3 switches are reporting control plane failures and that they are running at a high CPU load.

The switches experience frequent MAC address table changes. If a loop exists, a switch might see a frame with a certain source MAC address coming in on one port and then see another frame with the same source MAC address coming in on a different port a fraction of a second later. This will cause the switch to update the MAC address table twice for the same MAC address.

Because of the combination of very high load on all links and the switch CPUs running at maximum load, these devices typically become unreachable. This makes it very difficult to diagnose the problem while it is happening.

### Repairing a Spanning Tree Problem (2.3.3.5)

One way to correct spanning tree failure is to manually remove redundant links in the switched network, either physically or through configuration, until all loops are eliminated from the topology. When the loops are broken, the traffic and CPU loads should quickly drop to normal levels, and connectivity to devices should be restored.

Although this intervention restores connectivity to the network, it is not the end of the troubleshooting process. All redundancy from the switched network has been removed, and now the redundant links must be restored.

If the underlying cause of the spanning tree failure has not been fixed, chances are that restoring the redundant links will trigger a new broadcast storm. Before restoring the redundant links, determine and correct the cause of the spanning tree failure. Carefully monitor the network to ensure that the problem is fixed.

**Interactive Graphic**

**Activity 2.3.3.6: Troubleshoot STP Configuration Issues**

Go to the course online to perform this practice activity.

# First Hop Redundancy Protocols (2.4)

The term First Hop Redundancy Protocol (FHRP) refers to a collection of protocols that transparently provide end users with at least one redundant default gateway.

# Concept of First Hop Redundancy Protocols (2.4.1)

With redundant routers and redundant links, it is possible to configure a redundant default gateway.

## Default Gateway Limitations (2.4.1.1)

Spanning tree protocols enable physical redundancy in a switched network. However, a host at the access layer of a hierarchical network also benefits from alternate default gateways. If a router or router interface (that serves as a default gateway) fails, the hosts configured with that default gateway are isolated from outside networks. A mechanism is needed to provide alternate default gateways in switched networks where two or more routers are connected to the same VLANs.

> **Note**
>
> For the purposes of the discussion on router redundancy, there is no functional difference between a multilayer switch and a router at the distribution layer. In practice, it is common for a multilayer switch to act as the default gateway for each VLAN in a switched network. This discussion focuses on the functionality of *routing*, regardless of the physical device used.

In a switched network, each client receives only one default gateway. There is no way to configure a secondary gateway, even if a second path exists to carry packets off the local segment.

In Figure 2-38, R1 is responsible for routing packets from PC1.

If R1 becomes unavailable, the routing protocols can dynamically converge. R2 now routes packets from outside networks that would have gone through R1. However, traffic from the inside network associated with R1, including traffic from workstations, servers, and printers configured with R1 as their default gateway, is still sent to R1 and dropped.

End devices are typically configured with a single IP address for a default gateway. This address does not change when the network topology changes. If that default gateway IP address cannot be reached, the local device is unable to send packets off the local network segment, effectively disconnecting it from the rest of the network. Even if a redundant router exists that could serve as a default gateway for that segment, there is no dynamic method by which these devices can determine the address of a new default gateway.

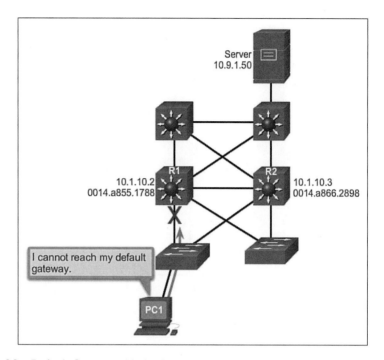

**Figure 2-38**    Default Gateway Limitations

## Router Redundancy (2.4.1.2)

One way to prevent a single point of failure at the default gateway is to implement a virtual router. To implement this type of router redundancy, multiple routers are configured to work together to present the illusion of a single router to the hosts on the LAN, as shown in Figure 2-39. By sharing an IP address and a MAC address, two or more routers can act as a single virtual router.

The IP address of the virtual router is configured as the default gateway for the workstations on a specific IP segment. When frames are sent from host devices to the default gateway, the hosts use ARP to resolve the MAC address that is associated with the IP address of the default gateway. The ARP resolution returns the MAC address of the virtual router. Frames that are sent to the MAC address of the virtual router can then be physically processed by the currently active router within the virtual router group. A protocol is used to identify two or more routers as the devices that are responsible for processing frames that are sent to the MAC or IP address of a single virtual router. Host devices send traffic to the address of the virtual router. The physical router that forwards this traffic is transparent to the host devices.

**Figure 2-39**   Router Redundancy

A redundancy protocol provides the mechanism for determining which router should take the active role in forwarding traffic. It also determines when the forwarding role must be taken over by a standby router. The transition from one forwarding router to another is transparent to the end devices.

The ability of a network to dynamically recover from the failure of a device acting as a default gateway is known as first hop redundancy.

## Steps for Router Failover (2.4.1.3)

When the active router fails, the redundancy protocol transitions the standby router to the new active router role, as shown in Figure 2-40.

These are the steps that take place when the active router fails:

1. The standby router stops seeing Hello messages from the forwarding router.

2. The standby router assumes the role of the forwarding router.

3. Because the new forwarding router assumes both the IP and MAC addresses of the virtual router, the host devices see no disruption in service.

**Activity 2.4.1.4: Identify FHRP Terminology**

Go to the course online to perform this practice activity.

**Figure 2-40**   Router Failover Example

# Varieties of First Hop Redundancy Protocols (2.4.2)

There are several options to choose from when configuring an FHRP.

## First Hop Redundancy Protocols (2.4.2.1)

The following list defines the options available for First Hop Redundancy Protocols (FHRP).

- *Hot Standby Router Protocol (HSRP):* A Cisco-proprietary FHRP designed to allow for transparent failover of a first hop IPv4 device. HSRP provides high network availability by providing first-hop routing redundancy for IPv4 hosts on networks configured with an IPv4 default gateway address. HSRP is used in a group of routers for selecting an active device and a standby device. In a group of device interfaces, the active device is the device that is used for routing packets; the standby device is the device that takes over when the active device fails, or when preset conditions are met. The function of the HSRP standby router is to monitor the operational status of the HSRP group and to quickly assume packet-forwarding responsibility if the active router fails.

- **HSRP for IPv6:** A Cisco-proprietary FHRP providing the same functionality of HSRP, but in an IPv6 environment. An HSRP IPv6 group has a virtual MAC address derived from the HSRP group number and a virtual IPv6 link-local address derived from the HSRP virtual MAC address. Periodic router advertisements (RA) are sent for the HSRP virtual IPv6 link-local address when the HSRP group is active. When the group becomes inactive, these RAs stop after a final RA is sent.

- *Virtual Router Redundancy Protocol* **version 2 (VRRPv2):** A nonproprietary election protocol that dynamically assigns responsibility for one or more virtual routers to the VRRP routers on an IPv4 LAN. This allows several routers on a multiaccess link to use the same virtual IPv4 address. A VRRP router is configured to run the VRRP protocol in conjunction with one or more other routers attached to a LAN. In a VRRP configuration, one router is elected as the virtual router master, with the other routers acting as backups, in case the virtual router master fails.

- **VRRPv3:** Provides the capability to support IPv4 and IPv6 addresses. VRRPv3 works in multivendor environments and is more scalable than VRRPv2.

- *Gateway Load Balancing Protocol* **(GLBP):** A Cisco-proprietary FHRP that protects data traffic from a failed router or circuit, like HSRP and VRRP, while also allowing load balancing (also called load sharing) between a group of redundant routers.

- **GLBP for IPv6:** A Cisco-proprietary FHRP providing the same functionality of GLBP, but in an IPv6 environment. GLBP for IPv6 provides automatic router backup for IPv6 hosts configured with a single default gateway on a LAN. Multiple first-hop routers on the LAN combine to offer a single virtual first-hop IPv6 router while sharing the IPv6 packet-forwarding load.

- *ICMP Router Discovery Protocol* **(IRDP):** Specified in RFC 1256, this is a legacy FHRP solution. IRDP allows IPv4 hosts to locate routers that provide IPv4 connectivity to other (nonlocal) IP networks.

**Interactive Graphic**

**Activity 2.4.2.2: Identify the Type of FHRP**

Go to the course online to perform this practice activity.

## FHRP Verification (2.4.3)

This topic briefly reviews the tasks necessary to configure and verify HSRP and GLBP.

### HSRP Verification (2.4.3.1)

Figure 2-41 shows an example topology for configuring either HSRP or GLBP.

**Figure 2-41**    FHRP Configuration Topology

An HSRP active router has the following characteristics:

- Responds to default gateway's ARP requests with the virtual router's MAC.
- Assumes active forwarding of packets for the virtual router.
- Sends Hello messages.
- Knows the virtual router IP address.

An HSRP standby router has the following characteristics:

- Listens for periodic Hello messages.
- Assumes active forwarding of packets if it does not hear from the active router.

Use the **show standby** command to verify the HSRP state. In Example 2-12, the output shows that R1 is in the active state.

**Example 2-12**    Verifying That R1 Is the HSRP Active Router

```
R1# show standby
FastEthernet0/1 - Group 10
  State is Active
    2 state changes, last state change 00:04:01
  Virtual IP address is 172.16.10.1
  Active virtual MAC address is 0000.0c07.ac0a
    Local virtual MAC address is 0000.0c07.ac0a (v1 default)
  Hello time 3 sec, hold time 10 sec
    Next hello sent in 0.528 secs
  Preemption disabled
  Active router is local
  Standby router is 172.16.10.3, priority 110 (expires in 10.576 sec)
  Priority 150 (configured 150)
  Group name is "hsrp-Fa0/1-10" (default)
```

## GLBP Verification (2.4.3.2)

Although HSRP and VRRP provide gateway resiliency, for the standby members of the redundancy group, the upstream bandwidth is not used while the device is in standby mode.

Only the active router in HSRP and VRRP groups forwards traffic for the virtual MAC address. Resources that are associated with the standby router are not fully utilized. You can accomplish some load balancing with these protocols by creating multiple groups and assigning multiple default gateways, but this configuration creates an administrative burden.

GLBP is a Cisco-proprietary solution to allow automatic selection and simultaneous use of multiple available gateways in addition to automatic failover between those gateways. Multiple routers share the load of frames that, from a client perspective, are sent to a single default gateway address, as shown in Figure 2-42.

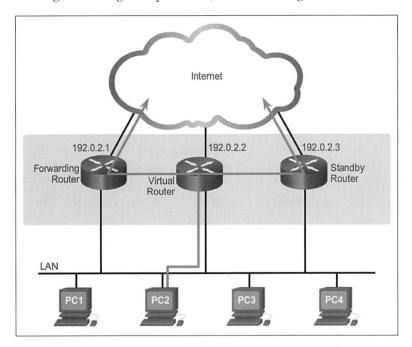

**Figure 2-42** Gateway Load-Balancing Protocol

With GLBP, you can fully utilize resources without the administrative burden of configuring multiple groups and managing multiple default gateway configurations. GLBP has the following characteristics:

- Allows full use of resources on all devices without the administrative burden of creating multiple groups.

- Provides a single virtual IP address and multiple virtual MAC addresses.

- Routes traffic to single gateway distributed across routers.

- Provides automatic rerouting in the event of any failure.

Use the **show glbp** command to verify the GLBP status. Example 2-13 for R1 shows that GLBP group 10 is in the active state with virtual IP address 172.16.10.1. R1 is the active router for Forwarder 2.

**Example 2-13**   Verifying R1 GLBP Forwarding Roles

```
R1# show glbp
FastEthernet0/1 - Group 10
  State is Active
    2 state changes, last state change 00:02:50
  Virtual IP address is 172.16.10.1
  Hello time 3 sec, hold time 10 sec
    Next hello sent in 1.408 secs
  Redirect time 600 sec, forwarder timeout 14400 sec
  Preemption disabled
  Active is local
  Standby is 172.16.10.3, priority 110 (expires in 7.776 sec)
  Priority 150 (configured)
  Weighting 100 (default 100), thresholds: lower 1, upper 100
  Load balancing: round-robin
  Group members:
    0016.c8ee.131a (172.16.10.3)
    001b.d4ef.5091 (172.16.10.2) local
  There are 2 forwarders (1 active)
  Forwarder 1
    State is Listen
      2 state changes, last state change 00:00:09
    MAC address is 0007.b400.0a01 (learnt)
    Owner ID is 0016.c8ee.131a
    Redirection enabled, 597.792 sec remaining (maximum 600 sec)
    Time to live: 14397.792 sec (maximum 14400 sec)
    Preemption enabled, min delay 30 sec
    Active is 172.16.10.3 (primary), weighting 100 (expires in 9.920 sec)
  Forwarder 2
    State is Active
      1 state change, last state change 00:05:57
    MAC address is 0007.b400.0a02 (default)
    Owner ID is 001b.d4ef.5091
    Redirection enabled
    Preemption enabled, min delay 30 sec
    Active is local, weighting 100
```

## Syntax Checker — HSRP and GLBP (2.4.3.3)

Configuration of HSRP and GLBP is beyond the scope of this course. However, familiarity with the commands used to enable HSRP and GLBP aid in understanding the configuration output. For this reason, the syntax checker and subsequent lab are available as optional exercises.

**Lab 2.4.3.4: Configuring HSRP and GLBP**

In this lab, you will complete the following objectives:

- Part 1: Build the Network and Verify Connectivity
- Part 2: Configure First Hop Redundancy Using HSRP
- Part 3: Configure First Hop Redundancy Using GLBP

# Summary (2.5)

**Class Activity 2.5.1.1: Documentation Tree**

The employees in your building are having difficulty accessing a web server on the network. You look for the network documentation that the previous network engineer used before he transitioned to a new job; however, you cannot find any network documentation whatsoever.

Therefore, you decide to create your own network record-keeping system. You decide to start at the access layer of your network hierarchy. This is where redundant switches are located, as well as the company servers, printers, and local hosts.

You create a matrix to record your documentation and include access layer switches on the list. You also decide to document switch names, ports in use, cabling connections, root ports, designated ports, and alternate ports.

---

Problems that can result from a redundant Layer 2 network include broadcast storms, MAC database instability, and duplicate unicast frames. STP is a Layer 2 protocol that ensures that there is only one logical path between all destinations on the network by intentionally blocking redundant paths that could cause a loop.

STP sends BPDU frames for communication between switches. One switch is elected as the root bridge for each instance of spanning tree. An administrator can control this election by changing the bridge priority. Root bridges can be configured to enable spanning tree load balancing by VLAN or by a group of VLANs, depending on the spanning tree protocol used. STP then assigns a port role to each participating port using a path cost. The path cost is equal to the sum of all the port costs along the path to the root bridge. A port cost is automatically assigned to each port; however, it can also be manually configured. Paths with the lowest cost become preferred, and all other redundant paths are blocked.

PVST+ is the default configuration of IEEE 802.1D on Cisco switches. It runs one instance of STP for each VLAN. A newer, faster-converging spanning tree protocol, RSTP, can be implemented on Cisco switches on a per-VLAN basis in the form of Rapid PVST+. Multiple Spanning Tree (MST) is the Cisco implementation of Multiple Spanning Tree Protocol (MSTP), where one instance of spanning tree runs for a defined group of VLANs. Features such as PortFast and BPDU guard ensure that hosts in the switched environment are provided immediate access to the network without interfering with spanning tree operation.

First Hop Redundancy Protocols, such as HSRP, VRRP, and GLBP, provide alternate default gateways for hosts in the redundant router or multilayer switched environment. Multiple routers share a virtual IP address and MAC address that is used as the default gateway on a client. This ensures that hosts maintain connectivity in the event of the failure of one device serving as a default gateway for a VLAN or set of VLANs. When using HSRP or VRRP, one router is active or forwarding for a particular group while others are in standby mode. GLBP allows the simultaneous use of multiple gateways in addition to providing automatic failover.

# Practice

The following activities provide practice with the topics introduced in this chapter. The Labs and Class Activities are available in the companion *Scaling Networks Lab Manual* (ISBN 978-1-58713-325-1). The Packet Tracer Activities PKA files are found in the online course.

## Class Activities

- Class Activity 2.0.1.2: Stormy Traffic
- Class Activity 2.5.1.1: Documentation Tree

## Labs

- Lab 2.1.2.10: Building a Switched Network with Redundant Links
- Lab 2.3.2.3: Configuring Rapid PVST+, PortFast, and BPDU Guard
- Lab 2.4.3.4: Configuring HSRP and GLBP

Packet Tracer
☐ Activity

## Packet Tracer Activities

- Packet Tracer Activity 2.1.1.5: Examining a Redundant Design
- Packet Tracer Activity 2.3.1.5: Configuring PVST+
- Packet Tracer Activity 2.3.2.2: Configuring Rapid PVST+

# Check Your Understanding Questions

Complete all the review questions listed here to test your understanding of the topics and concepts in this chapter. The appendix "Answers to 'Check Your Understanding' Questions" lists the answers.

1. What is an accurate description of redundancy?

   A. Configuring a router with a complete MAC address database to ensure that all frames can be forwarded to the correct destination

   B. Designing a network to use multiple paths between switches to ensure that there is no single point of failure

   C. Designing a network to use multiple virtual devices to ensure that all traffic uses the best path through the internetwork

   D. Configuring a switch with proper security to ensure that all traffic forwarded through an interface is filtered

2. Which of the following issues are the result of a broadcast storm? (Choose two.)

   A. During a broadcast storm, constant changes to the MAC address table prevent a switch from accurately forwarding frames.

   B. In a network saturated with broadcast traffic, new traffic arriving at the switch will be forwarded into the broadcast domain, which further consumes available bandwidth.

   C. During a broadcast storm, switches with high-speed interfaces will forward traffic in half-duplex mode to conserve available bandwidth.

   D. Because of high processing demands during a broadcast storm, communication can fail between end stations in the broadcast domain.

   E. During a broadcast storm, a switch will forward a received broadcast out every port on the switch.

3. During the implementation of Spanning Tree Protocol, all switches are rebooted by the network administrator. What is the first step of the spanning-tree election process?

   A. Each switch determines the best path to forward traffic.

   B. Each switch determines what port to block to prevent a loop from occurring.

   C. Each switch with a lower root ID than its neighbor will not send BPDUs.

   D. All the switches send out BPDUs advertising themselves as the root bridge.

4. After the election of the root bridge has been completed, how will switches find the best paths to the root bridge?

   A. Each switch will analyze the sum of all port costs to reach the root and use the path with the lowest cost.

   B. Each switch will analyze the port states of all neighbors and use the designated ports to forward traffic to the root.

   C. Each switch will analyze the sum of the hops to reach the root and use the path with the fewest hops.

   D. Each switch will analyze the BID of all neighbors to reach the root and use the path through the lowest BID neighbors.

5. When PVST is running over a switched network, which port state can participate in BPDU frame forwarding based on BPDUs received, but does not forward data frames?

   A. Disabled

   B. Blocking

   C. Listening

   D. Forwarding

6. What are expectations of configuring PortFast on a switch port? (Choose two.)

   A. The switch port immediately transitions from the listening to the forwarding state.

   B. The switch port immediately processes any BPDUs before transitioning to the forwarding state.

   C. The switch port sends DHCP requests before transitioning to the forwarding state.

   D. The switch port should never receive BPDUs from end stations that are connected to the port.

   E. The switch port immediately transitions from the blocking to the forwarding state.

7. Which of the following port states are used by Rapid PVST+? (Choose three.)

   A. Learning

   B. Blocking

   C. Trunking

   D. Discarding

   E. Forwarding

   F. Listening

8. An administrator is troubleshooting a switch and wants to verify whether it is a root bridge. What command can be used to do this?

    A. **show vlan**

    B. **show spanning-tree**

    C. **show running-config**

    D. **show startup-config**

9. What is the initial approach that should be used to troubleshoot a broadcast storm in a switched network?

    A. Replace all instances of STP with RSTP.

    B. Insert redundant links to replace the failed STP links.

    C. Manually remove redundant links in the switched network.

    D. Replace the cables on failed STP links.

10. When first hop redundancy protocols are used, which of the following items will be shared by a set of routers that are presenting the illusion of being a single router? (Choose two.)

    A. Host name

    B. BID

    C. MAC address

    D. IP address

    E. Static route

11. A network administrator is overseeing the implementation of first hop redundancy protocols. Which of the following protocols will not be able to function with multivendor devices? (Choose two.)

    A. VRRP

    B. HSRP

    C. IRDP

    D. GLBP

12. Indicate the STP protocol the matches the description.

    _____ is a legacy standard that runs all VLANs in a single spanning tree instance.

    _____ is a Cisco enhancement of RSTP that provides a spanning tree instance for each VLAN.

    _____ allows multiple VLANs to run in a single spanning tree instance.

13. List the three steps that an FHRP initiates during a router failover process.

# CHAPTER 3

# LAN Aggregation

## Objectives

Upon completion of this chapter, you will be able to answer the following questions:

- What is link aggregation?

- What is EtherChannel technology?

- What are the commands to configure EtherChannel?

- What are the methods to troubleshoot link aggregation with EtherChannel?

## Key Terms

This chapter uses the following key terms. You can find the definitions in the Glossary.

# Introduction (3.0.1.1)

Link aggregation is the ability to create one logical link using multiple physical links between two devices. This allows load sharing among the physical links, rather than having STP block one or more of the links. EtherChannel is a form of link aggregation used in switched networks.

This chapter describes EtherChannel and the methods used to create an Ether-Channel. An EtherChannel can be manually configured or can be negotiated by using the Cisco-proprietary protocol *Port Aggregation Protocol (PAgP)* or the IEEE 802.3ad–defined protocol *Link Aggregation Control Protocol (LACP)*. The configuration, verification, and troubleshooting of EtherChannel are discussed.

**Class Activity 3.0.1.2: Imagine This**

It is the end of the work day. In your small- to medium-sized business, you are trying to explain to the network engineers about EtherChannel and how it looks when it is physically set up. The network engineers have difficulty envisioning how two switches could possibly be connected through several links that collectively act as one channel or connection. Your company is definitely considering implementing an EtherChannel network.

Therefore, you end the meeting with an assignment for the engineers. To prepare for the next day's meeting, they are to perform some research and bring to the meeting one graphic representation of an EtherChannel network connection. They are tasked with explaining how an EtherChannel network operates to the other engineers.

When researching EtherChannel, a good question to search for is "What does Ether-Channel look like?" Prepare a few slides to demonstrate your research that will be presented to the network engineering group. These slides should provide a solid grasp of how EtherChannels are physically created within a network topology. Your goal is to ensure that everyone leaving the next meeting will have a good idea as to why he or she would consider moving to a network topology using EtherChannel as an option.

# Link Aggregation Concepts (3.1)

In this section, we discuss link aggregation and EtherChannel, a Layer 2 link aggregation technology.

# Link Aggregation (3.1.1)

Link aggregation is the process of using multiple redundant links as one logical link in order to take advantage of underutilized links to increase bandwidth.

## Introduction to Link Aggregation (3.1.1.1)

In Figure 3-1, traffic coming from several links (usually 100 or 1000 Mb/s) aggregates on the access switch and must be sent to distribution switches. Because of the traffic aggregation, links with higher bandwidth must be available between the access and distribution switches.

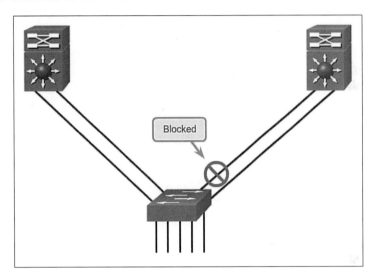

**Figure 3-1**   Redundant Links with STP

It might be possible to use faster links, such as 10 Gb/s, on the aggregated link between the access and distribution layer switches. However, adding faster links is expensive. Additionally, as the speed increases on the access links, even the fastest possible port on the aggregated link is no longer fast enough to aggregate the traffic coming from all access links.

It is also possible to multiply the number of physical links between the switches to increase the overall speed of switch-to-switch communication. However, by default, STP is enabled on switch devices. STP will block redundant links to prevent routing loops.

For these reasons, the best solution is to implement an EtherChannel configuration.

## Advantages of EtherChannel (3.1.1.2)

Figure 3-2 shows a conceptual view of links aggregated using EtherChannel.

**Figure 3-2**    EtherChannel Topology Example

EtherChannel technology was originally developed by Cisco as a LAN switch-to-switch technique of grouping several Fast Ethernet or Gigabit Ethernet ports into one logical channel. When an EtherChannel is configured, the resulting virtual interface is called a port channel. The physical interfaces are bundled together into a port channel interface.

EtherChannel technology has many advantages:

- Most configuration tasks can be done on the EtherChannel interface instead of on each individual port, ensuring configuration consistency throughout the links.

- EtherChannel relies on existing switch ports. There is no need to upgrade the link to a faster and more expensive connection to have more bandwidth.

- Load balancing takes place between links that are part of the same Ether-Channel. Depending on the hardware platform, one or more load-balancing methods can be implemented. These methods include source MAC to destination MAC load balancing, or source IP to destination IP load balancing, across the physical links.

- EtherChannel creates an aggregation that is seen as one logical link. When several EtherChannel bundles exist between two switches, STP can block one of the bundles to prevent switching loops. When STP blocks one of the redundant links, it blocks the entire EtherChannel. This blocks all the ports belonging to that EtherChannel link. Where there is only one EtherChannel link, all physical links in the EtherChannel are active because STP sees only one (logical) link.

- EtherChannel provides redundancy because the overall link is seen as one logical connection. Additionally, the loss of one physical link within the channel does not create a change in the topology; therefore a spanning tree recalculation is not required. Assuming that at least one physical link is present, the EtherChannel remains functional, even if its overall throughput decreases because of a lost link within the EtherChannel.

## EtherChannel Operation (3.1.2)

This section reviews the restrictions to implementing EtherChannel and the two EtherChannel protocols.

### Implementation Restrictions (3.1.2.1)

EtherChannel can be implemented by grouping multiple physical ports into one or more logical EtherChannel links.

---
**Note**

Interface types cannot be mixed. For example, Fast Ethernet and Gigabit Ethernet cannot be mixed within a single EtherChannel.

---

The EtherChannel provides full-duplex bandwidth up to 800 Mb/s (Fast EtherChannel) or 8 Gb/s (Gigabit EtherChannel) between one switch and another switch or host. Currently each EtherChannel can consist of up to eight compatibly configured Ethernet ports. The Cisco IOS switch can currently support six EtherChannels. However, as new IOSs are developed and platforms change, some cards and platforms can support increased numbers of ports within an EtherChannel link, as well as support an increased number of Gigabit EtherChannels. The concept is the same no matter the speeds or number of links that are involved. When configuring EtherChannel on switches, be aware of the hardware platform boundaries and specifications.

The original purpose of EtherChannel was to increase speed capability on aggregated links between switches. However, this concept was extended as EtherChannel technology became more popular, and now many servers also support link aggregation with EtherChannel. EtherChannel creates a one-to-one relationship; that is, one EtherChannel link connects only two devices. An EtherChannel link can be created between two switches, or an EtherChannel link can be created between an EtherChannel-enabled server and a switch. However, traffic cannot be sent to two different switches through the same EtherChannel link.

The individual EtherChannel group member port configuration must be consistent on both devices. If the physical ports of one side are configured as trunks, the physical ports of the other side must also be configured as trunks within the same native VLAN. Additionally, all ports in each EtherChannel link must be configured as Layer 2 ports.

**Note**

Layer 3 EtherChannels can be configured on Cisco Catalyst multilayer switches, such as the Catalyst 3560, but these are not explored in this course. A Layer 3 EtherChannel has a single IP address associated with the logical aggregation of switch ports in the EtherChannel.

Each EtherChannel has a logical port channel interface, shown in Figure 3-3. A configuration applied to the port channel interface affects all physical interfaces that are assigned to that interface.

**Figure 3-3** EtherChannel Logical Groupings

## Port Aggregation Protocol (3.1.2.2)

EtherChannels can be formed through negotiation using one of two protocols, PAgP or LACP. These protocols allow ports with similar characteristics to form a channel through dynamic negotiation with adjoining switches.

**Note**

It is also possible to configure a static or unconditional EtherChannel without PAgP or LACP.

## PAgP

PAgP is a Cisco-proprietary protocol that aids in the automatic creation of Ether-Channel links, as shown in Figure 3-4.

**Figure 3-4**   PAgP Topology

When an EtherChannel link is configured using PAgP, PAgP packets are sent between EtherChannel-capable ports to negotiate the forming of a channel. When PAgP identifies matched Ethernet links, it groups the links into an EtherChannel. The EtherChannel is then added to the spanning tree as a single port.

When enabled, PAgP also manages the EtherChannel. PAgP packets are sent every 30 seconds. PAgP checks for configuration consistency and manages link additions and failures between two switches. It ensures that when an EtherChannel is created, all ports have the same type of configuration.

**Note**

In EtherChannel, it is mandatory that all ports have the same speed, duplex setting, and VLAN information. Any port modification after the creation of the channel also changes all other channel ports.

PAgP helps create the EtherChannel link by detecting the configuration of each side and ensuring that links are compatible so that the EtherChannel link can be enabled when needed.

- **On:** This mode forces the interface to channel without PAgP. Interfaces configured in the on mode do not exchange PAgP packets.

- *PAgP desirable*: This PAgP mode places an interface in an active negotiating state in which the interface initiates negotiations with other interfaces by sending PAgP packets.

- *PAgP auto*: This PAgP mode places an interface in a passive negotiating state in which the interface responds to the PAgP packets that it receives, but does not initiate PAgP negotiation.

Table 3-1 summarizes the result for PAgP channel establishment based on the configuration of each side of a link in Figure 3-4.

**Table 3-1**　PAgP Channel Establishment

| S1 | S2 | Established? |
|---|---|---|
| On | On | Yes |
| Auto/Desirable | Desirable | Yes |
| On/Auto/Desirable | Not Configured | No |
| On | Desirable | No |
| Auto/On | Auto | No |

The modes must be compatible on each side. If one side is configured to be in auto mode, it is placed in a passive state, waiting for the other side to initiate the Ether-Channel negotiation. If the other side is also set to auto, the negotiation never starts and the EtherChannel does not form. If all modes are disabled by using the **no** command, or if no mode is configured, the EtherChannel is disabled.

The on mode manually places the interface in an EtherChannel, without any negotiation. It works only if the other side is also set to on. If the other side is set to negotiate parameters through PAgP, no EtherChannel forms, because the side that is set to on mode does not negotiate.

## Link Aggregation Control Protocol (3.1.2.3)

LACP is part of an IEEE specification (802.3ad) that allows several physical ports to be bundled to form a single logical channel, as shown in Figure 3-5.

**Figure 3-5**　LACP Topology

LACP allows a switch to negotiate an automatic bundle by sending LACP packets to the peer. It performs a function similar to PAgP with Cisco EtherChannel. Because LACP is an IEEE standard, it can be used to facilitate EtherChannels in multivendor environments. On Cisco devices, both protocols are supported.

**Note**

LACP was originally defined as IEEE 802.3ad. However, LACP is now defined in the newer IEEE 802.1AX standard for local and metropolitan-area networks.

LACP provides the same negotiation benefits as PAgP. LACP helps create the Ether-Channel link by detecting the configuration of each side and making sure that they are compatible so that the EtherChannel link can be enabled when needed. Figure 3-5 shows the modes for LACP.

■ **On:** This mode forces the interface to channel without LACP. Interfaces configured in the on mode do not exchange LACP packets.

■ *LACP active*: This LACP mode places a port in an active negotiating state. In this state, the port initiates negotiations with other ports by sending LACP packets.

■ *LACP passive*: This LACP mode places a port in a passive negotiating state. In this state, the port responds to the LACP packets that it receives, but does not initiate LACP packet negotiation.

Just as with PAgP, modes must be compatible on both sides for the EtherChannel link to form. The on mode is repeated, because it creates the EtherChannel configuration unconditionally, without PAgP or LACP dynamic negotiation. Table 3-2 summarizes the results for LACP channel establishment based on the configuration of each side of a link in Figure 3-5.

**Table 3-2**   LACP Channel Establishment

| S1 | S2 | Established? |
|---|---|---|
| On | On | Yes |
| Active/Passive | Active | Yes |
| On/Active/Passive | Not Configured | No |
| On | Active | No |
| Passive/On | Passive | No |

**Interactive Graphic**

**Activity 3.1.2.4: Identify the PAgP and LACP Modes**

Go to the course online to perform this practice activity.

# Link Aggregation Configuration (3.2)

This section discusses EtherChannel configuration, verification, and troubleshooting.

## Configuring EtherChannel (3.2.1)

Configuring EtherChannel is simple enough as long as the network administrator is aware of the limitations.

### Configuration Guidelines (3.2.1.1)

The following guidelines and restrictions are useful for configuring EtherChannel:

- **EtherChannel support:** All Ethernet interfaces on all modules must support EtherChannel with no requirement that interfaces be physically contiguous, or on the same module.

- **Speed and duplex:** Configure all interfaces in an EtherChannel to operate at the same speed and in the same duplex mode, as shown in Figure 3-6.

- **VLAN match:** All interfaces in the EtherChannel bundle must be assigned to the same VLAN, or be configured as a trunk (also shown in Figure 3-6).

- **Range of VLANs:** An EtherChannel supports the same allowed range of VLANs on all the interfaces in a trunking EtherChannel. If the allowed range of VLANs is not the same, the interfaces do not form an EtherChannel, even when set to auto or desirable mode.

Figure 3-6 shows example topologies. In the top topology, a channel is established because none of the restrictions apply. In the bottom topology, the duplex mode doesn't match, so a channel is not established.

If these settings must be changed, configure them in port channel interface configuration mode. After the port channel interface is configured, any configuration that is applied to the port channel interface also affects individual interfaces. However, configurations that are applied to the individual interfaces do not affect the port channel interface. Therefore, making configuration changes to an interface that is part of an EtherChannel link can cause interface compatibility issues.

**Figure 3-6**   EtherChannel Configuration Restrictions Example

## Configuring Interfaces (3.2.1.2)

Configuring EtherChannel with LACP is based on two steps:

**Step 1.**    Specify the interfaces that compose the EtherChannel group using the
**interface range** *interface* global configuration mode command. The **range**
keyword allows you to select several interfaces and configure them all
together. A good practice is to start by shutting down those interfaces so
that any incomplete configuration does not create activity on the link.

**Step 2.**    Create the port channel interface with the **channel-group** *identifier* **mode
active** command in interface range configuration mode. The identifier
specifies a channel group number. The **mode active** keywords identify this
as an LACP EtherChannel configuration.

**Note**

EtherChannel is disabled by default.

Figure 3-7 shows the topology that is used for the configuration, verification, and
troubleshooting examples in this section.

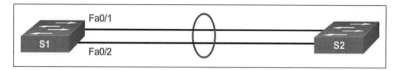

**Figure 3-7**    EtherChannel Configuration Topology

In Example 3-1, the FastEthernet0/1 and FastEthernet0/2 interfaces are bundled into EtherChannel interface port channel 1. To change Layer 2 settings on the port channel interface, enter port channel interface configuration mode using the inter-face **port-channel** command, followed by the interface identifier. In the example, the EtherChannel is configured as a trunk interface with allowed VLANs specified. Interface port channel 1 is configured as a trunk with allowed VLANs 1, 2, and 20.

**Example 3-1**    Configuring EtherChannel with LACP

```
S1(config)# interface range FastEthernet0/1 - 2
S1(config-if-range)# channel-group 1 mode active
S1(config-if-range)# interface port-channel 1
S1(config-if)# switchport mode trunk
S1(config-if)# switchport trunk allowed vlan 1,2,20
```

**Packet Tracer Activity 3.2.1.3: Configuring EtherChannel**

Three switches have just been installed. There are redundant uplinks between the switches. Usually, only one of these links could be used; otherwise, a bridging loop might occur. However, using only one link utilizes only half of the available bandwidth. EtherChannel allows up to eight redundant links to be bundled together into one logical link. In this lab, you will configure Port Aggregation Protocol (PAgP), a Cisco EtherChannel protocol, and Link Aggregation Control Protocol (LACP), an IEEE 802.3ad open standard version of EtherChannel.

**Lab 3.2.1.4: Configuring EtherChannel**

In this lab, you will complete the following objectives:

- Part 1: Configure Basic Switch Settings
- Part 2: Configure PAgP
- Part 3: Configure LACP

# Verifying and Troubleshooting EtherChannel (3.2.2)

This topic discusses several useful commands available for verifying and trouble-shooting EtherChannel.

### Verifying EtherChannel (3.2.2.1)

There are a number of commands to verify an EtherChannel configuration. First, the **show interface port-channel** command displays the general status of the port channel interface. In Example 3-2, the Port Channel 1 interface is up.

**Example 3-2   show interface port-channel** Command

```
S1# show interface Port-channel1
Port-channel1 is up, line protocol is up (connected)
  Hardware is EtherChannel, address is 0cd9.96e8.8a01 (bia 0cd9.96e8.8a01)
  MTU 1500 bytes, BW 200000 Kbit/sec, DLY 100 usec,
     reliability 255/255, txload 1/255, rxload 1/255
  Encapsulation ARPA, loopback not set
<output omitted>
```

When several port channel interfaces are configured on the same device, use the **show etherchannel summary** command to simply display one line of information per port channel. In Example 3-3, the switch has one EtherChannel configured; group 1 uses LACP.

**Example 3-3   show etherchannel summary** Command

```
S1# show etherchannel summary
Flags:  D - down        P - bundled in port-channel
        I - stand-alone s - suspended
        H - Hot-standby (LACP only)
        R - Layer3       S - Layer2
        U - in use       f - failed to allocate aggregator

        M - not in use, minimum links not met
        u - unsuitable for bundling
        w - waiting to be aggregated
        d - default port


Number of channel-groups in use:  1
Number of aggregators:             1
```

```
Group  Port-channel  Protocol    Ports
------+-------------+-----------+----------------------------------------------
1       Po1(SU)        LACP      Fa0/1(P)    Fa0/2(P)
```

The interface bundle consists of the FastEthernet0/1 and FastEthernet0/2 interfaces. Group 1 is a Layer 2 EtherChannel and is in use, as indicated by the letters SU next to the port channel number.

Use the **show etherchannel port-channel** command to display information about a specific port channel interface, as shown in Example 3-4.

**Example 3-4    show etherchannel port-channel** Command

```
S1# show etherchannel Port-channel
        Channel-group listing:
        ----------------------


Group: 1
----------
        Port-channels in the group:
        --------------------------


Port-channel: Po1    (Primary Aggregator)


------------

Age of the Port-channel    = 0d:00h:25m:17s
Logical slot/port    = 2/1           Number of ports = 2
HotStandBy port = null
Port state            = Port-channel Ag-Inuse
Protocol              =    LACP
Port security         = Disabled

Ports in the Port-channel:


Index   Load   Port     EC state          No of bits
------+------+------+-----------------+-----------
  0     00    Fa0/1    Active              0
  0     00    Fa0/2    Active              0


Time since last port bundled:    0d:00h:05m:41s    Fa0/2
Time since last port Un-bundled: 0d:00h:05m:48s    Fa0/2
```

In the example, the Port Channel 1 interface consists of two physical interfaces, FastEthernet0/1 and FastEthernet0/2. It uses LACP in active mode. It is properly connected to another switch with a compatible configuration, which is why the port channel is said to be in use.

On any physical interface member of an EtherChannel bundle, the **show interfaces etherchannel** command can provide information about the role of the interface in the EtherChannel, as shown in Example 3-5. The interface FastEthernet 0/1 is part of the EtherChannel bundle 1. The protocol for this EtherChannel is LACP.

**Example 3-5    show interfaces f0/1 etherchannel** Command

```
S1# show interfaces f0/1 etherchannel
Port state      = Up Mstr Assoc In-Bndl
Channel group = 1            Mode = Active       Gcchange = -
Port-channel  = Po1          GC   =  -           Pseudo port-channel = Po1
Port index    = 0            Load = 0x00         Protocol =    LACP


Flags:  S - Device is sending Slow LACPDUs   F - Device is sending fast LACPDUs.
        A - Device is in active mode.         P - Device is in passive mode.


Local information:
                              LACP port    Admin    Oper    Port      Port
Port        Flags   State     Priority     Key      Key     Number    State
Fa0/1       SA      bndl      32768        0x1      0x1     0x102     0x3D


Partner's information:

                      LACP port                  Admin  Oper  Port    Port
Port        Flags   Priority  Dev ID       Age   key    Key   Number  State
Fa0/1       SA      32768     0cd9.96d2.4000  4s  0x0    0x1   0x102   0x3D
```

## Troubleshooting EtherChannel (3.2.2.2)

All interfaces within an EtherChannel must have the same configuration of speed and duplex mode, native and allowed VLANs on trunks, and access VLAN on access ports:

■ Assign all ports in the EtherChannel to the same VLAN, or configure them as trunks. Ports with different native VLANs cannot form an EtherChannel.

■ When configuring an EtherChannel from trunk ports, verify that the trunking mode is the same on all the trunks. Inconsistent trunk modes on EtherChannel ports can cause EtherChannel not to function and ports to be shut down (errdisable state).

- An EtherChannel supports the same allowed range of VLANs on all the ports. If the allowed range of VLANs is not the same, the ports do not form an Ether-Channel, even when PAgP is set to the auto or desirable mode.

- The dynamic negotiation options for PAgP and LACP must be compatibly configured on both ends of the EtherChannel.

**Note**

It is easy to confuse PAgP or LACP with the Dynamic Trunking Protocol (DTP), because they are protocols used to automate behavior on trunk links. PAgP and LACP are used for link aggregation (EtherChannel). DTP is used for automating the creation of trunk links. When an EtherChannel trunk is configured, typically EtherChannel (PAgP or LACP) is configured first and then DTP.

In Example 3-6, interfaces F0/1 and F0/2 on switches S1 and S2 are connected with an EtherChannel. The output indicates that the EtherChannel is down.

**Example 3-6** Troubleshooting Scenario 1

```
S1# show etherchannel summary
Flags:  D - down         P - bundled in port-channel
        I - stand-alone s - suspended
        H - Hot-standby (LACP only)
        R - Layer3       S - Layer2
        U - in use       f - failed to allocate aggregator
        M - not in use, minimum links not met
        u - unsuitable for bundling
        w - waiting to be aggregated
        d - default port


Number of channel-groups in use: 1
Number of aggregators:           1


Group  Port-channel  Protocol    Ports
------+-------------+-----------+---------------------------------------------
1      Po1(SD)          -        Fa0/1(D)    Fa0/2(D)
```

In Example 3-7, more detailed output indicates that there are incompatible PAgP modes configured on S1 and S2.

**Example 3-7**   Troubleshooting Scenario 2

```
S1# show run | begin interface Port-channel
interface Port-channel1
 switchport mode trunk
!
interface FastEthernet0/1
 switchport mode trunk
 channel-group 1 mode on
!
interface FastEthernet0/2
 switchport mode trunk
 channel-group 1 mode on
!
<output omitted>
S2# show run | begin interface Port-channel
interface Port-channel1
 switchport mode trunk
!
interface FastEthernet0/1
 switchport mode trunk
 channel-group 1 mode desirable
!
interface FastEthernet0/2
 switchport mode trunk
 channel-group 1 mode desirable
!
<output omitted>
```

In Example 3-8, the PAgP mode on the EtherChannel is changed to desirable and the EtherChannel becomes active.

**Example 3-8**   Troubleshooting Scenario 3

```
S1(config)# no interface Port-channel 1
S1(config)# interface range f0/1 - 2
S1(config-if-range)# channel-group 1 mode desirable
Creating a port-channel interface Port-channel 1
S1(config-if-range)# no shutdown
S1(config-if-range)# interface Port-channel 1
S1(config-if)# switchport mode trunk
S1(config-if)# end
S1# show etherchannel summary
```

```
Flags:  D - down          P - bundled in port-channel
        I - stand-alone   s - suspended
        H - Hot-standby (LACP only)
        R - Layer3        S - Layer2
        U - in use        f - failed to allocate aggregator
        M - not in use, minimum links not met
        u - unsuitable for bundling
        w - waiting to be aggregated
        d - default port

Number of channel-groups in use: 1
Number of aggregators:           1

Group  Port-channel  Protocol    Ports
------+-------------+-----------+-----------------------------------------------
1      Po1(SU)         PAgP       Fa0/1(P)    Fa0/2(P)
```

---

**Note**

EtherChannel and spanning tree must interoperate. For this reason, the order in which EtherChannel-related commands are entered is important, which is why (in Example 3-8) you see interface Port-Channel 1 removed and then re-added with the **channel-group** command, as opposed to directly changed. If one tries to change the configuration directly, spanning tree errors cause the associated ports to go into the blocking or errdisabled state.

---

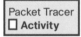

**Packet Tracer Activity 3.2.2.3: Troubleshooting EtherChannel**

Four switches were recently configured by a junior technician. Users are complaining that the network is running slowly and would like you to investigate.

---

**Lab 3.2.2.4: Troubleshooting EtherChannel**

In this lab, you will complete the following objectives:

- Part 1: Build the Network and Load Device Configurations
- Part 2: Troubleshoot EtherChannel

# Summary (3.3)

### Class Activity 3.3.1.1: Linking Up

Many bottlenecks occur on your small- to medium-sized business network, even though you have configured VLANs, STP, and other network traffic options on the company's switches.

Instead of keeping the switches as they are currently configured, you would like to try EtherChannel as an option for, at least, part of the network to see whether it will decrease traffic congestion between your access and distribution layer switches.

Your company uses Catalyst 3560 switches at the distribution layer and Catalyst 2960 and 2950 switches at the access layer of the network. To verify whether these switches can perform EtherChannel, you visit the site "The System Requirements to Implement EtherChannel on Catalyst Switches." This site allows you to gather more information to determine whether EtherChannel is a good option for the equipment and network currently in place.

After researching the models, you decide to use a simulation software program to practice configuring EtherChannel before implementing it live on your network. As a part of this procedure, you ensure that the equipment simulated in Packet Tracer will support these practice configurations.

---

### Packet Tracer Activity 3.3.1.2: Skills Integration Challenge

In this activity, two routers are configured to communicate with each other. You are responsible for configuring subinterfaces to communicate with the switches. You will configure VLANs, trunking, and EtherChannel with PVST. The Internet devices are all preconfigured.

---

EtherChannel aggregates multiple switched links together to load-balance over redundant paths between two devices. All ports in one EtherChannel must have the same speed, duplex setting, and VLAN information on all interfaces on the devices at both ends. Settings configured in the port channel interface configuration mode will also be applied to the individual interfaces in that EtherChannel. Settings configured on individual interfaces will not be applied to the EtherChannel or to the other interfaces in the EtherChannel.

PAgP is a Cisco-proprietary protocol that aids in the automatic creation of Ether-Channel links. PAgP modes are on, PAgP desirable, and PAgP auto. LACP is part of an IEEE specification that also allows multiple physical ports to be bundled into one logical channel. The LACP modes are on, LACP active, and LACP passive. PAgP and LACP do not interoperate. The on mode is repeated in both PAgP and LACP because it creates an EtherChannel unconditionally, without the use of PAgP or LACP. The default for EtherChannel is that no mode is configured.

# Practice

The following activities provide practice with the topics introduced in this chapter. The Labs and Class Activities are available in the companion *Scaling Networks Lab Manual* (ISBN 978-1-58713-325-1). The Packet Tracer Activities PKA files are found in the online course.

## Class Activities

- Class Activity 3.0.1.2: Imagine This
- Class Activity 3.3.1.1: Linking Up

## Labs

- Lab 3.2.1.4: Configuring EtherChannel
- Lab 3.2.2.4: Troubleshooting EtherChannel

Packet Tracer
☐ Activity

## Packet Tracer Activities

- Packet Tracer Activity 3.2.1.3: Configuring EtherChannel
- Packet Tracer Activity 3.2.2.3: Troubleshooting EtherChannel
- Packet Tracer Activity 3.3.1.2: Skills Integration Challenge

# Check Your Understanding Questions

Complete all the review questions listed here to test your understanding of the topics and concepts in this chapter. The appendix "Answers to 'Check Your Understanding' Questions" lists the answers.

1. Which statement is true about EtherChannel technology?

   A. EtherChannel relies on existing switch ports.

   B. STP does not run on EtherChannel links.

   C. Configuration tasks must be done on individual ports.

   D. Links must be upgraded to support EtherChannel.

2. What are advantages of using EtherChannel technology? (Choose three.)

   A. EtherChannel uses multiple logical links to provide redundancy.

   B. Load balancing is not needed with EtherChannel.

   C. The Spanning Tree Protocol shuts down the unused interfaces in the bundle to avoid loops.

   D. A spanning tree recalculation is not required when a single link within the channel goes down.

   E. There is no need to upgrade links to faster connections to increase bandwidth.

   F. Configuration tasks can be done on the EtherChannel interface.

3. Refer to Figure 3-8. An administrator tried to implement an EtherChannel between two switches by grouping the six physical ports as shown. However, the administrator was not successful. What is the reason for that?

**Figure 3-8**   Question 3 Exhibit

   A. An EtherChannel link can only be implemented on Fast Ethernet interfaces.

   B. An EtherChannel link can only be implemented on Gigabit Ethernet interfaces.

   C. An EtherChannel link can only be formed by grouping interfaces of the same type.

   D. An EtherChannel link can only be created between Layer 3 switches.

4. Refer to Figure 3-9. An administrator wants to form an EtherChannel between the two switches by using the Port Aggregation Protocol. If switch S1 is configured to be in auto mode, which mode should be configured on S2 to form the EtherChannel?

**Figure 3-9**   Question 4 Exhibit

   A. On

   B. Auto

   C. Desirable

   D. Off

5. When a range of ports is being configured for EtherChannel, which mode will configure PAgP so that it initiates the EtherChannel negotiation?

   A. Active

   B. Auto

   C. Desirable

   D. Passive

6. Which of the following protocols are used to implement EtherChannel? (Choose two.)

   A. Spanning Tree Protocol

   B. Rapid Spanning Tree Protocol

   C. Port Aggregation Protocol

   D. Link Aggregation Control Protocol

   E. Cisco Discovery Protocol

7. What will happen if a network administrator puts a port that is part of an EtherChannel bundle into a different VLAN than the other ports in that bundle?

   A. The EtherChannel bundle will stay up only if PAgP is used.

   B. The EtherChannel bundle will stay up only if LACP is used.

   C. The EtherChannel bundle will stay up if either PAgP or LACP is used.

   D. The EtherChannel bundle will stay up if the ports were configured with no negotiation between the switches to form the EtherChannel.

   E. The EtherChannel will fail.

8. Refer to Example 3-9. On the basis of the output that is shown, what can be determined about the EtherChannel bundle?

**Example 3-9**   Question 8 Exhibit

```
S1# show etherchannel summary
Flags:  D - down        P - bundled in port-channel
        I - stand-alone s - suspended
        H - Hot-standby (LACP only)
        R - Layer3       S - Layer2
        U - in use       f - failed to allocate aggregator
        M - not in use, minimum links not met
        u - unsuitable for bundling
        w - waiting to be aggregated
        d - default port


Number of channel-groups in use: 1
Number of aggregators:           1


Group  Port-channel  Protocol    Ports
------+-------------+-----------+------------------------------------------------
1      Po1(SU)         PAgP      Fa0/1(P)    Fa0/2(P)
```

A. Two Gigabit Ethernet ports are used to form the EtherChannel.

B. A Cisco-proprietary protocol was used to negotiate the EtherChannel link.

C. The EtherChannel bundle is down.

D. The EtherChannel bundle is operating at both Layer 2 and Layer 3.

9. Which of the following interface parameters must match for an EtherChannel to form? (Choose three.)

A. Trunking mode

B. Native VLAN

C. EtherChannel mode

D. Spanning-tree state

E. Allowed VLANs

F. PortFast mode

10. Which command displays only one line of information per port channel?

# CHAPTER 4

# Wireless LANs

## Objectives

Upon completion of this chapter, you will be able to answer the following questions:

- What are the wireless LAN technologies and standards?

- What components make up a wireless LAN infrastructure?

- What are the wireless topologies?

- What is the structure of the 802.11 frame?

- What is the media access method used by wireless technologies?

- What is channel management in a WLAN?

- What are the threats to wireless LANs?

- What security mechanisms are available for wireless LANs?

- What are the steps to configure a wireless router to support a remote site?

- What are the steps to configure a wireless client to connect to a wireless router?

- What are some solutions to troubleshooting common wireless issues?

## Key Terms

This chapter uses the following key terms. You can find the definitions in the Glossary.

# Introduction (4.0.1.1)

Wireless networks can provide client mobility, the ability to connect from any location and at any time, and the ability to roam while staying connected. A *Wireless LAN* (WLAN) is a classification of wireless network that is commonly used in homes, offices, and campus environments. Although it uses radio frequencies instead of cables, it is commonly implemented in a switched network environment and its frame format is similar to Ethernet.

This chapter covers WLAN technology, components, security, planning, implementation, and troubleshooting. The types of network attacks to which wireless networks are particularly susceptible are discussed.

**Class Activity 4.0.1.2: Make Mine Wireless**

As the network administrator for your small- to medium-sized business, you realize that your wireless network needs updating, both inside and outside of your building. Therefore, you decide to research how other businesses and educational and community groups set up their WLANs for better access to their employees and clients.

To research this topic, you visit the "Customer Case Studies and Research" website to see how other businesses use wireless technology. After viewing a few of the videos, or reading some of the case study PDFs, you decide to select two to show to your CEO to support upgrading to a more robust wireless solution for your company.

# Wireless Concepts (4.1)

This section is an overview of wireless concepts, including wireless benefits, technologies, components, and topologies.

## Introduction to Wireless (4.1.1)

You most likely use wireless technologies daily, whether it's your cell phone, laptop, computer, or other mobile device. You might be reading this book on a wireless device. For many businesses, supporting wireless device access really is no longer an option. This topic discusses the benefits of wireless and the standards that make wireless possible.

## Supporting Mobility (4.1.1.1)

Business networks today are evolving to support people who are on the move. People are connected using multiple devices, including computers, laptops, tablets, and smart phones. This is the vision of mobility, where people can take their connection to the network along with them on the road.

There are many different infrastructures (wired LAN, service provider networks) that make this type of mobility possible, but in a business environment, the most important is the wireless LAN (WLAN).

Productivity is no longer restricted to a fixed work location or a defined time period. People now expect to be connected at any time and place, from the office to the airport or the home. Traveling employees used to be restricted to pay phones for checking messages and returning a few phone calls between flights. Now employees can check email, voice mail, and the status of projects on smart phones.

Users now expect to be able to roam wirelessly. Roaming enables a wireless device to maintain Internet access without losing connection.

**Video**

**Video 4.1.1.1**

View the video in the online course for an example of how wireless networks enable mobility.

## Benefits of Wireless (4.1.1.2)

There are many benefits to supporting wireless networking, both in the business environment and at home. Some of the benefits include increased flexibility, increased productivity, reduced costs, and the ability to grow and adapt to changing requirements.

Most businesses rely on switch-based LANs for day-to-day operation within the office. However, employees are becoming more mobile and want to maintain access to their business LAN resources from locations other than their desks. Workers want to take their wireless devices to meetings, coworkers' offices, conference rooms, and even customer sites, all while maintaining access to office resources. Wireless networking provides this type of flexibility. Instead of spending a significant amount of time transporting necessary company material or locating wired connections to access network resources, using the wireless network, LAN resources can be easily made available to a variety of wireless devices.

Although hard to measure, wireless access can result in increased productivity and more relaxed employees. With wireless networking, employees have the flexibility to work when they want, where they want. They can respond to customer inquiries whether at the office or out to dinner. They can access email and other work-related resources quickly and easily, providing better management, better and faster results for customers, and increased profits.

Wireless networking can also reduce costs. In businesses with a wireless infrastructure already in place, savings are realized anytime equipment changes or moves are required, such as when relocating an employee within a building, reorganizing equipment or a lab, or moving to temporary locations or project sites.

Another important benefit of wireless networking is the ability to adapt to changing needs and technologies. Adding new equipment to the network is fairly seamless with wireless networking. Consider the wireless connectivity of the home. Users can surf the web from their kitchen table, living rooms, or even outdoors. Home users connect new devices, such as smart phones and smart pads, laptops, and smart televisions. A wireless home router allows the user to connect to these devices without the additional cost or inconvenience of running cables to different locations in the home.

## Wireless Technologies (4.1.1.3)

Wireless communications are used in a variety of professions.

Although the mix of wireless technologies is continually expanding, the focus of this discussion is on wireless networks that allow users to be mobile. Wireless networks can be classified broadly as

- *Wireless Personal-Area Networks (WPAN)*: Operate in the range of a few feet. Bluetooth or Wi-Fi direct-enabled devices are used in WPANs.

- **Wireless LANs (WLAN)**: Operate in the range of a few hundred feet, such as in a room, home, office, and even campus environment.

- *Wireless Wide-Area Networks (WWAN)*: Operate in the range of miles, such as a metropolitan area, cellular hierarchy, or even on intercity links through microwave relays.

The various wireless technologies available to connect devices to these wireless networks include the following:

- *Bluetooth*: Originally an IEEE 802.15 WPAN standard that uses a device-pairing process to communicate over distances up to 0.05 mile (100m). Newer Bluetooth versions are standardized by the Bluetooth Special Interest Group (www.bluetooth.org).

- *Wi-Fi (wireless fidelity)*: An IEEE 802.11 WLAN standard commonly deployed to provide network access to home and corporate users, to include data and voice and video traffic, to distances up to 300m (0.18 mile).

- *WiMAX (Worldwide Interoperability for Microwave Access)*: An IEEE 802.16 WWAN standard that provides wireless broadband access of up to 30 miles (50 km). WiMAX is an alternative to cable and DSL broadband connections. Mobility was added to WiMAX in 2005 and can now be used by service providers to provide cellular broadband.

- *Cellular broadband*: Consists of various corporate, national, and international organizations using service provider cellular access to provide mobile broadband network connectivity. First available with second-generation cell phones in 1991 (2G), with higher speeds becoming available in 2001 and 2006 as part of the third (3G) and fourth (4G) generations of mobile communication technology.

- *Satellite broadband*: Provides network access to remote sites through the use of a directional satellite dish that is aligned with a specific geostationary Earth orbit (GEO) satellite. It is usually more expensive and requires a clear line of sight.

There are many types of wireless technologies available. However, the focus of this chapter is on 802.11 WLANs.

## Radio Frequencies (4.1.1.4)

All wireless devices operate in the radio waves range of the electromagnetic spectrum. It is the responsibility of the *International Telecommunication Union: Radiocommunication Sector* (ITU-R) to regulate the allocation of the radio frequency (RF) spectrum. Ranges of frequencies, called bands, are allocated for various purposes. Some bands in the electromagnetic spectrum are heavily regulated and are used for applications such as air traffic control and emergency responder communications networks. Other bands are license free, such as the Industrial, Scientific, and Medical (ISM) and the national information infrastructure (UNII) frequency bands.

**Note**

WLAN networks operate in the ISM 2.4-GHz frequency band and the UNII 5-GHz band.

Wireless communication occurs in the radio waves range (that is, 3 Hz to 300 GHz) of the electromagnetic spectrum, as shown in Figure 4-1.

**Note**

Refer to the online curriculum for additional information provided in this interactive graphic.

The radio waves range is subdivided into a radio frequencies section and a microwave frequencies section. Notice that WLANs, Bluetooth, cellular, and satellite communication all operate in the microwave UHF, SHF, and EHF ranges.

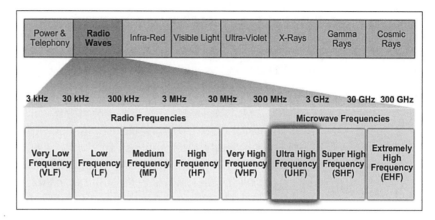

**Figure 4-1**   Radio Waves of the Electromagnetic Spectrum

Wireless LAN devices have transmitters and receivers tuned to specific frequencies of the radio waves range. Specifically, the following frequency bands are allocated to 802.11 wireless LANs:

- *2.4 GHz (UHF)*: 802.11b/g/n/ad

- *5 GHz (SHF)*: 802.11a/n/ac/ad

- *60 GHz (EHF)*: 802.11ad

## 802.11 Standards (4.1.1.5)

The IEEE 802.11 WLAN standard defines how RF in the unlicensed ISM frequency bands is used for the physical layer and the MAC sublayer of wireless links.

Various implementations of the IEEE 802.11 standard have been developed over the years. The following highlights these standards:

- *IEEE 802.11*: Released in 1997 and now obsolete, this is the original WLAN specification that operated in the 2.4-GHz band and offered speeds of up to 2 Mb/s. When it was released, wired LANs were operating at 10 Mb/s, so the new wireless technology was not enthusiastically adopted. Wireless devices have one antenna to transmit and receive wireless signals.

- *IEEE 802.11a*: Released in 1999, it operates in the less crowded 5-GHz frequency band and offers speeds of up to 54 Mb/s. Because this standard operates at higher frequencies, it has a smaller coverage area and is less effective at penetrating building structures. Wireless devices have one antenna to transmit and receive wireless signals. Devices operating under this standard are not interoperable with the 802.11b and 802.11g standards.

- *IEEE 802.11b*: Released in 1999, it operates in the 2.4-GHz frequency band and offers speeds of up to 11 Mb/s. Devices implementing this standard have a longer range and are better able to penetrate building structures than devices based on 802.11a. Wireless devices have one antenna to transmit and receive wireless signals.

- *IEEE 802.11g*: Released in 2003, it operates in the 2.4-GHz frequency band and offers speeds of up to 54 Mb/s. Devices implementing this standard, therefore, operate at the same radio frequency and range as 802.11b, but with the bandwidth of 802.11a. Wireless devices have one antenna to transmit and receive wireless signals. It is backward compatible with 802.11b. However, when supporting an 802.11b client, the overall bandwidth is reduced.

- *IEEE 802.11n*: Released in 2009, it operates in the 2.4-GHz and 5-GHz frequency bands and is referred to as a dual-band device. Typical data rates range from 150 Mb/s to 600 Mb/s with a distance range of up to 70m (0.5 mile). However, to achieve the higher speeds, APs and wireless clients require multiple antennas using the multiple-input and multiple-output (MIMO) technology. MIMO uses multiple antennas as both the transmitter and receiver to improve communication performance. Up to four antennas can be supported. The 802.11n standard is backward compatible with 802.11a/b/g devices. However, supporting a mixed environment limits the expected data rates.

- *IEEE 802.11ac*: Released in 2013, this operates in the 5-GHz frequency band and provides data rates ranging from 450 Mb/s to 1.3 Gb/s (1300 Mb/s). It uses MIMO technology to improve communication performance. Up to eight antennas can be supported. The 802.11ac standard is backward compatible with 802.11a/n devices; however, supporting a mixed environment limits the expected data rates.

- *IEEE 802.11ad*: Scheduled for release in 2014 and also known as "WiGig," it uses a tri-band Wi-Fi solution using 2.4 GHz, 5 GHz, and 60 GHz, and offers theoretical speeds of up to 7 Gb/s. However, the 60-GHz band is a line-of-site technology and, therefore, cannot penetrate through walls. When a user is roaming, the device switches to the lower 2.4-GHz and 5-GHz bands. It is backward compatible with existing Wi-Fi devices. However, supporting a mixed environment limits the expected data rates.

Table 4-1 summarizes each 802.11 standard.

**Table 4-1**   Comparing 802.11 Standards

| IEEE Standard | Maximum Speed | Frequency | Backward Compatibility with... |
|---|---|---|---|
| 802.11 | 2 Mbps | 2.4 GHz | None |
| 802.11a | 54 Mbps | 5 GHz | None |
| 802.11b | 11 Mbps | 2.4 GHz | None |
| 802.11g | 54 Mbps | 2.4 GHz | 802.11b |
| 802.11n | 600 Mbps | 2.4 GHz and 5 GHz | 802.11a/b/g |
| 802.11ac | 1.3 Gbps | 5 GHz | 802.11a/n |
| 802.11ad | 7 Gbps | 2.4 GHz, 5 GHz, and 60 GHz | 802.11a/b/g/n/ac |

## Wi-Fi Certification (4.1.1.6)

Standards ensure interoperability between devices made by different manufacturers. Internationally, the three organizations influencing WLAN standards are

- **ITU-R:** Regulates the allocation of the RF spectrum and satellite orbits.

- **IEEE:** Specifies how RF is modulated to carry information. It maintains the standards for local- and metropolitan-area networks (MAN) with the IEEE 802 LAN/MAN family of standards. The dominant standards in the IEEE 802 family are 802.3 Ethernet and 802.11 WLAN. Although the IEEE has specified standards for RF modulation devices, it has not specified manufacturing standards; therefore, interpretations of the 802.11 standards by different vendors can cause interoperability problems between their devices.

- *Wi-Fi Alliance*: The Wi-Fi Alliance (www.wi-fi.org) is a global, nonprofit, industry trade association devoted to promoting the growth and acceptance of WLANs. It is an association of vendors whose objective is to improve the interoperability of products that are based on the 802.11 standard by certifying vendors for conformance to industry norms and adherence to standards.

The Wi-Fi Alliance certifies Wi-Fi and the following product compatibility:

- IEEE 802.11a/b/g/n/ac/ad compatible

- IEEE 802.11i secure using WPA2 and Extensible Authentication Protocol (EAP)

- Wi-Fi Protected Setup (WPS) to simplify device connections

- Wi-Fi Direct to share media between devices

- Wi-Fi Passpoint to simplify securely connecting to Wi-Fi hotspot networks

- Wi-Fi Miracast to seamlessly display video between devices

**Note**

Other Wi-Fi certification products are available such as WMM (Wi-Fi Multimedia), Tunneled Direct Link Setup (TDLS), and WMM-Power Save.

Figure 4-2 displays the Wi-Fi Alliance logos identifying specific feature compatibility. Devices displaying specific logos support the identified feature. A device can display a combination of these logos.

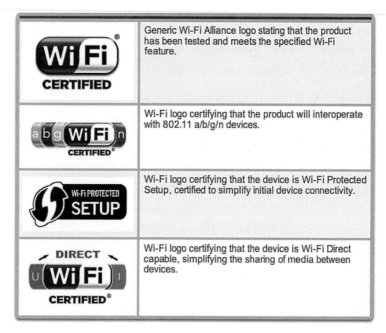

**Figure 4-2**   Common Wi-Fi Certified Logos

**Video**

**Videos 4.1.1.6**

View three videos in the online course that explain the Wi-Fi Direct, Wi-Fi Passpoint, and Wi-Fi Miracast features. The videos can be found on figure buttons 2, 3, and 4.

## Comparing WLANs to a LAN (4.1.1.7)

WLANs share a similar origin with Ethernet LANs. The IEEE has adopted the 802 LAN/MAN portfolio of computer network architecture standards. The two dominant 802 working groups are 802.3 Ethernet and 802.11 WLAN. However, there are important differences between the two, as shown in Table 4-2.

**Table 4-2**   WLANs Versus LANs

| Characteristic | 802.11 Wireless LAN | 802.3 Ethernet LANs |
|---|---|---|
| Physical Layer | Radio Frequency (RF) | Cable |
| Media Access | Collision Avoidance | Collision Detection |
| Availability | Anyone with a radio NIC in range of an access point | Cable connection required |
| Signal Interference | Yes | Inconsequential |
| Regulation | Additional regulation by country authorities | IEEE standard dictates |

WLANs use RF instead of cables at the physical layer and MAC sublayer of the data link layer. In comparison to cable, RF has the following characteristics:

- RF does not have boundaries, such as the limits of a wire in a sheath. This allows data frames traveling over the RF media to be available to anyone who can receive the RF signal.

- RF is unprotected from outside signals, whereas cable is in an insulating sheath. Radios operating independently in the same geographic area, but using the same or a similar RF, can interfere with each other.

- RF transmission is subject to the same challenges inherent in any wave-based technology, such as consumer radio. For example, as the radio travels farther away from the source, radio stations can start playing over each other and static noise increases. Eventually the signal is completely lost. Wired LANs have cables that are of an appropriate length to maintain signal strength.

- RF bands are regulated differently in various countries. The use of WLANs is subject to additional regulations and sets of standards that are not applied to wired LANs.

WLANs also differ from wired LANs as follows:

- WLANs connect clients to the network through a wireless access point (AP) or wireless router, instead of an Ethernet switch.

- WLANs connect mobile devices that are often battery powered, as opposed to plugged-in LAN devices. Wireless NICs tend to reduce the battery life of a mobile device.

- WLANs support hosts that contend for access on the RF media (frequency bands). 802.11 prescribes collision avoidance (CSMA/CA) instead of collision detection (CSMA/CD) for media access to proactively avoid collisions within the media.

- WLANs use a different frame format than wired Ethernet LANs. WLANs require additional information in the Layer 2 header of the frame.

- WLANs raise more privacy issues because radio frequencies can reach outside the facility.

Interactive
Graphic

### Activity 4.1.1.8: Identify the Wireless Technology

Go to the course online to perform this practice activity.

Interactive
Graphic

### Activity 4.1.1.9: Compare Wireless Standards

Go to the course online to perform this practice activity.

Interactive
Graphic

### Activity 4.1.1.10: Compare WLANs and LANs

Go to the course online to perform this practice activity.

## Components of WLANs (4.1.2)

This topic discusses all the various devices and components that are needed for an end device to connect to a WLAN. Some of these devices and components are transparent to the end user in that they are embedded in the device or environment. Ideally, these types of components require no interaction from the user. Other devices might require end-user interaction to become operational, such as configuring usernames and passwords.

### Wireless NICs (4.1.2.1)

The simplest wireless network requires a minimum of two devices. Each device must have a radio transmitter and a radio receiver tuned to the same frequencies.

However most wireless deployments require

- End devices with wireless NICs

- An infrastructure device, such as a wireless router or wireless AP

To communicate wirelessly, end devices require a wireless NIC that incorporates a radio transmitter/receiver and the required software driver to make it operational. Laptops, tablets, and smart phones now all include integrated wireless NICs. However, if a device does not have an integrated wireless NIC, a USB wireless adapter can be used.

Figure 4-3 displays two USB wireless adapters.

| Linksys AE6000 Mini USB Wi-Fi Wireless-AC Dual-Band Adapter 2.4 or 5 GHz 802.11ac | Linksys AE3000 High Performance Dual-Band N USB Adapter |

**Figure 4-3**    Wireless USB Adapters

## Wireless Home Router (4.1.2.2)

The type of infrastructure device that an end device associates and authenticates with varies on the size and requirement of the WLAN.

For example, a home user typically interconnects wireless devices using a small, integrated wireless router. These smaller, integrated routers serve as

- **Access point:** Provides 802.11a/b/g/n/ac wireless access

- **Switch:** Provides a four-port, full-duplex, 10/100/1000 Ethernet switch to connect wired devices

- **Router:** Provides a default gateway for connecting to other network infrastructures

For example, the Cisco Linksys EA6500 router, shown in Figure 4-4, is commonly implemented as a small-business or residential wireless access device.

**Figure 4-4**   Typical Home Network

The wireless router connects to the ISP DLS modem and advertises its services by sending beacons containing its shared *service set identifier (SSID)*. Internal devices wirelessly discover the router SSID and attempt to associate and authenticate with it to access the Internet.

The expected load on the Linksys EA6500 router, in this environment, is low enough that it should be able to manage the provision of WLAN, 802.3 Ethernet, and connect to an ISP. It also provides advanced features, such as high-speed access, support for video streaming, IPv6, QoS, and USB ports to connect printers or portable drives.

Additionally, for home users who want to extend their network services, both wireless and wired, wireless Powerline adapters can be implemented. With these devices, a device can connect directly to the network through electrical outlets, which is ideal for HD video streaming and online gaming. The home user can conveniently set this up by plugging into a wall outlet or power strip and connecting the device without the need of outside technical advice or support.

**Video 4.1.2.2**

Video

View the video in the online course to see an overview of the Linksys Powerline adapters.

## Business Wireless Solutions (4.1.2.3)

Organizations providing wireless connectivity to their users require a WLAN infra-structure to provide additional connectivity options.

The small-business network shown in Figure 4-5 is an 802.3 Ethernet LAN.

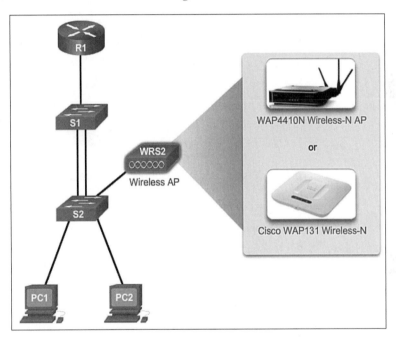

**Figure 4-5**    Access Point Connected to Wired Infrastructure

Each client (that is, PC1 and PC2) connects to a switch using a network cable. The switch is the point where the clients gain access to the network. Notice that the wireless AP also connects to the switch. In this example, an AP such as the Cisco WAP4410N AP or the WAP131 AP could be used to provide wireless network connectivity.

Wireless clients use a wireless NIC to discover nearby APs that are advertising an SSID. Clients then attempt to associate and authenticate with an AP, as shown in Figure 4-6. After being authenticated, wireless users have access to network resources.

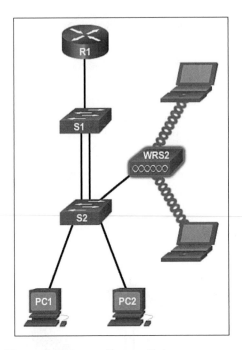

**Figure 4-6**    Wireless Clients Connect to Access Point

**Note**

The wireless needs of a small organization differ from those of a large organization. Large, wireless deployments require additional wireless hardware to simplify the installation and management of the wireless network.

## Wireless Access Points (4.1.2.4)

APs can be categorized as either autonomous APs or controller-based APs.

### Autonomous APs

Autonomous APs, sometimes referred to as heavy APs, are standalone devices configured using the Cisco CLI or a GUI. Autonomous APs are useful in situations where only a couple of APs are required in the network. Optionally, multiple APs can be controlled using wireless domain services (WDS) and managed using Cisco-Works Wireless LAN Solution Engine (WLSE).

**Note**

A home router is an example of an autonomous AP because the entire AP configuration resides on the device.

Figure 4-7 displays an autonomous AP in a small network.

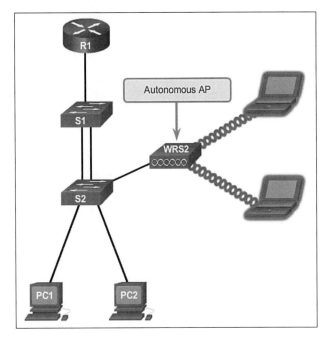

**Figure 4-7**   Autonomous AP

If the wireless demands increase, more APs would be required. Each AP would operate independent of other APs and require manual configuration and management.

## Controller-Based APs

Controller-based APs are server-dependent devices that require no initial configuration. Cisco offers two controller-based solutions. Controller-based APs are useful in situations where many APs are required in the network. As more APs are added, each AP is automatically configured and managed by a WLAN controller.

Figure 4-8 displays a controller-based AP in a small network.

Notice how a WLAN controller is now required to manage the APs. The benefit of the controller is that it can be used to manage many APs.

**Note**

Some AP models can operate in either autonomous mode or in controller-based mode.

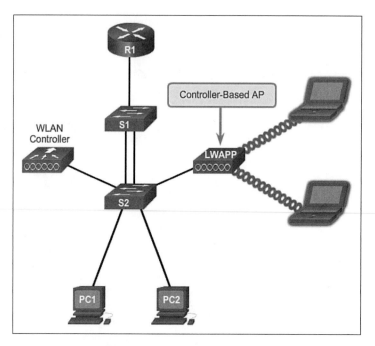

**Figure 4-8**   Controller-Based AP

## Small Wireless Deployment Solutions (4.1.2.5)

For small wireless deployment requirements, Cisco offers the following wireless autonomous AP solutions:

- **Cisco WAP4410N AP:** This AP is ideal for small organizations requiring two APs and supporting a small group of users.

- **Cisco WAP121 and WAP321 APs:** These APs are ideal for small organizations that want to simplify their wireless deployment using several APs.

- **Cisco AP541N AP:** This AP is ideal for small- to mid-sized organizations that want robust and an easily manageable cluster of APs.

### Note

Most enterprise-level APs also support Power over Ethernet (PoE).

Figure 4-9 displays and summarizes the Cisco small-business APs.

Figure 4-10 displays a sample topology for a small-business network using the WAP4410N APs. Each AP is configured and managed individually. This can become a problem when several APs are required.

**Figure 4-9**    Cisco Small-Business Autonomous APs

**Figure 4-10**    Simple WLAN Using WAP4410N APs

For this reason, the WAP121, WAP321, and AP541N APs support the clustering of APs without the use of a controller. The cluster provides a single point of administration and enables the administrator to view the deployment of APs as a single wireless network, rather than a series of separate wireless devices. The clustering capability makes it easy to set up, configure, and manage a growing wireless network. Multiple APs can be deployed and push a single configuration to all the devices within the cluster, managing the wireless network as a single system without worrying about interference between APs, and without configuring each AP as a separate device.

Specifically, the WAP121 and WAP321 support Single Point Setup (SPS), which makes AP deployment easier and faster, as shown in Figure 4-11.

**Figure 4-11**   Simple WLAN Using a Cluster of WAP321 APs

SPS helps to enable the wireless LAN to scale up to four WAP121 and up to eight WAP321 devices to provide broader coverage and support additional users as business needs change and grow. The Cisco AP541N AP can cluster up to 10 APs together and can support multiple clusters.

A cluster can be formed between two APs if the following conditions are met:

- Clustering mode is enabled on the APs.

- The APs joining the cluster have the same Cluster Name.

- The APs are connected on the same network segment.

- The APs use the same radio mode (that is, both radios use 802.11n).

Access an online AP541N emulator at www.cisco.com/assets/sol/sb/AP541N_GUI/
AP541N_1_9_2/Getting_Started.htm.

## Large Wireless Deployment Solutions (4.1.2.6, 4.1.2.7)

Organizations requiring the clustering of multiple APs require a more robust and
scalable solution. For larger organizations with many APs, Cisco provides controller-
based managed solutions, including the Cisco Meraki Cloud Managed Architecture
and the Cisco Unified Wireless Network Architecture.

---

**Note**

There are other controller-based solutions, such as the controllers using Flex mode. Visit
www.cisco.com for more information.

---

### Cisco Meraki Cloud Managed Architecture

The Cisco Meraki cloud architecture is a management solution used to simplify the
wireless deployment. Using this architecture, APs are managed centrally from a controller in the cloud, as shown in Figure 4-12.

**Figure 4-12**   Cloud Managed Wireless AP

Cloud networking and management provide centralized management, visibility, and
control without the cost and complexity of controller appliances or overlay management software.

This process reduces costs and complexity. The controller pushes management settings, such as firmware updates, security settings, wireless network, and SSID settings
to the Meraki APs.

**Note**

Only management data flows through the Meraki cloud infrastructure. No user traffic passes through Meraki's data centers. Therefore, if the Cisco Meraki cannot access the cloud, the network continues to function normally. This means that users can still authenticate, firewall rules remain in place, and traffic flows at full line rate. Only management functions, such as reports and configuration tools, are interrupted.

The Cisco Meraki cloud managed architecture requires the following:

- **Cisco MR Cloud Managed Wireless APs:** Various models exist to address a broad range of wireless deployment.

- **Meraki Cloud Controller (MCC):** The MCC provides centralized management, optimization, and monitoring of a Meraki WLAN system. The MCC is not an appliance that must be purchased and installed to manage wireless APs. Rather, the MCC is a cloud-based service that constantly monitors, optimizes, and reports the behavior of the network.

- **Web-based Dashboard:** Meraki's web-based Dashboard performs configuration and diagnostics remotely.

Figure 4-13 shows components of the Cisco Meraki architecture.

Visit the online curriculum to interact with the figure and learn more about each component.

**Figure 4-13**   MR Cloud Managed Wireless Access Points

## Cisco Unified Wireless Network Architecture

The Cisco Unified wireless network architecture solution, using a split MAC design, controls APs using a WLAN controller (WLC) and can be optionally managed using Cisco Wireless Control Systems (WCS). The *lightweight APs* communicate with the WLAN controller using the Lightweight Access Control Point Protocol (LWAPP). The controller has all the intelligence for communication, and the AP is a "dumb terminal" that simply processes packets.

The Cisco Unified wireless network architecture requires the following devices:

- **Lightweight APs:** Cisco Aironet 1600, 2600, or 3600 wireless AP models provide robust, dependable wireless network access for hosts.

- **Controllers for small- and medium-sized businesses:** The Cisco 2500 Series Wireless Controllers, Cisco Virtual Wireless Controller, or Cisco Wireless Controller Module for Cisco ISR G2 provides small-branch or single-site enterprise WLAN deployments with entry-level wireless for data.

Other WLAN controllers of greater capacity are also available. For example, the Cisco 5760 Wireless Controller and the Cisco 8500 Series Controller are designed to cost-effectively manage, secure, and optimize the performance of sizeable wireless networks, such as service provider and large campus deployments.

Figure 4-14 summarizes the lightweight APs.

**Cisco Aironet 1600, 2600, and 3600 Series**
Robust controller-based APs

**Cisco Aironet 600 Series OfficeExtend**
Used to extend 802.11n wireless coverage to the home teleworking environment

**Cisco 1552 Series Outdoor Rugged APs**
Robust outdoor controller-based AP

**Figure 4-14**   Controller-Based Wireless APs

Figure 4-15 shows small- and medium-sized business controllers.

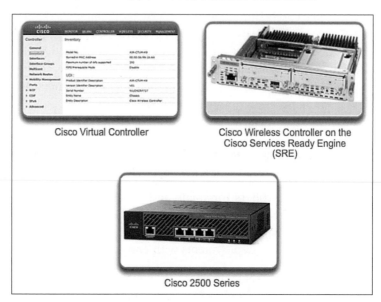

Cisco Virtual Controller

Cisco Wireless Controller on the
Cisco Services Ready Engine
(SRE)

Cisco 2500 Series

**Figure 4-15**   Controllers for Small- and Medium-Sized Businesses

Visit the online curriculum to interact with the figure and learn more information about the controllers for small- and medium-sized businesses.

## Wireless Antennas (4.1.2.8)

Most business-class APs require the use of external antennas to make them fully functioning units. Cisco has developed antennas specifically designed for use with 802.11 APs while accommodating specific deployment conditions, including physical layout, distance, and aesthetics.

Cisco Aironet APs can use

- *Omnidirectional Wi-Fi Antennas*: Factory Wi-Fi gear often uses basic dipole antennas, also referred to as a "rubber duck" design, similar to those used on walkie-talkie radios. Omnidirectional antennas provide 360-degree coverage and are ideal in open office areas, hallways, conference rooms, and outside areas.

- *Directional Wi-Fi Antennas*: Directional antennas focus the radio signal in a given direction. This enhances the signal to and from the AP in the direction the antenna is pointing, providing stronger signal strength in one direction and less signal strength in all other directions.

- *Yagi antennas*: A type of directional radio antenna that can be used for long-distance Wi-Fi networking. These antennas are typically used to extend the range of outdoor hotspots in a specific direction, or to reach an outbuilding.

Figure 4-16 displays various Cisco indoor and outdoor antennas.

**Figure 4-16**   Various Wireless Cisco Antennas

IEEE 802.11n/ac/ad use *MIMO* technology to increase available bandwidth. Specifically, MIMO uses multiple antennas to exchange more data than would be possible using a single antenna. Up to four antennas can be used to increase throughput.

**Note**

Not all wireless routers are the same. For example, entry-level 802.11n routers support 150-Mb/s bandwidth using one Wi-Fi radio and one antenna attached to the unit. To support the higher data rates, an 802.11n router requires more radios and antennas to manage more channels of data in parallel. For example, two radios and two antennas on an 802.11n router support up to 300 Mb/s, while 450 and 600 Mb/s require three and four radios and antennas, respectively.

**Activity 4.1.2.9: Identify WLAN Component Terminology**

Go to the course online to perform this practice activity.

**Lab 4.1.2.10: Investigating Wireless Implementations**

In this lab, you will complete the following objectives:

- Part 1: Explore Integrated Wireless Routers
- Part 2: Explore Wireless Access Points

# 802.11 WLAN Topologies (4.1.3)

This topic discusses the two basic WLAN topologies: ad hoc mode and infrastructure mode.

## 802.11 Wireless Topology Modes (4.1.3.1)

Wireless LANs can accommodate various network topologies. The 802.11 standard identifies two main wireless topology modes:

- *Ad hoc mode*: When two devices connect wirelessly without the aid of an infrastructure device, such as a wireless router or AP. Examples include Bluetooth and Wi-Fi Direct.

- *Infrastructure mode*: When wireless clients interconnect through a wireless router or AP, such as in WLANs. APs connect to the network infrastructure using the wired distribution system (DS), such as Ethernet.

Figure 4-17 displays an example of ad hoc mode.

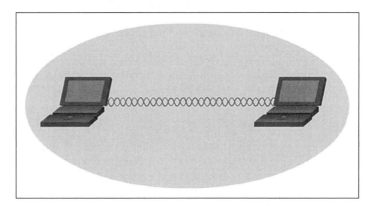

**Figure 4-17**  Ad Hoc Mode

Figure 4-18 displays an example of infrastructure mode.

## Ad Hoc Mode (4.1.3.2)

An ad hoc wireless network, like the one shown in Figure 4-17, is when two wireless devices communicate in a peer-to-peer (P2P) manner without using APs or wireless routers. For example, a client workstation with wireless capability can be configured to operate in ad hoc mode, enabling another device to connect to it. Bluetooth and Wi-Fi Direct are examples of ad hoc mode.

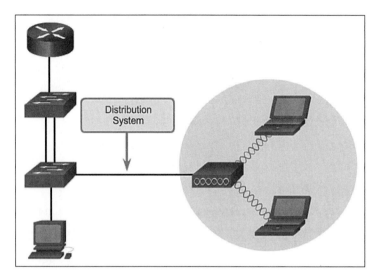

**Figure 4-18**   Infrastructure Mode

A variation of the ad hoc topology is when a smart phone or tablet with cellular data access is enabled to create a personal hotspot. This feature is sometimes referred to as *tethering*. A hotspot is usually a temporary quick solution that enables a smart phone to provide the wireless services of a Wi-Fi router. Other devices can associate and authenticate with the smart phone to use the Internet connection. The Apple iPhone refers to this as the Personal Hotspot feature, while Android devices refer to it as either Tethering or Portable Hotspot.

## Infrastructure Mode (4.1.3.3)

The IEEE 802.11 architecture consists of several components that interact to provide a WLAN that supports clients. It defines two infrastructure mode topology building blocks: a *Basic Service Set* (BSS) and an *Extended Service Set* (ESS).

### Basic Service Set

A BSS consists of a single AP interconnecting all associated wireless clients. In Figure 4-19, two BSS topologies are displayed.

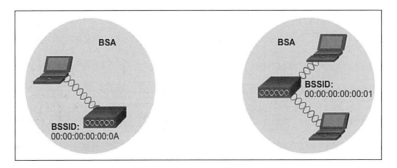

**Figure 4-19**    Basic Service Set Topologies

The circles depict the coverage area within which the wireless clients of the BSS can remain in communication. This area is called the *Basic Service Area* (BSA). If a wireless client moves out of its BSA, it can no longer directly communicate with other wireless clients within the BSA. The BSS is the topology building block, while the BSA is the actual coverage area (the terms BSA and BSS are often used interchangeably).

The Layer 2 MAC address of the AP is used to uniquely identify each BSS, which is called the *Basic Service Set Identifier* (BSSID). Therefore, the BSSID is the formal name of the BSS and is always associated with only one AP.

### Extended Service Set

When a single BSS provides insufficient RF coverage, two or more BSSs can be joined through a common distribution system (DS) into an ESS, as shown in Figure 4-20.

**Figure 4-20**    Extended Service Set Topology

An ESS is the union of two or more BSSs interconnected by a wired DS. Wireless clients in one BSA can now communicate with wireless clients in another BSA within the same ESS. Roaming mobile wireless clients can move from one BSA to another (within the same ESS) and seamlessly connect.

The rectangular area depicts the coverage area within which members of an ESS can communicate. This area is called the *Extended Service Area* (ESA). An ESA typically involves several BSSs in overlapping and/or separated configurations.

Each ESS is identified by an SSID, and in an ESS, each BSS is identified by its BSSID. For security reasons, additional SSIDs can be propagated through the ESS to segregate the level of network access.

> **Note**
>
> The 802.11 standard refers to ad hoc mode as an IBSS.

**Interactive Graphic**

**Activity 4.1.3.4: Identify WLAN Topology Terminology**

Go to the course online to perform this practice activity.

# Wireless LAN Operations (4.2)

This section discusses the inner workings of WLAN standards, including frame structure, access control, AP association, and channel management.

## 802.11 Frame Structure (4.2.1)

Not surprisingly, IEEE used a familiar frame structure to develop the 802.11 frame. This topic discusses the 802.11 frame with focus on the frame control fields.

### Wireless 802.11 Frame (4.2.1.1)

All Layer 2 frames consist of a header, payload, and FCS section, as shown in the top portion of Figure 4-21.

The 802.11 frame format is similar to the Ethernet frame format, with the exception that it contains more fields.

**Figure 4-21**    Wireless 802.11 Frame Header

As shown in the top portion of Figure 4-21, all 802.11 wireless frames contain the following fields:

- **Frame Control:** Identifies the type of wireless frame and contains subfields for protocol version, frame type, address type, power management, and security settings.

- **Duration:** Typically used to indicate the remaining duration needed to receive the next frame transmission.

- **Address1:** Usually contains the MAC address of the receiving wireless device or AP.

- **Address2:** Usually contains the MAC address of the transmitting wireless device or AP.

- **Address3:** Sometimes contains the MAC address of the destination, such as the router interface (default gateway) to which the AP is attached.

- **Sequence Control:** Contains the Sequence Number and the Fragment Number subfields. The Sequence Number indicates the sequence number of each frame. The Fragment Number indicates the number of each frame sent as a fragmented frame.

- **Address4:** Usually missing because it is used only in ad hoc mode.

- **Payload:** Contains the data for transmission.

- **FCS:** Frame Check Sequence; used for Layer 2 error control.

Figure 4-22 displays a Wireshark capture of a WLAN beacon frame.

Notice how the Frame Control field has also been expanded to display its subfields.

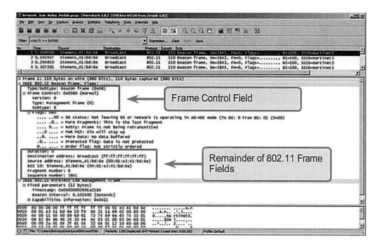

**Figure 4-22**   Wireshark Capture 1: 802.11 Frame

## Frame Control Field (4.2.1.2)

The Frame Control field contains multiple subfields, as shown in Figure 4-23.

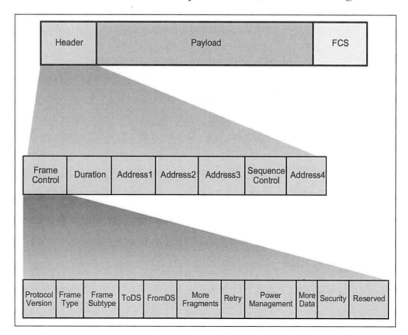

**Figure 4-23**   Frame Control Field

Specifically, the Frame Control field contains the following subfields:

- **Protocol Version:** Provides the current version of the 802.11 protocol used. Receiving devices use this value to determine whether the version of the protocol of the received frame is supported.

- **Frame Type** and **Frame Subtype:** Determine the function of the frame. A wireless frame can be a control frame, data frame, or management frame. There are multiple subtype fields for each frame type. Each subtype determines the specific function to perform for its associated frame type.

- **ToDS** and **FromDS:** Indicate whether the frame is going to or exiting from the DS, and is only used in data frames of wireless clients associated with an AP.

- **More Fragments:** Indicates whether more fragments of the frame, either data or management type, are to follow.

- **Retry:** Indicates whether the frame, for either data or management frame types, is being retransmitted.

- **Power Management:** Indicates whether the sending device is in active mode or power-save mode.

- **More Data:** Indicates to a device in power-save mode that the AP has more frames to send. It is also used for APs to indicate that additional broadcast/multicast frames are to follow.

- **Security:** Indicates whether encryption and authentication are used in the frame. It can be set for all data frames and management frames, which have the subtype set to authentication.

- **Reserved:** Can indicate that all received data frames must be processed in order.

Figure 4-24 displays a Wireshark capture of a WLAN beacon frame.

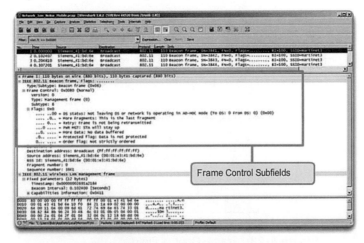

**Figure 4-24**  Wireshark Capture 2: Frame Control Subfields

Notice that the Frame Type field and the Frame Subtype fields identify whether the frame is a management frame, a control frame, or a data frame. In the example, the Frame Type is 0x0, identifying it as a management frame. The subtype value 8 identifies this as a *beacon* frame. The frame is specifically identified as 0x08.

## Wireless Frame Type (4.2.1.3)

**Note**

The Frame Type and Frame Subtype fields are used to identify the type of wireless transmission. As shown in Figure 4-25, a wireless frame can be one of three frame types:

- **Management Frame:** Used in the maintenance of communication, such as finding, authenticating, and associating with an AP.
- **Control Frame:** Used to facilitate the exchange of data frames between wireless clients.
- **Data Frame:** Used to carry the payload information, such as web pages and files.

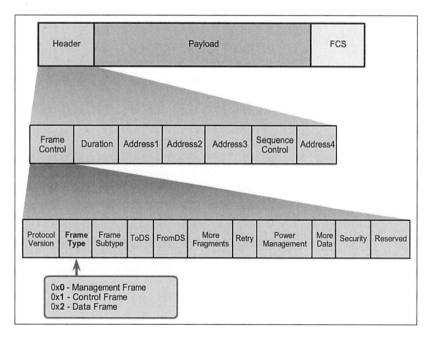

**Figure 4-25**   Frame Type Field

## Management Frames (4.2.1.4)

Management frames are used exclusively to find, authenticate, and associate with an AP.

Figure 4-26 displays the field value of common management frames including

- **Association request frame:** (0x00) Sent from a wireless client, it enables the AP to allocate resources and synchronize. The frame carries information about the wireless connection including supported data rates and the SSID of the network to the wireless client that wants to associate. If the request is accepted, the AP reserves memory and establishes an association ID for the device.

- **Association response frame:** (0x01) Sent from an AP to a wireless client containing the acceptance or rejection to an association request. If it is an acceptance, the frame contains information, such as an association ID and supported data rates.

- **Reassociation request frame:** (0x02) A device sends a reassociation request when it drops from the range of the currently associated AP and finds another AP with a stronger signal. The new AP coordinates the forwarding of any information that might still be contained in the buffer of the previous AP.

- **Reassociation response frame:** (0x03) Sent from an AP containing the acceptance or rejection to a device reassociation request frame. The frame includes information required for association, such as the association ID and supported data rates.

- **Probe request frame:** (0x04) Sent from a wireless client when it requires information from another wireless client.

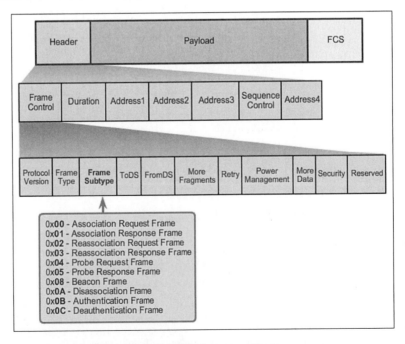

**Figure 4-26**   Frame Subtype Field in a Management Frame

- **Probe response frame:** (0x05) Sent from an AP containing capability information, such as the supported data rates, after receiving a probe request frame.

- **Beacon frame:** (0x08) Sent periodically from an AP to announce its presence and provide the SSID and other preconfigured parameters.

- **Disassociation frame:** (0x0A) Sent from a device wanting to terminate a connection. Allows the AP to relinquish memory allocation and remove the device from the association table.

- **Authentication frame:** (0x0B) The sending device sends an authentication frame to the AP containing its identity.

- **Deauthentication frame:** (0x0C) Sent from a wireless client wanting to terminate a connection from another wireless client.

Beacons are the only management frame that can regularly be broadcast by an AP. All other probing, authentication, and association frames are used only during the association (or reassociation) process.

Figure 4-27 displays a sample Wireshark screen capture of a management frame.

**Figure 4-27**    Wireshark Capture 3: Beacon Management Frame

The field values change to reflect the purpose of the frame.

**Note**

The example provided was captured using Wireshark. However, Wireshark must be specifically configured to capture WLAN traffic. The ability to capture traffic varies between operating systems and might require a special wireless NIC.

## Control Frames (4.2.1.5)

Control frames are used to manage the information exchange between a wireless client and an AP. They help prevent collisions from occurring on the wireless medium.

Figure 4-28 displays the field value of common control frames.

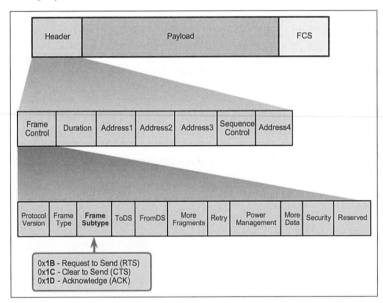

**Figure 4-28**   Frame Subtype Field in a Control Frame

These values include the following:

- **Request to Send (RTS) frame:** The RTS and CTS frames provide an optional collision reduction scheme for APs with hidden wireless clients. A wireless client sends an RTS frame as the first step in the two-way handshake, which is required before sending data frames.

- **Clear to Send (CTS) frame:** A wireless AP responds to an RTS frame with a CTS frame. It provides clearance for the requesting wireless client to send a data frame. The CTS contributes to collision control management by including a time value. This time delay minimizes the chance that other wireless clients will transmit while the requesting client transmits.

- **Acknowledgment (ACK) frame:** After receiving a data frame, the receiving wireless client sends an ACK frame to the sending client if no errors are found. If the sending client does not receive an ACK frame within a predetermined period of time, the sending client resends the frame.

Control frames are integral to wireless transmission and play a significant role in the media contention method used by wireless, known as Carrier Sense Multiple Access with Collision Avoidance (CSMA/CA).

**Interactive Graphic**

**Activity 4.2.1.6: Identify the 802.11 Frame Control Fields**

Go to the course online to perform this practice activity.

## Wireless Operation (4.2.2)

Like Ethernet, 802.11 is multiaccess technology. This topic discusses the mechanisms for avoiding collisions and controlling wireless access in a WLAN.

### Carrier Sense Multiple Access with Collision Avoidance (4.2.2.1)

Recall that the media contention method is the method in which devices determine how and when to access the media when traffic must be forwarded across the network. The IEEE 802.11 WLANs use the MAC protocol *Carrier Sense Multiple Access with Collision Avoidance* (CSMA/CA). While the name is similar to the Ethernet CSMA/CD, the operating concept is completely different.

Wi-Fi systems are half-duplex, shared media configurations; therefore, wireless clients can transmit and receive on the same radio channel. This creates a problem because a wireless client cannot hear while it is sending, thus making it impossible to detect a collision. To address this problem, the IEEE developed an additional collision avoidance mechanism called the *Distributed Coordination Function* (DCF). Using DCF, a wireless client transmits only if the channel is clear. All transmissions are acknowledged; therefore, if a wireless client does not receive an acknowledgment, it assumes that a collision occurred and retries after a random waiting interval.

Wireless clients and APs use the RTS and CTS control frames to facilitate the actual data transfer.

Figure 4-29 shows a control frame sent between a client and AP.

When a wireless client sends data, it first senses the media to determine whether other devices are transmitting. If not, it then sends an RTS frame to the AP. This frame is used to request dedicated access to the RF medium for a specified duration. The AP receives the frame and, if available, grants the wireless client access to the RF medium by sending a CTS frame of the same time duration. All other wireless devices observing the CTS frame relinquish the media to the transmitting node for transmission.

The CTS control frame includes the time duration that the transmitting node is allowed to transmit. Other wireless clients withhold transmissions for at least the specified duration.

Figure 4-30 displays a flowchart detailing the CSMA/CA process.

**Figure 4-29**   Control Frames During Data Transfer

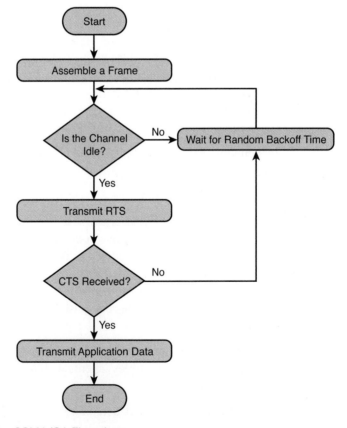

**Figure 4-30**   CSMA/CA Flowchart

## Wireless Clients and Access Point Association (4.2.2.2)

For wireless devices to communicate over a network, they must first associate with an AP or wireless router. An important part of the 802.11 process is discovering a WLAN and subsequently connecting to it.

As shown in Figure 4-31, management frames are used by wireless devices to complete the following three-stage process:

- Discover new wireless AP.

- Authenticate with AP.

- Associate with AP.

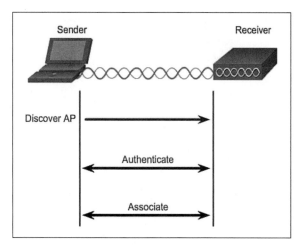

**Figure 4-31**   Discover, Authenticate, and Associate

To associate, a wireless client and an AP must agree on specific parameters. Parameters must be configured on the AP and subsequently on the client to enable the negotiation of these processes.

## Association Parameters (4.2.2.3)

Figure 4-32 displays the wireless settings on a Linksys EA6500 wireless router.

**Figure 4-32**   Wireless Settings Window

Common configurable wireless parameters include

- **SSID:** An SSID is a unique identifier that wireless clients use to distinguish between multiple wireless networks in the same vicinity. The SSID name appears in the list of available wireless network on a client. Depending on the network configuration, several APs on a network can share an SSID. Names are usually 2 to 32 characters long.

- **Password:** Required from the wireless client to authenticate to the AP. A password is sometimes called the security key. It prevents intruders and other unwanted users from accessing the wireless network.

- **Network mode:** Refers to the 802.11a/b/g/n/ac/ad WLAN standards. APs and wireless routers can operate in a Mixed mode, meaning that they can simultaneously use multiple standards.

- **Security mode:** Refers to the security parameter settings, such as WEP, WPA, or WPA2. Always enable the highest security level supported.

- **Channel settings:** Refers to the frequency bands being used to transmit wireless data. Wireless routers and APs can choose the channel setting, or it can be set manually if there is interference with another AP or wireless device.

Notice that the Linksys EA6500 supports 2.4-GHz and 5-GHz radios.

Figure 4-33 displays the options for the 2.4-GHz radio Network mode.

Notice that it can support Mixed, Wireless-N Only, or Wireless-G Only. The Mixed setting provides more flexibility, but it can also slow communication. For example, if all the wireless clients connecting to the router are using 802.11n, they all enjoy the better data rates provided. If 802.11g wireless clients associate with the AP, all the faster wireless clients contending for the channel must wait on the 802.11g clients to clear the channel before transmitting. However, if all wireless clients support 802.11n, select Wireless-N Only for best performance.

Figure 4-34 displays the Network mode options for the 5-GHz radio.

**Figure 4-33**  2.4-GHz Radio Network Modes

**Figure 4-34**  5-GHz Radio Network Modes

Notice that it also supports a Mixed setting, along with the Wireless-N Only and Wireless-AC Only settings.

Notice that the Linksys EA6500 does not support 802.11ad.

The Security options listed in Figure 4-35 are choices of security protocols available on the Linksys EA6500 wireless router.

**Figure 4-35**   Security Settings

Home users should choose WPA2/WPA Mixed Personal, while business users would typically choose WPA2/WPA Mixed Enterprise. The 5-GHz radio offers the identical choices. The wireless end device must also support the selected security option to associate.

---

**Note**

All wireless routers and APs should be secured using the highest available settings. The None or WEP options should be avoided and only used in situations where security is of no concern.

---

Figure 4-36 displays the Channel settings for the 2.4-GHz radio.

The preferred option to use is Auto; however, a specific channel could be selected if there were other APs or other devices nearby interfering with the channel selected by the router. Although the 5-GHz radio also has the Auto option, in the example, it lists a specific channel (153) and channel width.

**Figure 4-36**  Wireless Frequency Channels

## Discovering APs (4.2.2.4)

Wireless devices must discover and connect to an AP or wireless router. Wireless clients connect to the AP using a scanning (probing) process. This process can be

- **Passive mode:** The AP openly advertises its service by periodically sending broadcast beacon frames containing the SSID, supported standards, and security settings. The primary purpose of the beacon is to allow wireless clients to learn which networks and APs are available in a given area, thereby allowing them to choose which network and AP to use.

- **Active mode:** Wireless clients must know the name of the SSID. The wireless client initiates the process by broadcasting a probe request frame on multiple channels. The probe request includes the SSID name and standards supported. Active mode might be required if an AP or wireless router is configured to not broadcast beacon frames.

Figure 4-37 illustrates how passive mode works with the AP broadcasting a beacon frame every so often.

Figure 4-38 illustrates how active mode works with a wireless client broadcasting a probe request for a specific SSID. The AP with that SSID responds with a probe response frame.

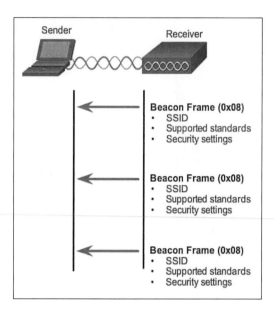

**Figure 4-37**   Client Devices Listen for an AP

**Figure 4-38**   AP Broadcasts Periodic Beacon Frames

A wireless client could also send a probe request without an SSID name to discover nearby WLAN networks. APs configured to broadcast beacon frames would respond to the wireless client with a probe response and provide the SSID name. APs with the broadcast SSID feature disabled do not respond.

## Authentication (4.2.2.5)

The 802.11 standard was originally developed with two authentication mechanisms:

- **Open authentication:** Fundamentally a NULL authentication where the wireless client says "authenticate me" and the AP responds with "yes." Open authentication provides wireless connectivity to any wireless device and should only be used in situations where security is of no concern.

- **Shared key authentication:** Technique is based on a key that is preshared between the client and the AP.

Figure 4-39 provides a simple overview of the authentication process.

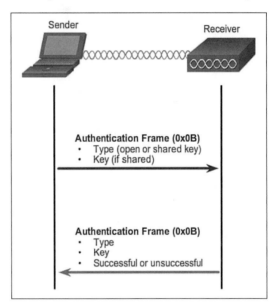

**Figure 4-39**   Client and AP Authenticate

However, in most shared key authentication installations, the exchange is as follows:

1. The wireless client sends an authentication frame to the AP.

2. The AP responds with a challenge text to the client.

3. The client encrypts the message using its shared key and returns the encrypted text to the AP.

4. The AP then decrypts the encrypted text using its shared key.

5. If the decrypted text matches the challenge text, the AP authenticates the client. If the messages do not match, the wireless client is not authenticated and wireless access is denied.

After a wireless client has been authenticated, the AP proceeds to the association stage. As shown in Figure 4-40, the association stage finalizes settings and establishes the data link between the wireless client and the AP.

**Figure 4-40** Client and AP Associate

As part of this stage

- The wireless client forwards an Association Request frame that includes its MAC address.

- The AP responds with an Associate Response that includes the AP BSSID, which is the AP MAC address.

- The AP maps a logical port known as the association identifier (AID) to the wireless client. The AID is equivalent to a port on a switch and allows the infrastructure switch to keep track of frames destined for the wireless client to be forwarded.

After a wireless client has associated with an AP, traffic is now able to flow between the client and the AP.

**Interactive Graphic**

**Activity 4.2.2.6: Order the Steps in the Client and AP Association Process**

Go to the course online to perform this practice activity.

# Channel Management (4.2.3)

Managing channel access is an important part of the 802.11 standard. This topic discusses the methods 802.11 has used during its evolution to choose a channel within the electromagnetic spectrum.

## Frequency Channel Saturation (4.2.3.1)

As previously explained, wireless LAN devices have transmitters and receivers tuned to specific frequencies of radio waves to communicate. A common practice is for frequencies to be allocated as ranges. Such ranges are then split into smaller ranges called channels.

If the demand for a specific channel is too high, that channel is likely to become oversaturated. The saturation of the wireless medium degrades the quality of the communication. Over the years, a number of techniques have been created to improve wireless communication and alleviate saturation. The following techniques mitigate channel saturation by using the channels in a more efficient way:

- *Direct-sequence spread spectrum* (DSSS): DSSS is a spread-spectrum modulation technique, as shown in Figure 4-41.

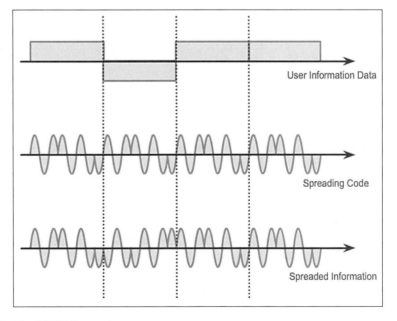

**Figure 4-41**    DSSS Example

Spread-spectrum is designed to spread a signal over a larger frequency band, making it more resistant to interference. With DSSS, the signal is multiplied by a "crafted noise" known as a spreading code. Because the receiver knows about the spreading code and when it was added, it can mathematically remove it and reconstruct the original signal. In effect, this creates redundancy in the transmitted signal in an effort to counter quality loss in the wireless medium. DSSS is used by 802.11b. It is also used by cordless phones operating in the 900-MHz, 2.4-GHz, and 5.8-GHz bands; by CDMA cellular; and by GPS networks.

- *Frequency-hopping spread spectrum* (**FHSS**): FHSS also relies on spread-spectrum methods to communicate, as shown in Figure 4-42.

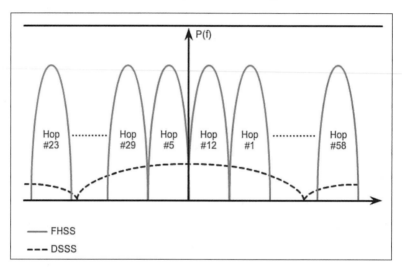

**Figure 4-42**   FHSS Example

FHSS is similar to DSSS but transmits radio signals by rapidly switching a carrier signal among many frequency channels. With FHSS, the sender and receiver must be synchronized to "know" which channel to jump. This channel-hopping process allows for a more efficient usage of the channels, decreasing channel congestion. Walkie-talkies and 900-MHz cordless phones also use FHSS, and Bluetooth uses a variation of FHSS. FHSS is also used by the original 802.11 standard.

- *Orthogonal frequency-division multiplexing* (**OFDM**): OFDM is a subset of frequency-division multiplexing in which a single channel utilizes multiple subchannels on adjacent frequencies, as shown in Figure 4-43.

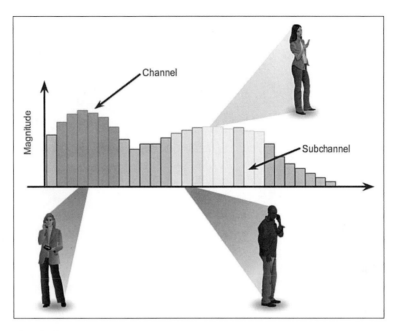

**Figure 4-43**    OFDM Example

Subchannels in an OFDM system are precisely orthogonal to one another, which allows the subchannels to overlap without interfering. As a result, OFDM systems are able to maximize spectral efficiency without causing adjacent channel interference. In effect, this makes it easier for a receiving station to "hear" the signal. Because OFDM uses subchannels, channel usage is very efficient. OFDM is used by a number of communication systems, including 802.11a/g/n/ac.

## Selecting Channels (4.2.3.2)

The IEEE 802.11b/g/n standards all operate in the microwave frequencies of the radio spectrum. The IEEE 802.11b/g/n standards operate in the 2.4-GHz to 2.5-GHz spectrum, while 802.11a/n/ac standards operate in the more heavily regulated 5-GHz band. Figure 4-44 highlights which 802.11 standard operates in the 2.4-GHz, 5-GHz, and 60-GHz bands.

Each spectrum is subdivided into channels with a center frequency and bandwidth, analogous to the way that radio bands are subdivided.

**Figure 4-44**    802.11 Microwave Frequencies

The 2.4-GHz band is subdivided into multiple channels. The overall, combined channel bandwidth is 22 MHz, with each channel separated by 5 MHz. The 802.11b standard identifies 11 channels for North America. The 22-MHz bandwidth, combined with the 5-MHz separation between frequencies, results in an overlap between successive channels, as shown in Figure 4-45.

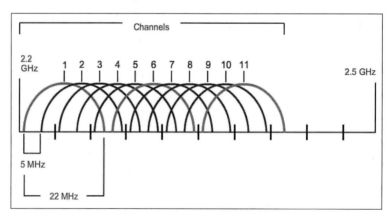

**Figure 4-45**    802.11b Channels

**Note**

In Europe, there are 13 802.11b channels.

Interference occurs when an undesired signal overlaps a channel reserved for a desired signal, causing possible distortion. The solution to interference is to use non-overlapping channels. Specifically, channels 1, 6, and 11 are nonoverlapping 802.11b channels, as shown in Figure 4-46.

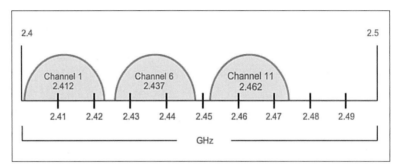

**Figure 4-46**   802.11b (DSSS) Channel Width 22 MHz

A best practice for WLANs requiring multiple APs is to use nonoverlapping channels. If there are three adjacent APs, use channels 1, 6, and 11. If there are just two, select any two that are five channels apart, such as channels 5 and 10. Most APs can automatically select a channel based on adjacent channels used. Some products continuously monitor the radio space to adjust the channel settings dynamically in response to environmental changes.

As enterprise WLANs migrate to 802.11n, they can use channels in the larger, less-crowded 5-GHz band, reducing "accidental denial of service (DoS)." For example, the 802.11n standard uses OFDM and can support four nonoverlapping channels, as shown in Figure 4-47.

**Figure 4-47**   802.11g/n (OFDM) Channel Width 20 MHz

802.11n can also use channel bonding, which combines two 20-MHz channels into one 40-MHz channel, as shown in Figure 4-48.

**Figure 4-48**    802.11n (OFDM) Channel Width 40 MHz

Channel bonding increases throughput by using two channels at one time to deliver data. Most modern APs can auto-adjust channels to circumvent interference.

**Note**

IEEE 802.11ac uses OFDM, with channel widths of 80,160, and 80+80.

## Planning a WLAN Deployment (4.2.3.3)

Implementing a WLAN that takes the best advantage of resources and delivers the best service can require careful planning. WLANs can range from relatively simple installations to very complex and intricate designs. There should be a well-documented plan before a wireless network can be implemented.

The number of users a WLAN can support is not a straightforward calculation. The number or users depends on the geographical layout of the facility, including the number of bodies and devices that can fit in a space, the data rates users expect, the use of nonoverlapping channels by multiple APs in an ESS, and transmit power settings.

Refer to the floor plan in Figure 4-49.

When planning the location of APs, the administrator cannot simply draw coverage area circles and drop them over a plan. The approximate circular coverage area is important, but there are some additional recommendations:

- If APs are to use existing wiring or if there are locations where APs cannot be placed, note these locations on the map.

- Position APs above obstructions.

- Position APs vertically near the ceiling in the center of each coverage area, if possible.

- Position APs in locations where users are expected to be. For example, conference rooms are typically a better location for APs than a hallway.

**Figure 4-49**    BSA Coverage

When these points have been addressed, estimate the expected coverage area of an AP. This value varies depending on the WLAN standard or mix of standards that are deployed, the nature of the facility, the transmit power that the AP is configured for, and so on. Always consult the specifications for the AP when planning for coverage areas.

BSAs represent the coverage area provided by a single channel. An ESS should have 10 to 15 percent overlap between BSAs in an ESS, as shown in Figure 4-49. With a 15 percent overlap between BSAs, an SSID, and nonoverlapping channels (that is, one cell on channel 1 and the other on channel 6), roaming capability can be created.

Other factors include site surveys, which are detailed analyses of where to locate the various APs.

**Interactive Graphic**

**Activity 4.2.3.4: Identify Channel Management Terminology**

Go to the course online to perform this practice activity.

**Interactive Graphic**

**Activity 4.2.3.5: Cisco Wireless Explorer Game**

Go to the course online to perform this practice activity.

# Wireless LAN Security (4.3)

As with all network access technologies, wireless security is of paramount importance. This section discusses WLAN security threats and the methods for securing WLANs.

## WLAN Threats (4.3.1)

Security is a major concern in WLANs because the frequencies of WLANs are open to anyone with a device within the range of an AP. This topic discusses the unique threats to WLANs.

### Securing Wireless (4.3.1.1)

The difficulties in keeping a wired network secure are amplified with a wireless network. Security should be a priority for anyone who uses or administers networks.

A WLAN is open to anyone within range of an AP and the appropriate credentials to associate to it. With a wireless NIC and knowledge of cracking techniques, an attacker might not have to physically enter the workplace to gain access to a WLAN.

Security concerns are even more significant when dealing with business networks, because the livelihood of the business relies on the protection of its information. Security breaches for a business can have major repercussions, especially if the business maintains financial information associated with its customers. Wireless networks are increasingly being deployed in enterprises and, in many cases, have evolved from a convenience to a mission-critical part of the network. Although WLANs have always been a target for attacks, with their rise in popularity increasing, they are now a major target.

Attacks can be generated by outsiders and disgruntled employees, and even unintentionally by employees. Wireless networks are specifically susceptible to several threats, including

- **Wireless intruders:** Unauthorized users attempting to access network resources. The solution is to deter intruders using authentication.

- **Rogue apps:** Unauthorized APs installed by a well-intentioned user or willingly for malicious purpose. Use wireless management software to detect rogue APs.

- **Interception of data:** Wireless data can easily be captured by eavesdroppers. Protect data exchanged between client and AP using encryption.

- **Denial of service (DoS) attacks:** WLANs services can be compromised either accidentally or for malicious intent. Various solutions exist depending on the source of DoS attacks.

**Note**

Other threats, such as AP/wireless client MAC spoofing, cracking, and infrastructure attacks, are outside the scope of this chapter.

## DoS Attack (4.3.1.2)

Wireless DoS attacks can be the result of

- **Improperly configured devices:** Configuration errors can disable the WLAN. For example, an administrator could accidentally alter a configuration and disable the network, or an intruder with administrator privileges could intentionally disable a WLAN.

- **A malicious user intentionally interfering with the wireless communication:** His goal is to disable the wireless network completely or to the point where no legitimate device can access the medium.

- **Accidental interference:** WLANs operate in the unlicensed frequency bands and, therefore, all wireless networks, regardless of security features, are prone to interference from other wireless devices. Accidental interference can occur from such devices as microwave ovens, cordless phones, baby monitors, and more. The 2.4-GHz band is more prone to interference than the 5-GHz band.

To minimize the risk of a DoS attack because of improperly configured devices and malicious attack, harden all devices, keep passwords secure, create backups, and ensure that all configuration changes are incorporated off-hours.

Accidental interference only happens when another wireless device is introduced. The best solution is to monitor the WLAN for any interference problems and address them as they appear. Because the 2.4-GHz band is more prone to interference, the 5-GHz band could be used in areas prone to interference. Some WLAN solutions enable APs to automatically adjust channels and use the 5-GHz band to compensate for interference. For example, some 802.11n/ac/ad solutions automatically adjust to counter interference.

Figure 4-50 illustrates how a cordless phone, or even a microwave, can interfere with WLAN communication.

The Cisco CleanAir technology enables devices to identify and locate non-802.11 interference sources. It creates a network that has the ability to adjust automatically to changes in its environment.

**Figure 4-50**   Accidental Interference

## Management Frame DoS Attacks (4.3.1.3)

Although unlikely, a malicious user could intentionally initiate a DoS attack using RF jamming devices that produce accidental interference. It is more likely that they will attempt to manipulate management frames to consume the AP resources and keep channels too busy to service legitimate user traffic.

Management frames can be manipulated to create various types of DoS attacks. Two common management frame attacks include

- **A spoofed disconnect attack:** This occurs when an attacker sends a series of "disassociate" commands to all wireless clients within a BSS. These commands cause all clients to disconnect. When disconnected, the wireless clients immediately try to reassociate, which creates a burst of traffic. The attacker continues sending disassociate frames and the cycle repeats itself.

- **A CTS flood:** This occurs when an attacker takes advantage of the CSMA/CA contention method to monopolize the bandwidth and deny all other wireless clients access to the AP. To accomplish this, the attacker repeatedly floods the BSS with Clear to Send (CTS) frames to a bogus STA. All other wireless clients sharing the RF medium receive the CTS and withhold their transmissions until the attacker stops transmitting the CTS frames.

Figure 4-51 displays how a wireless client and an AP normally use CSMA/CA to access the medium.

**Figure 4-51**   Normal Operation with CSMA/CA

Figure 4-52 illustrates how a CTS flood is created by an attacker sending out CTS frames to a bogus wireless client.

**Figure 4-52**   Attacker Creating a CTS Flood DoS Attack

All other clients must now wait the specified duration in the CTS frame. However, the attacker keeps sending CTS frames, thus making the other clients wait indefinitely. The attacker now has control of the medium.

**Note**

This is only one example of a management frame attack. Many others exist.

To mitigate many of these attacks, Cisco has developed a variety of solutions, including the Cisco Management Frame Protection (MFP) feature, which also provides complete proactive protection against frame and device spoofing. The Cisco Adaptive Wireless IPS contributes to this solution by an early detection system where the attack signatures are matched.

The IEEE 802.11 committee has also released two standards in regard to wireless security. The 802.11i standard, which is based on Cisco MFP, specifies security mechanisms for wireless networks, while the 802.11w management frame protection standard addresses the problem of manipulating management frames.

## Rogue Access Points (4.3.1.4)

A rogue AP is an AP or wireless router that has either been

- Connected to a corporate network without explicit authorization and against corporate policy. Anyone with access to the premises can install (maliciously or nonmaliciously) an inexpensive wireless router that can potentially allow access to secure network resources.

- Connected or enabled by an attacker to capture client data such as the MAC addresses of clients (both wireless and wired), or to capture and disguise data packets, to gain access to network resources, or to launch a *man-in-the-middle attack*.

Another consideration is how easy it is to create a personal network hotspot. For example, a user with secure network access enables his authorized Windows host to become a Wi-Fi AP. Doing so circumvents the security measures, and other unauthorized devices can now access network resources as a shared device.

To prevent the installation of rogue APs, organizations must use monitoring software to actively monitor the radio spectrum for unauthorized APs. For example, the sample Cisco Prime Infrastructure network management software screenshot in Figure 4-53 displays an RF map identifying the location of an intruder with a spoofed MAC address detected.

**Figure 4-53**    Sample Screenshot of a Rogue AP Detection

**Note**

Cisco Prime is network management software that works with other management software to provide a common look and central location for all network information. It is usually deployed in very large organizations.

## Man-in-the-Middle Attack (4.3.1.5)

One of the more sophisticated attacks a malicious user can use is called a man-in-the-middle (MITM) attack. There are many ways in which to create a MITM attack.

A popular wireless MITM attack is called the "evil twin AP" attack, where an attacker introduces a rogue AP and configures it with the same SSID as a legitimate AP. Locations offering free Wi-Fi, such as airports, cafes, and restaurants, are hotbeds for this type of attack because of the open authentication.

Connecting wireless clients would see two APs offering wireless access. Those near the rogue AP find the stronger signal and most likely associate with the evil twin AP. User traffic is now sent to the rogue AP, which in turn captures the data and forwards it to the legitimate AP. Return traffic from the legitimate AP is sent to the rogue AP, captured, and then forwarded to the unsuspecting STA. The attacker can steal the user's password, take personal information, gain network access, and compromise the user's system.

For example, in Figure 4-54, a malicious user is in "Bob's Latte" coffee shop and wants to capture traffic from unsuspecting wireless clients.

**Figure 4-54**    Malicious User Launches Evil Twin Attack

The attacker launches software that enables his laptop to become an evil twin AP, matching the same SSID and channel as the legitimate wireless router.

In Figure 4-55, a user sees two wireless connections available, but chooses and associates with the evil twin AP.

**Figure 4-55**    Evil Twin Attack Successful

The attacker captures the user data and forwards it to the legitimate AP, which in turn directs the return traffic back to the evil twin AP. The evil twin AP captures the return traffic and forwards the information to the unsuspecting user.

Defeating an attack like an MITM attack depends on the sophistication of the WLAN infrastructure and the vigilance in monitoring activity on the network. The process begins with identifying legitimate devices on the WLAN. To do this, users must be authenticated. After all the legitimate devices are known, the network can be monitored for abnormal devices or traffic.

Enterprise WLANs that use state-of-the-art WLAN devices provide administrators with tools that work together as a wireless intrusion prevention system (IPS). These tools include scanners that identify rogue APs and ad hoc networks, and radio resource management (RRM), which monitors the RF band for activity and AP load. An AP that is busier than normal alerts the administrator of possible unauthorized traffic.

## Securing WLANs (4.3.2)

Securing access to the WLAN involves implementing several solutions, including SSID cloaking, MAC address filtering, and a strong authentication method.

### Wireless Security Overview (4.3.2.1)

Security has always been a concern with Wi-Fi because the network boundary has moved. Wireless signals can travel through solid matter, such as ceilings, floors, and walls, and outside of the home or office space. Without stringent security measures in place, installing a WLAN can be the equivalent of putting Ethernet ports everywhere, even outside.

To address the threats of keeping wireless intruders out and protecting data, two early security features were used:

- *SSID cloaking*: APs and some wireless routers allow the SSID beacon frame to be disabled. Wireless clients must manually identify the SSID to connect to the network.

- **MAC addresses filtering:** An administrator can manually allow or deny clients' wireless access based on their physical MAC hardware address.

Although these two features would deter most users, the reality is that neither SSID cloaking nor MAC address filtering would deter a crafty intruder. SSIDs are easily discovered even if APs do not broadcast them, and the MAC addresses can be spoofed. The best way to secure a wireless network is to use authentication and encryption systems. Two types of authentication were introduced with the original 802.11 standard:

- **Open system authentication:** Any wireless client should easily be able to connect, and should only be used in situations where security is of no concern, such as in locations providing free Internet access like cafes, hotels, and in remote areas.

- **Shared key authentication:** Provides mechanisms, such as WEP, WPA, or WPA2, to authenticate and encrypt data between a wireless client and AP. However, the password must be preshared between both parties to connect.

The chart in Figure 4-56 summarizes the various types of authentication with a focus on the characteristics of open authentication.

**Figure 4-56**   Authentication Methods: Open

## Shared Key Authentication Methods (4.3.2.2)

Figure 4-57 shows a summary of the three shared key authentication techniques available:

- *Wired Equivalent Privacy* **(WEP):** Original 802.11 specification designed to provide privacy similar to connecting to a network using a wired connection. The data is secured using the RC4 encryption method with a static key. However, the key never changes when exchanging packets, making it easy to hack.

- *Wi-Fi Protected Access* **(WPA):** A Wi-Fi Alliance standard that uses WEP, but secures the data with the much stronger Temporal Key Integrity Protocol (TKIP) encryption algorithm. TKIP changes the key for each packet, making it much more difficult to hack.

- *IEEE 802.11i/WPA2*: IEEE 802.11i is the industry standard for securing wireless networks. The Wi-Fi Alliance version is called WPA2. 802.11i and WPA2 both use the Advanced Encryption Standard (AES) for encryption. AES is currently considered the strongest encryption protocol.

**Figure 4-57**   Authentication Methods: Shared Key

WEP is no longer recommended. Its shared WEP keys have proven to be flawed and, therefore, should never be used. To counteract shared WEP key weakness, the very first approach by companies was to try techniques such as cloaking SSIDs and filtering MAC addresses. These techniques have also proven to be too weak.

Following the weakness of WEP-based security, there was a period of interim security measures. Vendors like Cisco, wanting to meet the demand for better security, developed their own systems while simultaneously helping to evolve the 802.11i standard. On the way to 802.11i, the TKIP encryption algorithm was created, which was linked to the Wi-Fi Alliance WPA security method.

Modern wireless networks should always use the 802.11i/WPA2 standard. WPA2 is the Wi-Fi version of 802.11i, and therefore, the terms WPA2 and 802.11i are often used interchangeably.

Since 2006, any device that bears the Wi-Fi Certified logo is WPA2 certified.

**Note**

Wireless-N networks should use the WPA2-Personal security mode for best performance.

Table 4-3 summarizes the three types of shared key authentication methods.

**Table 4-3** Comparing Shared Key Authentication Characteristics

| Characteristic | WEP | WPA | 802.11i/WPA2 |
|---|---|---|---|
| Authentication Method | Pre-shared key | PSK or 802.1x | PSK or 802.1x |
| Encryption | RC4 | TKIP | AES |
| Message Integrity | CRC-32 | MIC | CCMP |
| Security | Weak | Strong | Stronger |

## Encryption Methods (4.3.2.3)

Encryption is used to protect data. If an intruder has captured encrypted data, he would not be able to decipher it in any reasonable amount of time.

The IEEE 802.11i and the Wi-Fi Alliance WPA and WPA2 standards use the following encryption protocols:

- *Temporal Key Integrity Protocol* (**TKIP**): TKIP is the encryption method used by WPA. It provides support for legacy WLAN equipment by addressing the original flaws associated with the 802.11 WEP encryption method. It makes use of WEP, but encrypts the Layer 2 payload using TKIP, and carries out a Message Integrity Check (MIC) in the encrypted packet to ensure that the message has not been tampered with.

- *Advanced Encryption Standard* (**AES**): AES is the encryption method used by WPA2. It is the preferred method because it aligns with the industry-standard IEEE 802.11i. AES performs the same functions as TKIP, but it is a far stronger method of encryption. It uses the Counter Cipher Mode with Block Chaining Message Authentication Code Protocol (CCMP), which allows destination hosts to recognize whether the encrypted and nonencrypted bits have been tampered with.

### Note

Always choose WPA2 with AES when possible.

## Authenticating a Home User (4.3.2.4)

Figure 4-58 displays the security mode choices of the Linksys EA6500 wireless router.

Notice how the security mode for the 2.4-GHz network uses open authentication (that is, None) and no password is required, while the security mode for the 5-GHz network uses WPA2/WPA Mixed Personal authentication and a password is required.

**Figure 4-58**   Mixed Authentication Example

The Security Mode drop-down list of the 2.4-GHz network displays the security methods available on the Linksys EA6500 router. It lists the weakest (that is, None) to the strongest (that is, WPA2/WPA Mixed Enterprise). The 5-GHz network includes the same drop-down list.

WPA and WPA2 support two types of authentication:

- **Personal:** Intended for home or small-office networks, users authenticate using a preshared key (PSK). Wireless clients authenticate with the AP using a preshared password. No special authentication server is required.

- **Enterprise:** Intended for enterprise networks but requires a Remote Authentication Dial-In User Service (RADIUS) authentication server. Although more complicated to set up, it provides additional security. The device must be authenticated by the RADIUS server and then users must authenticate using the 802.1X standard, which uses the Extensible Authentication Protocol (EAP) for authentication.

## Authentication in the Enterprise (4.3.2.5)

In networks that have stricter security requirements, an additional authentication or login is required to grant wireless clients such access. The Enterprise security mode choices require an Authentication, Authorization, and Accounting (AAA) RADIUS server.

Refer to the example in Figure 4-59.

**Figure 4-59**   RADIUS Server Configuration

Notice the new fields displayed when choosing an Enterprise version of WPA or WPA2. These fields are necessary to supply the AP with the required information to contact the AAA server:

- **RADIUS Server IP address:** This is the reachable address of the RADIUS server.

- **UDP port numbers:** Officially assigned UDP ports 1812 for RADIUS Authentication and 1813 for RADIUS Accounting, but could also operate using UDP ports 1645 and 1646.

- **Shared key:** Used to authenticate the AP with the RADIUS server.

The shared key is not a parameter that must be configured on an STA. It is only required on the AP to authenticate with the RADIUS server.

**Note**

There is no Password field listed, because the actual user authentication and authorization is handled by the 802.1X standard, which provides a centralized, server-based authentication of end users.

The 802.1X login process uses EAP to communicate with the AP and RADIUS server. EAP is a framework for authenticating network access. It can provide a secure authentication mechanism and negotiate a secure private key that can then be used for a wireless encryption session utilizing TKIP or AES encryption.

**Interactive
Graphic**

**Activity 4.3.2.6: Identify the WLAN Authentication Characteristics**

Go to the course online to perform this practice activity.

# Wireless LAN Configuration (4.4)

WLAN implementation includes tasks for configuring the AP or wireless router, tasks for configuring wireless clients, as well as tasks for troubleshooting any issues that might arise during operation.

## Configure a Wireless Router (4.4.1)

This topic discusses the configuration of a specific type of wireless router: the Linksys EAS65000. However, configuration is similar on any wireless router that implements the same technology.

### Configuring a Wireless Router (4.4.1.1)

Modern wireless routers offer a variety of features, and most are designed to be functional right out of the box with the default settings. However, it is good practice to change initial, default configurations.

Home wireless routers are configured using a GUI web interface.

The basic approach to wireless implementation, as with any basic networking, is to configure and test incrementally. For example, before implementing any wireless devices, verify that the existing wired network is operational and that wired hosts can access Internet services.

After the wired network operation has been confirmed, the implementation plan consists of the following:

**Step 1.** Start the WLAN implementation process with a single AP and a single wireless client, without enabling wireless security.

**Step 2.** Verify that the client has received a DHCP IP address and can ping the local wired default router and then browse to the external Internet.

**Step 3.**   Configure wireless security using WPA2/WPA Mixed Personal. Never use WEP unless no other options exist.

**Step 4.**   Back up the configuration.

Before installing a wireless router, consider the following settings:

- **SSID Name:** Name of the WLAN network.

- **Network Password (if required):** If prompted, this is the password required to associate and access the SSID.

- **Router Password:** This is a management router password equivalent to the **enable secret** privileged EXEC mode password.

- **Guest Network SSID Name:** For security reasons, guests can be isolated to a different SSID.

- **Guest Network Password:** This is the password to access the guest SSID.

- **Linksys Smart Wi-Fi Username:** Internet account required to access the router remotely over the Internet.

- **Linksys Smart Wi-Fi Password:** Password to access the router remotely.

Table 4-4 outlines example settings used to configure the Linksys EA6500 wireless router.

**Table 4-4**   Management Parameters and Settings

| Management Parameters | Settings |
|---|---|
| Network Name (SSID) | Home-Net |
| Network Password | cisco123 |
| Router Password | class123 |
| Guest Network Name (SSID) | Home-Net-Guest |
| Guest Network Password | cisco |
| Linksys Smart Wi-Fi Username | My-Name |
| Linksys Smart Wi-Fi Password | class12345 |

## Setting Up and Installing Initial Linksys EA6500 (4.4.1.2)

The Linksys EA6500 wireless router is packaged with a Setup CD.

To set up and install the Linksys EA6500 router software, perform the following steps:

**Step 1.**   Insert the CD into the CD or DVD drive and the Setup should start auto-matically. If the Setup CD is not available, download the Setup program from http://Linksys.com/support. Figure 4-60 displays the initial Connect your Linksys EA6500 window, with instructions to connect the router power and the Internet connection.

**Figure 4-60**   Initial Instructions

**Note**

In our example, the wireless router will not be connected to the Internet.

**Step 2.**   Click **Next** to begin the installation.

The Setup program begins the installation and displays a status window, as shown in Figure 4-61.

**Figure 4-61**    Router Setup Status

During this time, the Setup program attempts to configure and enable the Internet connection. In the example, the Internet connection is unavailable, and after a few prompts to connect to the Internet, the option to skip this step displays.

The Linksys router settings window displays, as shown in Figure 4-62. This is where the SSID, wireless password, and administrative password are configured.

**Figure 4-62**    Enter the Linksys Router Settings

**Step 3.** Click **Next** to display the summary router settings screen, as shown in Figure 4-63. Record these settings if the initial table was not previously completed.

**Figure 4-63**    Summary of Router Settings

**Step 4.** Click **Next** to display the option to configure the Linksys Smart Wi-Fi account window, as shown in Figure 4-64.

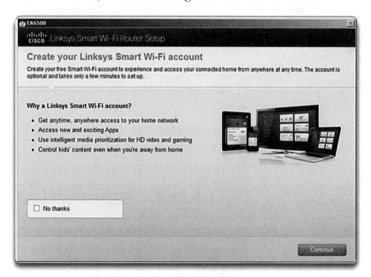

**Figure 4-64**    Create Smart Wi-Fi Account

This window enables you to manage the router remotely over the Internet. In this example, the Linksys Smart Wi-Fi account is not set up because there is no Internet access.

Step 5.    Click **Continue** to display the Sign In window, as shown in Figure 4-65. Because the Internet connection has not been configured, the administrative router password is required.

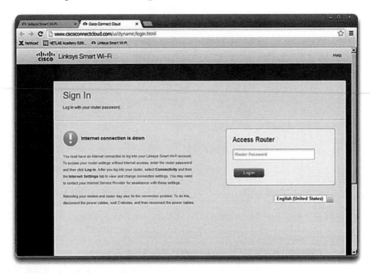

**Figure 4-65**    Log in to the Router

Step 6.    When the password is entered, click **Log in** to display the Linksys Smart Wi-Fi Home page, as shown in Figure 4-66.

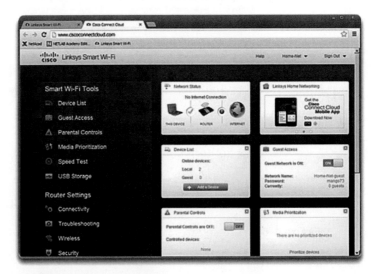

**Figure 4-66**    EA6500 Web Dashboard

## Configuring the Linksys Smart Wi-Fi Home Page (4.4.1.3)

As shown in Figures 4-67 to 4-69, the Linksys Smart-Wi-Fi Home page is divided into the following three main sections:

- **Smart Wi-Fi Tools:** Use this section to see who is currently connected to the network, create a separate network for guests, configure parental control to keep kids safe, prioritize bandwidth to specific devices and applications, test the Internet connection speed, and control access to shared files.

**Figure 4-67**   Smart Wi-Fi Tools

- **Smart Wi-Fi Router Settings:** Use this section to alter settings for connectivity, troubleshooting, wireless, and security.

**Figure 4-68**   Smart Wi-Fi Router Settings

- **Smart Wi-Fi Widgets:** Provides a quick summary of the Smart Wi-Fi Tools section.

**Figure 4-69**   Smart Wi-Fi Widgets

**Video 4.4.1.3**

View the video in the online course launched from Figure button 4 to see a short explanation on the Smart Wi-Fi interface.

## Smart Wi-Fi Settings (4.4.1.4)

As shown in Figures 4-70 to 4-73, the Smart Wi-Fi settings enable you to

- Configure the router's basic settings for the local network. This tool can be used to configure a DHCP reservation, change the router's administration password, change the IP address of the Linksys router, set up the Linksys routers with a static route, set up the router with cable Internet service, and configure the MTU settings of the Linksys router.

- Diagnose and troubleshoot connectivity issues on the network. The Troubleshooting page contains the current status of the router and connected devices. It can also be used to perform a ping test and a traceroute, to back up and restore the router's current settings, to check the WAN IP address, to reboot and reset the router to factory defaults, and to maintain the router's status.

- Secure and personalize the wireless network. The Wireless settings page can also be used to enable and configure wireless MAC filters and connect devices easily using WPS.

- Keep the network safe from Internet threats by configuring the DMZ feature.

- View connected computers and devices on the network, and set up port forwarding.

**Figure 4-70**   Connectivity Settings

**Figure 4-71**   Troubleshooting Settings

**Figure 4-72**   Wireless Settings

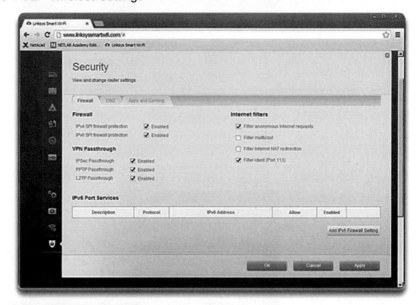

**Figure 4-73**   Security Settings

## Smart Wi-Fi Tools (4.4.1.5)

As shown in Figures 4-74 to 4-79, the Smart Wi-Fi tools provide additional services including

- **Device List:** View to see who is connected to the WLAN. Device names and icons can be personalized. Devices can also be connected with this service.

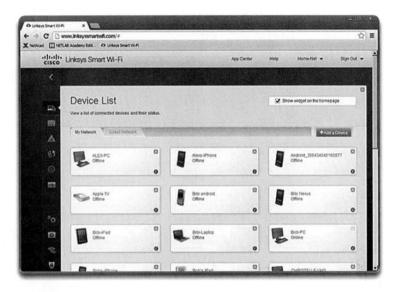

**Figure 4-74**   Device List

- **Guest Access:** Create a separate network for up to 50 guests at home while keeping network files safe with the Guest Access Tool.

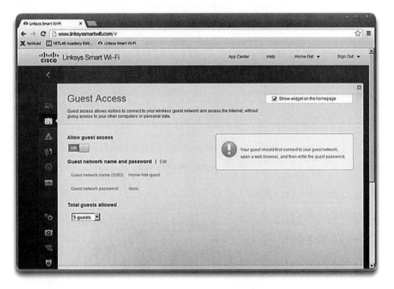

**Figure 4-75**   Guest Access

- **Parental Controls:** Protect kids and family members by restricting access to potentially harmful websites. This tool is used to restrict Internet access on specific devices, control the time and days of specific devices that can access the Internet, block specific websites for certain devices, disable restrictions on Internet access, and disable the Parental Controls feature.

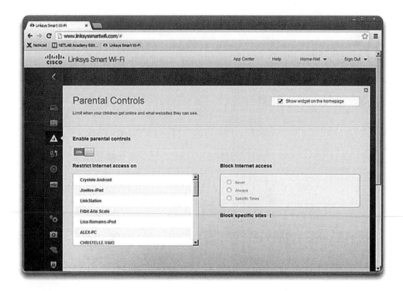

**Figure 4-76**    Parental Controls

■ **Media Prioritization:** Prioritize bandwidth to specific devices and applications. With this tool, optimize the online experience by prioritizing bandwidth on applications and devices that need it the most. This tool can be used to utilize the Settings feature of the Media Prioritization Tool, add more applications to be assigned with a specific bandwidth, and allocate higher bandwidth to an application, device, or online game by setting the bandwidth priority.

**Figure 4-77**    Media Prioritization

■ **Speed Test:** A tool used to test the upload and download speed of the Internet link. Useful for baselining.

**Figure 4-78**   Speed Test

■ **USB Storage:** Controls access to shared files. Configures how users can access shared files. With this tool, users can access USB storage in the local network, create shares on a USB storage device, configure the Folder Access settings, configure how devices and computers within the network can access the FTP server, and configure the access to a Media Server.

**Figure 4-79**   USB Storage

## Backing Up a Configuration (4.4.1.6)

Just like the IOS of a Cisco router should be backed up in case of failure, so should the configuration of a home router. If a home router is left to its default configuration, backing up the configuration is not warranted. However, if many of the Smart Wi-Fi tools have been customized, it might be advantageous to back up the configuration.

Backing up the configuration is easy to do with the Linksys EA6500 wireless router:

**Step 1.** Log in to the Smart Wi-Fi Home page. Click the **Troubleshooting** icon to display the Troubleshooting Status window, as shown in Figure 4-80.

**Figure 4-80** Troubleshooting Window

**Step 2.** Click the **Diagnostic** tab to open the Diagnostics Troubleshooting window, as shown in Figure 4-81.

**Step 3.** Under the Router configuration title, click **Backup** and save the file to an appropriate folder.

---

**Note**

To upload a previously saved backup, click **Restore**, locate the file, and start the restore process.

---

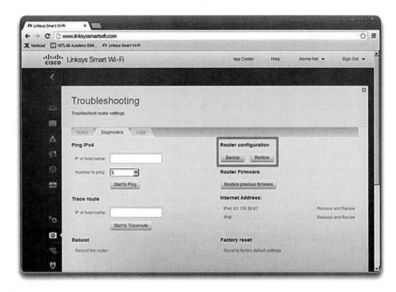

**Figure 4-81**   Diagnostics Troubleshooting Window

## Configuring Wireless Clients (4.4.2)

This short topic reviews how a client would connect to a Linksys EAS6500.

### Connecting Wireless Clients (4.4.2.1)

When the AP or wireless router has been configured, the wireless NIC on the client must be configured to allow it to connect to the WLAN. The user should also verify that the client has successfully connected to the correct wireless network, especially because there might be many WLANs available with which to connect.

**Video**

**Video 4.4.2.1**

View the video in the online course launched from Figure button 1 to see a short explanation on how to connect a Windows computer to the WLAN.

**Video**

**Video 4.4.2.2**

View the video in the online course launched from Figure button 2 to see a short explanation on how to connect an iPod, iPhone, and iPad to the WLAN.

**Packet Tracer Activity 4.4.2.2: Configuring Wireless LAN Access**

In this activity, you will configure a Linksys wireless router, allowing for remote access from PCs as well as wireless connectivity with WPA2 security. You will manually configure PC wireless connectivity by entering the Linksys router SSID and password.

**Lab 4.4.2.3: Configuring a Wireless Router and Client**

In this lab, you will complete the following objectives:

- Part 1: Configure Basic Settings on a Linksys EA Series Router
- Part 2: Secure the Wireless Network
- Part 3: Review Additional Features on a Linksys EA Series Router
- Part 4: Connect a Wireless Client

## Troubleshoot WLAN Issues (4.4.3)

This topic discusses three troubleshooting approaches and some of the more common errors you might encounter in a WLAN.

### Troubleshooting Approaches (4.4.3.1)

Troubleshooting any sort of network problem should follow a systematic approach. Logical networking models, such as the OSI and TCP/IP models, separate network functionality into modular layers.

When troubleshooting, these layered models can be applied to the physical network to isolate network problems. For example, if the symptoms suggest a physical connection problem, the network technician can focus on troubleshooting the circuit that operates at the physical layer. If that circuit functions properly, the technician looks at areas in another layer that could be causing the problem.

There are three main troubleshooting approaches used to resolve network problems that focus on using layers in the OSI model:

- **Bottom-up:** Start at Layer 1 and work up through the layers.
- **Top-down:** Start at Layer 7 and work down through the layers.
- **Divide-and-conquer:** Ping the destination. If the pings fail, verify the lower layers. If the pings are successful, verify the upper layers. This methodology is shown in Figure 4-82.

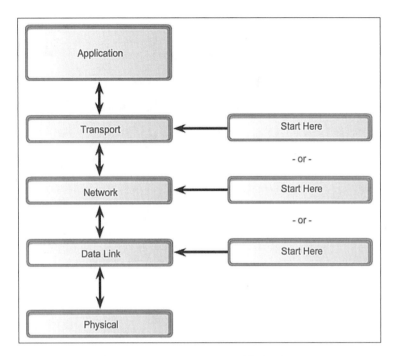

**Figure 4-82**   Divide-and-Conquer Troubleshooting Method

## Wireless Client Not Connecting (4.4.3.2)

When troubleshooting a WLAN, a process of elimination is recommended.

In Figure 4-83, a wireless client is not connecting to the WLAN. If there is no connectivity, check the following:

- Confirm the network configuration on the PC using the **ipconfig** command. Verify that the PC has received an IP address through DHCP or is configured with a static IP address.

- Confirm that the device can connect to the wired network. Connect the device to the wired LAN and ping a known IP address.

- If necessary, reload drivers as appropriate for the client. It might be necessary to try a different wireless NIC.

- If the wireless NIC of the client is working, check the security mode and encryption settings on the client. If the security settings do not match, the client cannot gain access to the WLAN.

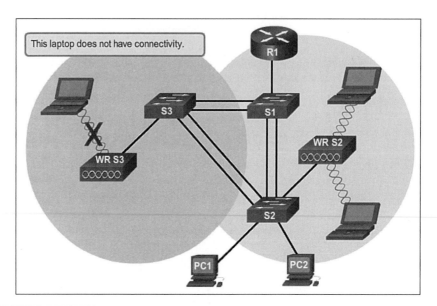

**Figure 4-83**  Wireless Connectivity Problem

If the PC is operational but the wireless connection is performing poorly, check the following:

- How far is the PC from an AP? Is the PC out of the planned coverage area (BSA)?

- Check the channel settings on the wireless client. The client software should detect the appropriate channel as long as the SSID is correct.

- Check for the presence of other devices in the area that might be interfering with the 2.4-GHz band. Examples of other devices are cordless phones, baby monitors, microwave ovens, wireless security systems, and potentially rogue APs. Data from these devices can cause interference in the WLAN and intermittent connection problems between a wireless client and AP.

Next, ensure that all the devices are actually in place. Consider a possible physical security issue. Is there power to all devices and are they powered on?

Finally, inspect links between cabled devices, looking for bad connectors or damaged or missing cables. If the physical plant is in place, verify the wired LAN by pinging devices, including the AP. If connectivity still fails at this point, perhaps something is wrong with the AP or its configuration.

When the user PC is eliminated as the source of the problem, and the physical status of devices is confirmed, begin investigating the performance of the AP. Check the power status of the AP.

## Troubleshooting When the Network Is Slow (4.4.3.3)

To optimize and increase the bandwidth of 802.11n/ac dual-band routers, either

- **Upgrade your wireless clients:** Older 802.11b and even 802.11g devices can slow the entire WLAN. For the best performance, all wireless devices should support the same highest acceptable standard.

- **Split the traffic:** The easiest way to improve wireless performance is to split the wireless traffic between the 802.11n 2.4-GHz band and the 5-GHz band. Therefore, 802.11n (or better) can use the two bands as two separate wireless networks to help manage the traffic. For example, use the 2.4-GHz network for basic Internet tasks, such as web browsing, email, and downloads, and use the 5-GHz band for streaming multimedia, as shown in Figure 4-84.

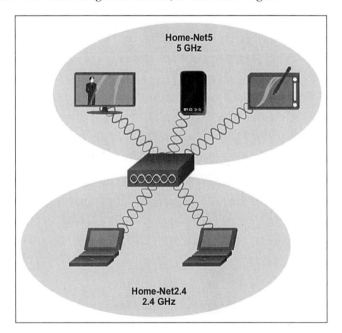

**Figure 4-84**   Splitting Traffic Between 2.4- and 5-GHz Bands

There are several reasons for using a split-the-traffic approach:

- The 2.4-GHz band can be suitable for basic Internet traffic that is not time-sensitive.

- The bandwidth can still be shared with other nearby WLANs.

- The 5-GHz band is much less crowded than the 2.4-GHz band and is ideal for streaming multimedia.

- The 5-GHz band has more channels; therefore, the channel chosen is likely interference-free.

By default, dual-band routers use the same network name on both the 2.4-GHz band and the 5-GHz band. The simplest way to segment traffic is to rename one of the wireless networks. With a separate, descriptive name, it is easier to connect to the right network.

To improve the range of a wireless network, ensure that the physical wireless router location is free of obstructions, such as furniture, fixtures, and tall appliances. These block the signal, which shortens the range of the WLAN. If this still does not solve the problem, a Wi-Fi Range Extender or Powerline wireless technology can be used.

### Updating Firmware (4.4.3.4)

The IOS of the Linksys EA6500 router is called firmware. The firmware might need to be upgraded if there is a problem with the device or if there is a new feature included with a new firmware update. Regardless of the reason, most modern wireless home routers offer upgradeable firmware.

You can easily upgrade the Linksys EA6500 Smart Wi-Fi router firmware by performing the following steps:

**Step 1.**   Access the Linksys Smart Wi-Fi Home page.

**Step 2.**   Click the **Connectivity** icon to open the Connectivity window, as shown in Figure 4-85.

**Figure 4-85**   Updating the Firmware

**Step 3.**   Under the Firmware Update label, click **Check for Updates.**

The router either responds with "No updates found" or it prompts you to download and install the new firmware.

**Note**

Some routers require that the firmware file be downloaded ahead of time and then manually uploaded. To do so, select **Choose File.** If a firmware upgrade fails or makes the situation worse, you can load the previous firmware by clicking **Troubleshooting, Diagnostics,** and then selecting **Restore previous firmware,** as shown in Figure 4-86.

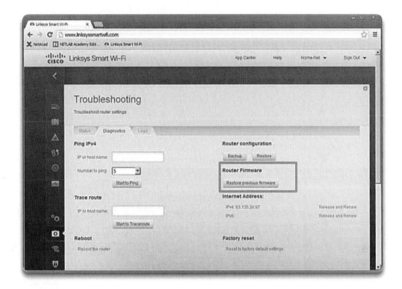

**Figure 4-86**   Restoring the Previous Firmware

**Caution**

Do not upgrade the firmware unless there are problems with the AP or the new firmware has a desired feature.

**Activity 4.4.3.5: Identify the Troubleshooting Solution**

Go to the course online to perform this practice activity.

# Summary (4.5)

### Class Activity 4.5.1.1: Inside and Outside Control

An assessment has been completed to validate the need for an upgrade to your small- to medium-sized wireless network. Approved for purchase are indoor and outdoor access points and one wireless controller. You must compare equipment models and their specifications before you purchase.

Therefore, you visit the "Wireless Compare Products and Services" website and see a features chart for indoor and outdoor wireless access points and controller devices. After reviewing the chart, you note there is some terminology with which you are unfamiliar:

- Federal Information Processing Standard (FIPS)
- MIMO
- Cisco CleanAir Technology
- Cisco FlexConnect
- Band Select

Research these terms. Prepare a chart with your company's most important requirements listed for purchasing the indoor and outdoor wireless access points and wireless controller. This chart will assist in validating your purchase order to your accounting manager and CEO.

---

Packet Tracer
☐ Activity

### Packet Tracer Activity 4.5.1.2: Skills Integration Challenge

In this challenge activity, you will configure VLANs and inter-VLAN routing, DHCP, and Rapid PVST+. You will also be required to configure a Linksys router for wireless connectivity with wireless security. At the end of the activity, the PCs will not be able to ping each other but should be able to ping the outside host.

---

WLANs are often implemented in homes, offices, and campus environments. Only the 2.4-GHz, 5.0-GHz, and 60-GHz frequencies are used for 802.11 WLANs. The ITU-R regulates the allocation of the RF spectrum, while the IEEE provides the 802.11 standards to define how these frequencies are used for the physical and MAC sublayer of wireless networks. The Wi-Fi Alliance certifies that vendor products conform to industry standards and norms.

A wireless client uses a wireless NIC to connect to an infrastructure device, such as a wireless router or wireless AP. Wireless clients connect using an SSID. APs can be implemented as standalone devices, in small clusters, or in a larger controller-base network.

A Cisco Aironet AP can use an omnidirectional antenna, a directional antenna, or a Yagi antenna to direct signals. IEEE 802.11n/ac/ad use MIMO technology to improve throughput and support up to four antennas simultaneously.

In ad hoc mode or IBSS, two wireless devices connect to each other in a P2P manner.

In infrastructure mode, APs connect to the network infrastructure using the wired DS. Each AP defines a BSS and is uniquely identified by its BSSID. Multiple BSSs can be joined into an ESS. Using a particular SSID in an ESS provides seamless roaming capabilities among the BSSs in the ESS. Additional SSIDs can be used to segregate the level of network access defined by which SSID is in use.

A wireless client first authenticates with an AP and then associates with that AP. The 802.11i/WPA2 authentication standard should be used. AES is the encryption method that should be used with WPA2.

When planning a wireless network, nonoverlapping channels should be used when deploying multiple APs to cover a particular area. There should be a 10–15 percent overlap between BSAs in an ESS. Cisco APs support PoE to simplify installation.

Wireless networks are specifically susceptible to threats, such as wireless intruders, rogue APs, data interception, and DoS attacks. Cisco has developed a range of solutions to mitigate these types of threats.

# Practice

The following activities provide practice with the topics introduced in this chapter. The Labs and Class Activities are available in the companion *Scaling Networks Lab Manual* (ISBN 978-1-58713-325-1). The Packet Tracer Activities PKA files are found in the online course.

## Class Activities

- Class Activity 4.0.1.2: Make Mine Wireless
- Class Activity 4.5.1.1: Inside and Outside Control

## Labs

- Lab 4.1.2.10: Investigating Wireless Implementations
- Lab 4.4.2.3: Configuring a Wireless Router and Client

```
Packet Tracer
☐ Activity
```

# Packet Tracer Activities

- Packet Tracer Activity 4.4.2.2: Configuring Wireless LAN Access
- Packet Tracer Activity 4.5.1.2: Skills Integration Challenge

# Check Your Understanding Questions

Complete all the review questions listed here to test your understanding of the topics and concepts in this chapter. The appendix "Answers to 'Check Your Understanding' Questions" lists the answers.

1. Which wireless RF band do IEEE 802.11b/g devices use?

   A. 900 MHz

   B. 2.4 GHz

   C. 5 GHz

   D. 60 GHz

2. What is a characteristic of a Yagi antenna that is used by Cisco Aironet Access Points?

   A. It can be used for long-distance Wi-Fi networking.

   B. It is also referred to as a "rubber duck" design.

   C. It has the same characteristics as an omnidirectional Wi-Fi antenna.

   D. It provides 360-degree coverage.

3. Which statement describes an ESS?

   A. Bluetooth is an example of ESS infrastructure mode.

   B. It involves several BSSs that are joined through a common distribution system.

   C. An ESS is a connection of a BSS to an ad hoc wireless network.

   D. An ESS consists of two or more BSSs that are interconnected wirelessly by a DS.

4. What Wi-Fi management frame is regularly broadcast by APs to announce their presence?

   A. Authentication

   B. Association

   C. Probe

   D. Beacon

5. What type of frames are used for advertising, authenticating, and associating with a wireless AP?

   A. Management

   B. Control

   C. Data

   D. Acknowledgment

6. An IEEE 802.11n network has been configured for mixed mode and has clients that are using 802.11n and 802.11g radios on the network. The 802.11n clients are complaining of slower than normal speeds. What is the problem?

   A. The access point is failing.

   B. This is the normal behavior of a mixed-mode network.

   C. The authentication is not allowing roaming.

   D. Roaming between access points is disabled.

7. Which of the following recommendations should an administrator follow when planning the location of multiple APs? (Choose two.)

   A. Position APs horizontally near the ceiling in the center of each coverage area, if possible.

   B. Overlap channels to provide roaming capability.

   C. Always consult the specifications for the AP when planning for coverage areas.

   D. Position APs in locations where users are expected to be.

   E. An ESS should have 20 to 25 percent overlap between BSAs in an ESS.

8. The company handbook states that employees cannot have microwave ovens in their offices. Instead, all employees must use the microwave ovens located in the employee cafeteria. What wireless security risk is the company trying to avoid?

   A. Interception of data

   B. Rogue access points

   C. Improperly configured devices

   D. Accidental interference

9. Which combination of WLAN authentication and encryption is recommended as a best practice for home users?

   A. EAP and AES

   B. WPA and PSK

   C. WPA2 and AES

   D. WEP and TKIP

   E. WEP and RC4

10. If an administrator is troubleshooting a WLAN using a bottom-up approach, which action would be taken first?

   A. Make sure all devices are powered on.

   B. Verify that the GUI interface is accessible from a client.

   C. Update the firmware on the AP.

   D. Ping the AP.

11. Fill in the blank. Known as "WiGig," the IEEE 802.11 _____ standard provides average speeds of up to 7 Gb/s, but will switch to a lower-GHz band when roaming is employed.

12. Fill in the blank. A network administrator discovers a rogue AP in the network. The rogue AP is capturing traffic and then forwarding it on to the legitimate AP. This type of attack is known as a _____ attack.

13. Fill in the blank. What wireless technology is described by each of the following statements?

   _____ is an alternative to cable and DSL that can communicate over distances up to 50 km.

   _____ provides network access within a home with connectivity distances of up to 300 meters.

   _____ is useful in remote areas, but requires a clear line of sight.

   _____ uses device pairing to communicate over distances of up to 100 meters.

# CHAPTER 5

# Adjust and Troubleshoot Single-Area OSPF

## Objectives

Upon completion of this chapter, you will be able to answer the following questions:

- What are the commands to modify the OSPF interface priority to influence DR/BDR election?

- What are the commands to configure OSPF to propagate a default route?

- What commands are available to modify OSPF interface settings to improve network performance?

- What are the commands to configure OSPF authentication to secure routing updates?

- What are the process and tools available to troubleshoot a single-area OSPF network?

- What is the process to troubleshoot missing route entries in a single-area OSPFv2 routing table?

- What is the process to troubleshoot missing route entries in a single-area OSPFv3 routing table?

## Key Terms

This chapter uses the following key terms. You can find the definitions in the Glossary.

# Introduction (5.0.1.1)

OSPF is a popular link-state routing protocol that can be fine-tuned in many ways. Some of the most common methods of fine-tuning include manipulating the Designated Router/Backup Designated Router (DR/BDR) election process, propagating default routes, fine-tuning the OSPFv2 and OSPFv3 interfaces, and enabling authentication.

This chapter of OSPF describes these tuning features, the configuration mode commands to implement these features for both IPv4 and IPv6, and the components and commands used to troubleshoot OSPFv2 and OSPFv3.

### Class Activity 5.0.1.2: DR and BDR Election

You are trying to decide how to influence the selection of the designated router and backup designated router for your OSPF network. This activity simulates that process.

Three separate designated-router election scenarios will be presented. The focus is on electing a DR and BDR for your group. Refer to the PDF for this activity for the remaining instructions.

If additional time is available, two groups can be combined to simulate DR and BDR elections.

# Advanced Single-Area OSPF Configurations (5.1)

This section assumes a certain level of expertise in basic OSPF configuration. However, it does include a brief review to help refresh the reader before proceeding to the more advanced topics of OSPF operation in multiaccess networks, default route propagation, fine-tuning OSPF interfaces, and securing OSPF routing updates.

## Routing in the Distribution and Core Layers (5.1.1)

This topic briefly reviews routing concepts and single-area OSPF configuration.

### Routing Versus Switching (5.1.1.1)

A scalable network requires a hierarchical network design. The focus of the preceding chapters was on the access and distribution layers. Layer 2 switches, link aggregation, LAN redundancy, and wireless LANs are all technologies that provide or enhance user access to network resources.

Scalable networks also require optimal reachability between sites. Remote network reachability is provided by routers and Layer 3 switches, which operate in the distribution and core layers, as shown in Figure 5-1.

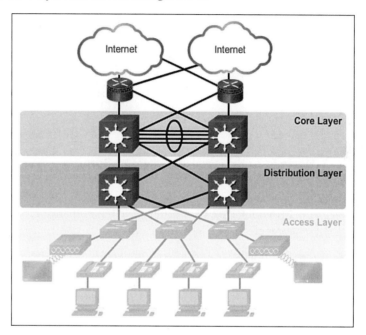

**Figure 5-1**   Routing in the Distribution and Core Layers

Routers and Layer 3 switches learn about remote networks in one of two ways:

- **Manually:** Remote networks are manually entered into the route table using static routes.

- **Dynamically:** Remote routes are automatically learned using a dynamic routing protocol such as Enhanced Interior Gateway Routing Protocol (EIGRP) or Open Shortest Path First (OSPF).

## Static Routing (5.1.1.2)

The example in Figure 5-2 provides a sample scenario of static routing.

A network administrator can manually configure a static route to reach a specific network. Unlike a dynamic routing protocol, static routes are not automatically updated and must be manually reconfigured anytime the network topology changes. A static route does not change until the administrator manually reconfigures it.

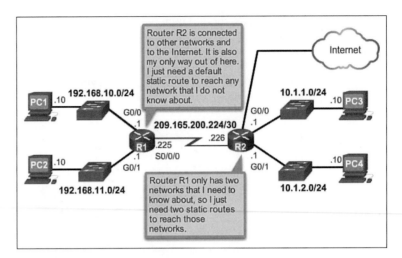

**Figure 5-2** Static and Default Route Scenario

Static routing has three primary uses:

- Providing ease of routing table maintenance in smaller networks that are not expected to grow significantly.

- Routing to and from stub networks. A stub network is a network accessed by a single route, and the router has only one neighbor.

- Using a single default route to represent a path to any network that does not have a more specific match with another route in the routing table. Default routes are used to send traffic to any destination beyond the next upstream router.

### Dynamic Routing Protocols (5.1.1.3)

Routing protocols allow routers to dynamically share information about remote networks, as shown in Figure 5-3.

Routers receiving the update automatically add this information to their own routing tables. The routing protocols then determine the best path, or route, to each network. A primary benefit of dynamic routing protocols is that routers exchange routing information when there is a topology change. This exchange allows routers to automatically learn about new networks and also to find alternate paths when there is a link failure to a current network.

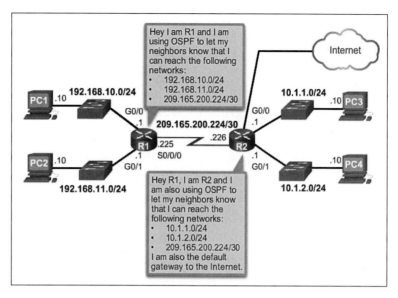

**Figure 5-3**   Dynamic Routing Scenario

Compared to static routing, dynamic routing protocols require less administrative overhead. However, the expense of using dynamic routing protocols is dedicating part of a router's resources for protocol operation, including CPU time and network link bandwidth. Despite the benefits of dynamic routing, static routing still has its place. There are times when static routing is more appropriate and other times when dynamic routing is the better choice. However, it is important to understand that static and dynamic routing are not mutually exclusive. Rather, most networks use a combination of dynamic routing protocols and static routes.

The two most common dynamic routing protocols are EIGRP and OSPF. The focus of this chapter is on OSPF.

**Note**

All dynamic routing protocols are capable of advertising and propagating static routes in their routing updates.

## Open Shortest Path First (5.1.1.4)

OSPF is a commonly implemented link-state routing protocol. It was developed as a replacement for the distance vector routing protocol Routing Information Protocol (RIP). However, OSPF has significant advantages over RIP in that it offers faster convergence and scales to much larger network implementations.

OSPF features include

- *Classless*: It is classless by design; therefore, it supports VLSM and CIDR.

- **Efficient:** Routing changes trigger routing updates (no periodic updates). It uses the SPF algorithm to choose the best path.

- **Fast convergence:** It quickly propagates network changes.

- **Scalable:** It works well in small and large network sizes. Routers can be grouped into areas to support a hierarchical system.

- **Secure:** It supports Message Digest 5 (MD5) authentication. When enabled, OSPF routers only accept encrypted routing updates from peers with the same preshared password.

## Configuring Single-Area OSPF (5.1.1.5)

The focus of this chapter is to adjust and troubleshoot OSPF. However, it is a good idea to review a basic implementation of the OSPF routing protocol. Figure 5-4 displays the topology used for configuring OSPFv2.

**Figure 5-4**   OSPFv2 Reference Topology

The routers in the topology have a starting configuration, including enabled interface addresses. There is currently no static routing or dynamic routing configured on any of the routers. All interfaces on Routers R1, R2, and R3 (except the loopback on R2) are within the OSPF backbone area. The ISP router is used as the routing domain's gateway to the Internet.

Example 5-1 shows the configuration for R1.

**Example 5-1**   Basic Single-Area OSPFv2 Configuration for R1

```
R1(config)# interface gigabitethernet 0/0
R1(config-if)# bandwidth 1000000
R1(config-if)# router ospf 10
R1(config-router)# router-id 1.1.1.1
R1(config-router)# auto-cost reference-bandwidth 1000
R1(config-router)# network 172.16.1.0 0.0.0.255 area 0
R1(config-router)# network 172.16.3.0 0.0.0.255 area 0
R1(config-router)# network 192.168.10.4 0.0.0.3 area 0
R1(config-router)# passive-interface g0/0
```

The Gigabit Ethernet 0/0 interface is configured to reflect its true bandwidth of 1,000,000 kilobits (that is 1,000,000,000 b/s). Next, from OSPF router configuration mode, the router ID is assigned, the reference bandwidth is adjusted to account for fast interfaces, and the three networks attached to R1 are advertised. Notice how the wildcard mask is used to identify the specific networks.

Example 5-2 shows the configuration for R2.

**Example 5-2**   Basic Single-Area OSPFv2 Configuration for R2

```
R2(config)# interface gigabitethernet 0/0
R2(config-if)# bandwidth 1000000
R2(config-if)# router ospf 10
R2(config-router)# router-id 2.2.2.2
R2(config-router)# auto-cost reference-bandwidth 1000
R2(config-router)# network 172.16.2.1 0.0.0.0 area 0
R2(config-router)# network 172.16.3.2 0.0.0.0 area 0
R2(config-router)# network 192.168.10.9 0.0.0.0 area 0
R2(config-router)# passive-interface g0/0
```

The Gigabit Ethernet 0/0 interface is configured to reflect its true bandwidth, the router ID is assigned, the reference bandwidth is adjusted to account for fast interfaces, and the three networks attached to R2 are advertised. Notice how the use of the wildcard mask can be avoided by identifying the actual router interface with a quad-zero mask. This effectively makes OSPF use the subnet mask assigned to the router interface as the advertised network mask.

Example 5-3 shows the configuration for R3, which is similar to R1 and R2.

**Example 5-3**   Basic Single-Area OSPFv2 Configuration for R3

```
R3(config)# interface GigabitEthernet0/0
R3(config-if)# bandwidth 1000000
R3(config-if)# router ospf 10
R3(config-router)# router-id 3.3.3.3
R3(config-router)# auto-cost reference-bandwidth 1000
R3(config-router)# network 192.168.1.1 0.0.0.0 area 0
R3(config-router)# network 192.168.10.6 0.0.0.0 area 0
R3(config-router)# network 192.168.10.10 0.0.0.0 area 0
R3(config-router)# passive-interface g0/0
R3(config-router)#
*Aug 28 17:15:26.547: %OSPF-5-ADJCHG: Process 10, Nbr 1.1.1.1 on Serial0/0/0 from
  LOADING to FULL, Loading Done
*Aug 28 17:15:26.863: %OSPF-5-ADJCHG: Process 10, Nbr 2.2.2.2 on Serial0/0/1 from
  LOADING to FULL, Loading Done
R3(config-router)#
```

Notice the informational messages displaying that R3 has established a full neighbor adjacency with R1 with router ID 1.1.1.1 and R2 with router ID 2.2.2.2. The OSPF network has converged.

## Verifying Single-Area OSPF (5.1.1.6)

Useful commands to verify OSPF include the following:

- **show ip ospf neighbor:** This command verifies that the router has formed an adjacency with its neighboring routers. If the router ID of the neighboring router is not displayed, or if it does not show as being in a state of FULL, the two routers have not formed an OSPF adjacency. Example 5-4 shows output for R2.

**Example 5-4**   **show ip ospf neighbor** Command

```
R2# show ip ospf neighbor

Neighbor ID     Pri   State          Dead Time   Address         Interface
3.3.3.3           0   FULL/  -       00:00:39    192.168.10.10   Serial0/0/1
1.1.1.1           0   FULL/  -       00:00:32    172.16.3.1      Serial0/0/0
```

- **show ip protocols:** This command provides a quick way to verify vital OSPF configuration information. This includes the OSPF process ID, the router ID, networks the router is advertising, the neighbors the router is receiving updates from, and the default administrative distance, which is 110 for OSPF. Example 5-5 shows the output for R2.

**Example 5-5   show ip protocols** Command

```
R2# show ip protocols
*** IP Routing is NSF aware ***


Routing Protocol is "ospf 10"
  Outgoing update filter list for all interfaces is not set
  Incoming update filter list for all interfaces is not set
  Router ID 2.2.2.2
  Number of areas in this router is 1. 1 normal 0 stub 0 nssa
  Maximum path: 4
  Routing for Networks:
    172.16.2.1 0.0.0.0 area 0
    172.16.3.2 0.0.0.0 area 0
    192.168.10.9 0.0.0.0 area 0
  Passive Interface(s):
    GigabitEthernet0/0
  Routing Information Sources:
    Gateway         Distance      Last Update
    3.3.3.3               110      00:34:32
    1.1.1.1               110      00:35:05
  Distance: (default is 110)
```

- **show ip ospf:** This command is used to display the OSPF process ID and router ID as well as the OSPF SPF and OSPF area information. Example 5-6 shows the output for R2.

**Example 5-6   show ip ospf** Command

```
R2# show ip ospf
 Routing Process "ospf 10" with ID 2.2.2.2
 Start time: 01:37:24.332, Time elapsed: 01:32:17.412
 Supports only single TOS(TOS0) routes
 Supports opaque LSA
 Supports Link-local Signaling (LLS)
 Supports area transit capability
 Supports NSSA (compatible with RFC 3101)
 Event-log enabled, Maximum number of events: 1000, Mode: cyclic
 Router is not originating router-LSAs with maximum metric
 Initial SPF schedule delay 5000 msecs
 Minimum hold time between two consecutive SPFs 10000 msecs
 Maximum wait time between two consecutive SPFs 10000 msecs
 Incremental-SPF disabled
 Minimum LSA interval 5 secs
```

```
Minimum LSA arrival 1000 msecs
LSA group pacing timer 240 secs
Interface flood pacing timer 33 msecs
Retransmission pacing timer 66 msecs
Number of external LSA 0. Checksum Sum 0x000000
Number of opaque AS LSA 0. Checksum Sum 0x000000
Number of DCbitless external and opaque AS LSA 0
Number of DoNotAge external and opaque AS LSA 0
Number of areas in this router is 1. 1 normal 0 stub 0 nssa
Number of areas transit capable is 0
External flood list length 0
IETF NSF helper support enabled
Cisco NSF helper support enabled
Reference bandwidth unit is 1000 mbps
    Area BACKBONE(0)
        Number of interfaces in this area is 3
      Area has no authentication
      SPF algorithm last executed 01:30:07.268 ago
      SPF algorithm executed 3 times
      Area ranges are
      Number of LSA 3. Checksum Sum 0x02033A
      Number of opaque link LSA 0. Checksum Sum 0x000000
      Number of DCbitless LSA 0
      Number of indication LSA 0
      Number of DoNotAge LSA 0
      Flood list length 0
```

- **show ip ospf interface:** This command provides a detailed list for every OSPF-enabled interface and is very useful to determine whether the **network** statements were correctly composed. Example 5-7 shows the output for the Serial 0/0/1 interface on R2.

**Example 5-7    show ip ospf interface Command**

```
R2# show ip ospf interface serial 0/0/1
Serial0/0/1 is up, line protocol is up
  Internet Address 192.168.10.9/30, Area 0, Attached via Network Statement
  Process ID 10, Router ID 2.2.2.2, Network Type POINT_TO_POINT, Cost: 976
  Topology-MTID    Cost    Disabled    Shutdown       Topology Name
        0           976       no          no             Base
  Transmit Delay is 1 sec, State POINT_TO_POINT
```

```
Timer intervals configured, Hello 10, Dead 40, Wait 40, Retransmit 5
  oob-resync timeout 40
  Hello due in 00:00:03
Supports Link-local Signaling (LLS)
Cisco NSF helper support enabled
IETF NSF helper support enabled
Index 3/3, flood queue length 0
Next 0x0(0)/0x0(0)
Last flood scan length is 1, maximum is 1
Last flood scan time is 0 msec, maximum is 0 msec
Neighbor Count is 1, Adjacent neighbor count is 1
  Adjacent with neighbor 3.3.3.3
Suppress hello for 0 neighbor(s)
```

- **show ip ospf interface brief:** This command is useful to display a summary and status of OSPF-enabled interfaces. Example 5-8 shows the output for R2.

**Example 5-8   show ip ospf interface brief Command**

```
R2# show ip ospf interface brief
Interface    PID    Area         IP Address/Mask    Cost   State Nbrs F/C
Gi0/0        10     0            172.16.2.1/24      1      DR    0/0
Se0/0/1      10     0            192.168.10.9/30    647    P2P   1/1
Se0/0/0      10     0            172.16.3.2/30      647    P2P   1/1
```

## Configuring Single-Area OSPFv3 (5.1.1.7)

The following is a review of a basic implementation of the OSPFv3 routing protocol for IPv6. Figure 5-5 displays the topology used for configuring OSPFv3.

The routers in the topology have a starting configuration, including enabled interface IPv6 addresses. There is currently no static routing or dynamic routing configured on any of the routers. All interfaces on Routers R1, R2, and R3 (except the loopback on R2) are within the OSPF backbone area. Example 5-9 shows the OSPFv3 configuration for R1.

**Figure 5-5**   OSPFv3 Reference Topology

**Example 5-9**   Basic Single-Area OSPFv3 Configuration for R1

```
R1(config)# ipv6 router ospf 10
R1(config-rtr)# router-id 1.1.1.1
R1(config-rtr)# auto-cost reference-bandwidth 1000
R1(config-rtr)# interface GigabitEthernet0/0
R1(config-if)# bandwidth 1000000
R1(config-if)# ipv6 ospf 10 area 0
R1(config-if)# interface Serial0/0/0
R1(config-if)# ipv6 ospf 10 area 0
R1(config-if)# interface Serial0/0/1
R1(config-if)# ipv6 ospf 10 area 0
```

From OSPFv3 router configuration mode on R1, the router ID is manually assigned and the reference bandwidth is adjusted to account for fast interfaces. Next the interfaces participating in OSPFv3 are configured. The Gigabit Ethernet 0/0 is also configured to reflect its true bandwidth. Notice how there is no wildcard mask required when configuring OSPFv3.

**Note**

Except for the router ID value, the configuration is the same for R2 and R3.

## Verifying Single-Area OSPFv3 (5.1.1.8)

Useful commands to verify OSPFv3 include the following:

- **show ipv6 ospf neighbor:** This command verifies that the router has formed an adjacency with its neighboring routers. If the router ID of the neighboring router is not displayed, or if it does not show as being in a state of FULL, the two routers have not formed an OSPF adjacency. Example 5-10 shows the output for R1.

**Example 5-10   show ipv6 ospf neighbor Command**

```
R1# show ipv6 ospf neighbor

          OSPFv3 Router with ID (1.1.1.1) (Process ID 10)


Neighbor ID     Pri   State          Dead Time   Interface ID   Interface
3.3.3.3           0   FULL/  -       00:00:39    6              Serial0/0/1
2.2.2.2           0   FULL/  -       00:00:36    6              Serial0/0/0
```

- **show ipv6 protocols:** This command provides a quick way to verify vital OSPFv3 configuration information, including the OSPF process ID, the router ID, and the interfaces enabled for OSPFv3. Example 5-11 shows the output for R1.

**Example 5-11   show ipv6 protocols Command**

```
R1# show ipv6 protocols
IPv6 Routing Protocol is "connected"
IPv6 Routing Protocol is "ND"
IPv6 Routing Protocol is "ospf 10"
  Router ID 1.1.1.1
  Number of areas: 1 normal, 0 stub, 0 nssa
  Interfaces (Area 0):
    Serial0/0/1
    Serial0/0/0
    GigabitEthernet0/0
  Redistribution:
    None
```

- **show ipv6 route ospf:** This command provides specifics about OSPFv3 routes in the routing table. Example 5-12 shows the output for R1.

**Example 5-12   show ipv6 route ospf** Command

```
R1# show ipv6 route ospf
IPv6 Routing Table - default - 10 entries
Codes: C - Connected, L - Local, S - Static, U - Per-user Static route
       B - BGP, R - RIP, H - NHRP, I1 - ISIS L1
       I2 - ISIS L2, IA - ISIS interarea, IS - ISIS summary, D - EIGRP
       EX - EIGRP external, ND - ND Default, NDp - ND Prefix, DCE - Destination
       NDr - Redirect, O - OSPF Intra, OI - OSPF Inter, OE1 - OSPF ext 1
       OE2 - OSPF ext 2, ON1 - OSPF NSSA ext 1, ON2 - OSPF NSSA ext 2
O   2001:DB8:CAFE:2::/64 [110/657]
     via FE80::2, Serial0/0/0
O   2001:DB8:CAFE:3::/64 [110/1304]
     via FE80::2, Serial0/0/0
O   2001:DB8:CAFE:A002::/64 [110/1294]
     via FE80::2, Serial0/0/0
```

- **show ipv6 ospf interface brief:** This command is useful to display a summary and status of OSPFv3-enabled interfaces. Example 5-13 shows the output for R1.

**Example 5-13   show ipv6 ospf interface** Command

```
R1# show ipv6 ospf interface serial 0/0/0
Serial0/0/0 is up, line protocol is up
  Link Local Address FE80::1, Interface ID 7
  Area 0, Process ID 10, Instance ID 0, Router ID 1.1.1.1
  Network Type POINT_TO_POINT, Cost: 647
  Transmit Delay is 1 sec, State POINT_TO_POINT
  Timer intervals configured, Hello 10, Dead 40, Wait 40, Retransmit 5
    Hello due in 00:00:01
  Graceful restart helper support enabled
  Index 1/3/3, flood queue length 0
  Next 0x0(0)/0x0(0)/0x0(0)
  Last flood scan length is 2, maximum is 4
  Last flood scan time is 0 msec, maximum is 0 msec
  Neighbor Count is 1, Adjacent neighbor count is 1
    Adjacent with neighbor 2.2.2.2
  Suppress hello for 0 neighbor(s)
```

**Lab 5.1.1.9: Configuring Basic Single-Area OSPFv2**

In this lab, you will complete the following objectives:

- Part 1: Build the Network and Configure Basic Device Settings

- Part 2: Configure and Verify OSPF Routing

- Part 3: Change Router ID Assignments

- Part 4: Configure OSPF Passive Interfaces

- Part 5: Change OSPF Metrics

# OSPF in Multiaccess Networks (5.1.2)

In a multiaccess environment, OSPF incorporates a mechanism to reduce the amount of OSPF message overhead. This topic discusses OSPF network types and the details of the DR/BDR election process.

## OSPF Network Types (5.1.2.1)

To configure OSPF adjustments, start with a basic implementation of the OSPF routing protocol.

OSPF defines the following five network types:

- *Point-to-point*: Two routers interconnected over a common link. No other routers are on the link. This is often the configuration in WAN links, as shown in Figure 5-6.

**Figure 5-6**   OSPF Point-to-Point Networks

- *Broadcast multiaccess*: Multiple routers interconnected over an Ethernet network, as shown in Figure 5-7.

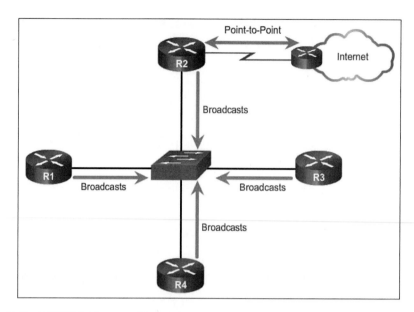

**Figure 5-7**    OSPF Multiaccess Network

- *Nonbroadcast multiaccess (NBMA)*: Multiple routers interconnected in a network that does not allow broadcasts, such as Frame Relay, as shown in Figure 5-8.

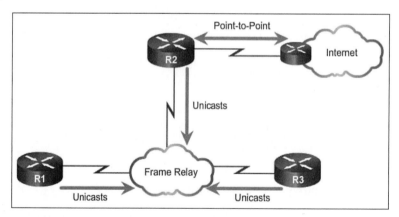

**Figure 5-8**    OSPF Nonbroadcast Multiaccess Network

- *Point-to-multipoint*: Multiple routers interconnected in a hub-and-spoke topology over an NBMA network. Often used to connect branch sites (spokes) to a central site (hub), as shown in Figure 5-9.

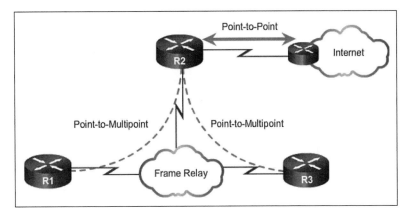

**Figure 5-9**    OSPF Point-to-Multipoint Network

- *Virtual links*: Special OSPF network used to interconnect distant OSPF areas to the backbone area, as shown in Figure 5-10.

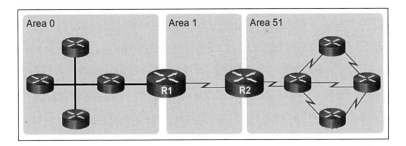

**Figure 5-10**    OSPF Virtual Link Network

A multiaccess network is a network with multiple devices on the same shared media, which are sharing communications. Ethernet LANs are the most common example of broadcast multiaccess networks. In broadcast networks, all devices on the network see all broadcast and multicast frames. They are multiaccess networks because there can be numerous hosts, printers, routers, and other devices that are all members of the same network.

## Challenges in Multiaccess Networks (5.1.2.2)

Multiaccess networks can create two challenges for OSPF regarding the flooding of LSAs:

- **Creation of multiple adjacencies:** Ethernet networks could potentially interconnect many OSPF routers over a common link. Creating adjacencies with every router is unnecessary and undesirable. This would lead to an excessive number of LSAs exchanged between routers on the same network.

- **Extensive flooding of LSAs:** Link-state routers flood their link-state packets when OSPF is initialized, or when there is a change in the topology. This flooding can become excessive.

The following formula can be used to calculate the number of required adjacencies. The number of adjacencies required for any number of routers (designated as *n*) on a multiaccess network is:

$$n (n - 1) / 2$$

Figure 5-11 shows a simple topology of four routers, all of which are attached to the same multiaccess Ethernet network.

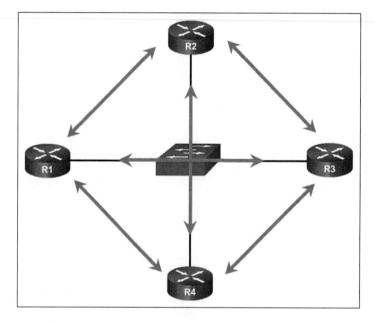

**Figure 5-11**   Establishing Six Neighbor Adjacencies

Without some type of mechanism to reduce the number of adjacencies, collectively these routers would form six adjacencies: 4 (4 − 1) / 2 = 6. Table 5-1 shows that as routers are added to the network, the number of adjacencies increases dramatically.

**Table 5-1**   More Routers = More Adjacencies

| Routers | Adjacencies |
| --- | --- |
| *n* | *n* (*n* − 1) / 2 |
| 4 | 6 |
| 5 | 10 |

| Routers | Adjacencies |
|---------|-------------|
| 10 | 45 |
| 20 | 190 |
| 50 | 1225 |

## OSPF Designated Router (5.1.2.3)

The solution to managing the number of adjacencies and the flooding of LSAs on a multiaccess network is the *designated router (DR)*. On multiaccess networks, OSPF elects a DR to be the collection and distribution point for LSAs sent and received. A *backup designated router (BDR)* is also elected in case the DR fails. The BDR listens passively to this exchange and maintains a relationship with all the routers. If the DR stops producing Hello packets, the BDR promotes itself and assumes the role of DR.

All other non-DR or non-BDR routers become a *DROTHER* (a router that is neither the DR nor the BDR). DROTHERs only form full adjacencies with the DR and BDR in the network. Instead of flooding LSAs to all routers in the network, DROTHERs only send their LSAs to the DR and BDR using the multicast address 224.0.0.6 (all DR routers).

In Figure 5-12, R1 sends LSAs to the DR. The BDR also listens.

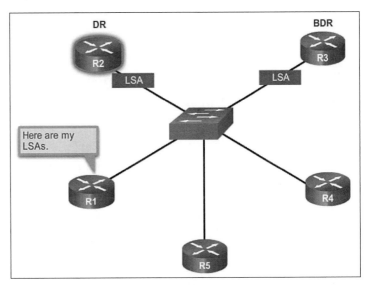

**Figure 5-12**   R1 Sends LSAs to DR and BDR

The DR is responsible for forwarding the LSAs from R1 to all other routers. The DR uses the multicast address 224.0.0.5 (all OSPF routers). The end result is that there is only one router doing all the flooding of all LSAs in the multiaccess network, as shown in Figure 5-13.

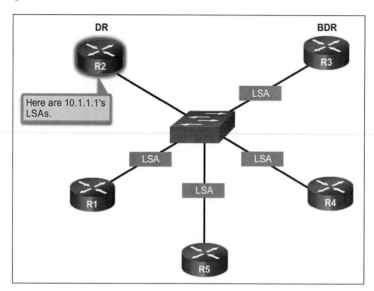

**Figure 5-13**   DR Sends LSAs

**Note**

DR/BDR elections only occur in multiaccess networks and do not occur in point-to-point networks.

## Verifying DR/BDR Roles (5.1.2.4)

In the multiaccess topology shown in Figure 5-14, there are three routers interconnected over a common Ethernet multiaccess network, 192.168.1.0/28. Each router is configured with the indicated IP address on the Gigabit Ethernet 0/0 interface.

Because the routers are connected over a common multiaccess broadcast network, OSPF has automatically elected a DR and BDR. In this example, R3 has been elected as the DR because its router ID is 3.3.3.3, which is the highest in this network. R2 is the BDR because it has the second-highest router ID in the network.

To verify the roles of the router, use the **show ip ospf interface** command, as shown in Figure 5-15.

**Figure 5-14**    OSPF Multiaccess Broadcast Reference Topology

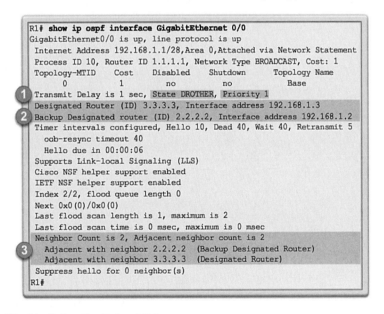

**Figure 5-15**    Verifying the Role of R1

The output generated by R1 confirms that

- R1 is not the DR or BDR, but is a DROTHER with a default priority of 1. (1)

- The DR is R3 with router ID 3.3.3.3 at IP address 192.168.1.3, while the BDR is R2 with router ID 2.2.2.2 at IP address 192.168.1.2. (2)

- R1 has two adjacencies: one with the BDR and one with the DR. (3)

Figure 5-16 shows the output for R2.

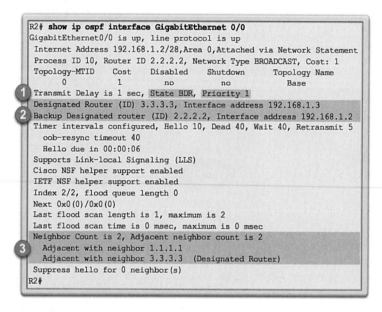

**Figure 5-16**    Verifying the Role of R2

The output for R2 confirms that

- R2 is the BDR with a default priority of 1. (1)

- The DR is R3 with router ID 3.3.3.3 at IP address 192.168.1.3, while the BDR is R2 with router ID 2.2.2.2 at IP address 192.168.1.2. (2)

- R2 has two adjacencies: one with a neighbor with router ID 1.1.1.1 (R1) and the other with the DR. (3)

Figure 5-17 shows the output for R3.

The output for R3 confirms that

- R3 is the DR with a default priority of 1. (1)

- The DR is R3 with router ID 3.3.3.3 at IP address 192.168.1.3, while the BDR is R2 with router ID 2.2.2.2 at IP address 192.168.1.2. (2)

- R3 has two adjacencies: one with a neighbor with router ID 1.1.1.1 (R1) and the other with the BDR. (3)

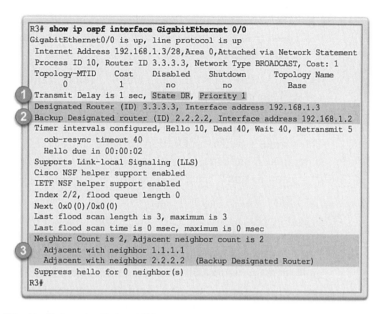

```
R3# show ip ospf interface GigabitEthernet 0/0
GigabitEthernet0/0 is up, line protocol is up
  Internet Address 192.168.1.3/28,Area 0,Attached via Network Statement
  Process ID 10, Router ID 3.3.3.3, Network Type BROADCAST, Cost: 1
  Topology-MTID    Cost    Disabled    Shutdown    Topology Name
       0             1        no          no           Base
  Transmit Delay is 1 sec, State DR, Priority 1
  Designated Router (ID) 3.3.3.3, Interface address 192.168.1.3
  Backup Designated router (ID) 2.2.2.2, Interface address 192.168.1.2
  Timer intervals configured, Hello 10, Dead 40, Wait 40, Retransmit 5
    oob-resync timeout 40
    Hello due in 00:00:02
  Supports Link-local Signaling (LLS)
  Cisco NSF helper support enabled
  IETF NSF helper support enabled
  Index 2/2, flood queue length 0
  Next 0x0(0)/0x0(0)
  Last flood scan length is 3, maximum is 3
  Last flood scan time is 0 msec, maximum is 0 msec
  Neighbor Count is 2, Adjacent neighbor count is 2
    Adjacent with neighbor 1.1.1.1
    Adjacent with neighbor 2.2.2.2  (Backup Designated Router)
  Suppress hello for 0 neighbor(s)
R3#
```

**Figure 5-17**   Verifying the Role of R3

## Verifying DR/BDR Adjacencies (5.1.2.5)

To verify the OSPF adjacencies, use the **show ip ospf neighbor** command, as shown in Figure 5-18.

```
R1# show ip ospf neighbor

Neighbor ID Pri State        Dead Time  Address       Interface
2.2.2.2      1   FULL/BDR    00:00:36  192.168.1.2  GigabitEthernet0/0

3.3.3.3      1   FULL/DR     0:00:35   192.168.1.3  GigabitEthernet0/0

R1#
```

**Figure 5-18**   Verifying the Neighbor Adjacencies on R1

Unlike serial links that only display a state of FULL/-, the state of neighbors in multiaccess networks can be

- **FULL/DROTHER:** This is a DR or BDR router that is fully adjacent with a non-DR or BDR router. These two neighbors can exchange Hello packets, updates, queries, replies, and acknowledgments.

- **FULL/DR:** The router is fully adjacent with the indicated DR neighbor. These two neighbors can exchange Hello packets, updates, queries, replies, and acknowledgments.

- **FULL/BDR:** The router is fully adjacent with the indicated BDR neighbor. These two neighbors can exchange Hello packets, updates, queries, replies, and acknowledgments.

- **2-WAY/DROTHER:** The non-DR or BDR router has a neighbor relationship with another non-DR or BDR router. These two neighbors exchange Hello packets.

The normal state for an OSPF router is usually FULL. If a router is stuck in another state, it is an indication that there are problems in forming adjacencies. The only exception to this is the 2-WAY state, which is normal in a multiaccess broadcast network.

In multiaccess networks, DROTHERs only form FULL adjacencies with the DR and BDR. However, DROTHERs will still form a 2-WAY neighbor adjacency with any DROTHERs that join the network. This means that all DROTHER routers in the multiaccess network still receive Hello packets from all other DROTHER routers. In this way, they are aware of all routers in the network. When two DROTHER routers form a neighbor adjacency, the neighbor state displays as 2-WAY/DROTHER.

The output generated by R1 confirms that R1 has adjacencies with router

- R2 with router ID 2.2.2.2 is in a FULL state, and the role of R2 is BDR. (1)

- R3 with router ID 3.3.3.3 is in a FULL state, and the role of R3 is DR. (2)

Figure 5-19 shows the output for R2.

**Figure 5-19** Verifying the Neighbor Adjacencies on R2

The output for R2 confirms that R2 has adjacencies with router

- R1 with router ID 1.1.1.1 is in a FULL state, and R1 is neither the DR nor BDR. (1)

- R3 with router ID 3.3.3.3 is in a FULL state, and the role of R3 is DR. (2)

Figure 5-20 shows the output for R3.

**Figure 5-20**   Verifying the Neighbor Adjacencies on R3

The output for R3 confirms that R3 has adjacencies with router

- R1 with router ID 1.1.1.1 is in a FULL state, and R1 is neither the DR nor BDR. (1)

- R2 with router ID 2.2.2.2 is in a FULL state, and the role of R2 is BDR. (2)

## Default DR/BDR Election Process (5.1.2.6)

How do the DR and BDR get elected? The OSPF DR and BDR election decision is based on the following criteria, in sequential order:

1. The routers in the network elect the router with the highest interface priority as the DR. The router with the second-highest interface priority is elected as the BDR. The priority can be configured to be any number between 0 and 255. The higher the priority, the more likely the router will be selected as the DR. If the priority is set to 0, the router is not capable of becoming the DR. The default priority of multiaccess broadcast interfaces is 1. Therefore, unless otherwise configured, all routers have an equal priority value and must rely on another tie-breaking method during the DR/BDR election.

2. If the interface priorities are equal, the router with the highest router ID is elected the DR. The router with the second-highest router ID is the BDR.

Recall that the router ID is determined in one of three ways:

- The router ID can be manually configured.

- If no router IDs are configured, the router ID is determined by the highest loopback IP address.

- If no loopback interfaces are configured, the router ID is determined by the highest active IPv4 address.

> **Note**
>
> In an IPv6 network, if there are no IPv4 addresses configured on the router, the router ID must be manually configured with the **router-id** *rid* command; otherwise, OSPFv3 does not start.

All Ethernet router interfaces have a default priority of 1. As a result, based on the selection criteria previously listed, the OSPF router ID is used to elect the DR and BDR. R3, with the highest router ID, becomes the DR, and R2, with the second-highest router ID, becomes the BDR.

> **Note**
>
> Serial interfaces have default priorities set to 0; therefore, they do not elect DR and BDRs.

The DR and BDR election process takes place as soon as the first router with an OSPF-enabled interface is active on the multiaccess network. This can happen when the routers are powered on, or when the OSPF **network** command for that interface is configured. The election process only takes a few seconds. If all of the routers on the multiaccess network have not finished booting, it is possible that a router with a lower router ID becomes the DR. (This can be a lower-end router that takes less time to boot.)

## DR/BDR Election Process (5.1.2.7)

OSPF DR and BDR elections are not preemptive. If a new router with a higher priority or higher router ID is added to the network after the DR and BDR election, the newly added router does not take over the DR or the BDR role. This is because those roles have already been assigned. The addition of a new router does not initiate a new election process.

After the DR is elected, it remains the DR until one of the following events occurs:

- The DR fails
- The OSPF process on the DR fails or is stopped
- The multiaccess interface on the DR fails or is shut down

If the DR fails, the BDR is automatically promoted to DR. This is the case even if another DROTHER with a higher priority or router ID is added to the network after the initial DR/BDR election. However, after a BDR is promoted to DR, a new BDR election occurs and the DROTHER with the higher priority or router ID is elected as the new BDR.

Figures 5-21 to 5-24 illustrate various scenarios relating to the DR and BDR election process.

In Figure 5-21, the current DR (R3) fails; therefore, the preelected BDR (R2) assumes the role of DR. Subsequently, an election is held to choose a new BDR. Because R1 is the only DROTHER, it is elected as the BDR.

**Figure 5-21**   Current DR Fails

In Figure 5-22, R3 has rejoined the network after several minutes of being unavailable. Because the DR and BDR already exist, R3 does not take over either role; instead, it becomes a DROTHER.

**Figure 5-22**   Old DR Rejoins the Network

In Figure 5-23, a new router (R4) with a higher router ID is added to the network. DR (R2) and BDR (R1) retain the DR and BDR roles. R4 automatically becomes a DROTHER.

**Figure 5-23**   New Router Joins the Network

In Figure 5-24, R2 has failed. The BDR (R1) automatically becomes the DR, and an election process selects R4 as the BDR because it has the higher router ID.

**Figure 5-24**   New DR Fails

## The OSPF Priority (5.1.2.8)

The DR becomes the focal point for the collection and distribution of LSAs; therefore, this router must have sufficient CPU and memory capacity to handle the workload. It is possible to influence the DR/BDR election process through configurations.

If the interface priorities are equal on all routers, the router with the highest router ID is elected the DR. It is possible to configure the router ID to manipulate the DR/BDR election. However, this process only works if there is a stringent plan for setting the router ID on all routers. In large networks, this can be cumbersome.

Instead of relying on the router ID, it is better to control the election by setting interface priorities. Priorities are an interface-specific value, which means that it provides better control on a multiaccess network. This also allows a router to be the DR in one network and a DROTHER in another.

To set the priority of an interface, use the following commands:

- **ip ospf priority** *value*: OSPFv2 interface command
- **ipv6 ospf priority** *value*: OSPFv3 interface command

The *value* can be

- **0:** Does not become a DR or BDR.
- **1 – 255:** The higher the priority value, the more likely the router becomes the DR or BDR on the interface.

In the multiaccess broadcast topology shown in Figure 5-14, all routers have an equal OSPF priority because the priority value defaults to 1 for all router interfaces. Therefore, the router ID is used to determine the DR (R3) and BDR (R2). Changing the priority value on an interface from 1 to a higher value would enable the router to become a DR or BDR router during the next election.

If the interface priority is configured after OSPF is enabled, the administrator must shut down the OSPF process on all routers, and then reenable the OSPF process, to force a new DR/BDR election.

## Changing the OSPF Priority (5.1.2.9)

Recall in Figure 5-14 that R3 is the DR and R2 is the BDR. It has been decided that

- R1 should be the DR and will be configured with a priority of 255.
- R2 should be the BDR and will be left with the default priority of 1.
- R3 should never be a DR or BDR and will be configured with a priority of 0.

Example 5-14 shows the commands to change the R1 interface Gigabit 0/0 priority from 1 to 255 and to change the R3 interface Gigabit 0/0 priority from 1 to 0.

**Example 5-14**   Changing the Interface Priority

```
R1(config)# interface GigabitEthernet 0/0
R1(config-if)# ip ospf priority 255
R1(config-if)# end
R1#

R3(config)# interface GigabitEthernet 0/0
R3(config-if)# ip ospf priority 0
R3(config-if)# end
R3#
```

The changes do not automatically take effect because the DR and BDR are already elected. Therefore, the OSPF election must be negotiated using one of the following methods:

- Shut down the router interfaces and then reenable them starting with the DR, then the BDR, and then all other routers.

- Reset the OSPF process using the **clear ip ospf process** privileged EXEC mode command on all routers.

Example 5-15 displays how to clear the OSPF process on R1.

**Example 5-15**   Clearing the OSPF Process on R1

```
R1# clear ip ospf process
Reset ALL OSPF processes? [no]: yes
R1#
*Apr  6 16:00:44.282: %OSPF-5-ADJCHG: Process 10, Nbr 2.2.2.2 on GigabitEthernet0/0
  from FULL to DOWN, Neighbor Down: Interface down or detached
*Apr  6 16:00:44.282: %OSPF-5-ADJCHG: Process 10, Nbr 3.3.3.3 on GigabitEthernet0/0
  from FULL to DOWN, Neighbor Down: Interface down or detached
R1#
```

Assume that the **clear ip ospf process** privileged EXEC mode command has also been configured on R2 and R3. Notice the OSPF state information generated.

The output displayed in Example 5-16 confirms that R1 is now the DR with a priority of 255 and identifies the new neighbor adjacencies of R1.

**Example 5-16**   Verifying Role and Adjacencies on R1

```
R1# show ip ospf interface GigabitEthernet 0/0
GigabitEthernet0/0 is up, line protocol is up
  Internet Address 192.168.1.1/28, Area 0, Attached via Network Statement
  Process ID 10, Router ID 1.1.1.1, Network Type BROADCAST, Cost: 1
  Topology-MTID    Cost    Disabled    Shutdown      Topology Name
        0           1         no          no            Base
  Transmit Delay is 1 sec, State DR, Priority 255
  Designated Router (ID) 1.1.1.1, Interface address 192.168.1.1
  Backup Designated router (ID) 2.2.2.2, Interface address 192.168.1.2
  Timer intervals configured, Hello 10, Dead 40, Wait 40, Retransmit 5
    oob-resync timeout 40
    Hello due in 00:00:05
  Supports Link-local Signaling (LLS)
  Cisco NSF helper support enabled
  IETF NSF helper support enabled
  Index 2/2, flood queue length 0
  Next 0x0(0)/0x0(0)
  Last flood scan length is 1, maximum is 2
  Last flood scan time is 0 msec, maximum is 0 msec
  Neighbor Count is 2, Adjacent neighbor count is 2
    Adjacent with neighbor 2.2.2.2  (Backup Designated Router)
    Adjacent with neighbor 3.3.3.3
  Suppress hello for 0 neighbor(s)

R1# show ip ospf neighbor

Neighbor ID      Pri   State           Dead Time   Address        Interface
2.2.2.2            1   FULL/BDR        00:00:30    192.168.1.2    GigabitEthernet0/0
3.3.3.3            0   FULL/DROTHER    00:00:38    192.168.1.3    GigabitEthernet0/0
R1#
```

**Interactive Graphic**

### Activity 5.1.2.10: Identify OSPF Network Type Terminology

Go to the course online to perform this practice activity.

**Interactive Graphic**

### Activity 5.1.2.11: Select the Designated Router

Go to the course online to perform this practice activity.

**Packet Tracer Activity 5.1.2.12: Determining the DR and BDR**

In this activity, you will examine DR and BDR roles and watch the roles change when there is a change in the network. You will then modify the priority to control the roles and force a new election. Finally, you will verify that routers are filling the desired roles.

**Lab 5.1.2.13: Configuring OSPFv2 on a Multiaccess Network**

In this lab, you will complete the following objectives:

- Part 1: Build the Network and Configure Basic Device Settings
- Part 2: Configure and Verify OSPFv2 on the DR, BDR, and DROTHER
- Part 3: Configure OSPFv2 Interface Priority to Determine the DR and BDR

# Default Route Propagation (5.1.3)

Without some mechanism for advertising a default route to other OSPF routers in the organization, each router would need to be configured with a static default route. This topic discusses how to configure a router to send other OSPF routers a default route.

## Propagating a Default Static Route in OSPFv2 (5.1.3.1)

With OSPF, the router connected to the Internet is used to propagate a default route to other routers in the OSPF routing domain. This router is sometimes called the edge, the entrance, or the gateway router. However, in OSPF terminology, the router located between an OSPF routing domain and a non-OSPF network is also called the *autonomous system boundary router (ASBR)*.

In Figure 5-25, R2 is *single-homed* to a service provider. Therefore, all that is required for R2 to reach the Internet is a default static route to the service provider.

> **Note**
>
> In this example, a loopback interface with IP address 209.165.200.225 is used to simulate the connection to the service provider.

**Figure 5-25**  OSPFv2 Topology with Default Route

To propagate a default route, the edge router (R2) must be configured with

- A default static route using the **ip route 0.0.0.0 0.0.0.0** {*ip-address* | *exit-intf*} command.

- The **default-information originate** router configuration mode command. This instructs R2 to be the source of the default route information and propagate the default static route in OSPF updates.

Example 5-17 shows how to configure a fully specified default static route to the service provider and then propagate that route in the OSPF process.

**Example 5-17**  Configuring and Propagating a Default Route in OSPFv2

```
R2(config)# ip route 0.0.0.0 0.0.0.0 loopback 0 209.165.200.226
R2(config)# router ospf 10
R2(config-router)# default-information originate
R2(config-router)# end
R2#
```

## Verifying the Propagated Default Route (5.1.3.2)

Verify the default route settings on R2 using the **show ip route** command, as shown in Example 5-18.

**Example 5-18**    Verifying the Default Route on R2

```
R2# show ip route | begin Gateway

Gateway of last resort is 209.165.200.226 to network 0.0.0.0

S*     0.0.0.0/0 [1/0] via 209.165.200.226, Loopback0
       172.16.0.0/16 is variably subnetted, 5 subnets, 3 masks
O         172.16.1.0/24 [110/65] via 172.16.3.1, 00:01:44, Serial0/0/0
C         172.16.2.0/24 is directly connected, GigabitEthernet0/0
L         172.16.2.1/32 is directly connected, GigabitEthernet0/0
C         172.16.3.0/30 is directly connected, Serial0/0/0
L         172.16.3.2/32 is directly connected, Serial0/0/0
O      192.168.1.0/24 [110/65] via 192.168.10.10, 00:01:12, Serial0/0/1
       192.168.10.0/24 is variably subnetted, 3 subnets, 2 masks
O         192.168.10.4/30 [110/128] via 192.168.10.10, 00:01:12, Serial0/0/1
                          [110/128] via 172.16.3.1, 00:01:12, Serial0/0/0
C         192.168.10.8/30 is directly connected, Serial0/0/1
L         192.168.10.9/32 is directly connected, Serial0/0/1
       209.165.200.0/24 is variably subnetted, 2 subnets, 2 masks
C         209.165.200.224/30 is directly connected, Loopback0
L         209.165.200.225/32 is directly connected, Loopback0
```

The output in Example 5-19 verifies that the default route has been propagated to R1.

**Example 5-19**    Verifying That R1 Received the Default Route

```
R1# show ip route | begin Gateway

Gateway of last resort is 172.16.3.2 to network 0.0.0.0

O*E2  0.0.0.0/0 [110/1] via 172.16.3.2, 00:19:37, Serial0/0/0
       172.16.0.0/16 is variably subnetted, 5 subnets, 3 masks
C         172.16.1.0/24 is directly connected, GigabitEthernet0/0
L         172.16.1.1/32 is directly connected, GigabitEthernet0/0
O         172.16.2.0/24 [110/65] via 172.16.3.2, 00:21:19, Serial0/0/0
C         172.16.3.0/30 is directly connected, Serial0/0/0
L         172.16.3.1/32 is directly connected, Serial0/0/0
O      192.168.1.0/24 [110/65] via 192.168.10.6, 00:20:49, Serial0/0/1
       192.168.10.0/24 is variably subnetted, 3 subnets, 2 masks
C         192.168.10.4/30 is directly connected, Serial0/0/1
L         192.168.10.5/32 is directly connected, Serial0/0/1
O         192.168.10.8/30 [110/128] via 192.168.10.6, 00:20:49, Serial0/0/1
                          [110/128] via 172.16.3.2, 00:20:49, Serial0/0/0
R1#
```

Notice that the route source is **O*E2**, signifying that it was learned using OSPF. The asterisk identifies this as a good candidate for the default route. The E2 designation identifies that it is an external route.

External routes are either external type 1 or external type 2. The difference between the two is in the way the cost (metric) of the route is being calculated. The cost of a type 2 route is always the external cost, regardless of the interior cost to reach that route. A type 1 cost is the addition of the external cost and the internal cost used to reach that route. A type 1 route is always preferred over a type 2 route for the same destination.

## Propagating a Default Static Route in OSPFv3 (5.1.3.3)

The process of propagating a default static route in OSPFv3 is almost identical to that in OSPFv2.

In Figure 5-26, R2 is single-homed to a service provider. Therefore, all that is required for R2 to reach the Internet is a default static route to the service provider.

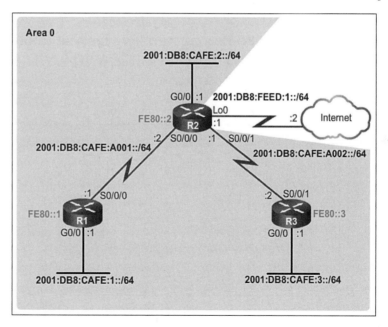

**Figure 5-26**   OSPFv3 Topology with Default Route

---

**Note**

In this example, a loopback interface with the IP address of 2001:DB8:FEED:1::1/64 is used to simulate the connection to the service provider.

---

To propagate a default route, the edge router (R2) must be configured with

- A default static route using the **ipv6 route ::/0** {*ipv6-address* | *exit-intf*} command.

- The **default-information originate** router configuration mode command. This instructs R2 to be the source of the default route information and propagate the default static route in OSPF updates.

Example 5-20 shows how to configure a fully specified default static route to the service provider and propagate that route in OSPF.

**Example 5-20**   Configuring and Propagating a Default Route in OSPFv3

```
R2(config)# ipv6 route 0::/0 loopback0 2001:DB8:FEED:1::2
R2(config)# ipv6 router ospf 10
R2(config-rtr)# default-information originate
R2(config-rtr)# end
R2#
```

## Verifying the Propagated IPv6 Default Route (5.1.3.4)

Verify the default static route setting on R2 using the **show ipv6 route** command, as shown in Example 5-21.

**Example 5-21**   Verifying the Default Route on R2

```
R2# show ipv6 route static
IPv6 Routing Table - default - 12 entries
Codes: C - Connected, L - Local, S - Static, U - Per-user Static route
       B - BGP, R - RIP, H - NHRP, I1 - ISIS L1
       I2 - ISIS L2, IA - ISIS interarea, IS - ISIS summary, D - EIGRP
       EX - EIGRP external, ND - ND Default, NDp - ND Prefix, DCE - Destination
       NDr - Redirect, O - OSPF Intra, OI - OSPF Inter, OE1 - OSPF ext 1
       OE2 - OSPF ext 2, ON1 - OSPF NSSA ext 1, ON2 - OSPF NSSA ext 2
S    ::/0 [1/0]
      via 2001:DB8:FEED:1::2, Loopback0
```

The output in Example 5-22 verifies that the default route has been propagated to R1.

**Example 5-22**   Verifying That R1 Received the Default Route

```
R1# show ipv6 route ospf | begin OE2 ::/0
OE2 ::/0 [110/1], tag 10
      via FE80::2, Serial0/0/0
```

```
O    2001:DB8:CAFE:2::/64 [110/648]
        via FE80::2, Serial0/0/0
O    2001:DB8:CAFE:3::/64 [110/648]
        via FE80::2, Serial0/0/0
O    2001:DB8:CAFE:A002::/64 [110/1294]
        via FE80::2, Serial0/0/0
```

Notice that the route source is **OE2**, signifying that it was learned using OSPFv3. The E2 designation identifies that it is an external route. Unlike the IPv4 routing table, IPv6 does not use the asterisk to signify that the route is a good candidate for the default route.

### Packet Tracer Activity 5.1.3.5: Propagating a Default Route in OSPFv2

In this activity, you will configure an IPv4 default route to the Internet and propagate that default route to other OSPF routers. You will then verify that the default route is in downstream routing tables and that hosts can now access a web server on the Internet.

## Fine-Tuning OSPF Interfaces (5.1.4)

In some situations, the default behavior of OSPF might not be acceptable. This topic discusses how to modify the timer values on OSPF interfaces to fine-tune the operation of OSPF.

### OSPF Hello and Dead Intervals (5.1.4.1)

The *OSPF Hello and Dead intervals* are configurable on a per-interface basis. The OSPF intervals must match or a neighbor adjacency does not occur.

To verify the currently configured interface intervals, use the **show ip ospf interface** command, as shown in Example 5-23. The Serial 0/0/0 Hello and Dead intervals are set to the default 10 seconds and 40 seconds, respectively.

**Example 5-23**   Verifying the OSPF Intervals on R1

```
R1# show ip ospf interface serial 0/0/0
Serial0/0/0 is up, line protocol is up
  Internet Address 172.16.3.1/30, Area 0, Attached via Network Statement
  Process ID 10, Router ID 1.1.1.1, Network Type POINT_TO_POINT, Cost: 64
  Topology-MTID    Cost    Disabled    Shutdown    Topology Name
        0           64        no          no          Base
```

```
Transmit Delay is 1 sec, State POINT_TO_POINT
Timer intervals configured, Hello 10, Dead 40, Wait 40, Retransmit 5
  oob-resync timeout 40
  Hello due in 00:00:03
Supports Link-local Signaling (LLS)
Cisco NSF helper support enabled
IETF NSF helper support enabled
Index 2/2, flood queue length 0
Next 0x0(0)/0x0(0)
Last flood scan length is 1, maximum is 1
Last flood scan time is 0 msec, maximum is 0 msec
Neighbor Count is 1, Adjacent neighbor count is 1
  Adjacent with neighbor 2.2.2.2
Suppress hello for 0 neighbor(s)
R1#
```

Example 5-24 provides an example of using a filtering technique to display the OSPF intervals for the OSPF-enabled interface Serial 0/0/0 on R1.

**Example 5-24**   Filtering for OSPF Timer Intervals on R1

```
R1# show ip ospf interface | include Timer
  Timer intervals configured, Hello 10, Dead 40, Wait 40, Retransmit 5
  Timer intervals configured, Hello 10, Dead 40, Wait 40, Retransmit 5
  Timer intervals configured, Hello 10, Dead 40, Wait 40, Retransmit 5
R1#
```

In Example 5-25, the **show ip ospf neighbor** command is used on R1 to verify that R1 is adjacent to R2 and R3.

**Example 5-25**   Verifying OSPF Dead Timer Values on R1

```
R1# show ip ospf neighbor

Neighbor ID     Pri   State       Dead Time   Address        Interface
3.3.3.3           0   FULL/   -   00:00:35    192.168.10.6   Serial0/0/1
2.2.2.2           0   FULL/   -   00:00:33    172.16.3.2     Serial0/0/0
R1#
```

Notice in the output that the Dead Time is counting down from 40 seconds. By default, this value is refreshed every 10 seconds when R1 receives a Hello from the neighbor.

## Modifying OSPFv2 Intervals (5.1.4.2)

It might be desirable to change the OSPF timers so that routers detect network failures in less time. Doing this increases traffic, but sometimes the need for quick convergence is more important than the extra traffic it creates.

> **Note**
>
> The default Hello and Dead intervals are based on best practices and should only be altered in rare situations.

OSPF Hello and Dead intervals can be modified manually using the following interface configuration mode commands:

- **ip ospf hello-interval** *seconds*
- **ip ospf dead-interval** *seconds*

Use the **no ip ospf hello-interval** and **no ip ospf dead-interval** commands to reset the intervals to their default.

In Example 5-26, the Hello interval is modified to 5 seconds.

**Example 5-26**   Modifying the OSPFv2 Timer Intervals on R1

```
R1(config)# interface Serial 0/0/0
R1(config-if)# ip ospf hello-interval 5
R1(config-if)# ip ospf dead-interval 20
R1(config-if)# end
*Apr  7 17:28:21.529: %OSPF-5-ADJCHG: Process 10, Nbr 2.2.2.2 on Serial0/0/0 from
  FULL to DOWN, Neighbor Down: Dead timer expired
R1#
```

Immediately after changing the Hello interval, the Cisco IOS automatically modifies the Dead interval to four times the Hello interval. However, it is always good practice to explicitly modify the timer instead of relying on an automatic IOS feature so that modifications are documented in the configuration. Therefore, the Dead interval is also manually set to 20 seconds on the R1 Serial 0/0/0 interface.

As displayed by the highlighted OSPFv2 adjacency message in Example 5-26, when the Dead Timer on R1 expires, R1 and R2 lose adjacency. This is because the values have only been altered on one side of the serial link between R1 and R2. Recall that the OSPF Hello and Dead intervals must match between neighbors.

Use the **show ip ospf neighbor** command on R1 to verify the neighbor adjacencies, as shown in Example 5-27.

**Example 5-27**    Verifying Lost Neighbor Adjacency with R2

```
R1# show ip ospf neighbor

Neighbor ID     Pri    State         Dead Time    Address        Interface
3.3.3.3           0    FULL/  -      00:00:37     192.168.10.6   Serial0/0/1
R1#
```

Notice that the only neighbor listed is the 3.3.3.3 (R3) router and that R1 is no longer adjacent with the 2.2.2.2 (R2) neighbor. The timers set on Serial 0/0/0 do not affect the neighbor adjacency with R3.

To restore adjacency between R1 and R2, the R2 Serial 0/0/0 interface Hello interval is set to **5** seconds, as shown in Example 5-28.

**Example 5-28**    Modifying the OSPFv2 Hello Interval on R2

```
R2(config)# interface serial 0/0/0
R2(config-if)# ip ospf hello-interval 5
*Apr  7 17:41:49.001: %OSPF-5-ADJCHG: Process 10, Nbr 1.1.1.1 on Serial0/0/0 from
  LOADING to FULL, Loading Done
R2(config-if)# end
R2#
```

Almost immediately, the IOS displays a message that adjacency has been established with a state of FULL. Verify the interface intervals using the **show ip ospf interface** command, as shown in Example 5-29.

**Example 5-29**    Verifying Reestablished Neighbor Adjacency with R1

```
R2# show ip ospf interface s0/0/0 | include Timer
  Timer intervals configured, Hello 5, Dead 20, Wait 20, Retransmit 5
R2#
R2# show ip ospf neighbor

Neighbor ID     Pri    State         Dead Time    Address         Interface
3.3.3.3           0    FULL/  -      00:00:35     192.168.10.10   Serial0/0/1
1.1.1.1           0    FULL/  -      00:00:17     172.16.3.1      Serial0/0/0
R2#
```

Notice that the Hello time is 5 seconds and that the Dead Time was automatically set to 20 seconds instead of the default 40 seconds. Remember that the OSPF automatically sets the Dead interval to four times the Hello interval.

## Modifying OSPFv3 Intervals (5.1.4.3)

Like OSPFv2, OSPFv3 intervals can also be adjusted.

OSPFv3 Hello and Dead intervals can be modified manually using the following interface configuration mode commands:

- **ipv6 ospf hello-interval** *seconds*
- **ipv6 ospf dead-interval** *seconds*

**Note**

Use the **no ipv6 ospf hello-interval** and **no ipv6 ospf dead-interval** commands to reset the intervals to their default.

Refer to the IPv6 topology shown previously in Figure 5-26. Assume that the network has converged using OSPFv3. Example 5-30 shows the commands to modify the OSPFv3 Hello interval to 5 seconds.

**Example 5-30**   Modifying the OSPFv3 Timer Intervals on R1

```
R1(config)# interface Serial 0/0/0
R1(config-if)# ipv6 ospf hello-interval 5
R1(config-if)# ipv6 ospf dead-interval 20
R1(config-if)# end
R1#
*Apr 10 15:03:51.175: %OSPFv3-5-ADJCHG: Process 10, Nbr 2.2.2.2 on Serial0/0/0 from
  FULL to DOWN, Neighbor Down: Dead timer expired
R1#
```

Immediately after changing the Hello interval, the Cisco IOS automatically modifies the Dead interval to four times the Hello interval. However, as with OSPFv2, it is always good practice to explicitly modify the timer instead of relying on an automatic IOS feature so that modifications are documented in the configuration. Therefore, the Dead interval is also manually set to 20 seconds on the R1 Serial 0/0/0 interface.

After the Dead timer on R1 expires, R1 and R2 lose adjacency, as displayed by the highlighted OSPFv3 adjacency message in Example 5-30, because the values have only been altered on one side of the serial link between R1 and R2. Recall that the OSPFv3 Hello and Dead intervals must be equivalent between neighbors.

Use the **show ipv6 ospf neighbor** command on R1 to verify the neighbor adjacencies, as shown in Example 5-31.

**Example 5-31**   Verifying Lost Neighbor Adjacency with R2

```
R1# show ipv6 ospf neighbor
R1#
```

Notice that R1 is no longer adjacent with the 2.2.2.2 (R2) neighbor. To restore adjacency between R1 and R2, the R2 Serial 0/0/0 interface Hello interval is set to 5 seconds, as shown in Example 5-32.

**Example 5-32**   Modifying the OSPFv3 Hello Interval on R3

```
R2(config)# interface serial 0/0/0
R2(config-if)# ipv6 ospf hello-interval 5
R2(config-if)#
*Apr 10 15:07:28.815: %OSPFv3-5-ADJCHG: Process 10, Nbr 1.1.1.1 on Serial0/0/0 from
  LOADING to FULL, Loading Done
R2(config-if)# end
R2#
```

Almost immediately, the IOS displays a message that adjacency has been established with a state of FULL. Verify the interface intervals using the **show ipv6 ospf interface** command, as shown in Example 5-33.

**Example 5-33**   Verifying Reestablished Neighbor Adjacency with R1

```
R2# show ipv6 ospf interface s0/0/0 | include Timer
  Timer intervals configured, Hello 5, Dead 20, Wait 20, Retransmit 5
R2#
R2# show ipv6 ospf neighbor

          OSPFv3 Router with ID (2.2.2.2) (Process ID 10)

Neighbor ID     Pri   State           Dead Time   Interface ID   Interface
3.3.3.3           0   FULL/  -        00:00:38    7              Serial0/0/1
1.1.1.1           0   FULL/  -        00:00:19    6              Serial0/0/0
R2#
```

Notice that the Hello timer is 5 seconds and that the Dead timer was automatically set to 20 seconds instead of the default 40 seconds. Remember that the OSPF automatically sets the Dead interval to four times the Hello interval.

# Secure OSPF (5.1.5)

As long as OSPF is configured correctly between two neighbors, the OSPF messages will be received and used to update the link-state database. This means that anyone knowing or guessing the correct configurations can manipulate the routing behavior of an unsuspecting OSPF router. This topic discusses the importance of authenticating routing updates and how to enable authentication in OSPFv2.

## Routers Are Targets (5.1.5.1)

The role of routers in a network is so crucial that they are often the targets of network attacks. Network administrators must be aware that routers are at risk from attack just as much as end-user systems.

In general, routing systems can be attacked by disrupting the routing peers or by falsifying the information carried within the routing protocol. Falsified routing information can generally be used to cause systems to misinform (lie to) each other, cause a denial of service (DoS) attack, or cause traffic to follow a path it would not normally follow. The consequences of falsifying routing information are

- Redirecting traffic to create routing loops (shown in Figure 5-27)

**Figure 5-27**   Routing Table Attack Example

- Redirecting traffic so that it can be monitored on an insecure link

- Redirecting traffic to discard it

For example, in Figure 5-27, an attacker has been able to connect directly to the link between Routers R1 and R2. The attacker injects false routing information destined to Router R1 only, indicating that R2 is the preferred destination to the 192.168.10.10/32 host route. Although R1 has a routing table entry to the directly connected 192.168.10.0/24 network, it adds the injected route to its routing table because of the longer subnet mask. A route with a longer matching subnet mask is considered to be superior to a route with a shorter subnet mask. Consequently, when a router receives a packet, it selects the longer subnet mask, because it is a more precise route to the destination.

When PC3 sends a packet to PC1 (192.168.10.10/24), R1 does not forward the packet to the PC1 host. Instead, it routes the packet to Router R2, because the apparent best path to 192.168.10.10/32 is through R2. When R2 gets the packet, it looks in its routing table and forwards the packet back to R1, which creates the loop.

To mitigate against routing protocol attacks, configure OSPF authentication.

## Secure Routing Updates (5.1.5.2)

When neighbor authentication has been configured on a router, the router authenticates the source of each routing update packet that it receives. This is accomplished by the exchange of an authenticating key (sometimes referred to as a password) that is known to both the sending and the receiving router.

To exchange routing update information in a secure manner, enable OSPF authentication. OSPF authentication can either be none (or null), simple, or Message Digest 5 (MD5).

OSPF supports three types of authentication:

- **Null:** This is the default method and means that no authentication is used for OSPF.

- **Simple password authentication:** This is also referred to as plaintext authentication because the password in the update is sent in plaintext over the network. This is considered to be a legacy method of OSPF authentication.

- *MD5 authentication*: This is the most secure and recommended method of authentication. MD5 authentication provides higher security because the password is never exchanged between peers. Instead it is calculated using the MD5 algorithm. Matching results authenticate the sender.

Figure 5-28 shows an example of MD5 authentication between two neighbors.

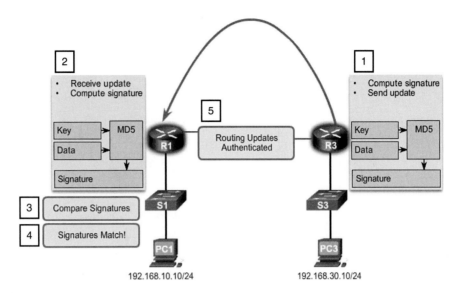

**Figure 5-28**   Routing Update with MD5 Authentication

In the figure, R3 uses the MD5 algorithm to generate a signature (sometimes called a "hash") and includes it in the authentication field inside the message header for routing update (1). R1 receives the message and does the same MD5 calculation (2). R1 then compares the generated signature with the one received from R3 (3). If the signatures match (4), the routing update is authenticated (5) and will be used by R1 to make routing decisions. If the signatures do not match, R1 discards the message.

**Note**

RIPv2, EIGRP, OSPF, IS-IS, and BGP all support various forms of MD5 authentication.

## MD5 Authentication (5.1.5.3)

Figure 5-29 shows another example of how MD5 authentication is used to authenticate two neighboring OSPF routers.

In the figure, R1 combines the routing message with the preshared secret key and calculates the signature using the MD5 algorithm. The signature is also known as a hash value. R1 adds the signature to the routing message and sends it to R2. MD5 does not encrypt the message; therefore, the content is easily readable. R2 opens the packet, combines the routing message with the preshared secret key, and calculates the signature using the MD5 algorithm.

- If the signatures match, R2 accepts the routing update.

- If the signatures do not match, R2 discards the update.

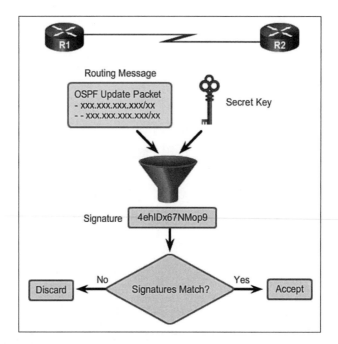

**Figure 5-29**   Operation of the MD5 Algorithm

OSPFv3 (OSPF for IPv6) does not include any authentication capabilities of its own. Instead it relies entirely on IPsec to secure communications between neighbors using the **ipv6 ospf authentication ipsec spi** interface configuration mode command. This is beneficial in simplifying the OSPFv3 protocol and standardizing its authentication mechanism.

## Configuring OSPF MD5 Authentication (5.1.5.4)

OSPF supports routing protocol authentication using MD5. MD5 authentication can be enabled globally for all interfaces or on a per-interface basis.

To enable OSPF MD5 authentication globally, configure

- The **ip ospf message-digest-key** *key* **md5** *password* interface configuration mode command

- The **area** *area-id* **authentication message-digest** router configuration mode command

This method forces authentication on all OSPF-enabled interfaces. If an interface is not configured with the **ip ospf message-digest-key** command, it will not be able to form adjacencies with other OSPF neighbors.

To provide more flexibility, authentication is now supported on a per-interface basis. To enable MD5 authentication on a per-interface basis, configure

- The **ip ospf message-digest-key** *key* **md5** *password* interface configuration mode command

- The **ip ospf authentication message-digest** interface configuration mode command

Global and per-interface OSPF MD5 authentication can be used on the same router. However, the interface setting overrides the global setting. MD5 authentication passwords do not have to be the same throughout an area; however, they do need to be the same between neighbors.

For example, assume that all routers in the previous Figure 5-25 have converged using OSPF and that routing is functioning properly. OSPF authentication will be implemented on all routers.

## OSPF MD5 Authentication Example (5.1.5.5)

Example 5-34 shows the configurations for R1 to enable OSPF MD5 authentication on all interfaces.

**Example 5-34**   Enabling MD5 Authentication Globally on R1

```
R1(config)# router ospf 10
R1(config-router)# area 0 authentication message-digest
R1(config-router)# exit
*Apr  8 09:58:09.899: %OSPF-5-ADJCHG: Process 10, Nbr 2.2.2.2 on Serial0/0/0 from
  FULL to DOWN, Neighbor Down: Dead timer expired
*Apr  8 09:58:28.627: %OSPF-5-ADJCHG: Process 10, Nbr 3.3.3.3 on Serial0/0/1 from
  FULL to DOWN, Neighbor Down: Dead timer expired
R1(config)# interface GigabitEthernet 0/0
R1(config-if)# ip ospf message-digest-key 1 md5 CISCO-123
R1(config-if)# exit
R1(config)# interface Serial 0/0/0
R1(config-if)# ip ospf message-digest-key 1 md5 CISCO-123
R1(config-if)# exit
R1(config)# interface Serial 0/0/1
R1(config-if)# ip ospf message-digest-key 1 md5 CISCO-123
R1(config-if)#
```

Notice the informational messages stating that the OSPF neighbor adjacencies with R2 and R3 have changed to the Down state, because R2 and R3 have not yet been configured to support MD5 authentication.

As an alternative to globally enabling MD5 authentication, Example 5-35 demonstrates how to configure R1 to enable OSPF MD5 authentication on a per-interface basis.

**Example 5-35**   Enabling OSPF MD5 Authentication on the R1 Interfaces

```
R1(config)# interface GigabitEthernet 0/0
R1(config-if)# ip ospf message-digest-key 1 md5 CISCO-123
R1(config-if)# ip ospf authentication message-digest
R1(config-if)# exit
R1(config)# interface Serial 0/0/0
R1(config-if)# ip ospf message-digest-key 1 md5 CISCO-123
R1(config-if)# ip ospf authentication message-digest
R1(config-if)# exit
R1(config)# interface Serial 0/0/1
R1(config-if)# ip ospf message-digest-key 1 md5 CISCO-123
R1(config-if)# ip ospf authentication message-digest
R1(config-if)# exit
R1(config)#
*Apr  8 10:20:10.647: %OSPF-5-ADJCHG: Process 10, Nbr 2.2.2.2 on Serial0/0/0 from
  FULL to DOWN, Neighbor Down: Dead timer expired
*Apr  8 10:20:50.007: %OSPF-5-ADJCHG: Process 10, Nbr 3.3.3.3 on Serial0/0/1 from
  FULL to DOWN, Neighbor Down: Dead timer expired
R1(config)#
```

Again, notice how the OSPF neighbor adjacencies have changed to the Down state.

## Verifying OSPF MD5 Authentication (5.1.5.6)

Assume that R2 and R3 are correctly configured for authentication. To verify that OSPF MD5 authentication is enabled, use the **show ip ospf interface** privileged EXEC mode command. By verifying that the routing table is complete, successful authentication can be confirmed.

Example 5-36 verifies the OSPF MD5 authentication on the Serial 0/0/0 interface on R1.

**Example 5-36**   Verifying the OSPF MD5 Authentication Settings on R1

```
R1# show ip ospf interface Serial 0/0/0
Serial0/0/0 is up, line protocol is up
  Internet Address 172.16.3.1/30, Area 0, Attached via Network Statement
  Process ID 10, Router ID 1.1.1.1, Network Type POINT_TO_POINT, Cost: 64
  Topology-MTID    Cost    Disabled    Shutdown      Topology Name
        0           64        no          no             Base
  Transmit Delay is 1 sec, State POINT_TO_POINT
  Timer intervals configured, Hello 5, Dead 20, Wait 20, Retransmit 5
```

```
   oob-resync timeout 40
   Hello due in 00:00:02
  Supports Link-local Signaling (LLS)
  Cisco NSF helper support enabled
  IETF NSF helper support enabled
  Index 2/2, flood queue length 0
  Next 0x0(0)/0x0(0)
  Last flood scan length is 1, maximum is 1
  Last flood scan time is 0 msec, maximum is 0 msec
  Neighbor Count is 1, Adjacent neighbor count is 1
    Adjacent with neighbor 2.2.2.2
  Suppress hello for 0 neighbor(s)
  Message digest authentication enabled
    Youngest key id is 1
R1# show ip ospf interface | include Message
  Message digest authentication enabled
  Message digest authentication enabled
  Message digest authentication enabled
R1#
```

Example 5-37 confirms that the authentication is successful. R1 has received routes from both R2 and R3.

**Example 5-37**   Verifying the Routing Table on R1

```
R1# show ip route ospf | begin Gateway

Gateway of last resort is 172.16.3.2 to network 0.0.0.0

O*E2  0.0.0.0/0 [110/1] via 172.16.3.2, 00:33:17, Serial0/0/0
       172.16.0.0/16 is variably subnetted, 5 subnets, 3 masks
O        172.16.2.0/24 [110/65] via 172.16.3.2, 00:33:17, Serial0/0/0
O      192.168.1.0/24 [110/65] via 192.168.10.6, 00:30:43, Serial0/0/1
       192.168.10.0/24 is variably subnetted, 3 subnets, 2 masks
O        192.168.10.8/30 [110/128] via 192.168.10.6, 00:30:43, Serial0/0/1
                         [110/128] via 172.16.3.2, 00:33:17, Serial0/0/0
R1#
```

**Packet Tracer Activity 5.1.5.7: Configuring OSPFv2 Advanced Features**

In this activity, OSPF is already configured and all end devices currently have full connectivity. You will modify the default OSPF routing configuration by changing the Hello and Dead timers, adjusting the bandwidth of a link, and enabling OSPF authentication. Then you will verify that full connectivity is restored for all end devices.

**Lab 5.1.5.8: Configuring OSPFv2 Advanced Features**

In this lab, you will complete the following objectives:

- Part 1: Build the Network and Configure Basic Device Settings

- Part 2: Configure and Verify OSPF Routing

- Part 3: Change OSPF Metrics

- Part 4: Configure and Propagate a Static Default Route

- Part 5: Configure OSPF Authentication

# Troubleshooting Single-Area OSPF Implementations (5.2)

Troubleshooting is a key skill for a network administrator. This section reviews the unique aspects of troubleshooting single-area OSPFv2 and OSPFv3.

## Components of Troubleshooting Single-Area OSPF (5.2.1)

This topic reviews the OSPF states and common OSPF verification commands. Using these commands in a systematic troubleshooting method is then discussed.

### Overview (5.2.1.1)

OSPF is a popularly implemented routing protocol used in large enterprise networks. Troubleshooting problems related to the exchange of routing information is one of the most essential skills for a network professional who is involved in the implementation and maintenance of large, routed enterprise networks that use OSPF as the IGP.

Issues with forming OSPF adjacencies include

- The interfaces are not on the same network.

- OSPF network types do not match.

- OSPF Hello or Dead timers do not match.

- The interface to neighbor is incorrectly configured as passive.

- There is a missing or incorrect OSPF **network** command.

- Authentication is misconfigured.

## OSPF States (5.2.1.2)

To troubleshoot OSPF, it is important to understand how OSPF routers traverse different OSPF states when adjacencies are being established. Figure 5-30 shows the OSPF states from DOWN to FULL.

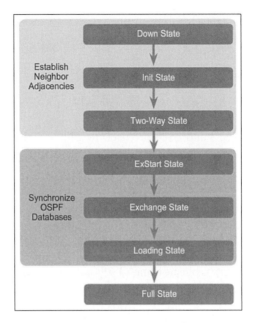

**Figure 5-30**    Transitioning Through the OSPF States

The following reviews some specific details about the OSPF states:

Down State

- No Hello packets received = Down.

- Router sends Hello packets.

- Transition to Init state.

Init State

- Hello packets are received from the neighbor.

- They contain the sending router's router ID.

- Transition to Two-Way state.

Two-Way State

- On Ethernet links, elect a DR and a BDR.

- Transition to ExStart state.

ExStart State

- Negotiate master/slave relationship and DBD packet sequence number.

- The master initiates the DBD packet exchange.

Exchange State

- Routers exchange DBD packets.

- If additional router information is required, transition to Loading; otherwise, transition to Full.

Loading State

- LSRs and LSUs are used to gain additional route information.

- Routes are processed using the SPF algorithm.

- Transition to the Full state.

Full State

- Routers have converged.

When troubleshooting OSPF neighbors, be aware that the FULL or 2WAY state is normal. All other states are transitory; that is, the router should not remain in those states for extended periods of time.

## OSPF Troubleshooting Commands (5.2.1.3)

There are many different OSPF commands that can be used to help in the troubleshooting process. The following summarizes the most common of these commands:

- **show ip protocols** (Example 5-38): Used to verify vital OSPF configuration information, including the OSPF process ID, the router ID, networks the router is advertising, the neighbors the router is receiving updates from, and the default administrative distance, which is 110 for OSPF.

**Example 5-38**  Verify the OSPF Settings on R1

```
R1# show ip protocols
*** IP Routing is NSF aware ***

Routing Protocol is "ospf 10"
  Outgoing update filter list for all interfaces is not set
  Incoming update filter list for all interfaces is not set
  Router ID 1.1.1.1
  Number of areas in this router is 1. 1 normal 0 stub 0 nssa
```

```
Maximum path: 4
Routing for Networks:
  172.16.1.1 0.0.0.0 area 0
  172.16.3.1 0.0.0.0 area 0
  192.168.10.5 0.0.0.0 area 0
Passive Interface(s):
  GigabitEthernet0/0
Routing Information Sources:
  Gateway          Distance      Last Update
  3.3.3.3               110      00:08:35
  2.2.2.2               110      00:08:35
Distance: (default is 110)

R1#
```

- **show ip ospf neighbor** (Example 5-39): Used to verify that the router has formed an adjacency with its neighboring routers. Displays the neighbor router ID, neighbor priority, OSPF state, Dead timer, neighbor interface IP address, and interface that the neighbor is accessible through. If the router ID of the neighboring router is not displayed, or if it does not show as a state of FULL or 2WAY, the two routers have not formed an OSPF adjacency. If two routers do not establish adjacency, link-state information will not be exchanged. Incomplete link-state databases can cause inaccurate SPF trees and routing tables. Routes to destination networks might not exist or might not be the most optimum path.

**Example 5-39**   Verify the OSPF Neighbor Adjacencies on R1

```
R1# show ip ospf neighbor

Neighbor ID     Pri   State        Dead Time   Address       Interface
2.2.2.2           1   FULL/BDR     00:00:30    192.168.1.2   GigabitEthernet0/0
3.3.3.3           0   FULL/DROTHER 00:00:38    192.168.1.3   GigabitEthernet0/0
R1#
```

- **show ip ospf interface** (Example 5-40): Used to display the OSPF parameters configured on an interface, such as the OSPF process ID that the interface is assigned to, the area that the interfaces are in, the cost of the interface, and the Hello and Dead intervals. Adding the interface name and number to the command displays output for a specific interface.

**Example 5-40**    Verify the OSPF Interface Settings of S0/0/0 on R1

```
R1# show ip ospf interface Serial 0/0/0
Serial0/0/0 is up, line protocol is up
  Internet Address 172.16.3.1/30, Area 0, Attached via Network Statement
  Process ID 10, Router ID 1.1.1.1, Network Type POINT_TO_POINT, Cost: 64
  Topology-MTID    Cost    Disabled    Shutdown       Topology Name
       0            64        no          no             Base
  Transmit Delay is 1 sec, State POINT_TO_POINT
  Timer intervals configured, Hello 5, Dead 20, Wait 20, Retransmit 5
    oob-resync timeout 40
    Hello due in 00:00:02
  Supports Link-local Signaling (LLS)
  Cisco NSF helper support enabled
  IETF NSF helper support enabled
  Index 2/2, flood queue length 0
  Next 0x0(0)/0x0(0)
  Last flood scan length is 1, maximum is 1
  Last flood scan time is 0 msec, maximum is 0 msec
  Neighbor Count is 1, Adjacent neighbor count is 1
    Adjacent with neighbor 2.2.2.2
  Suppress hello for 0 neighbor(s)
  Message digest authentication enabled
    Youngest key id is 1
R1#
```

■ **show ip ospf** (Example 5-41): Used to examine the OSPF process ID and router ID. Additionally, this command displays the OSPF area information, as well as the last time the SPF algorithm was calculated.

**Example 5-41**    Displaying the OSPF Parameters on R1

```
R1# show ip ospf
Routing Process "ospf 10" with ID 1.1.1.1
 Start time: 00:02:19.116, Time elapsed: 00:01:00.796
 Supports only single TOS(TOS0) routes
 Supports opaque LSA
 Supports Link-local Signaling (LLS)
 Supports area transit capability
 Supports NSSA (compatible with RFC 3101)
 Event-log enabled, Maximum number of events: 1000, Mode: cyclic
 Router is not originating router-LSAs with maximum metric
 Initial SPF schedule delay 5000 msecs
 Minimum hold time between two consecutive SPFs 10000 msecs
 Maximum wait time between two consecutive SPFs 10000 msecs
```

```
Incremental-SPF disabled
Minimum LSA interval 5 secs
Minimum LSA arrival 1000 msecs
LSA group pacing timer 240 secs
Interface flood pacing timer 33 msecs
Retransmission pacing timer 66 msecs
Number of external LSA 1. Checksum Sum 0x00A1FF
Number of opaque AS LSA 0. Checksum Sum 0x000000
Number of DCbitless external and opaque AS LSA 0
Number of DoNotAge external and opaque AS LSA 0
Number of areas in this router is 1. 1 normal 0 stub 0 nssa
Number of areas transit capable is 0
External flood list length 0
IETF NSF helper support enabled
Cisco NSF helper support enabled
Reference bandwidth unit is 100 mbps
    Area BACKBONE(0)
        Number of interfaces in this area is 3
      Area has no authentication
      SPF algorithm last executed 00:00:36.936 ago
      SPF algorithm executed 3 times
      Area ranges are
      Number of LSA 3. Checksum Sum 0x016D60
      Number of opaque link LSA 0. Checksum Sum 0x000000
      Number of DCbitless LSA 0
      Number of indication LSA 0
      Number of DoNotAge LSA 0
      Flood list length 0

R1#
```

- **show ip route ospf** (Example 5-42): Used to display only the OSPF-learned routes in the routing table. The output shows that R1 has learned about four remote networks through OSPF.

**Example 5-42**    Verify the OSPF Routes in the Routing Table on R1

```
R1# show ip route ospf | begin Gateway
Gateway of last resort is 172.16.3.2 to network 0.0.0.0

O*E2  0.0.0.0/0 [110/1] via 172.16.3.2, 00:33:17, Serial0/0/0
      172.16.0.0/16 is variably subnetted, 5 subnets, 3 masks
O        172.16.2.0/24 [110/65] via 172.16.3.2, 00:33:17, Serial0/0/0
O      192.168.1.0/24 [110/65] via 192.168.10.6, 00:30:43, Serial0/0/1
```

```
        192.168.10.0/24 is variably subnetted, 3 subnets, 2 masks
O          192.168.10.8/30 [110/128] via 192.168.10.6, 00:30:43, Serial0/0/1
                           [110/128] via 172.16.3.2, 00:33:17, Serial0/0/0
R1#
```

- **clear ip ospf** [ *process-id* ] **process:** Used to reset the OSPFv2 neighbor adjacencies.

## Components of Troubleshooting OSPF (5.2.1.4)

As shown in Figure 5-31, OSPF problems usually relate to

- Neighbor adjacencies
- Missing routes
- Path selection

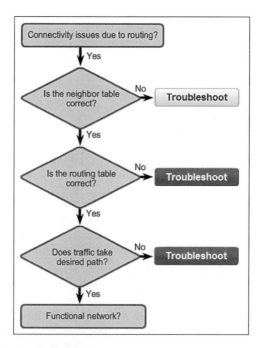

**Figure 5-31**   Troubleshooting OSPF

When troubleshooting neighbor issues, verify whether the router has established adjacencies with neighboring routers using the **show ip ospf neighbors** command. If there is no adjacency, the routers cannot exchange routes. Verify whether interfaces are operational and enabled for OSPF using the **show ip interface brief** and the **show ip ospf interface** commands. If the interfaces are operational and enabled for

OSPF, ensure that interfaces on both routers are configured for the same OSPF area and the interfaces are not configured as passive interfaces.

If adjacency between two routers is established, verify that there are OSPF routes in the routing table using the **show ip route ospf** command. If there are no OSPF routes, verify that there are no other routing protocols with lower administrative distances running in the network. Verify whether all the required networks are advertised into OSPF. Also verify whether an access list is configured on a router that would filter either incoming or outgoing routing updates.

If all the required routes are in the routing table, but the path that traffic takes is not correct, verify the OSPF cost on interfaces on the path. Also be careful in cases where the interfaces are faster than 100 Mb/s, because all interfaces above this bandwidth have the same OSPF cost by default.

**Interactive Graphic**

**Activity 5.2.1.5: Identify the Troubleshooting Command**

Go to the course online to perform this practice activity.

# Troubleshoot Single-Area OSPFv2 Routing Issues (5.2.2)

This topic discusses a specific example of troubleshooting a single-area OSPFv2 issue.

## Troubleshooting Neighbor Issues (5.2.2.1)

This example will highlight how to troubleshoot neighbor problems. In the previous OSPFv2 topology, shown in Figure 5-25, all the routers have been configured to support OSPF routing. A quick look at the R1 routing table, as shown in Example 5-43, reveals that it is not adding any OSPF routes.

**Example 5-43**   OSPF Routes Not Installed in R1 Routing Table

```
R1# show ip route | begin Gateway

Gateway of last resort is not set

      172.16.0.0/16 is variably subnetted, 4 subnets, 3 masks
C        172.16.1.0/24 is directly connected, GigabitEthernet0/0
L        172.16.1.1/32 is directly connected, GigabitEthernet0/0
C        172.16.3.0/30 is directly connected, Serial0/0/0
L        172.16.3.1/32 is directly connected, Serial0/0/0
R1#
```

There are multiple reasons why this could be. However, a prerequisite for the neighbor relationship to form between two routers is OSI Layer 3 connectivity. The output in Example 5-44 confirms that the S0/0/0 interface is up and active. The successful ping also confirms that the R2 serial interface is active.

**Example 5-44**   Verify Layer 3 Connectivity to R2

```
R1# show ip interface brief
Interface                  IP-Address      OK?  Method Status                 Protocol
Embedded-Service-Engine0/0 unassigned      YES  unset  administratively down  down
GigabitEthernet0/0         172.16.1.1      YES  manual up                     up
GigabitEthernet0/1         unassigned      YES  unset  administratively down  down
Serial0/0/0                172.16.3.1      YES  manual up                     up
Serial0/0/1                unassigned      YES  TFTP   up                     up
R1#
R1# ping 172.16.3.2
Type escape sequence to abort.
Sending 5, 100-byte ICMP Echos to 172.16.3.2, timeout is 2 seconds:
!!!!!
Success rate is 100 percent (5/5), round-trip min/avg/max = 12/14/16 ms
R1#
```

A successful ping does not mean that an adjacency will form because it is possible to have overlapping subnets. You still have to verify that interfaces on the connected devices share the same subnet. If the ping was not successful, check the cabling and verify that interfaces on connected devices are configured correctly and operational.

For an interface to be enabled for OSPF, a matching **network** command must be configured under the OSPF routing process. Active OSPF interfaces can be verified using the **show ip ospf interface** command. The output in Example 5-45 verifies that the Serial 0/0/0 interface is enabled for OSPF. If connected interfaces on two routers are not enabled for OSPF, the neighbors will not form an adjacency.

**Example 5-45**   Verify That OSPF Is Enabled on the R1 Interfaces

```
R1# show ip ospf interface serial 0/0/0
Serial0/0/0 is up, line protocol is up
  Internet Address 172.16.3.1/30, Area 0, Attached via Network Statement
  Process ID 10, Router ID 1.1.1.1, Network Type POINT_TO_POINT, Cost: 64
  Topology-MTID    Cost    Disabled     Shutdown      Topology Name
       0            64        no           no            Base
  Transmit Delay is 1 sec, State POINT_TO_POINT
  Timer intervals configured, Hello 5, Dead 20, Wait 20, Retransmit 5
    oob-resync timeout 40
```

```
   No Hellos (Passive interface)
 Supports Link-local Signaling (LLS)
 Cisco NSF helper support enabled
 IETF NSF helper support enabled
 Index 2/2, flood queue length 0
 Next 0x0(0)/0x0(0)
 Last flood scan length is 1, maximum is 1
 Last flood scan time is 0 msec, maximum is 0 msec
 Neighbor Count is 0, Adjacent neighbor count is 0
 Suppress hello for 0 neighbor(s)
 Message digest authentication enabled
   Youngest key id is 1
R1#
```

Verify the OSPF settings using the **show ip protocols** command. The output in Example 5-46 verifies that OSPF is enabled and also lists the networks being advertised as enabled by the **network** command.

**Example 5-46**   Verify OSPF Settings on R1

```
R1# show ip protocols
*** IP Routing is NSF aware ***

Routing Protocol is "ospf 10"
  Outgoing update filter list for all interfaces is not set
  Incoming update filter list for all interfaces is not set
  Router ID 1.1.1.1
  Number of areas in this router is 1. 1 normal 0 stub 0 nssa
  Maximum path: 4
  Routing for Networks:
    172.16.1.1 0.0.0.0 area 0
    172.16.3.1 0.0.0.0 area 0
  Passive Interface(s):
    GigabitEthernet0/0
    Serial0/0/0
  Routing Information Sources:
    Gateway         Distance      Last Update
    3.3.3.3              110       00:50:03
    2.2.2.2              110       04:27:25
  Distance: (default is 110)

R1#
```

If an IP address on an interface falls within a network that has been enabled for OSPF, the interface will be enabled for OSPF. However, notice that the Serial 0/0/0 interface is listed as passive. Recall that the **passive-interface** command stops both outgoing and incoming routing updates because the effect of the command causes the router to stop sending and receiving Hello packets over an interface. For this reason, the routers will not become neighbors.

To disable the interface as passive, use the **no passive-interface** router configuration mode command, as shown in Example 5-47.

**Example 5-47**   Removing the **passive-interface** Command

```
R1(config)# router ospf 10
R1(config-router)# no passive-interface s0/0/0
R1(config-router)#
*Apr  9 13:14:15.454: %OSPF-5-ADJCHG: Process 10, Nbr 2.2.2.2 on Serial0/0/0 from
  LOADING to FULL, Loading Done
R1(config-router)# end
R1#
```

After you disable the passive interface, the routers become adjacent, as indicated by the automatically generated information message. A quick verification of the routing table, as shown in Example 5-48, confirms that OSPF is now exchanging routing information.

**Example 5-48**   Verify That OSPF Routes Are Now in the R1 Routing Table

```
R1# show ip route ospf | begin Gateway

Gateway of last resort is 172.16.3.2 to network 0.0.0.0

O*E2  0.0.0.0/0 [110/1] via 172.16.3.2, 00:00:18, Serial0/0/0
      172.16.0.0/16 is variably subnetted, 5 subnets, 3 masks
O        172.16.2.0/24 [110/65] via 172.16.3.2, 00:00:18, Serial0/0/0
O     192.168.1.0/24 [110/129] via 172.16.3.2, 00:00:18, Serial0/0/0
      192.168.10.0/30 is subnetted, 1 subnets
O        192.168.10.8 [110/128] via 172.16.3.2, 00:00:18, Serial0/0/0
R1#
```

Another problem that can arise is when two neighboring routers have mismatched MTU sizes on their connecting interfaces. The MTU size is the largest network layer packet that the router will forward out each interface. Routers default to an MTU size of 1500 bytes. However, this value can be changed for IPv4 packets using the **ip mtu** *size* interface configuration command or the **ipv6 mtu** *size* interface command for IPv6 packets. If two connecting routers had mismatched MTU values, they would still attempt to form an adjacency but they would not exchange their LSDBs and the neighbor relationship would fail.

## Troubleshooting OSPF Routing Table Issues (5.2.2.2)

Again, referring to the previous OSPFv2 topology in Figure 5-25 all the routers have been configured to support OSPF routing.

A quick look at the R1 routing table in Example 5-49 reveals that it receives default route information, the R2 LAN (172.16.2.0/24) and the link between R2 and R3 (192.168.10.8/30). However, it does not receive the R3 LAN OSPF route.

**Example 5-49**   Verify OSPF Routes in the R1 Routing Table

```
R1# show ip route | begin Gateway

Gateway of last resort is 172.16.3.2 to network 0.0.0.0

O*E2  0.0.0.0/0 [110/1] via 172.16.3.2, 00:05:26, Serial0/0/0
      172.16.0.0/16 is variably subnetted, 5 subnets, 3 masks
C         172.16.1.0/24 is directly connected, GigabitEthernet0/0
L         172.16.1.1/32 is directly connected, GigabitEthernet0/0
O         172.16.2.0/24 [110/65] via 172.16.3.2, 00:05:26, Serial0/0/0
C         172.16.3.0/30 is directly connected, Serial0/0/0
L         172.16.3.1/32 is directly connected, Serial0/0/0
      192.168.10.0/30 is subnetted, 1 subnets
O         192.168.10.8 [110/128] via 172.16.3.2, 00:05:26, Serial0/0/0
R1#
```

The output in Example 5-50 verifies the OSPF settings on R3. Notice that R3 only advertises the link between R3 and R2. It does not advertise the R3 LAN (192.168.1.0/24).

**Example 5-50**   Verify OSPF Settings on R3

```
R3# show ip protocols
*** IP Routing is NSF aware ***

Routing Protocol is "ospf 10"
  Outgoing update filter list for all interfaces is not set
  Incoming update filter list for all interfaces is not set
  Router ID 3.3.3.3
  Number of areas in this router is 1. 1 normal 0 stub 0 nssa
  Maximum path: 4
```

```
   Routing for Networks:
      192.168.10.8 0.0.0.3 area 0
   Passive Interface(s):
      Embedded-Service-Engine0/0
      GigabitEthernet0/0
      GigabitEthernet0/1
      GigabitEthernet0/3
      RG-AR-IF-INPUT1
   Routing Information Sources:
      Gateway          Distance       Last Update
      1.1.1.1               110       00:02:48
      2.2.2.2               110       00:02:48
   Distance: (default is 110)

R3#
```

For an interface to be enabled for OSPF, a matching **network** command must be configured under the OSPF routing process. The output in Example 5-51 confirms that the R3 LAN is not advertised in OSPF.

**Example 5-51**    Verify the OSPF Router Configuration on R3

```
R3# show running-config | section router ospf
router ospf 10
 router-id 3.3.3.3
 passive-interface default
 no passive-interface Serial0/0/1
 network 192.168.10.8 0.0.0.3 area 0
R3#
```

The configuration in Example 5-52 adds a **network** command for the R3 LAN. R3 should now advertise the R3 LAN to its OSPF neighbors.

**Example 5-52**    Add R3 LAN to Routing Configuration

```
R3# conf t
Enter configuration commands, one per line.  End with CNTL/Z.
R3(config)# router ospf 10
R3(config-router)# network 192.168.1.0 0.0.0.255 area 0
R3(config-router)# end
R3#
```

The output in Example 5-53 verifies that the R3 LAN is now in the routing table of R1.

**Example 5-53**    Verify R1 Now Has Route to R3 LAN

```
R1# show ip route ospf | begin Gateway

Gateway of last resort is 172.16.3.2 to network 0.0.0.0

O*E2  0.0.0.0/0 [110/1] via 172.16.3.2, 00:08:38, Serial0/0/0
       172.16.0.0/16 is variably subnetted, 5 subnets, 3 masks
O        172.16.2.0/24 [110/65] via 172.16.3.2, 00:08:38, Serial0/0/0
O      192.168.1.0/24 [110/129] via 172.16.3.2, 00:00:37, Serial0/0/0
       192.168.10.0/30 is subnetted, 1 subnets
O        192.168.10.8 [110/128] via 172.16.3.2, 00:08:38, Serial0/0/0
R1#
```

**Packet Tracer Activity 5.2.2.3: Troubleshooting Single-Area OSPFv2**

In this activity, you will troubleshoot OSPF routing issues using **ping** and **show** commands to identify errors in the network configuration. Then, you will document the errors you discover and implement an appropriate solution. Finally, you will verify that end-to-end connectivity is restored.

## Troubleshoot Single-Area OSPFv3 Routing Issues (5.2.3)

This topic discusses a specific example of troubleshooting a single-area OSPFv3 issue.

### OSPFv3 Troubleshooting Commands (5.2.3.1)

Refer back to the OSPFv3 topology in Figure 5-26. Troubleshooting OSPFv3 is almost identical to OSPFv2; therefore, many OSPFv3 commands and troubleshooting criteria also apply to OSPFv3.

For example, the following are the equivalent commands used with OSPFv3:

■ **show ipv6 protocols** (Example 5-54): This command is used to verify vital OSPFv3 configuration information, including the OSPFv3 process ID, the router ID, and the interfaces the router is receiving updates from.

**Example 5-54**   Verify the OSPFv3 Settings on R1

```
R1# show ipv6 protocols
IPv6 Routing Protocol is "connected"
IPv6 Routing Protocol is "ND"
IPv6 Routing Protocol is "ospf 10"
  Router ID 1.1.1.1
  Number of areas: 1 normal, 0 stub, 0 nssa
  Interfaces (Area 0):
    Serial0/0/0
    GigabitEthernet0/0
  Redistribution:
    None
R1#
```

■ **show ipv6 ospf neighbor** (Example 5-55): Used to verify that the router has formed an adjacency with its neighboring routers. This output displays the neighbor router ID, the neighbor priority, OSPFv3 state, Dead timer, neighbor interface ID, and the interface that the neighbor is accessible through. If the router ID of the neighboring router is not displayed, or if it does not show as a state of FULL or 2WAY, the two routers have not formed an OSPFv3 adjacency. If two routers do not establish adjacency, link-state information will not be exchanged. Incomplete link-state databases can cause inaccurate SPF trees and routing tables. Routes to destination networks might not exist, or they might not be the most optimum paths.

**Example 5-55**   Verify the OSPFv3 Neighbor Adjacencies on R1

```
R1# show ipv6 ospf neighbor

Neighbor ID  Pri   State      Dead Time    Interface ID    Interface
2.2.2.2        1   FULL/-     00:00:33         7            Serial0/0/0
R1#
```

■ **show ipv6 ospf interface** (Example 5-56): Used to display the OSPFv3 parameters configured on an interface, such as the OSPFv3 process ID that the interface is assigned to, the area that the interfaces are in and the cost of the interface, and the Hello and Dead intervals. Adding the interface name and number to the command displays output for a specific interface.

**Example 5-56**   Verify the OSPFv3 Interface Settings of S0/0/0 on R1

```
R1# show ipv6 ospf interface s0/0/0
Serial0/0/0 is up, line protocol is up
  Link Local Address FE80::1, Interface ID 6
  Area 0, Process ID 10, Instance ID 0, Router ID 1.1.1.1
  Network Type POINT_TO_POINT, Cost: 647
  Transmit Delay is 1 sec, State POINT_TO_POINT
  Timer intervals configured, Hello 10, Dead 40, Wait 40, Retransmit 5
    Hello due in 00:00:08
  Graceful restart helper support enabled
  Index 1/2/2, flood queue length 0
  Next 0x0(0)/0x0(0)/0x0(0)
  Last flood scan length is 2, maximum is 6
  Last flood scan time is 0 msec, maximum is 0 msec
  Neighbor Count is 1, Adjacent neighbor count is 1
    Adjacent with neighbor 2.2.2.2
  Suppress hello for 0 neighbor(s)
R1#
```

- **show ipv6 ospf** (Example 5-57): Used to examine the OSPF process ID and router ID, as well as information about the LSA transmissions.

**Example 5-57**   Verify the OSPFv3 Interface Settings of S0/0/0 on R1

```
R1# show ipv6 ospf
 Routing Process "ospfv3 10" with ID 1.1.1.1
 Event-log enabled, Maximum number of events: 1000, Mode: cyclic
 Router is not originating router-LSAs with maximum metric
 Initial SPF schedule delay 5000 msecs
 Minimum hold time between two consecutive SPFs 10000 msecs
 Maximum wait time between two consecutive SPFs 10000 msecs
 Minimum LSA interval 5 secs
 Minimum LSA arrival 1000 msecs
 LSA group pacing timer 240 secs
 Interface flood pacing timer 33 msecs
 Retransmission pacing timer 66 msecs
 Number of external LSA 1. Checksum Sum 0x0017E9
 Number of areas in this router is 1. 1 normal 0 stub 0 nssa
 Graceful restart helper support enabled
 Reference bandwidth unit is 1000 mbps
 RFC1583 compatibility enabled
    Area BACKBONE(0)
  Number of interfaces in this area is 2
```

```
SPF algorithm executed 8 times

Number of LSA 13. Checksum Sum 0x063D5D

Number of DCbitless LSA 0

Number of indication LSA 0

Number of DoNotAge LSA 0

Flood list length 0

R1#
```

- **show ipv6 route ospf** (Example 5-58): Used to display only the OSPFv3-learned routes in the routing table. The output shows that R1 has learned about four remote networks through OSPFv3.

**Example 5-58**   Verify the OSPFv3 Routes in the R1 Routing Table

```
R1# show ipv6 route ospf
IPv6 Routing Table - default - 9 entries
Codes: C - Connected, L - Local, S - Static, U - Per-user Static route
       B - BGP, R - RIP, H - NHRP, I1 - ISIS L1
       I2 - ISIS L2, IA - ISIS interarea, IS - ISIS summary, D - EIGRP
       EX - EIGRP external, ND - ND Default, NDp - ND Prefix, DCE - Destination
       NDr - Redirect, O - OSPF Intra, OI - OSPF Inter, OE1 - OSPF ext 1
       OE2 - OSPF ext 2, ON1 - OSPF NSSA ext 1, ON2 - OSPF NSSA ext 2
OE2 ::/0 [110/1], tag 10
     via FE80::2, Serial0/0/0
O    2001:DB8:CAFE:2::/64 [110/648]
     via FE80::2, Serial0/0/0
O    2001:DB8:CAFE:3::/64 [110/648]
     via FE80::2, Serial0/0/0
O    2001:DB8:CAFE:A002::/64 [110/1294]
     via FE80::2, Serial0/0/0
R1#
```

- **clear ipv6 ospf** [ *process-id* ] **process:** Used to reset the OSPFv3 neighbor adjacencies.

### Troubleshooting OSPFv3 (5.2.3.2)

Assume that all the routers in Figure 5-25 have been configured to support OSPFv3 routing. A quick look at the R1 IPv6 routing table in Example 5-59 reveals that it receives the default route, the R2 LAN (2001:DB8:CAFE:2::/64) and the link between R2 and R3 (2001:DB8:CAFE:A002::/64). However, it does not receive the R3 LAN OSPFv3 route (2001:DB8:CAFE:3::/64).

**Example 5-59**    Verify OSPFv3 Routes in the Routing Table of R1

```
R1# show ipv6 route ospf
IPv6 Routing Table - default - 8 entries
Codes: C - Connected, L - Local, S - Static, U - Per-user Static route
       B - BGP, R - RIP, H - NHRP, I1 - ISIS L1
       I2 - ISIS L2, IA - ISIS interarea, IS - ISIS summary, D - EIGRP
       EX - EIGRP external, ND - ND Default, NDp - ND Prefix, DCE - Destination
       NDr - Redirect, O - OSPF Intra, OI - OSPF Inter, OE1 - OSPF ext 1
       OE2 - OSPF ext 2, ON1 - OSPF NSSA ext 1, ON2 - OSPF NSSA ext 2
OE2 ::/0 [110/1], tag 10
     via FE80::2, Serial0/0/0
O    2001:DB8:CAFE:2::/64 [110/648]
     via FE80::2, Serial0/0/0
O    2001:DB8:CAFE:A002::/64 [110/1294]
     via FE80::2, Serial0/0/0
R1#
```

The output in Example 5-60 verifies the OSPFv3 settings on R3. Notice that OSPF is only enabled on the Serial 0/0/1 interface. It appears that it is not enabled on the G0/0 R3 interface.

**Example 5-60**    Verify OSPFv3 Settings on R3

```
R3# show ipv6 protocols
IPv6 Routing Protocol is "connected"
IPv6 Routing Protocol is "ND"
IPv6 Routing Protocol is "ospf 10"
  Router ID 3.3.3.3
  Number of areas: 1 normal, 0 stub, 0 nssa
  Interfaces (Area 0):
    Serial0/0/1
  Redistribution:
    None
R3#
```

Unlike OSPFv2, OSPFv3 does not use the **network** command. Instead, OSPFv3 is enabled directly on the interface. The output in Example 5-61 confirms that the R3 interface is not enabled for OSPFv3.

**Example 5-61**    Verify the OSPFv3 Router Configuration on R3

```
R3# show running-config interface g0/0
Building configuration...

Current configuration : 196 bytes
!
interface GigabitEthernet0/0
 description R3 LAN
 no ip address
 duplex auto
 speed auto
 ipv6 address FE80::3 link-local
 ipv6 address 2001:DB8:CAFE:3::1/64
end

R3#
```

The configuration in Example 5-62 enables OSPFv3 on the R3 Gigabit Ethernet 0/0 interface. R3 should now advertise the R3 LAN to its OSPFv3 neighbors.

**Example 5-62**    Enable OSPFv3 on the R3 LAN

```
R3# conf t
Enter configuration commands, one per line.  End with CNTL/Z.
R3(config)# interface g0/0
R3(config-if)# ipv6 ospf 10 area 0
R3(config-if)# end
R3#
```

The output in Example 5-63 verifies that the R3 LAN is now in the routing table of R1.

**Example 5-63**    Verify OSPFv3 Routes in the Routing Table of R1

```
R1# show ipv6 route ospf
IPv6 Routing Table - default - 9 entries
Codes: C - Connected, L - Local, S - Static, U - Per-user Static route
       B - BGP, R - RIP, H - NHRP, I1 - ISIS L1
       I2 - ISIS L2, IA - ISIS interarea, IS - ISIS summary, D - EIGRP
       EX - EIGRP external, ND - ND Default, NDp - ND Prefix, DCE - Destination
       NDr - Redirect, O - OSPF Intra, OI - OSPF Inter, OE1 - OSPF ext 1
       OE2 - OSPF ext 2, ON1 - OSPF NSSA ext 1, ON2 - OSPF NSSA ext 2
```

```
OE2 ::/0 [110/1], tag 10
     via FE80::2, Serial0/0/0
O   2001:DB8:CAFE:2::/64 [110/648]
     via FE80::2, Serial0/0/0
O   2001:DB8:CAFE:3::/64 [110/1295]
     via FE80::2, Serial0/0/0
O   2001:DB8:CAFE:A002::/64 [110/1294]
     via FE80::2, Serial0/0/0
R1#
```

**Lab 5.2.3.3: Troubleshooting Basic Single-Area OSPFv2 and OSPFv3**

In this lab, you will complete the following objectives:

- Part 1: Build the Network and Load Device Configurations

- Part 2: Troubleshoot Layer 3 Connectivity

- Part 3: Troubleshoot OSPFv2

- Part 4: Troubleshoot OSPFv3

**Lab 5.2.3.4: Troubleshooting Advanced Single-Area OSPFv2**

In this lab, you will complete the following objectives:

- Part 1: Build the Network and Load Device Configurations

- Part 2: Troubleshoot OSPF

# Summary (5.3)

### Class Activity 5.3.1.1: OSPF Troubleshooting Mastery

You have decided to change your routing protocol from RIPv2 to OSPFv2. Your small- to medium-sized business network topology will not change from its original physical settings. Use the diagram on the PDF for this activity as your company's small- to medium-sized business network design.

Your addressing design is complete and you then configure your routers with IPv4 and VLSM. OSPF has been applied as the routing protocol. However, some routers are sharing routing information with each other and some are not.

Open the PDF file that accompanies this modeling activity and follow the directions to complete the activity.

When the steps in the directions are complete, regroup as a class and compare recorded activity correction times. The group taking the shortest time to find and fix the configuration error will be declared the winner only after successfully explaining how they found the error, fixed it, and proved that the topology is now working.

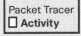

### Packet Tracer Activity 5.3.1.2: Skills Integration Challenge

In this Skills Integration Challenge, your focus is on OSPFv2 advanced configurations. IP addressing has been configured for all devices. You will configure OSPFv2 routing with passive interfaces and default route propagation. You will modify the OSPFv2 configuration by adjusting timers and establishing MD5 authentication. Finally, you will verify your configurations and test connectivity between end devices.

OSPF defines five network types: point-to-point, broadcast multiaccess, nonbroadcast multiaccess, point-to-multipoint, and virtual links.

Multiaccess networks can create two challenges for OSPF regarding the flooding of LSAs: creation of multiple adjacencies and extensive flooding of LSAs. The solution to managing the number of adjacencies and the flooding of LSAs on a multiaccess network is the DR and BDR. If the DR stops producing Hellos, the BDR promotes itself and assumes the role of DR.

The routers in the network elect the router with the highest interface priority as DR. The router with the second-highest interface priority is elected the BDR. The higher the priority, the more likely the router will be selected as the DR. If set to 0, the router is not capable of becoming the DR. The default priority of multiaccess broadcast interfaces is 1. Therefore, unless otherwise configured, all routers have an equal priority value and must rely on another tie-breaking method during the DR/BDR election. If the interface priorities are equal, the router with the highest router ID is elected the DR. The router with the second-highest router ID is the BDR. The addition of a new router does not initiate a new election process.

To propagate a default route in OSPF, the router must be configured with a default static route, and the **default-information originate** command must be added to the configuration. Verify routes with the **show ip route** or **show ipv6 route** command.

To assist OSPF in making the correct path determination, the reference bandwidth must be changed to a higher value to accommodate networks with links faster than 100 Mb/s. To adjust the reference bandwidth, use the **auto-cost reference-bandwidth** *Mbps* router configuration mode command. To adjust the interface bandwidth, use the **bandwidth** *kilobits* interface configuration mode command. The cost can be manually configured on an interface using the **ip ospf cost** *value* interface configuration mode command.

The OSPF Hello and Dead intervals must match or a neighbor adjacency does not occur. To modify these intervals, use the following interface commands:

- **ip ospf hello-interval** *seconds*
- **ip ospf dead-interval** *seconds*
- **ipv6 ospf hello-interval** *seconds*
- **ipv6 ospf dead-interval** *seconds*

OSPF supports three types of authentication: null, simple password authentication, and MD5 authentication. OSPF MD5 authentication can be configured globally or per interface. To verify that OSPF MD5 implementation is enabled, use the **show ip ospf interface** privileged EXEC mode command.

When troubleshooting OSPF neighbors, be aware that the FULL or 2WAY state is normal. The following commands summarize IPv4 OSPF troubleshooting:

- **show ip protocols**
- **show ip ospf neighbor**
- **show ip ospf interface**
- **show ip ospf**
- **show ip route ospf**
- **clear ip ospf** [*process-id*] **process**

Troubleshooting OSPFv3 is similar to OSPFv2. The following commands are the equivalent commands used with OSPFv3: **show ipv6 protocols**, **show ipv6 ospf neighbor**, **show ipv6 ospf interface**, **show ipv6 ospf**, **show ipv6 route ospf**, and **clear ipv6 ospf** [*process-id*] **process**.

# Practice

The following activities provide practice with the topics introduced in this chapter. The Labs and Class Activities are available in the companion *Scaling Networks Lab Manual* (ISBN 978-1-58713-325-1). The Packet Tracer Activities PKA files are found in the online course.

## Class Activities

■ Class Activity 5.0.1.2: DR and BDR Election

■ Class Activity 5.3.1.1: OSPF Troubleshooting Mastery

## Labs

■ Lab 5.1.1.9: Configuring Basic Single-Area OSPFv2

■ Lab 5.1.2.13: Configuring OSPFv2 on a Multiaccess Network

■ Lab 5.1.5.8: Configuring OSPFv2 Advanced Features

■ Lab 5.2.3.3: Troubleshooting Basic Single-Area OSPFv2 and OSPFv3

■ Lab 5.2.3.4: Troubleshooting Advanced Single-Area OSPFv2

Packet Tracer
□ Activity

## Packet Tracer Activities

■ Packet Tracer Activity 5.1.2.12: Determining the DR and BDR

■ Packet Tracer Activity 5.1.3.5: Propagating a Default Route in OSPFv2

■ Packet Tracer Activity 5.1.5.7: Configuring OSPFv2 Advanced Features

■ Packet Tracer Activity 5.2.2.3: Troubleshooting Single-Area OSPFv2

■ Packet Tracer Activity 5.3.1.2: Skills Integration Challenge

# Check Your Understanding Questions

Complete all the review questions listed here to test your understanding of the topics and concepts in this chapter. The appendix "Answers to 'Check Your Understanding' Questions" lists the answers.

1. What is one reason to use the **ip ospf priority** command when the OSPF routing protocol is in use?

    A. To provide a back door for connectivity during the convergence process

    B. To influence the DR/BDR election process

    C. To streamline and speed the convergence process

    D. To activate the OSPF neighboring process

2. Refer to the command output in Example 5-64. These four routers are connected together on the same LAN segment. Based on the output shown, which of these routers will be elected to be the DR for the segment?

**Example 5-64**   Command Output for Question 2

```
R1# show ip ospf interface fa0/0
FastEthernet0/0 is up, line protocol is up
  Internet Address 192.168.1.1/24, Area 0
  Process ID 1, Router ID 1.1.1.1, Network Type BROADCAST, Cost: 1
  Transmit Delay is 1 sec, <output omitted>, Priority 20


R2# show ip ospf interface fa0/0
FastEthernet0/0 is up, line protocol is up
  Internet Address 192.168.1.20/24, Area 0
  Process ID 1, Router ID 2.2.2.2, Network Type BROADCAST, Cost: 1
  Transmit Delay is 1 sec, <output omitted>, Priority 20
<output omitted>


R3# show ip ospf interface fa0/0
FastEthernet0/0 is up, line protocol is up
  Internet Address 192.168.1.33/24, Area 0
  Process ID 1, Router ID 3.3.3.3, Network Type BROADCAST, Cost: 1
  Transmit Delay is 1 sec, <output omitted>, Priority 1
<output omitted>


R4# show ip ospf interface fa0/0
FastEthernet0/0 is up, line protocol is up
  Internet Address 192.168.1.44/24, Area 0
  Process ID 100, Router ID 4.4.4.4, Network Type BROADCAST, Cost: 1
  Transmit Delay is 1 sec, <output omitted>, Priority 0
<output omitted>
```

A.  R1

B.  R2

C.  R3

D.  R4

3.  Which command will verify that a router running OSPFv3 has received a redistributed default static route from another OSPFv3 router?

A.  **show ip route**

B.  **default-information originate**

C.  **redistribute static**

D.  **show ipv6 route**

4.  Consider the R1(config-if)# **ip ospf message-digest-key 1 md5 CISCO-123** command. What is the function of the CISCO-123 portion of the command?

A.  It is used to name the OSPFv2 process.

B.  It is used as a password.

C.  It is used to choose the type of authentication.

D.  It is used as the key index.

5.  Which of the following parameters should match in order for a pair of routers to form an adjacency when running OSPFv2? (Choose three.)

A.  Router ID

B.  OSPFv2 type of network

C.  OSPFv2 process number

D.  Hello timer

E.  Interface priority

F.  Subnet mask

6. Refer to the command output in Example 5-65. R1 and R3 are connected to each other through the local Serial 0/0/0 interface. Why are they not forming an adjacency?

**Example 5-65**   Command Output for Question 6

```
R3# show running-config | section router ospf
router ospf 10
 router-id 10.10.10.3
 passive-interface default
 no passive-interface Serial0/0/0
 network 192.168.10.12 0.0.0.3 area 0

R1# show running-config | section router ospf
router ospf 1
 router-id 10.10.10.1
 passive-interface default
 no passive-interface Serial0/0/0
 network 192.168.10.8 0.0.0.3 area 0
```

A. The connecting interfaces are configured as passive.

B. They have different routing processes.

C. They have different router IDs.

D. They are in different subnets.

7. Refer to the command output in Example 5-66. Which command did an administrator issue to produce this output?

**Example 5-66**   Command Output for Question 7

```
Serial0/0/1 is up, line protocol is up
  Internet Address 172.16.30.1/30, Area 0, Attached via Network Statement
  Process ID 10, Router ID 2.2.2.2, Network Type POINT_TO_POINT, Cost: 64
  Topology-MTID    Cost    Disabled    Shutdown      Topology Name
        0           64        no          no            Base
  Transmit Delay is 1 sec, State POINT_TO_POINT
  Timer intervals configured, Hello 5, Dead 20, Wait 20, Retransmit 5
    oob-resync timeout 40
    Hello due in 00:00:02
  Supports Link-local Signaling (LLS)
  Cisco NSF helper support enabled
  IETF NSF helper support enabled
  Index 2/2, flood queue length 0
  Next 0x0(0)/0x0(0)
```

```
Last flood scan length is 1, maximum is 1
Last flood scan time is 0 msec, maximum is 0 msec
Neighbor Count is 1, Adjacent neighbor count is 1
   Adjacent with neighbor 1.1.1.1
Suppress hello for 0 neighbor(s)
Message digest authentication enabled
   Youngest key id is 1
R1#
```

A. R1# show ip route ospf

B. R1# show ip ospf neighbor

C. R1# show ip ospf

D. R1# show ip ospf interface serial0/0/1

8. What statement describes a feature of the reference bandwidth in OSPFv3?

A. It prevents the router from automatically adjusting the bandwidth.

B. It should be the same on all routers in the domain.

C. It is set to 1 Gb/s by default.

D. It increases the speed of the link.

9. Fill in the blank. Do not use abbreviations.

The _____ command is used when configuring an OSPFv2 router to redistribute only a static default route.

10. Refer to the command output in Example 5-67. Fill in the blank. Do not use abbreviations.

**Example 5-67**  Command Output for Question 10

```
IPv6 Routing Table - default - 8 entries
<output omitted>
OE2 ::/0 [110/1], tag 10
     via FE80::2, Serial 0/0/0
O   2001:DB8:CAFE:2::/64 [110/648]
     via FE80::2, Serial0/0/0
O   2001:DB8:CAFE:3::/64 [110/648]
     via FE80::2, Serial0/0/0
O   2001:DB8:CAFE:A002::/64 [110/1294]
     via FE80::2, Serial0/0/0
R1#
```

The _____ command is used to display only OSPFv3-learned routes.

**11.** Refer to the command output in Example 5-68. Fill in the blank. Use a number.

**Example 5-68**   Command Output for Question 11

```
R1# show ipv6 protocols
IPv6 Routing Protocol is connected
IPv6 Routing Protocol is ND
IPv6 Routing Protocol is ospf 10
  Router ID 1.1.1.1
  Number of areas: 1 normal, 0 stub, 0 nssa
  Interfaces (Area 0):
    Serial0/0/0
    GigabitEthernet0/0
  Redistribution:
    None
R1#
```

The process ID that is used for OSPFv3 on Router R1 is _____ .

**12.** Fill in the blanks. What OSPF state is described by each of the following statements?

A router enters the _____ state when it receives hello packets that contain the router ID of a neighboring device.

Routers enter the _____ state after a DR and BDR are elected.

Routers exchange DBD packets during the _____ state.

# CHAPTER 6

# Multiarea OSPF

## Objectives

Upon completion of this chapter, you will be able to answer the following questions:

- Why is multiarea OSPF used?

- How does multiarea OSPF use link-state advertisements to maintain routing tables?

- How does OSPF establish neighbor adjacencies in multiarea OSPF?

- What are the commands to configure multiarea OSPFv2 in a routed network?

- What are the commands to configure multiarea route summarization in a routed network?

- What are the commands to verify multiarea OSPFv2 operations?

## Key Terms

This chapter uses the following key terms. You can find the definitions in the Glossary.

# Introduction (6.0.1.1)

Multiarea OSPF is used to divide a large OSPF network. Having too many routers in one area increases the load on the CPU and creates a large link-state database. In this chapter, directions are provided to effectively partition a large single area into multiple areas. Area 0 used in a single-area OSPF is known as the *backbone area*.

Discussion is focused on the LSAs exchanged between areas. In addition, activities for configuring OSPFv2 and OSPFv3 are provided. The chapter concludes with the **show** commands used to verify OSPF configurations.

### Class Activity 6.0.1.2: Leaving on a Jet Plane

You and a classmate are starting a new airline to serve your continent.

In addition to your core area or headquarters airport, you will locate and map four intra-continental airport service areas and one transcontinental airport service area that can be used for additional source and destination travel.

Use the blank world map provided to design your airport locations. Additional instructions for completing this activity can be found in the accompanying PDF.

# Multiarea OSPF Operation (6.1)

This section discusses the reasons for using multiarea OSPF, the operation of multiarea OSPF, and the unique codes used to indicate multiarea OSPF routes in the routing table.

## Why Multiarea OSPF? (6.1.1)

When a network gets very large, the routing tables, databases, and SPF calculations can consume an unacceptable amount of router resources.

### Single-Area OSPF (6.1.1.1)

Single-area OSPF is useful in smaller networks, where the web of router links is not complex and paths to individual destinations are easily deduced.

However, if an area becomes too big, as shown in Figure 6-1, the following issues must be addressed (see the figure for illustration):

- **Large routing table:** OSPF does not perform route summarization by default. If the routes are not summarized, the routing table can become very large, depending on the size of the network.

- **Large link-state database (LSDB):** Because the LSDB covers the topology of the entire network, each router must maintain an entry for every network in the area, even if not every route is selected for the routing table.

- **Frequent SPF algorithm calculations:** In a large network, changes are inevitable, so the routers spend many CPU cycles recalculating the SPF algorithm and updating the routing table.

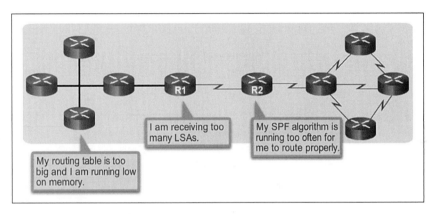

**Figure 6-1** Issues in a Large OSPF Single Area

To make OSPF more efficient and scalable, OSPF supports hierarchical routing using areas. An OSPF area is a group of routers that share the same link-state information in their link-state databases.

## Multiarea OSPF (6.1.1.2)

When a large OSPF area is divided into smaller areas, this is called multiarea OSPF. Multiarea OSPF is useful in larger network deployments to reduce processing and memory overhead.

For example, anytime a router receives new information about the topology, as with additions, deletions, or modifications of a link, the router must rerun the SPF algorithm, create a new SPF tree, and update the routing table. The SPF algorithm is CPU intensive, and the time it takes for calculation depends on the size of the area. Too many routers in one area make the LSDB larger and increase the load on the CPU. Therefore, arranging routers into areas effectively partitions one potentially large database into smaller and more manageable databases.

Multiarea OSPF requires a hierarchical network design. The main area is called the backbone area (area 0), and all other areas must connect to the backbone area. With hierarchical routing, routing still occurs between the areas (interarea routing), while many of the tedious routing operations, such as recalculating the database, are kept within an area.

As illustrated in Figure 6-2, the hierarchical topology possibilities of multiarea OSPF have these advantages:

- **Smaller routing tables:** There are fewer routing table entries as network addresses can be summarized between areas. For example, R1 summarizes the routes from area 1 to area 0 and R2 summarizes the routes from area 51 to area 0. R1 and R2 also propagate a default static route to area 1 and area 51.

- **Reduced link-state update overhead:** Minimizes processing and memory requirements, because there are fewer routers exchanging LSAs.

- **Reduced frequency of SPF calculations:** Localizes impact of a topology change within an area. For example, it minimizes routing update impacts, because LSA flooding stops at the area boundary.

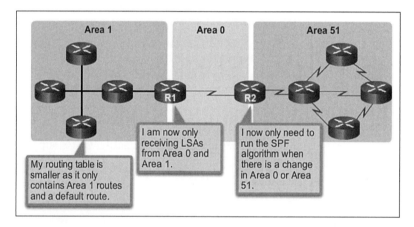

**Figure 6-2**  Multiarea OSPF Advantages

In Figure 6-3, assume that a link fails between two internal routers in area 51.

**Figure 6-3**  Multiarea OSPF Link Failure Example

Only the routers in area 51 exchange LSAs and rerun the SPF algorithm for this event. R1 does not receive LSAs from area 51 and does not recalculate the SPF algorithm.

## OSPF Two-Layer Area Hierarchy (6.1.1.3)

Multiarea OSPF is implemented in a two-layer area hierarchy, as shown in Figure 6-4:

- **Backbone (transit) area:** An OSPF area whose primary function is the fast and efficient movement of IP packets. Backbone areas interconnect with other OSPF area types. Generally, end users are not found within a backbone area. The backbone area is also called OSPF area 0. Hierarchical networking defines area 0 as the core to which all other areas directly connect.

- **Regular (nonbackbone) area:** Connects users and resources. Regular areas are usually set up along functional or geographical groupings. By default, a regular area does not allow traffic from another area to use its links to reach other areas. All traffic from other areas must cross a transit area.

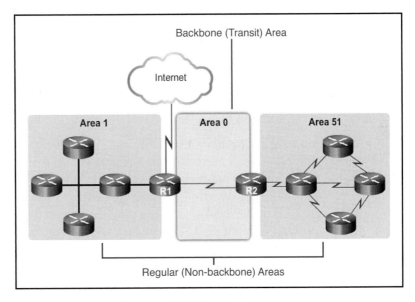

**Figure 6-4**   Backbone and Regular OSPF Areas

**Note**

A regular area can have a number of subtypes, including a standard area, stub area, totally stubby area, and not-so-stubby area (NSSA). Stub, totally stubby, and NSSAs are beyond the scope of this chapter.

OSPF enforces this rigid two-layer area hierarchy. The underlying physical connectivity of the network must map to the two-layer area structure, with all nonbackbone areas attaching directly to area 0. All traffic moving from one area to another area must traverse the backbone area. This traffic is referred to as interarea traffic.

The optimal number of routers per area varies based on factors such as network stability, but Cisco recommends the following guidelines:

- An area should have no more than 50 routers.

- A router should not be in more than three areas.

- Any single router should not have more than 60 neighbors.

## Types of OSPF Routers (6.1.1.4)

OSPF routers of different types control the traffic that goes in and out of areas. The OSPF routers are categorized based on the function they perform in the routing domain.

There are four different types of OSPF routers, as shown in Figure 6-5:

- *Internal router*: This is a router that has all its interfaces in the same area. All internal routers in an area have identical LSDBs. Internal routers are highlighted in Figure 6-5.

- *Backbone router*: This is a router in the backbone area. Generally, the backbone area is set to area 0. The backbone routers in Figure 6-4 are R1, R2, and the two internal routers in area 0.

- *Area Border Router (ABR)*: This is a router that has interfaces attached to multiple areas. It must maintain separate LSDBs for each area it is connected to, and it can route between areas. ABRs are exit points for the area, which means that routing information destined for another area can get there only through the ABR of the local area. ABRs can be configured to summarize the routing information from the LSDBs of their attached areas. ABRs distribute the routing information into the backbone. The backbone routers then forward the information to the other ABRs. In a multiarea network, an area can have one or more ABRs. The ABRs in Figure 6-5 are R1 and R2.

- **Autonomous System Boundary Router (ASBR)**: This is a router that has at least one interface attached to an external internetwork (another autonomous system), such as a non-OSPF network. An ASBR can import non-OSPF network information to the OSPF network, and vice versa, using a process called *route redistribution*. The ASBR in Figure 6-5 is R1.

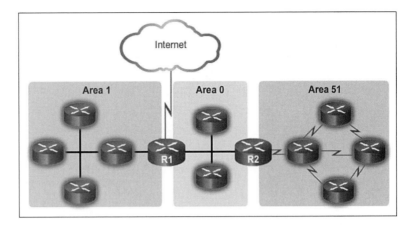

**Figure 6-5**   OSPF Router Types

Redistribution in multiarea OSPF occurs when an ASBR connects different routing domains (for example, EIGRP and OSPF) and configures them to exchange and advertise routing information between those routing domains.

A router can be classified as more than one router type. For example, if a router connects to area 0 and area 1 and, in addition, maintains routing information for another, non-OSPF network, it falls under three different classifications: a backbone router, an ABR, and an ASBR. In Figure 6-5, R1 is a backbone router, an ABR, and an ASBR.

**Interactive Graphic**

**Activity 6.1.1.5: Identify the Multiarea OSPF Terminology**

Go to the course online to perform this practice activity.

## Multiarea OSPF LSA Operation (6.1.2)

The propagation of OSPF messages is controlled by specific LSA types.

### OSPF LSA Types (6.1.2.1)

LSAs are the building blocks of the OSPF LSDB. Individually, they act as database records and provide specific OSPF network details. In combination, they describe the entire topology of an OSPF network or area.

The RFCs for OSPF currently specify up to 11 different LSA types, as shown in Table 6-1. However, any implementation of multiarea OSPF must support the first five LSAs: LSA 1 to LSA 5. The focus of this topic is on these first five LSAs.

**Table 6-1** Most Common OSPF LSA Types

| LSA Type | Description |
| --- | --- |
| 1 | Router LSA |
| 2 | Network LSA |
| 3 and 4 | Summary LSAs |
| 5 | AS External LSA |
| 6 | Multicast OSPF LSA |
| 7 | Defined for NSSAs |
| 8 | External Attributes LSA for BGP |
| 9, 10, or 11 | Opaque LSAs |

Each router link is defined as an LSA type. The LSA includes a link ID field that identifies, by network number and mask, the object to which the link connects. Depending on the type, the link ID has different meanings. LSAs differ on how they are generated and propagated within the routing domain.

**Note**

OSPFv3 includes additional LSA types.

## OSPF LSA Type 1 (6.1.2.2)

Figure 6-6 shows an example use of OSPF *LSA Type 1*.

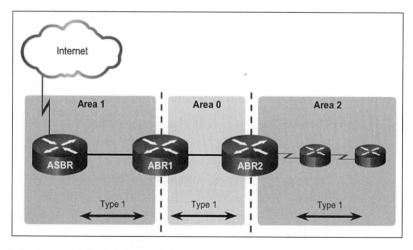

**Figure 6-6** Type 1 LSA Message Propagation

All routers advertise their directly connected OSPF-enabled links in a type 1 LSA and forward their network information to OSPF neighbors. The LSA contains a list of the directly connected interfaces, link types, and link states.

Type 1 LSA features are as follows:

- All routers generate type 1 LSAs.

- Type 1 LSAs include a list of directly connected network prefixes and link types.

- A type 1 LSA link-state ID is identified by the router ID of the originating router.

- Type 1 LSAs are also referred to as router link entries.

- Type 1 LSAs are flooded only within the area in which they originated. ABRs subsequently advertise the networks learned from the type 1 LSAs to other areas as type 3 LSAs.

## OSPF LSA Type 2 (6.1.2.3)

Figure 6-7 shows an example use of OSPF *LSA Type 2*.

**Figure 6-7**   Type 2 LSA Message Propagation

An LSA Type 2 only exists for multiaccess and nonbroadcast multiaccess (NBMA) networks where there is a DR elected and at least two routers on the multiaccess segment. The type 2 LSA contains the router ID and IP address of the DR, along with the router ID of all other routers on the multiaccess segment. A type 2 LSA is created for every multiaccess network in the area.

The purpose of a type 2 LSA is to give other routers information about multiaccess networks within the same area.

The DR floods type 2 LSAs only within the area in which they originated. Type 2 LSAs are not forwarded outside of an area.

Type 2 LSAs are also referred to as network link entries.

As shown in the figure, ABR1 is the DR for the Ethernet network in area 1. It generates the type 2 LSA and forwards it into area 1. ABR2 is the DR for the multiaccess network in area 0. There are no multiaccess networks in area 2, and therefore no type 2 LSAs are ever propagated in that area.

The link-state ID for a network LSA is the IP interface address of the DR that advertises it.

## OSPF LSA Type 3 (6.1.2.4)

Figure 6-8 shows an example use of OSPF *LSA Type 3*.

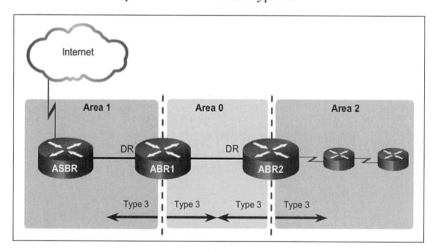

**Figure 6-8**   Type 3 LSA Message Propagation

LSA Type 3 is used by an ABR to advertise networks from other areas. ABRs collect type 1 LSAs in the LSDB. After an OSPF area has converged, the ABR creates a type 3 LSA for each of its learned OSPF networks. Therefore, an ABR with many OSPF routes must create type 3 LSAs for each network.

As shown in the figure, ABR1 and ABR2 flood type 3 LSAs from one area to other areas. The ABRs propagate the type 3 LSAs into other areas. In a large OSPF deployment with many networks, propagating type 3 LSAs can cause significant flooding problems. For this reason, it is strongly recommended that manual route summarization be configured on the ABR.

The link-state ID is set to the network number and the mask is also advertised.

Receiving a type 3 LSA into its area does not cause a router to run the SPF algorithm. The routes being advertised in the type 3 LSAs are appropriately added to or deleted from the router's routing table, but a full SPF calculation is not necessary.

## OSPF LSA Type 4 (6.1.2.5)

Figure 6-9 shows an example use of OSPF *LSA Type 4*.

**Figure 6-9**    Type 4 LSA Message Propagation

LSA Type 4 and LSA Type 5 are used collectively to identify an ASBR and advertise external networks into an OSPF routing domain.

A type 4 summary LSA is generated by an ABR only when an ASBR exists within an area. A type 4 LSA identifies the ASBR and provides a route to it. All traffic destined to an external autonomous system requires routing table knowledge of the ASBR that originated the external routes.

As shown in the figure, the ASBR sends a type 1 LSA, identifying itself as an ASBR. The LSA includes a special bit known as the external bit (e bit) that is used to identify the router as an ASBR. When ABR1 receives the type 1 LSA, it notices the e bit, it builds a type 4 LSA, and then floods the type 4 LSA to the backbone (area 0). Subsequent ABRs flood the type 4 LSA into other areas.

The link-state ID is set to the ASBR router ID.

## OSPF LSA Type 5 (6.1.2.6)

Figure 6-10 shows an example use of OSPF *LSA Type 5*.

**Figure 6-10**   Type 5 LSA Message Propagation

Type 5 external LSAs describe routes to networks outside the OSPF autonomous system. Type 5 LSAs are originated by the ASBR and are flooded to the entire autonomous system.

Type 5 LSAs are also referred to as autonomous system external LSA entries.

In the figure, the ASBR generates type 5 LSAs for each of its external routes and floods them into the area. Subsequent ABRs also flood the type 5 LSA into other areas. Routers in other areas use the information from the type 4 LSA to reach the external routes.

In a large OSPF deployment with many networks, propagating multiple type 5 LSAs can cause significant flooding problems. For this reason, it is strongly recommended that manual route summarization be configured on the ASBR.

The link-state ID is the external network number.

Interactive
Graphic

**Activity 6.1.2.7: Identify the OSPF LSA Type**

Go to the course online to perform this practice activity.

# OSPF Routing Table and Types of Routes (6.1.3)

Routes learned from multiple OSPF areas are immediately apparent because routes from other areas are identified with a unique code in the routing table.

## OSPF Routing Table Entries (6.1.3.1)

Figure 6-11 provides a sample routing table for a multiarea OSPF topology with a link to an external non-OSPF network.

```
R1# show ip route
Codes:L - local, C-connected, S-static, R-RIP, M-mobile, B-BGP
       D - EIGRP, EX - EIGRP external, O - OSPF, IA - OSPF inter area
       N1 - OSPF NSSA external type 1, N2 - OSPF NSSA external type 2
       E1 - OSPF external type 1, E2 - OSPF external type 2
       i - IS-IS, su-IS-IS summary, L1-IS-IS level-1, L2-IS-IS level-2
       ia - IS-IS inter area,*-candidate default,U-per-user static route
       o - ODR, P-periodic downloaded static route, H-NHRP, l-LISP
       + - replicated route, % - next hop override

Gateway of last resort is 192.168.10.2 to network 0.0.0.0

O*E2 0.0.0.0/0 [110/1] via 192.168.10.2, 00:00:19, Serial0/0/0
        10.0.0.0/8 is variably subnetted, 5 subnets, 2 masks
C       10.1.1.0/24 is directly connected, GigabitEthernet0/0
L       10.1.1.1/32 is directly connected, GigabitEthernet0/0
C       10.1.2.0/24 is directly connected, GigabitEthernet0/1
L       10.1.2.1/32 is directly connected, GigabitEthernet0/1
O       10.2.1.0/24 [110/648] via 192.168.10.2, 00:04:34, Serial0/0/0
O IA 192.168.1.0/24 [110/1295] via 192.168.10.2, 00:01:48,Serial0/0/0
O IA 192.168.2.0/24 [110/1295] via 192.168.10.2, 00:01:48,Serial0/0/0
        192.168.10.0/24 is variably subnetted, 3 subnets, 2 masks
C       192.168.10.0/30 is directly connected, Serial0/0/0
L       192.168.10.1/32 is directly connected, Serial0/0/0
O       192.168.10.4/30 [110/1294] via 192.168.10.2, 00:01:55,Serial0/0/0
R1#
```

**Figure 6-11**    OSPFv2 Routing Table

OSPF routes in an IPv4 routing table are identified using the following descriptors:

- **O:** Router (type 1) and network (type 2) LSAs describe the details within an area. The routing table reflects this link-state information with a designation of O, meaning that the route is intra-area.

- **O IA:** When an ABR receives summary LSAs, it adds them to its LSDB and regenerates them into the local area. When an ABR receives external LSAs, it adds them to its LSDB and floods them into the area. The internal routers then assimilate the information into their databases. Summary LSAs appear in the routing table as IA (interarea routes).

- **O E1 or O E2:** External LSAs appear in the routing table marked as external type 1 (E1) or external type 2 (E2) routes.

Figure 6-12 displays an IPv6 routing table with OSPF router, interarea, and external routing table entries.

```
R1# show ipv6 route
IPv6 Routing Table - default - 9 entries
Codes:C - Connected, L - Local, S - Static, U-Per-user Static route
       B - BGP, R - RIP, H - NHRP, I1 - ISIS L1
       I2 - ISIS L2, IA - ISIS interarea, IS - ISIS summary, D - EIGRP
       EX - EIGRP external, ND-ND Default,NDp-ND Prefix,DCE-Destination
       NDr - Redirect, O-OSPF Intra, OI-OSPF Inter, OE1-OSPF ext 1
       OE2 - OSPF ext 2, ON1 - OSPF NSSA ext 1, ON2 - OSPF NSSA ext 2
OE2 ::/0 [110/1], tag 10
       via FE80::2, Serial0/0/0
C   2001:DB8:CAFE:1::/64 [0/0]
       via GigabitEthernet0/0, directly connected
L   2001:DB8:CAFE:1::1/128 [0/0]
       via GigabitEthernet0/0, receive
O   2001:DB8:CAFE:2::/64 [110/648]
       via FE80::2, Serial0/0/0
OI  2001:DB8:CAFE:3::/64 [110/1295]
       via FE80::2, Serial0/0/0
C   2001:DB8:CAFE:A001::/64 [0/0]
       via Serial0/0/0, directly connected
L   2001:DB8:CAFE:A001::1/128 [0/0]
       via Serial0/0/0, receive
O   2001:DB8:CAFE:A002::/64 [110/1294]
       via FE80::2, Serial0/0/0
L   FF00::/8 [0/0]
       via Null0, receive
R1#
```

**Figure 6-12**   OSPFv3 Routing Table

## OSPF Route Calculation (6.1.3.2)

Each router uses the SPF algorithm against the LSDB to build the SPF tree. The SPF tree is used to determine the best paths. Refer to Figure 6-13.

```
R1# show ip route | begin Gateway
Gateway of last resort is 192.168.10.2 to network 0.0.0.0
O*E2 0.0.0.0/0 [110/1] via 192.168.10.2, 00:00:19, Serial0/0/0
       10.0.0.0/8 is variably subnetted, 5 subnets, 2 masks
C      10.1.1.0/24 is directly connected, GigabitEthernet0/0
L      10.1.1.1/32 is directly connected, GigabitEthernet0/0
C      10.1.2.0/24 is directly connected, GigabitEthernet0/1
L      10.1.2.1/32 is directly connected, GigabitEthernet0/1
O      10.2.1.0/24 [110/648] via 192.168.10.2, 00:04:34,Serial0/0/0
O IA 192.168.1.0/24 [110/1295] via 192.168.10.2, 00:01:48,Serial0/0/0
O IA 192.168.2.0/24 [110/1295] via 192.168.10.2, 00:01:48,Serial0/0/0
       192.168.10.0/24 is variably subnetted, 3 subnets, 2 masks
C      192.168.10.0/30 is directly connected, Serial0/0/0
L      192.168.10.1/32 is directly connected, Serial0/0/0
O      192.168.10.4/30 [110/1294] via 192.168.10.2, 00:01:55,Serial0/0/0
R1#
```

**Figure 6-13**   Steps to OSPF Convergence

In the figure, the order in which the best paths are calculated is as follows:

1. All routers calculate the best paths to destinations within their area (intra-area) and add these entries to the routing table. These are the type 1 and type 2 LSAs, which are noted in the routing table with a routing designator of O. (1)

2. All routers calculate the best paths to the other areas within the internetwork. These best paths are the interarea route entries, or type 3 and type 4 LSAs, and are noted with a routing designator of O IA. (2)

3. All routers (except those that are in a form of stub area) calculate the best paths to the external autonomous system (type 5) destinations. These are noted with either an O*E1 or an O*E2 route designator, depending on the configuration. (3)

When converged, a router can communicate with any network within or outside the OSPF autonomous system.

**Interactive Graphic**

**Activity 6.1.3.3: Order the Steps for OSPF Best Path Calculations**

Go to the course online to perform this practice activity.

# Configuring Multiarea OSPF (6.2)

This section discusses how to configure multiarea OSPF for both IPv4 and IPv6. In addition, summarizing OSPF routes and verifying the OSPF configuration are also covered.

## Configuring Multiarea OSPFv2 and OSPFv3 (6.2.1)

Configuring multiarea OSPF, whether for IPv4 or IPv6, is simply a matter of indicating the area to which a network belongs.

### Implementing Multiarea OSPF (6.2.1.1)

OSPF can be implemented as single-area or multiarea. The type of OSPF implementation chosen depends on the specific requirements and existing topology. There are four steps to implementing multiarea OSPF. Steps 1 and 2 are part of the planning process. Steps 3 and 4 are configuration and verification.

Step 1.    **Gather the network requirements and parameters.** This includes determining the number of host and network devices, the IP addressing scheme (if already implemented), the size of the routing domain, the size of the routing tables, the risk of topology changes, and other network characteristics.

**Step 2.** **Define the OSPF parameters.** Based on information gathered during Step 1, the network administrator must determine if single-area or multiarea OSPF is the preferred implementation. If multiarea OSPF is selected, there are several considerations the network administrator must take into account while determining the OSPF parameters:

- **IP addressing plan:** This governs how OSPF can be deployed and how well the OSPF deployment might scale. A detailed IP addressing plan, along with the IP subnetting information, must be created. A good IP addressing plan should enable the usage of OSPF multiarea design and summarization. This plan more easily scales the network, as well as optimizes OSPF behavior and the propagation of LSAs.

- **OSPF areas:** Dividing an OSPF network into areas decreases the LSDB size and limits the propagation of link-state updates when the topology changes. The routers that are to be ABRs and ASBRs must be identified, as are those that are to perform any summarization or redistribution.

- **Network topology:** This consists of links that connect the network equipment and belong to different OSPF areas in a multiarea OSPF design. Network topology is important to determine primary and backup links. Primary and backup links are defined by the changing OSPF cost on interfaces. A detailed network topology plan should also be used to determine the different OSPF areas, ABR, and ASBR, as well as summarization and redistribution points, if multiarea OSPF is used.

**Step 3.** **Configure the multiarea OSPF implementation based on the parameters.**

**Step 4.** **Verify the multiarea OSPF implementation based on the parameters.**

## Configuring Multiarea OSPF (6.2.1.2)

Figure 6-14 displays the reference multiarea OSPF topology.

In this topology

- R1 is an ABR because it has interfaces in area 1 and an interface in area 0.

- R2 is an internal backbone router because all its interfaces are in area 0.

- R3 is an ABR because it has interfaces in area 2 and an interface in area 0.

There are no special commands required to implement this multiarea OSPF network. A router simply becomes an ABR when it has two **network** statements in different areas.

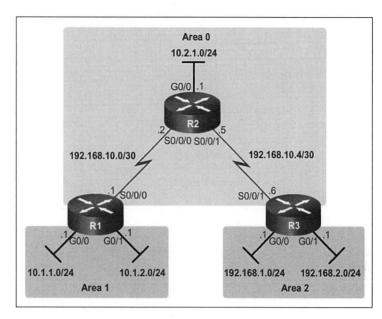

**Figure 6-14**    OSPFv2 Multiarea Topology

As shown in Example 6-1, R1 is assigned the router ID 1.1.1.1. This example enables OSPF on the two LAN interfaces in area 1. The serial interface is configured as part of OSPF area 0. Because R1 has interfaces connected to two different areas, it is an ABR.

**Example 6-1**    Configuring Multiarea OSPFv2

```
R1(config)# router ospf 10
R1(config-router)# router-id 1.1.1.1
R1(config-router)# network 10.1.1.1 0.0.0.0 area 1
R1(config-router)# network 10.1.2.1 0.0.0.0 area 1
R1(config-router)# network 192.168.10.1 0.0.0.0 area 0
R1(config-router)# end
R1#

R2(config)# router ospf 10
R2(config-router)# router-id 2.2.2.2
R2(config-router)# network 192.168.10.0 0.0.0.7 area 0
R2(config-router)# network 10.2.1.0 0.0.0.255 area 0
R2(config-router)# end
*Apr 19 18:11:04.029: %OSPF-5-ADJCHG: Process 10, Nbr 1.1.1.1 on Serial0/0/0 from
  LOADING to FULL, Loading Done
R2#
```

```
*Apr 19 18:11:06.781: %SYS-5-CONFIG_I: Configured from console by console
R2#

R3(config)#router ospf 10
R3(config-router)# router-id 3.3.3.3
R3(config-router)# network 192.168.10.6 0.0.0.0 area 0
R3(config-router)# network 192.168.1.1 0.0.0.0 area 2
R3(config-router)# network 192.168.2.1 0.0.0.0 area 2
R3(config-router)# end
*Apr 19 18:12:55.881: %OSPF-5-ADJCHG: Process 10, Nbr 2.2.2.2 on Serial0/0/1 from
  LOADING to FULL, Loading Done
R3#
```

In the example, the configuration for R2 uses the wildcard mask of the interface network address. Notice the informational messages informing of the adjacencies with R1 (1.1.1.1). The configuration for R3 uses the 0.0.0.0 wildcard mask for all networks. Notice the informational messages informing of an adjacency with R2 (2.2.2.2). Also notice how the IP addressing scheme used for the router ID makes it easy to identify the neighbor.

### Note

The inverse wildcard masks used to configure R2 and R3 purposely differ to demonstrate the two alternatives to entering **network** statements. The method used for R3 is simpler because the wildcard mask is always **0.0.0.0** and does not need to be calculated.

## Configuring Multiarea OSPFv3 (6.2.1.3)

Like OSPFv2, implementing the multiarea OSPFv3 topology shown in Figure 6-15 is simple.

There are no special commands required. A router simply becomes an ABR when it has two interfaces in different areas.

In Example 6-2, R1 is assigned the router ID 1.1.1.1. The example also shows how to enable OSPF on the two LAN interfaces in area 1 and the serial interface in area 0. Because R1 has interfaces connected to two different areas, it becomes an ABR.

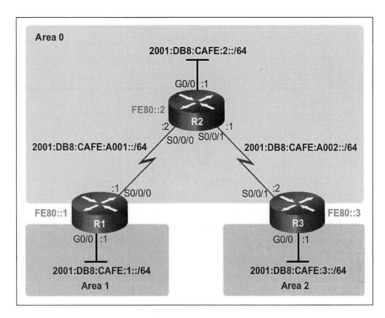

**Figure 6-15**    OSPFv3 Multiarea Topology

**Example 6-2**    Configuring Multiarea OSPFv3

```
R1(config)# ipv6 router ospf 10
R1(config-rtr)# router-id 1.1.1.1
R1(config-rtr)# exit
R1(config)# interface GigabitEthernet 0/0
R1(config-if)# ipv6 ospf 10 area 1
R1(config-if)# interface Serial0/0/0
R1(config-if)# ipv6 ospf 10 area 0
R1(config-if)# end
R1#


R2(config)# ipv6 router ospf 10
*Apr 24 14:18:10.463: %OSPFv3-4-NORTRID: Process OSPFv3-10-IPv6 could not pick a
   router-id, please configure manually
R2(config-rtr)# router-id 2.2.2.2
R2(config-rtr)# exit
R2(config)# interface g0/0
R2(config-if)# ipv6 ospf 10 area 0
R2(config-if)# interface s0/0/0
R2(config-if)# ipv6 ospf 10 area 0
R2(config-if)# interface s0/0/1
R2(config-if)# ipv6 ospf 10 area 0
```

```
*Apr 24 14:18:35.135: %OSPFv3-5-ADJCHG: Process 10, Nbr 1.1.1.1 on Serial0/0/0 from
  LOADING to FULL, Loading Done
R2(config-if)# end
R2#
```

```
R3(config)# ipv6 router ospf 10
*Apr 24 14:20:42.463: %OSPFv3-4-NORTRID: Process OSPFv3-10-IPv6 could not pick a
  router-id, please configure manually
R3(config-rtr)# router-id 3.3.3.3
R3(config-rtr)# exit
R3(config)# interface g0/0
R3(config-if)# ipv6 ospf 10 area 2
R3(config-if)# interface s0/0/1
R3(config-if)# ipv6 ospf 10 area 0
*Apr 24 14:21:01.439: %OSPFv3-5-ADJCHG: Process 10, Nbr 2.2.2.2 on Serial0/0/1 from
  LOADING to FULL, Loading Done
R3(config-if)# end
R3#
```

Notice that the configuration for R2 and R3 begins with the **ipv6 router ospf** command. Because a router ID in the IPv4 address format is required for OSPFv3, the router needs one explicitly configured before the OSPFv3 process can be started.

## OSPF Route Summarization (6.2.2)

Route summarization for OSPF requires special commands on an ASBR or ABR.

### OSPF Route Summarization (6.2.2.1)

Summarization helps keep routing tables small. It involves consolidating multiple routes into a single advertisement, which can then be propagated into the backbone area.

Normally, type 1 and type 2 LSAs are generated inside each area, translated into type 3 LSAs, and sent to other areas. If area 1 had 30 networks to advertise, 30 type 3 LSAs would be forwarded into the backbone. With route summarization, the ABR consolidates the 30 networks into one of two advertisements.

In Figure 6-16, R1 consolidates all the network advertisements into one summary LSA.

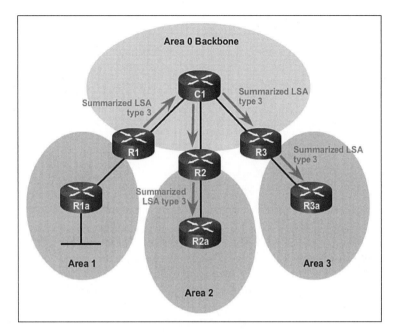

**Figure 6-16**   Propagating a Summary Route

Instead of forwarding individual LSAs for each route in area 1, R1 forwards a summary LSA to the core Router C1. C1 in turn, forwards the summary LSA to R2 and R3. R2 and R3 then forward it to their respective internal routers.

Summarization also helps increase the network's stability, because it reduces unnecessary LSA flooding. This directly affects the amount of bandwidth, CPU, and memory resources consumed by the OSPF routing process. Without route summarization, every specific-link LSA is propagated into the OSPF backbone and beyond, causing unnecessary network traffic and router overhead.

In Figure 6-17, a network link on R1a fails.

R1a sends an LSA to R1. However, R1 does not propagate the update, because it has a summary route configured. Specific-link LSA flooding outside the area does not occur.

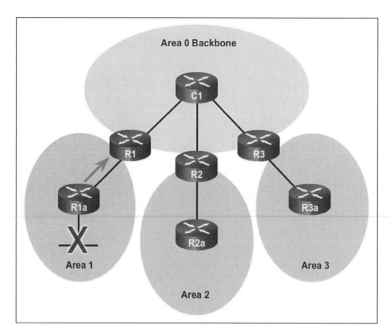

**Figure 6-17**    Suppressing Updates with Summarization

## Interarea and External Route Summarization (6.2.2.2)

In OSPF, summarization can only be configured on ABRs or ASBRs. Instead of advertising many specific networks, the ABR routers and ASBR routers advertise a summary route. ABR routers summarize type 3 LSAs and ASBR routers summarize type 5 LSAs.

By default, summary LSAs (type 3 LSAs) and external LSAs (type 5 LSAs) do not contain summarized (aggregated) routes; that is, by default, summary LSAs are not summarized.

Route summarization can be configured as follows:

- **Interarea route summarization:** Interarea route summarization, as shown in Figure 6-18, occurs on ABRs and applies to routes from within each area. It does not apply to external routes injected into OSPF through redistribution. To perform effective interarea route summarization, network addresses within areas should be assigned contiguously so that these addresses can be summarized into a minimal number of summary addresses.

**Figure 6-18**   Summarizing Interarea Routes on ABRs

- **External route summarization:** External route summarization is specific to external routes that are injected into OSPF through route redistribution. Again, it is important to ensure the contiguity of the external address ranges that are being summarized. Generally, only ASBRs summarize external routes. As shown in Figure 6-19, EIGRP external routes are summarized by ASBR R2 in a single LSA and sent to R1 and R3.

**Figure 6-19**   Summarizing External Routes on an ASBR

**Note**

External route summarization is configured on ASBRs using the **summary-address** *address mask* router configuration mode command.

## Interarea Route Summarization (6.2.2.3)

OSPF does not perform auto-summarization. Interarea summarization must be manually configured on ABRs.

Summarization of internal routes can only be done by ABRs. When summarization is enabled on an ABR, it injects into the backbone a single type 3 LSA describing the summary route. Multiple routes inside the area are summarized by the one LSA.

A summary route is generated if at least one subnet within the area falls in the summary address range. The summarized route metric is equal to the lowest cost of all subnets within the summary address range.

**Note**

An ABR can only summarize routes that are within the areas connected to the ABR.

Figure 6-20 shows a multiarea OSPF topology.

**Figure 6-20**  Summarizing Interarea Routes Example

In the following examples, the routing tables of R1 and R3 are examined to see the effect of the summarization.

Example 6-3 displays the R1 routing table before summarization is configured.

**Example 6-3**   Verify the R1 Routing Table Before Summarization

```
R1# show ip route ospf | begin Gateway
Gateway of last resort is not set


      10.0.0.0/8 is variably subnetted, 5 subnets, 2 masks
O        10.2.1.0/24 [110/648] via 192.168.10.2, 00:00:49, Serial0/0/0
O IA   192.168.1.0/24 [110/1295] via 192.168.10.2, 00:00:49, Serial0/0/0
O IA   192.168.2.0/24 [110/1295] via 192.168.10.2, 00:00:49, Serial0/0/0
      192.168.10.0/24 is variably subnetted, 3 subnets, 2 masks
O        192.168.10.4/30 [110/1294] via 192.168.10.2, 00:00:49, Serial0/0/0
R1#
```

Example 6-4 displays the R3 routing table before summarization.

**Example 6-4**   Verify the R3 Routing Table Before Summarization

```
R3# show ip route ospf | begin Gateway
Gateway of last resort is not set


      10.0.0.0/24 is subnetted, 3 subnets
O IA     10.1.1.0 [110/1295] via 192.168.10.5, 00:27:14, Serial0/0/1
O IA     10.1.2.0 [110/1295] via 192.168.10.5, 00:27:14, Serial0/0/1
O        10.2.1.0 [110/648] via 192.168.10.5, 00:27:57, Serial0/0/1
      192.168.10.0/24 is variably subnetted, 3 subnets, 2 masks
O        192.168.10.0/30 [110/1294] via 192.168.10.5, 00:27:57, Serial0/0/1
R3#
```

Notice how R3 currently has two interarea entries to the R1 area 1 networks.

## Calculating the Summary Route (6.2.2.4)

Figure 6-21 illustrates the three steps to summarizing networks into a single address.

The three steps shown in the figure are as follows:

**Step 1.**   List the networks in binary format. In the example, the two area 1 networks 10.1.1.0/24 and 10.1.2.0/24 are listed in binary format.

**Step 2.**   Count the number of far-left matching bits to determine the mask for the summary route. As highlighted, the first 22 far-left matching bits match. This results in the prefix /22 or subnet mask 255.255.252.0.

**Step 3.**   Copy the matching bits and then add zero bits to determine the summarized network address. In this example, the matching bits with zeros at the end result in a network address of 10.1.0.0/22. This summary address summarizes four networks: 10.1.0.0/24, 10.1.1.0/24, 10.1.2.0/24, and 10.1.3.0/24.

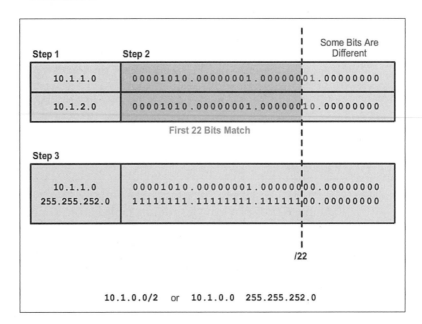

**Figure 6-21**   Calculating the Summary Route

In Figure 6-21, the summary address matches four networks, although only two networks exist.

## Configuring Interarea Route Summarization (6.2.2.5)

To demonstrate the effect of route summarization, Example 6-5 shows how R1 is configured to summarize the two internal area 1 routes into one OSPF interarea summary route.

**Example 6-5**   Summarizing Area 1 Routes on R1

```
R1(config)# router ospf 10
R1(config-router)# area 1 range 10.1.0.0 255.255.252.0
R1(config-router)#
```

As shown in the example, to manually configure interarea route summarization on an ABR, use the **area** *area-id* **range** *address mask* router configuration mode command. This instructs the ABR to summarize routes for a specific area before injecting them into a different area, through the backbone as type 3 summary LSAs. The summarized route 10.1.0.0/22 actually summarizes four network addresses, 10.1.0.0/24 to 10.1.3.0/24.

> **Note**
>
> In OSPFv3, the command is identical except for the IPv6 network address. The command syntax for OSPFv3 is **area** *area-id* **range** *prefix/prefix-length*.

Example 6-6 displays the IPv4 routing table of R1.

**Example 6-6**   Verify the R1 Routing Table After Summarization

```
R1# show ip route ospf | begin Gateway
Gateway of last resort is not set

      10.0.0.0/8 is variably subnetted, 6 subnets, 3 masks
O        10.1.0.0/22 is a summary, 00:00:09, Null0
O         10.2.1.0/24 [110/648] via 192.168.10.2, 00:00:09, Serial0/0/0
O IA  192.168.1.0/24 [110/1295] via 192.168.10.2, 00:00:09, Serial0/0/0
O IA  192.168.2.0/24 [110/1295] via 192.168.10.2, 00:00:09, Serial0/0/0
      192.168.10.0/24 is variably subnetted, 3 subnets, 2 masks
O         192.168.10.4/30 [110/1294] via 192.168.10.2, 00:00:09, Serial0/0/0
R1#
```

Notice how a new entry has appeared with a Null0 exit interface. The Cisco IOS automatically creates a bogus summary route to the Null0 interface when manual summarization is configured to prevent routing loops. A packet sent to a null interface is dropped.

For example, assume that R1 received a packet destined for 10.1.0.10. Although it would match the R1 summary route, R1 does not have a valid route in area 1. Therefore, R1 would refer to the routing table for the next longest match, which would be the Null0 entry. The packet would get forwarded to the Null0 interface and dropped. This prevents the router from forwarding the packet to a default route and possibly creating a routing loop.

Example 6-7 displays the updated R3 routing table.

**Example 6-7**   Verify the R3 Routing Table After Summarization

```
R3# show ip route ospf | begin Gateway
Gateway of last resort is not set

      10.0.0.0/8 is variably subnetted, 2 subnets, 2 masks
```

```
O IA      10.1.0.0/22 [110/1295] via 192.168.10.5, 00:00:06, Serial0/0/1
O         10.2.1.0/24 [110/648] via 192.168.10.5, 00:29:23, Serial0/0/1
       192.168.10.0/24 is variably subnetted, 3 subnets, 2 masks
O         192.168.10.0/30 [110/1294] via 192.168.10.5, 00:29:23, Serial0/0/1
R3#
```

Notice how there is now only one interarea entry going to the summary route 10.1.0.0/22. Although this example only reduced the routing table by one entry, summarization could be implemented to summarize many networks. This would reduce the size of routing tables.

The internal routes in area 2 can also be summarized on R3, as shown in Example 6-8.

**Example 6-8**   *Summarizing and Verifying Area 2 Routes on R3*

```
R3(config)# router ospf 10
R3(config-router)# area 2 range 192.168.0.0 255.255.252.0
R3(config-router)# end
R3# show ip route ospf | Gateway

Gateway of last resort is not set

      10.0.0.0/8 is variably subnetted, 2 subnets, 2 masks
O IA      10.1.0.0/22 [110/1295] via 192.168.10.5, 00:01:07, Serial0/0/1
O         10.2.1.0/24 [110/648] via 192.168.10.5, 00:01:07, Serial0/0/1
O      192.168.0.0/22 is a summary, 00:01:07, Null0
       192.168.10.0/24 is variably subnetted, 3 subnets, 2 masks
O         192.168.10.0/30 [110/1294] via 192.168.10.5, 00:01:07, Serial0/0/1
R3#
```

# Verifying Multiarea OSPF (6.2.3)

The commands used to verify multiarea OSPF are the same as single-area OSPF. However, the output is slightly different.

## Verifying Multiarea OSPF (6.2.3.1)

The same verification commands used to verify single-area OSPF also can be used to verify the multiarea OSPF topology:

- **show ip ospf neighbor**
- **show ip ospf**
- **show ip ospf interface**

Commands that verify specific multiarea information include

- **show ip protocols**
- **show ip ospf interface brief**
- **show ip route ospf**
- **show ip ospf database**

**Note**

For the equivalent OSPFv3 command, simply substitute **ip** with **ipv6**.

## Verify General Multiarea OSPF Settings (6.2.3.2)

Use the **show ip protocols** command to verify the OSPF status. The output of the command reveals which routing protocols are configured on a router. It also includes routing protocol specifics such as the router ID, number of areas in the router, and networks included within the routing protocol configuration.

Example 6-9 displays the OSPF settings of R1.

**Example 6-9**   Verifying Multiarea OSPF Status on R1

```
R1# show ip protocols
*** IP Routing is NSF aware ***

Routing Protocol is "ospf 10"
  Outgoing update filter list for all interfaces is not set
  Incoming update filter list for all interfaces is not set
  Router ID 1.1.1.1
  It is an area border router
  Number of areas in this router is 2. 2 normal 0 stub 0 nssa
  Maximum path: 4
  Routing for Networks:
    10.1.1.1 0.0.0.0 area 1
    10.1.2.1 0.0.0.0 area 1
    192.168.10.1 0.0.0.0 area 0
  Routing Information Sources:
    Gateway         Distance      Last Update
    3.3.3.3              110      02:20:36
    2.2.2.2              110      02:20:39
  Distance: (default is 110)

R1#
```

Notice that the command shows that there are two areas. The "Routing for Networks" section identifies the networks and their respective areas.

Use the **show ip ospf interface brief** command to display concise OSPF-related information of OSPF-enabled interfaces. This command reveals useful information, such as the OSPF process ID that the interface is assigned to, the area that the interfaces are in, and the cost of the interface.

Example 6-10 verifies the OSPF-enabled interfaces and the areas to which they belong.

**Example 6-10**   Verifying OSPF-Enabled Interface on R1

```
R1# show ip ospf interface brief
Interface     PID   Area         IP Address/Mask     Cost  State  Nbrs F/C
Se0/0/0       10    0            192.168.10.1/30     64    P2P    1/1
Gi0/1         10    1            10.1.2.1/24         1     DR     0/0
Gi0/0         10    1            10.1.1.1/24         1     DR     0/0
R1#
```

Example 6-11 shows the same verification commands for R2 and R3.

**Example 6-11**   Verifying Multiarea OSPF Status and Interfaces on R2 and R3

```
R2# show ip protocols
*** IP Routing is NSF aware ***

Routing Protocol is "ospf 10"
  Outgoing update filter list for all interfaces is not set
  Incoming update filter list for all interfaces is not set
  Router ID 2.2.2.2
  Number of areas in this router is 1. 1 normal 0 stub 0 nssa
  Maximum path: 4
  Routing for Networks:
    10.2.1.0 0.0.0.255 area 0
    192.168.10.0 0.0.0.7 area 0
  Routing Information Sources:
    Gateway         Distance      Last Update
    3.3.3.3              110      00:05:34
    1.1.1.1              110      00:05:34
  Distance: (default is 110)


R2# show ip ospf interface brief
Interface     PID   Area         IP Address/Mask     Cost  State  Nbrs F/C
Se0/0/1       10    0            192.168.10.5/30     647   P2P    1/1
```

```
Se0/0/0      10    0                   192.168.10.2/30  647  P2P  1/1
Gi0/0        10    0                   10.2.1.1/24      1    DR   0/0
R2#
```

```
R3# show ip protocols
*** IP Routing is NSF aware ***

Routing Protocol is "ospf 10"
  Outgoing update filter list for all interfaces is not set
  Incoming update filter list for all interfaces is not set
  Router ID 3.3.3.3
  It is an area border router
  Number of areas in this router is 2. 2 normal 0 stub 0 nssa
  Maximum path: 4
  Routing for Networks:
    192.168.1.1 0.0.0.0 area 2
    192.168.2.1 0.0.0.0 area 2
    192.168.10.4 0.0.0.3 area 0
  Routing Information Sources:
    Gateway         Distance      Last Update
    1.1.1.1              110      00:06:25
    2.2.2.2              110      00:06:25
  Distance: (default is 110)

R3# show ip ospf interface brief
Interface    PID   Area          IP Address/Mask   Cost  State Nbrs F/C
Se0/0/1      10    0             192.168.10.6/30   647   P2P   1/1
Gi0/1        10    2             192.168.2.1/24    1     DR    0/0
Gi0/0        10    2             192.168.1.1/24    1     DR    0/0
R3#
```

## Verify the OSPF Routes (6.2.3.3)

The most common command used to verify a multiarea OSPF configuration is the
**show ip route** command. Add the **ospf** parameter to display only OSPF-related
information. Example 6-12 displays the routing table of R1.

**Example 6-12**   Verifying Multiarea OSPF Routes on R1

```
R1# show ip route ospf | begin Gateway
Gateway of last resort is not set


      10.0.0.0/8 is variably subnetted, 5 subnets, 2 masks
```

```
O          10.2.1.0/24 [110/648] via 192.168.10.2, 00:26:03, Serial0/0/0
O IA   192.168.1.0/24 [110/1295] via 192.168.10.2, 00:26:03, Serial0/0/0
O IA   192.168.2.0/24 [110/1295] via 192.168.10.2, 00:26:03, Serial0/0/0
       192.168.10.0/24 is variably subnetted, 3 subnets, 2 masks
O          192.168.10.4/30 [110/1294] via 192.168.10.2, 00:26:03, Serial0/0/0
R1#
```

Notice how the O IA entries in the routing table identify networks learned from other areas. Specifically, O represents OSPF routes, and IA represents interarea, which means that the route originated from another area. Recall that R1 is in area 0, and the 192.168.1.0 and 192.168.2.0 subnets are connected to R3 in area 2. The [110/1295] entry in the routing table represents the administrative distance that is assigned to OSPF (110) and the total cost of the routes (cost of 1295).

Example 6-13 shows the OSPF routes for R2 and R3.

**Example 6-13**   Verifying Multiarea OSPF Routes on R2 and R3

```
R2# show ip route ospf | begin Gateway
Gateway of last resort is not set


       10.0.0.0/8 is variably subnetted, 4 subnets, 2 masks
O IA     10.1.1.0/24 [110/648] via 192.168.10.1, 00:07:52, Serial0/0/0
O IA     10.1.2.0/24 [110/648] via 192.168.10.1, 00:07:52, Serial0/0/0
O IA   192.168.1.0/24 [110/648] via 192.168.10.6, 00:07:52, Serial0/0/1
O IA   192.168.2.0/24 [110/648] via 192.168.10.6, 00:07:52, Serial0/0/1
R2#
```
```
R3# show ip route ospf | begin Gateway
Gateway of last resort is not set


       10.0.0.0/24 is subnetted, 3 subnets
O IA     10.1.1.0 [110/1295] via 192.168.10.5, 00:12:36, Serial0/0/1
O IA     10.1.2.0 [110/1295] via 192.168.10.5, 00:12:36, Serial0/0/1
O        10.2.1.0 [110/648] via 192.168.10.5, 00:12:36, Serial0/0/1
       192.168.10.0/24 is variably subnetted, 3 subnets, 2 masks
O          192.168.10.0/30 [110/1294] via 192.168.10.5, 00:12:36, Serial0/0/1
R3#
```

## Verify the Multiarea OSPF LSDB (6.2.3.4)

Use the **show ip ospf database** command to verify the contents of the LSDB. Example 6-14 displays the contents of the LSDB of R1.

**Example 6-14**    Verifying the OSPF LSDB on R1

```
R1# show ip ospf database

             OSPF Router with ID (1.1.1.1) (Process ID 10)

             Router Link States (Area 0)

Link ID         ADV Router      Age        Seq#       Checksum Link count
1.1.1.1         1.1.1.1         725        0x80000005 0x00F9B0 2
2.2.2.2         2.2.2.2         695        0x80000007 0x003DB1 5
3.3.3.3         3.3.3.3         681        0x80000005 0x00FF91 2


             Summary Net Link States (Area 0)

Link ID         ADV Router      Age        Seq#       Checksum
10.1.1.0        1.1.1.1         725        0x80000006 0x00D155
10.1.2.0        1.1.1.1         725        0x80000005 0x00C85E
192.168.1.0     3.3.3.3         681        0x80000006 0x00724E
192.168.2.0     3.3.3.3         681        0x80000005 0x006957

             Router Link States (Area 1)

Link ID         ADV Router      Age        Seq#       Checksum Link count
1.1.1.1         1.1.1.1         725        0x80000006 0x007D7C 2


             Summary Net Link States (Area 1)

Link ID         ADV Router      Age        Seq#       Checksum
10.2.1.0        1.1.1.1         725        0x80000005 0x004A9C
192.168.1.0     1.1.1.1         725        0x80000005 0x00B593
192.168.2.0     1.1.1.1         725        0x80000005 0x00AA9D
192.168.10.0    1.1.1.1         725        0x80000005 0x00B3D0
192.168.10.4    1.1.1.1         725        0x80000005 0x000E32
R1#
```

Notice that R1 has entries for area 0 and area 1, because ABRs must maintain a separate LSDB for each area to which they belong. In the output, "Router Link States" in area 0 identifies three routers. The "Summary Net Link States" section identifies networks learned from other areas and which neighbor advertised the network.

Example 6-15 shows the LSDB for R2 and R3 using the **show ip ospf database** command.

**Example 6-15**   Verifying the OSPF LSDB on R2 and R3

```
R2# show ip ospf database

            OSPF Router with ID (2.2.2.2) (Process ID 10)


            Router Link States (Area 0)


Link ID          ADV Router       Age        Seq#        Checksum Link count
1.1.1.1          1.1.1.1          843        0x80000002 0x00B961 2

2.2.2.2          2.2.2.2          839        0x80000004 0x007458 5

3.3.3.3          3.3.3.3          834        0x80000002 0x00BF42 2


            Summary Net Link States (Area 0)


Link ID          ADV Router       Age        Seq#        Checksum
10.1.1.0         1.1.1.1          117        0x80000002 0x00D951

10.1.2.0         1.1.1.1          117        0x80000002 0x00CE5B

192.168.1.0      3.3.3.3          103        0x80000003 0x00784B

192.168.2.0      3.3.3.3          103        0x80000002 0x006F54
R2#




R3# show ip ospf database

            OSPF Router with ID (3.3.3.3) (Process ID 10)


            Router Link States (Area 0)


Link ID          ADV Router       Age        Seq#        Checksum Link count
1.1.1.1          1.1.1.1          904        0x80000002 0x00B961 2

2.2.2.2          2.2.2.2          900        0x80000004 0x007458 5

3.3.3.3          3.3.3.3          893        0x80000002 0x00BF42 2


            Summary Net Link States (Area 0)


Link ID          ADV Router       Age        Seq#        Checksum
10.1.1.0         1.1.1.1          178        0x80000002 0x00D951

10.1.2.0         1.1.1.1          178        0x80000002 0x00CE5B

192.168.1.0      3.3.3.3          162        0x80000003 0x00784B

192.168.2.0      3.3.3.3          162        0x80000002 0x006F54
```

```
                    Router Link States (Area 2)

Link ID           ADV Router       Age        Seq#        Checksum Link count
3.3.3.3           3.3.3.3          162        0x80000003 0x00CF60 2


                    Summary Net Link States (Area 2)

Link ID           ADV Router       Age        Seq#        Checksum
10.1.1.0          3.3.3.3          892        0x80000003 0x0055B9
10.1.2.0          3.3.3.3          892        0x80000003 0x004AC3
10.2.1.0          3.3.3.3          892        0x80000002 0x00EEA9
192.168.10.0      3.3.3.3          892        0x80000003 0x00B2F8
192.168.10.4      3.3.3.3          892        0x80000002 0x003002
R3#
```

R2 only has interfaces in area 0; therefore, only one LSDB is required. Like R1, R3 contains two LSDBs.

## Verify Multiarea OSPFv3 (6.2.3.5)

Like OSPFv2, OSPFv3 provides similar OSPFv3 verification commands. Example 6-16 displays the OSPFv3 settings of R1.

**Example 6-16**   Verifying the Multiarea OSPFv3 Status on R1

```
R1# show ipv6 protocols
IPv6 Routing Protocol is "connected"
IPv6 Routing Protocol is "ND"
IPv6 Routing Protocol is "ospf 10"
  Router ID 1.1.1.1
  Area border router
  Number of areas: 2 normal, 0 stub, 0 nssa
  Interfaces (Area 0):
    Serial0/0/0
  Interfaces (Area 1):
    GigabitEthernet0/0
  Redistribution:
    None
R1#
```

Notice that the command confirms that there are now two areas. It also identifies each interface enabled for the respective area.

Example 6-17 verifies the OSPFv3-enabled interfaces and the area to which they belong.

**Example 6-17**   Verifying the OSPFv3-Enabled Interface on R1

```
R1# show ipv6 ospf interface brief
Interface    PID   Area          Intf ID    Cost   State Nbrs F/C
Se0/0/0      10    0             6          647    P2P   1/1
Gi0/0        10    1             3          1      DR    0/0
R1#
```

Example 6-18 displays the routing table of R1.

**Example 6-18**   Verifying the OSPFv3 Routing Table on R1

```
R1# show ipv6 route ospf
IPv6 Routing Table - default - 8 entries
Codes: C - Connected, L - Local, S - Static, U - Per-user Static route
       B - BGP, R - RIP, H - NHRP, I1 - ISIS L1
       I2 - ISIS L2, IA - ISIS interarea, IS - ISIS summary, D - EIGRP
       EX - EIGRP external, ND - ND Default, NDp - ND Prefix, DCE - Destination
       NDr - Redirect, O - OSPF Intra, OI - OSPF Inter, OE1 - OSPF ext 1
       OE2 - OSPF ext 2, ON1 - OSPF NSSA ext 1, ON2 - OSPF NSSA ext 2
O    2001:DB8:CAFE:2::/64 [110/648]
     via FE80::2, Serial0/0/0
OI   2001:DB8:CAFE:3::/64 [110/1295]
     via FE80::2, Serial0/0/0
O    2001:DB8:CAFE:A002::/64 [110/1294]
     via FE80::2, Serial0/0/0
R1#
```

Notice how the IPv6 routing table displays OI entries in the routing table to identify networks learned from other areas. Specifically, O represents OSPF routes and I represents interarea, which means that the route originated from another area. Recall that R1 is in area 0, and the 2001:DB8:CAFE3::/64 subnet is connected to R3 in area 2. The [110/1295] entry in the routing table represents the administrative distance that is assigned to OSPF (110) and the total cost of the routes (cost of 1295).

Example 6-19 displays the contents of the LSDB of R1.

**Example 6-19**   Verifying the OSPFv3 Database on R1

```
R1# show ipv6 ospf database


             OSPFv3 Router with ID (1.1.1.1) (Process ID 10)


            Router Link States (Area 0)


ADV Router       Age         Seq#       Fragment ID  Link count  Bits
 1.1.1.1         1617        0x80000002  0              1          B
 2.2.2.2         1484        0x80000002  0              2          None
 3.3.3.3         1485        0x80000001  0              1          B


            Inter Area Prefix Link States (Area 0)


ADV Router       Age         Seq#        Prefix
 1.1.1.1         1833        0x80000001  2001:DB8:CAFE:1::/64
 3.3.3.3         1476        0x80000001  2001:DB8:CAFE:3::/64


            Link (Type-8) Link States (Area 0)


ADV Router       Age         Seq#        Link ID    Interface
 1.1.1.1         1843        0x80000001  6          Se0/0/0
 2.2.2.2         1619        0x80000001  6          Se0/0/0


            Intra Area Prefix Link States (Area 0)


ADV Router       Age         Seq#        Link ID    Ref-lstype  Ref-LSID
 1.1.1.1         1843        0x80000001  0          0x2001      0
 2.2.2.2         1614        0x80000002  0          0x2001      0
 3.3.3.3         1486        0x80000001  0          0x2001      0


            Router Link States (Area 1)


ADV Router       Age         Seq#       Fragment ID  Link count  Bits
 1.1.1.1         1843        0x80000001  0              0          B


            Inter Area Prefix Link States (Area 1)


ADV Router       Age         Seq#        Prefix
 1.1.1.1         1833        0x80000001  2001:DB8:CAFE:A001::/64
 1.1.1.1         1613        0x80000001  2001:DB8:CAFE:A002::/64
 1.1.1.1         1613        0x80000001  2001:DB8:CAFE:2::/64
 1.1.1.1         1474        0x80000001  2001:DB8:CAFE:3::/64
```

```
                    Link (Type-8) Link States (Area 1)

ADV Router          Age           Seq#          Link ID     Interface
  1.1.1.1           1844          0x80000001   3            Gi0/0


                 Intra Area Prefix Link States (Area 1)

ADV Router          Age           Seq#          Link ID     Ref-lstype   Ref-LSID
  1.1.1.1           1844          0x80000001   0            0x2001       0
R1#
```

The command offers similar information to its OSPFv2 counterpart. However, the OSPFv3 LSDB contains additional LSA types not available in OSPFv2.

### Packet Tracer Activity 6.2.3.6: Configuring Multiarea OSPFv2

In this activity, you will configure multiarea OSPFv2. The network is already connected and interfaces are configured with IPv4 addressing. Your job is to enable multiarea OSPFv2, verify connectivity, and examine the operation of multiarea OSPFv2.

### Packet Tracer Activity 6.2.3.7: Configuring Multiarea OSPFv3

In this activity, you will configure multiarea OSPFv3. The network is already connected and interfaces are configured with IPv6 addressing. Your job is to enable multiarea OSPFv3, verify connectivity, and examine the operation of multiarea OSPFv3.

### Lab 6.2.3.8: Configuring Multiarea OSPFv2

In this lab, you will complete the following objectives:

- Part 1: Build the Network and Configure Basic Device Settings
- Part 2: Configure a Multiarea OSPFv2 Network
- Part 3: Configure Interarea Summary Routes

**Lab 6.2.3.9: Configuring Multiarea OSPFv3**

In this lab, you will complete the following objectives:

- Part 1: Build the Network and Configure Basic Device Settings
- Part 2: Configure Multiarea OSPFv3 Routing
- Part 3: Configure Interarea Route Summarization

**Lab 6.2.3.10: Troubleshooting Multiarea OSPFv2 and OSPFv3**

In this lab, you will complete the following objectives:

- Part 1: Build the Network and Load Device Configurations
- Part 2: Troubleshoot Layer 3 Connectivity
- Part 3: Troubleshoot OSPFv2
- Part 4: Troubleshoot OSPFv3

# Summary (6.3)

### Class Activity 6.3.1.1: Digital Trolleys

Your city has an aging digital trolley system based on a one-area design. All communications within this one area are taking longer to process as trolleys are being added to routes serving the population of your growing city. Trolley departures and arrivals are also taking a little longer, because each trolley must check large routing tables to determine where to pick up and deliver residents from their source and destination streets.

A concerned citizen has come up with the idea of dividing the city into different areas for a more efficient way to determine trolley routing information. It is thought that if the trolley maps are smaller, the system might be improved because of faster and smaller updates to the routing tables.

Your city board approves and implements the new area-based, digital trolley system. But to ensure that the new area routes are more efficient, the city board needs data to show the results at the next open board meeting.

Complete the directions found in the PDF for this activity. Share your answers with your class.

---

Packet Tracer
☐ Activity

Single-area OSPF is useful in smaller networks, but in larger networks, multiarea OSPF is a better choice. Multiarea OSPF solves the issues of a large routing table, large link-state database, and frequent SPF algorithm calculations.

The main area is called the backbone area (area 0), and all other areas must connect to the backbone area. Routing still occurs between the areas while many of the routing operations, such as recalculating the database, are kept within an area.

There are four different types of OSPF routers: Internal router, backbone router, Area Border Router (ABR), and Autonomous System Boundary Router (ASBR). A router can be classified as more than one router type.

Link-State Advertisements (LSAs) are the building blocks of OSPF. This chapter concentrated on LSA type 1 to LSA type 5. Type 1 LSAs are referred to as the router link entries. Type 2 LSAs are referred to as the network link entries and are flooded by a DR. Type 3 LSAs are referred to as the summary link entries and are created and propagated by ABRs. A type 4 summary LSA is generated by an ABR only when an ASBR exists within an area. Type 5 external LSAs describe routes to networks outside the OSPF autonomous system. Type 5 LSAs are originated by the ASBR and are flooded to the entire autonomous system.

OSPF routes in an IPv4 routing table are identified using the following descriptors: O, O IA, O*E1, or O*E2. Each router uses the SPF algorithm against the LSDB to build the SPF tree. The SPF tree is used to determine the best paths.

There are no special commands required to implement a multiarea OSPF network. A router simply becomes an ABR when it has two **network** statements in different areas.

Example 6-20 shows a multiarea OSPF configuration.

**Example 6-20**    Multiarea OSPFv2 Configuration

```
R1(config)# router ospf 10
R1(config-router)# router-id 1.1.1.1
R1(config-router)# network 10.1.1.1 0.0.0.0 area 1
R1(config-router)# network 10.1.2.1 0.0.0.0 area 1
R1(config-router)# network 192.168.10.1 0.0.0.0 area 0
```

OSPF does not perform auto-summarization. In OSPF, summarization can only be configured on ABRs or ASBRs. Interarea route summarization must be manually configured and occurs on ABRs and applies to routes from within each area. To manually configure interarea route summarization on an ABR, use the **area** *area-id* **range** *address mask* router configuration mode command.

External route summarization is specific to external routes that are injected into OSPF through route redistribution. Generally, only ASBRs summarize external routes. External route summarization is configured on ASBRs using the **summary-address** *address mask* router configuration mode command.

Commands that are used to verify OSPF configuration consist of the following:

- show ip ospf neighbor
- show ip ospf
- show ip ospf interface
- show ip protocols
- show ip ospf interface brief
- show ip route ospf
- show ip ospf database

# Practice

The following activities provide practice with the topics introduced in this chapter. The Labs and Class Activities are available in the companion *Scaling Networks Lab Manual* (ISBN 978-1-58713-325-1). The Packet Tracer Activities PKA files are found in the online course.

## Class Activities

- Class Activity 6.0.1.2: Leaving on a Jet Plane
- Class Activity 6.3.1.1: Digital Trolleys

## Labs

- Lab 6.2.3.8: Configuring Multiarea OSPFv2
- Lab 6.2.3.9: Configuring Multiarea OSPFv3
- Lab 6.2.3.10: Troubleshooting Multiarea OSPFv2 and OSPFv3

## Packet Tracer Activities

- Packet Tracer Activity 6.2.3.6: Configuring Multiarea OSPFv2
- Packet Tracer Activity 6.2.3.7: Configuring Multiarea OSPFv3

# Check Your Understanding Questions

Complete all the review questions listed to test your understanding of the topics and concepts in this chapter. The appendix "Answers to 'Check Your Understanding' Questions" lists the answers.

1. What are reasons for creating an OSPF network with multiple areas? (Choose two.)

   A. To reduce use of memory and processor resources
   B. To reduce SPF calculations
   C. To protect against the fact that not all routers support the OSPF backbone area
   D. To ensure that an area is used to connect the network to the Internet
   E. To simplify configuration

2. With multiarea OSPF, which OSPF router type has all interfaces in the same area?

   A.  Edge router

   B.  Internal router

   C.  Autonomous System Boundary Router

   D.  Area Border Router

3. Which of the following statements are OSPF characteristics? (Choose two.)

   A.  OSPF requires the **no auto-summary** command to prevent automatic route summarization.

   B.  OSPF routers within an area have the same link-state information.

   C.  OSPF requires many CPU cycles to calculate the shortest-path routes by using DUAL.

   D.  OSPF uses the SPF algorithm, which requires few CPU cycles.

   E.  OSPF routers can have large routing tables if routes are not summarized.

4. What is the correct order of statements for calculating the best path in an OSPF network?

   A.  All routers calculate the best path to other areas within the internetwork.

   B.  All routers calculate the best path to destinations within their area.

   C.  All routers calculate the best path to the external autonomous system destinations.

   A.  B, C, A

   B.  B, A, C

   C.  A, B, C

5. Which statement describes a characteristic of convergence in an OSPF network?

   A.  After it has converged, a router can communicate only within its autonomous system.

   B.  After it has converged, a router can communicate only with networks outside its autonomous system.

   C.  After it has converged, a router can communicate only with networks within its area.

   D.  After it has converged, a router can communicate with any network within or outside the OSPF autonomous system.

**6.** Refer to Example 6-21. Why are some of the entries marked O IA?

**Example 6-21**   Command Output for Question 6

```
R1# show ip route

<output omitted>

Gateway of last resort is 192.168.10.2 to network 0.0.0.0

O*E2  0.0.0.0/0 [110/1] via 192.168.10.2, 00:00:19, Serial0/0/0
           10.0.0.0/8 is variably subnetted, 5 subnets, 2 masks
C          10.1.1.0/24 is directly connected, GigabitEthernet0/0
L           10.1.1.1/32 is directly connected, GigabitEthernet0/0
C          10.1.2.0/24 is directly connected, GigabitEthernet0/1
L           10.1.2.1/32 is directly connected, GigabitEthernet0/1
O           10.2.1.0/24 [110/648] via 192.168.10.2, 00:04:34, Serial0/0/0
O IA  192.168.1.0/24 [110/1295] via 192.168.10.2, 00:01:48, Serial0/0/0
O IA  192.168.2.0/24 [110/1295] via 192.168.10.2, 00:01:48, Serial0/0/0
           192.168.10.0/24 is variably subnetted, 3 subnets, 2 masks
C          192.168.10.0/30 is directly connected, Serial0/0/0
L           192.168.10.1/32 is directly connected, Serial0/0/0
O         192.168.10.4/30 [110/1294] via 192.168.10.2, 00:01:55, Serial0/0/0
R1#
```

A.  They represent summary routes that are internal to the area.

B.  They correspond to entries that are learned from other areas.

C.  They are default routes that are learned from other routing protocols.

D.  They correspond to entries that are learned from other routing protocols.

**7.** Which type of routing table entry would indicate that an external route was redistributed into the multiarea OSPF process?

A.  S

B.  C

C.  O

D.  O IA

E.  O*E2

**8.** Refer to Example 6-22. A network administrator is configuring OSPFv3 on R1. Which command sequence is used to advertise the network that is attached to Gi0/0?

**Example 6-22** Configuration Commands for Question 8

```
R1(config)# interface GigabitEthernet 0/0
R1(config-if)# ipv6 address 2001:db8:acad:A::1/64
R1(config-if)# no shutdown
R1(config-if)# exit
R1(config)# ipv6 unicast-routing
R1(config)# ipv6 router ospf 3
R1(config-rtr)# router-id 1.1.1.1
R1(config-rtr)# exit
R1(config)#
```

A. R1(config)# **router ospf 3**

B. R1(config)# **interface GigabitEthernet 0/0**

   R1(config-if)# **ipv6 ospf network**

C. R1(config)# **ipv6 router ospf 3**

   R1(config-rtr)# **ipv6 ospf neighbor 2001:db8:acad:A::/64**

D. R1(config)# **interface GigabitEthernet 0/0**

   R1(config-if)# **ipv6 ospf 3 area 1**

**9.** Refer to Example 6-23. A network administrator is configuring OSPFv2 on R1. Which conclusion can be drawn based on the configuration?

**Example 6-23** Configuration Commands for Question 9

```
R1(config)# router ospf 3
R1(config-router)# router-id 1.1.1.1
R1(config-router)# network 172.16.1.64 0.0.0.63 area 1
R1(config-router)# network 172.16.1.192 0.0.0.63 area 1
R1(config-router)# network 192.168.10.0 0.0.0.7 area 0
R1(config-router)# end
R1#
```

A. R1 can advertise a summary route 172.16.64.0/25.

B. R1 has the lowest router ID in its area.

C. R1 is an ABR.

D. R1 runs three OSPFv2 processes.

10. A router has six networks that are connected to it with network IDs of 192.168.0.0/24, 192.168.1.0/24, 192.168.2.0/24, 192.168.3.0/24, 192.168.4.0/24, and 192.168.5.0/24. After summarization of these six networks, how many LSAs would be sent to advertise the summary route or routes?

    A. One

    B. Two

    C. Three

    D. Four

    E. Five

    F. Six

11. On which types of OSPF routers can route summarization be configured? (Choose two.)

    A. Internal

    B. ABR

    C. Boundary

    D. ASBR

12. Fill in the blank. What OSPF LSA type is described by each of the following statements?

    LSA type _____ identifies the ASBR and provides a route to it.

    LSA type _____ is used to advertise external (non-OSPF) network addresses.

    LSA type _____ identifies the routers and network address of the multiaccess link.

    LSA type _____ includes a list of directly attached network prefixes and link type.

    LSA type _____ is used by ABRs to advertise networks from other areas.

## Objectives

Upon completion of this chapter, you will be able to answer the following questions:

- What are the basic features of EIGRP?

- What types of packets are used to establish and maintain an EIGRP neighbor adjacency?

- How are EIGRP messages encapsulated?

- What are the commands to configure EIGRP for IPv4 in a small routed network?

- What are the commands to verify an EIGRP for IPv4 implementation in a small routed network?

- How are neighbor adjacencies formed using EIGRP?

- What is the purpose of the metrics used by EIGRP?

- How does DUAL operate and use the topology table?

- What events trigger EIGRP updates?

- What are the differences between the characteristics and operation of EIGRP for IPv4 and EIGRP for IPv6?

- What are the commands to configure EIGRP for IPv6 in a small routed network?

- What are the commands to verify an EIGRP for IPv6 implementation in a small routed network?

## Key Terms

This chapter uses the following key terms. You can find the definitions in the Glossary.

*Diffusing Update Algorithm (DUAL)* page 363

*Reliable Transport Protocol (RTP)* page 363

*partial updates* page 365

*bounded updates* page 365

*Hello packet* page 367

*Update packet* page 368

*Acknowledgment packet* page 369

*Query packet* page 369

*Reply packet* page 369

*type, length, value (TLV)* page 373

*Internet Assigned Numbers Authority (IANA)* page 379

*regional Internet registry (RIR)* page 380

*Border Gateway Protocol (BGP)* page 380

*composite metric* page 402

*Successor* page 413

*Feasible Distance (FD)* page 413

*Feasible Successor (FS)    page 413*

*Reported Distance (RD)    page 413*

*Advertised Distance (AD)    page 413*

*Feasible Condition (FC)    page 413*

*Finite State Machine (FSM)    page 414*

# Introduction (7.0.1.1)

Enhanced Interior Gateway Routing Protocol (EIGRP) is an advanced distance vector routing protocol developed by Cisco Systems. As the name suggests, EIGRP is an enhancement of another Cisco routing protocol, IGRP (Interior Gateway Routing Protocol). IGRP is an older classful, distance vector routing protocol, now obsolete since IOS Release 12.3.

EIGRP is a distance vector routing protocol that includes features found in link-state routing protocols. EIGRP is suited for many different topologies and media. In a well-designed network, EIGRP can scale to include multiple topologies and can provide extremely quick convergence times with minimal network traffic.

This chapter introduces EIGRP and provides basic configuration commands to enable it on a Cisco IOS router. It also explores the operation of the routing protocol and provides more detail on how EIGRP determines best path.

**Class Activity 7.0.1.2: Classless EIGRP**

EIGRP was introduced as a distance vector routing protocol in 1992. It was originally designed to work as a proprietary protocol on Cisco devices only. In 2013, EIGRP became a multivendor routing protocol, meaning that it can be used by other device vendors in addition to Cisco devices.

Complete the reflection questions that accompany the PDF file for this activity. Save your work and be prepared to share your answers with the class.

# Characteristics of EIGRP (7.1)

This section discusses the basic characteristics and operation of EIGRP, including packet types and the EIGRP message format.

## Basic Features of EIGRP (7.1.1)

Basic features of EIGRP include the *Diffusing Update Algorithm (DUAL)*, protocol-dependent modules (PDM), the *Reliable Transport Protocol (RTP)*, and authentication.

## Features of EIGRP (7.1.1.1)

Figure 7-1 shows all the current routing protocols for IPv4 and IPv6.

| | Interior Gateway Protocols | | | | Exterior Gateway Protocols |
|---|---|---|---|---|---|
| | Distance Vector Routing Protocols | | Link State Routing Protocols | | Path Vector |
| IPv4 | RIPv2 | EIGRP | OSPFv2 | IS-IS | BGP-4 |
| IPv6 | RIPng | EIGRP for IPv6 | OSPFv3 | IS-IS for IPv6 | BGP-4 for IPv6 |

**Figure 7-1**  Types of Routing Protocols

EIGRP was initially released in 1992 as a proprietary protocol available only on Cisco devices. In 2013, Cisco released a basic functionality of EIGRP as an open standard to the IETF as an informational RFC. This means that other networking vendors can now implement EIGRP on their equipment to interoperate with both Cisco and non-Cisco routers running EIGRP. However, advanced features of EIGRP, such as EIGRP stub, needed for the Dynamic Multipoint Virtual Private Network (DMVPN) deployment, will not be released to the IETF. As an informational RFC, Cisco will continue to maintain control of EIGRP.

EIGRP includes features of both link-state and distance vector routing protocols. However, EIGRP is still based on the key distance vector routing protocol principle, in which information about the rest of the network is learned from directly connected neighbors.

EIGRP is an advanced distance vector routing protocol that includes features not found in other distance vector routing protocols like RIP and IGRP.

### Diffusing Update Algorithm

As the computational engine that drives EIGRP, the Diffusing Update Algorithm (DUAL) resides at the center of the routing protocol. DUAL guarantees loop-free and backup paths throughout the routing domain. Using DUAL, EIGRP stores all available backup routes for destinations so that it can quickly adapt to alternate routes when necessary.

### Establishing Neighbor Adjacencies

EIGRP establishes relationships with directly connected routers that are also enabled for EIGRP. Neighbor adjacencies are used to track the status of these neighbors.

## Reliable Transport Protocol

The Reliable Transport Protocol (RTP) is unique to EIGRP and provides delivery of EIGRP packets to neighbors. RTP and the tracking of neighbor adjacencies set the stage for DUAL.

## Partial and Bounded Updates

EIGRP uses the terms *partial updates* and *bounded updates* when referring to its updates. Unlike RIP, EIGRP does not send periodic updates and route entries do not age out. The term *partial* means that the update only includes information about the route changes, such as a new link or a link becoming unavailable. The term *bounded* refers to the propagation of partial updates that are sent only to those routers that the changes affect. This minimizes the bandwidth that is required to send EIGRP updates.

## Equal and Unequal Cost Load Balancing

EIGRP supports equal cost load balancing and unequal cost load balancing, which allows administrators to better distribute traffic flow in their networks.

> **Note**
>
> The term *hybrid routing protocol* is used in some older documentation to define EIGRP. However, this term is misleading because EIGRP is not a hybrid between distance vector and link-state routing protocols. EIGRP is solely a distance vector routing protocol; therefore, Cisco no longer uses this term to refer to it.

## Protocol-Dependent Modules (7.1.1.2)

EIGRP has the capability to route several different protocols, including IPv4 and IPv6, using protocol-dependent modules (PDM). Although now obsolete, EIGRP also used PDMs to route Novell's IPX and Apple Computer's AppleTalk network layer protocols. EIGRP maintains three tables for each protocol, as shown in Figure 7-2.

PDMs are responsible for network layer protocol-specific tasks. An example is the EIGRP module that is responsible for sending and receiving EIGRP packets that are encapsulated in IPv4. This module is also responsible for parsing EIGRP packets and informing DUAL of the new information that is received. EIGRP asks DUAL to make routing decisions, but the results are stored in the IPv4 routing table.

**Figure 7-2** EIGRP Protocol-Dependent Modules (PDM)

PDMs are responsible for the specific routing tasks for each network layer protocol, including

- Maintaining the neighbor and topology tables of EIGRP routers that belong to that protocol suite

- Building and translating protocol-specific packets for DUAL

- Interfacing DUAL to the protocol-specific routing table

- Computing the metric and passing this information to DUAL

- Implementing filtering and access lists

- Performing redistribution functions to and from other routing protocols

- Redistributing routes that are learned by other routing protocols

When a router discovers a new neighbor, it records the neighbor's address and interface as an entry in the neighbor table. One neighbor table exists for each protocol-dependent module, such as IPv4. EIGRP also maintains a topology table. The topology table contains all destinations that are advertised by neighboring routers. There is also a separate topology table for each PDM.

## Reliable Transport Protocol (7.1.1.3)

EIGRP uses Reliable Transport Protocol (RTP) for the delivery and reception of EIGRP packets. EIGRP was designed as a network layer independent routing protocol; because of this design, EIGRP cannot use the services of UDP or TCP. This allows EIGRP to be used for protocols other than those from the TCP/IP protocol suite, such as IPX and AppleTalk. Figure 7-3 conceptually shows how RTP operates.

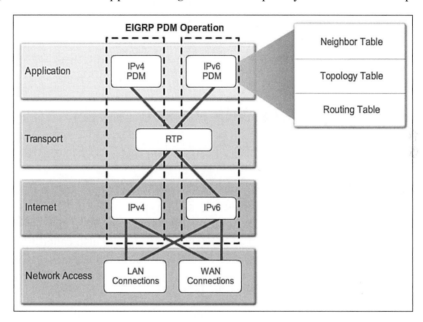

**Figure 7-3**   EIGRP Replaces TCP with RTP

Although "reliable" is part of its name, RTP includes both reliable delivery and unreliable delivery of EIGRP packets, similar to TCP and UDP, respectively. Reliable RTP requires an acknowledgment to be returned by the receiver to the sender. An unreliable RTP packet does not require an acknowledgment. For example, an EIGRP update packet is sent reliably over RTP and requires an acknowledgment. An EIGRP *Hello packet* is also sent over RTP, but unreliably. This means that EIGRP Hello packets do not require an acknowledgment.

RTP can send EIGRP packets as unicast or multicast.

- Multicast EIGRP packets for IPv4 use the reserved IPv4 multicast address 224.0.0.10.

- Multicast EIGRP packets for IPv6 are sent to the reserved IPv6 multicast address FF02::A.

## Authentication (7.1.1.4)

RIPv2, EIGRP, OSPF, IS-IS, and BGP can each be configured to authenticate their routing information.

It is a good practice to authenticate transmitted routing information. Doing so ensures that routers only accept routing information from other routers that have been configured with the same password or authentication information.

**Note**

Authentication does not encrypt the EIGRP routing updates.

# Types of EIGRP Packets (7.1.2)

EIGRP uses five messages to communicate with other EIGRP routers in the network.

## EIGRP Packet Types (7.1.2.1)

EIGRP uses five different packet types, some in pairs. EIGRP packets are sent using either RTP reliable or unreliable delivery and can be sent as a unicast, multicast, or sometimes both. EIGRP packet types are also called EIGRP packet formats or EIGRP messages. Table 7-1 lists and describes the five EIGRP packet types.

**Table 7-1** EIGRP Packet Types

| Packet Type | Description |
| --- | --- |
| Hello | Used to discover other EIGRP routers in the network |
| Acknowledgment | Used to acknowledge the receipt of any EIGRP packet |
| Update | Used to convey routing information to known destinations |
| Query | Used to request specific information from a neighbor router |
| Reply | Used to respond to a query |

**Hello packets:** Used for neighbor discovery and to maintain neighbor adjacencies.

- Sent with unreliable delivery
- Multicast (on most network types)

*Update packets*: Propagate routing information to EIGRP neighbors.

- Sent with reliable delivery
- Unicast or multicast

*Acknowledgment packets*: Used to acknowledge the receipt of an EIGRP message that was sent using reliable delivery.

- Sent with unreliable delivery
- Unicast

*Query packets*: Used to query routes from neighbors.

- Sent with reliable delivery
- Unicast or multicast

*Reply packets*: Sent in response to an EIGRP query.

- Sent with unreliable delivery
- Unicast

Figure 7-4 shows that EIGRP messages are typically encapsulated in IPv4 or IPv6 packets.

**Figure 7-4**    EIGRP Messages Are Sent Over IP

EIGRP for IPv4 messages use IPv4 as the network layer protocol. The IPv4 protocol field uses 88 to indicate that the data portion of the packet is an EIGRP for IPv4 message. EIGRP for IPv6 messages are encapsulated in IPv6 packets using the next header field of 88. Similar to the protocol field for IPv4, the IPv6 next header field indicates the type of data carried in the IPv6 packet.

## EIGRP Hello Packets (7.1.2.2)

EIGRP uses small Hello packets to discover other EIGRP-enabled routers on directly connected links. Hello packets are used by routers to form EIGRP neighbor adjacencies, also known as neighbor relationships.

EIGRP Hello packets are sent as IPv4 or IPv6 multicasts, and use RTP unreliable delivery. This means that the receiver does not reply with an acknowledgment packet.

- The reserved EIGRP multicast address for IPv4 is 224.0.0.10.

- The reserved EIGRP multicast address for IPv6 is FF02::A.

EIGRP routers discover neighbors and establish adjacencies with neighbor routers using the Hello packet. On most networks, EIGRP Hello packets are sent as multicast packets every five seconds. However, on multipoint, nonbroadcast multiple access (NBMA) networks, such as X.25, Frame Relay, and Asynchronous Transfer Mode (ATM) interfaces with access links of T1 (1.544 Mb/s) or slower, Hello packets are sent as unicast packets every 60 seconds. The default Hello intervals and hold timers are shown in Table 7-2.

**Table 7-2**    Default Hello Intervals and Hold Timers for EIGRP

| Bandwidth | Example Link | Default Hello Interval | Default Hold Time |
|---|---|---|---|
| 1.544 Mb/s | Multipoint Frame Relay | 60 seconds | 180 seconds |
| Greater than 1.544 Mb/s | T1, Ethernet | 5 seconds | 15 seconds |

EIGRP also uses Hello packets to maintain established adjacencies. An EIGRP router assumes that as long as it receives Hello packets from a neighbor, the neighbor and its routes remain viable.

EIGRP uses a Hold timer to determine the maximum time the router should wait to receive the next Hello before declaring that neighbor as unreachable. By default, the hold time is three times the Hello interval, or 15 seconds on most networks and 180 seconds on low-speed NBMA networks. If the hold time expires, EIGRP declares the route as down and DUAL searches for a new path by sending out queries.

## EIGRP Update and Acknowledgment Packets (7.1.2.3)

The first two packets discussed are Update and Acknowledgment packets.

## EIGRP Update Packets

EIGRP sends Update packets to propagate routing information. Update packets are sent only when necessary. EIGRP updates contain only the routing information needed and are sent only to those routers that require it.

Unlike RIP, EIGRP (another distance vector routing protocol) does not send periodic updates and route entries do not age out. Instead, EIGRP sends incremental updates only when the state of a destination changes. This can include when a new network becomes available, an existing network becomes unavailable, or a change occurs in the routing metric for an existing network.

EIGRP uses the terms *partial* and *bounded* when referring to its updates. The term *partial* means that the update only includes information about the route changes. The term *bounded* refers to the propagation of partial updates that are sent only to those routers that the changes affect.

By sending only the routing information that is needed only to those routers that need it, EIGRP minimizes the bandwidth that is required to send EIGRP updates.

EIGRP update packets use reliable delivery, which means that the sending router requires an acknowledgment. Update packets are sent as a multicast when required by multiple routers, or as a unicast when required by only a single router. In Figure 7-5, because the links are point-to-point, the updates are sent as unicasts.

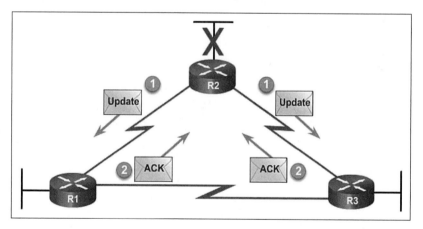

**Figure 7-5**    EIGRP Update and Acknowledgment Messages

## EIGRP Acknowledgment Packets

EIGRP sends Acknowledgment (ACK) packets when reliable delivery is used. An EIGRP acknowledgment is an EIGRP Hello packet without any data. RTP uses reliable delivery for EIGRP update, query, and reply packets. EIGRP acknowledgment packets are always sent as an unreliable unicast. Unreliable delivery makes sense; otherwise, there would be an endless loop of acknowledgments.

In Figure 7-5, R2 has lost connectivity to the LAN attached to its Gigabit Ethernet interface. R2 immediately sends an update to R1 and R3 noting the downed route. R1 and R3 respond with an acknowledgment to let R2 know that they have received the update.

**Note**

Some documentation refers to the Hello and Acknowledgment as a single type of EIGRP packet.

## EIGRP Query and Reply Packets (7.1.2.4)

The next two EIGRP packet types discussed are Query and Reply packets.

### EIGRP Query Packets

DUAL uses Query and Reply packets when searching for networks and other tasks. Queries and replies use reliable delivery. Queries can use multicast or unicast, whereas replies are always sent as unicast. In Figure 7-6, R2 has lost connectivity to the LAN and it sends out queries to all EIGRP neighbors searching for any possible routes to the LAN.

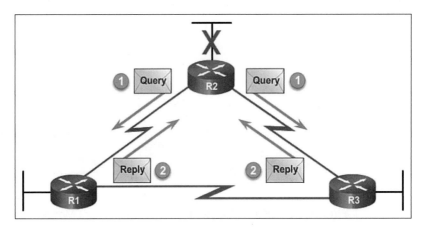

**Figure 7-6**   EIGRP Query and Reply Messages

Because queries use reliable delivery, the receiving router must return an EIGRP acknowledgment. The acknowledgment informs the sender of the query that it has received the query message. To keep this example simple, acknowledgments were omitted in the graphic.

### EIGRP Reply Packets

All neighbors must send a reply, regardless of whether they have a route to the downed network. Because replies also use reliable delivery, routers such as R2 must send an acknowledgment.

It might not be obvious why R2 would send out a query for a network it knows is down. Actually, only R2's interface that is attached to the network is down. Another router could be attached to the same LAN and have an alternate path to this same network. Therefore, R2 queries for such a router before completely removing the network from its topology table.

**Interactive Graphic**

**Activity 7.1.2.5: Identify the EIGRP Packet Type**

Go to the course online to perform this practice activity.

**Video**

**Video Demonstration 7.1.2.6: Observing EIGRP Protocol Communications**

Go to the course online to view this video.

## EIGRP Messages (7.1.3)

This topic discusses how the EIGRP message is encapsulated and the specific fields inside EIGRP messages.

### Encapsulating EIGRP Messages (7.1.3.1)

The data portion of an EIGRP message is encapsulated in a packet. This data field is called *type, length, value (TLV)*. The types of TLVs relevant to this course are EIGRP parameters, IP internal routes, and IP external routes.

The EIGRP packet header is included with every EIGRP packet, regardless of its type. The EIGRP packet header and TLV are then encapsulated in an IPv4 packet. In the IPv4 packet header, the protocol field is set to 88 to indicate EIGRP, and the IPv4 destination address is set to the multicast 224.0.0.10. If the EIGRP packet is encapsulated in an Ethernet frame, the destination MAC address is also a multicast address, 01-00-5E-00-00-0A.

Figure 7-7 shows the Data Link Ethernet Frame. EIGRP for IPv4 is encapsulated in an IPv4 packet. EIGRP for IPv6 would use a similar type of encapsulation. EIGRP for IPv6 is encapsulated using an IPv6 header. The IPv6 destination address would be the multicast address FF02::A, and the next header field would be set to 88.

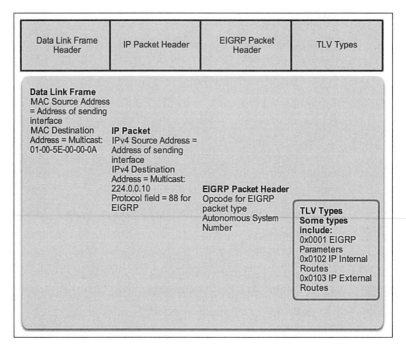

**Figure 7-7**   Encapsulated EIGRP Message

## EIGRP Packet Header and TLV (7.1.3.2)

Every EIGRP message includes the header, as shown in Figure 7-8.

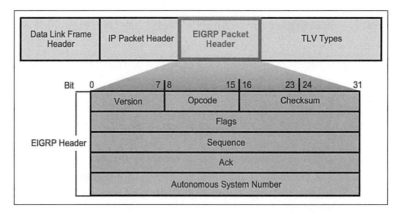

**Figure 7-8**   EIGRP Packet Header

Important fields include the Opcode field and the Autonomous System Number field. Opcode specifies the EIGRP packet type as follows:

- Update

- Query

- Reply

- Hello

The autonomous system number specifies the EIGRP routing process. Unlike RIP, multiple instances of EIGRP can run on a network; the autonomous system number is used to track each running EIGRP process.

Figure 7-9 shows the EIGRP parameter's TLV.

**Figure 7-9**  EIGRP TLV: Parameters

The EIGRP parameter's message includes the weights that EIGRP uses for its composite metric. By default, only bandwidth and delay are weighted. Both are weighted equally; therefore, the K1 field for bandwidth and the K3 field for delay are both set to 1. The other K values are set to 0.

The Hold Time is the amount of time the EIGRP neighbor receiving this message should wait before considering the advertising router to be down.

Figure 7-10 shows the IP Internal Routes TLV.

The IP internal message is used to advertise EIGRP routes within an autonomous system. Important fields include the metric fields (delay and bandwidth), the subnet mask field (prefix length), and the destination field.

Delay is calculated as the sum of delays from source to destination in units of 10 microseconds. Bandwidth is the lowest configured bandwidth of any interface along the route.

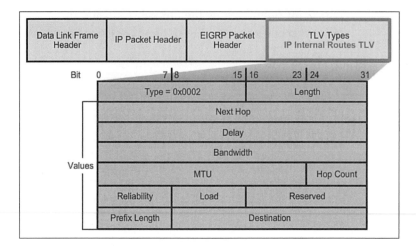

**Figure 7-10**   EIGRP TLV: Internal Routes

The subnet mask is specified as the prefix length or the number of network bits in the subnet mask. For example, the prefix length for the subnet mask 255.255.255.0 is 24, because 24 is the number of network bits.

The Destination field stores the address of the destination network. Although only 24 bits are shown in this figure, this field varies based on the value of the network portion of the 32-bit network address. For example, the network portion of 10.1.0.0/16 is 10.1; therefore, the Destination field stores the first 16 bits. Because the minimum length of this field is 24 bits, the remainder of the field is padded with 0s. If a network address is longer than 24 bits (192.168.1.32/27, for example), the Destination field is extended for another 32 bits (for a total of 56 bits) and the unused bits are padded with 0s.

Figure 7-11 shows the IP External Routes TLV.

The IP external message is used when external routes are imported into the EIGRP routing process. In this chapter, we will import or redistribute a default static route into EIGRP. Notice that the bottom half of the IP External Routes TLV includes all the fields used by the IP Internal TLV.

**Note**

The maximum transmission unit (MTU) is not a metric used by EIGRP. The MTU is included in the routing updates, but it is not used to determine the routing metric.

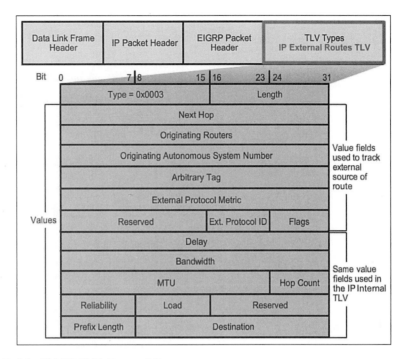

**Figure 7-11**   EIGRP TLV: External Routes

# Configuring EIGRP for IPv4 (7.2)

The section discusses the configuration and verification of EIGRP for IPv4.

## Configuring EIGRP with IPv4 (7.2.1)

Configuring EIGRP for IPv4 can be done very quickly with a few commands. However, this topic also discusses configuring the router ID and setting interfaces as passive.

### EIGRP Network Topology (7.2.1.1)

Figure 7-12 displays the topology that is used in this course to configure EIGRP for IPv4.

The types of serial interfaces and their associated bandwidths might not necessarily reflect the more common types of connections found in today's networks. The bandwidths of the serial links used in this topology were chosen to help explain the calculation of the routing protocol metrics and the process of best path selection.

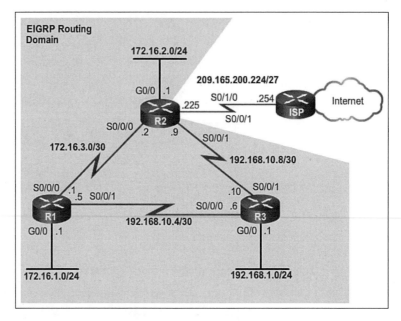

**Figure 7-12**   EIGRP for IPv4 Topology

The routers in the topology have a starting configuration, including addresses on the interfaces. There is currently no static routing or dynamic routing configured on any of the routers.

Example 7-1 shows the interface configurations for the three EIGRP routers in the topology. Only Routers R1, R2, and R3 are part of the EIGRP routing domain. The ISP router is used as the routing domain's gateway to the Internet.

**Example 7-1**   Interface Configurations

```
R1# show running-config
<Output omitted>
!
interface GigabitEthernet0/0
 ip address 172.16.1.1 255.255.255.0
!
interface Serial0/0/0
 ip address 172.16.3.1 255.255.255.252
 clock rate 64000
!
interface Serial0/0/1
 ip address 192.168.10.5 255.255.255.252
!
```

```
R2# show running-config
<Output omitted>
!
interface GigabitEthernet0/0
 ip address 172.16.2.1 255.255.255.0
!
interface Serial0/0/0
 ip address 172.16.3.2 255.255.255.252
!
interface Serial0/0/1
 ip address 192.168.10.9 255.255.255.252
 clock rate 64000
!
interface Serial0/1/0
 ip address 209.165.200.225 255.255.255.224
!
```

```
R3# show running-config
<Output omitted>
!
interface GigabitEthernet0/0
 ip address 192.168.1.1 255.255.255.0
!
interface Serial0/0/0
 ip address 192.168.10.6 255.255.255.252
 clock rate 64000
!
interface Serial0/0/1
 ip address 192.168.10.10 255.255.255.252
!
```

## Autonomous System Numbers (7.2.1.2)

EIGRP uses the **router eigrp** *autonomous-system* command to enable the EIGRP process. The autonomous system number referred to in the EIGRP configuration is not associated with the *Internet Assigned Numbers Authority (IANA)* globally assigned autonomous system numbers used by external routing protocols.

So what is the difference between the IANA globally assigned autonomous system number and the EIGRP autonomous system number?

An IANA globally assigned autonomous system is a collection of networks under the administrative control of a single entity that presents a common routing policy to the Internet. In Figure 7-13, companies A, B, C, and D are all under the administrative control of ISP1. ISP1 presents a common routing policy for all these companies when advertising routes to ISP2.

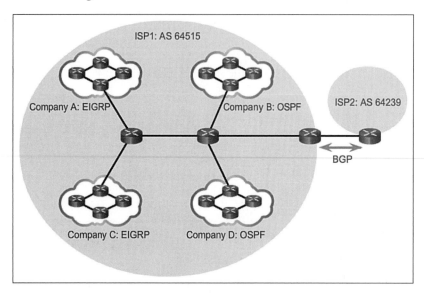

**Figure 7-13**   Autonomous Systems

The guidelines for the creation, selection, and registration of an autonomous system are described in RFC 1930. Global autonomous system numbers are assigned by IANA, the same authority that assigns IP address space. The local *regional Internet registry (RIR)* is responsible for assigning an autonomous system number to an entity from its block of assigned autonomous system numbers. Prior to 2007, autonomous system numbers were 16-bit numbers ranging from 0 to 65,535. Today, 32-bit autonomous system numbers are assigned, increasing the number of available autonomous system numbers to over 4 billion.

Usually Internet Service Providers (ISPs), Internet backbone providers, and large institutions connecting to other entities require an autonomous system number. These ISPs and large institutions use the exterior gateway routing protocol *Border Gateway Protocol (BGP)* to propagate routing information. BGP is the only routing protocol that uses an actual autonomous system number in its configuration.

The vast majority of companies and institutions with IP networks do not need an autonomous system number, because they are controlled by a larger entity, such as an ISP. These companies use interior gateway protocols, such as RIP, EIGRP, OSPF, and IS-IS to route packets within their own networks. They are one of many independent and separate networks within the autonomous system of the ISP. The ISP is responsible for the routing of packets within its autonomous system and between other autonomous systems.

The autonomous system number used for EIGRP configuration is only significant to the EIGRP routing domain. It functions as a process ID to help routers keep track of multiple, running instances of EIGRP. This is required because it is possible to have more than one instance of EIGRP running on a network. Each instance of EIGRP can be configured to support and exchange routing updates for different networks.

## The Router EIGRP Command (7.2.1.3)

The Cisco IOS includes the processes to enable and configure several different types of dynamic routing protocols. The **router** global configuration mode command is used to begin the configuration of any dynamic routing protocol. The topology shown in Figure 7-12 is used to demonstrate this command. As shown in Example 7-2, when followed by a question mark (**?**), the **router** global configuration mode command lists all the available routing protocols supported by this specific IOS release running on the router.

**Example 7-2**    Router Configuration Command

```
R1# conf t
Enter configuration commands, one per line.  End with CNTL/Z.
R1(config)# router ?
  bgp        Border Gateway Protocol (BGP)
  eigrp      Enhanced Interior Gateway Routing Protocol (EIGRP)
  isis       ISO IS-IS
  iso-igrp   IGRP for OSI networks
  lisp       Locator/ID Separation Protocol
  mobile     Mobile routes
  odr        On Demand stub Routes
  ospf       Open Shortest Path First (OSPF)
  rip        Routing Information Protocol (RIP)

R1(config)# router
```

The following global configuration mode command is used to enter the router configuration mode for EIGRP and begin the configuration of the EIGRP process:

```
Router(config)# router eigrp autonomous-system
```

The *autonomous-system* argument can be assigned to any 16-bit value between the number 1 and 65,535. All routers within the EIGRP routing domain must use the same autonomous system number.

Example 7-3 shows the configuration of the EIGRP process on Routers R1, R2, and R3. Notice that the prompt changes from a global configuration mode prompt to a router configuration mode.

**Example 7-3**  Router Configuration Command for All Three Routers

```
R1(config)# router eigrp 1
R1(config-router)#

R2(config)# router eigrp 1
R2(config-router)#

R3(config)# router eigrp 1
R3(config-router)#
```

In this example, **1** identifies this particular EIGRP process running on this router. To establish neighbor adjacencies, EIGRP requires all routers in the same routing domain to be configured with the same autonomous system number, as shown in Example 7-3.

**Note**

Both EIGRP and OSPF can support multiple instances of each routing protocol, although this type of multiple routing protocol implementation is not usually needed or recommended.

The **router eigrp** *autonomous-system* command does not start the EIGRP process itself. The router does not start sending updates. Rather, this command only provides access to configure the EIGRP settings.

To completely remove the EIGRP routing process from a device, use the **no router eigrp** *autonomous-system* global configuration mode command, which stops the EIGRP process and removes all existing EIGRP router configurations.

## EIGRP Router ID (7.2.1.4)

The EIGRP router ID is used to uniquely identify each router in the EIGRP routing domain. The router ID is used in both EIGRP and OSPF routing protocols, although the role of the router ID is more significant in OSPF.

In EIGRP IPv4 implementations, the use of the router ID is not that apparent. EIGRP for IPv4 uses the 32-bit router ID to identify the originating router for redistribution of external routes. The need for a router ID becomes more evident in the discussion of EIGRP for IPv6. While the router ID is necessary for redistribution, the details of EIGRP redistribution are beyond the scope of this curriculum. For purposes of this curriculum, it is only necessary to understand what the router ID is and how it is derived.

## Determining the Router ID

Cisco routers derive the router ID based on three criteria, in the following precedence:

1. Use the IPv4 address configured with the **eigrp router-id** router configuration mode command.

2. If the router ID is not configured, the router chooses the highest IPv4 address of any of its loopback interfaces.

3. If no loopback interfaces are configured, the router chooses the highest active IPv4 address of any of its physical interfaces.

If the network administrator does not explicitly configure a router ID using the **eigrp router-id** command, EIGRP generates its own router ID using either a loopback or physical IPv4 address. A loopback address is a virtual interface and is automatically in the up state when configured. The interface does not need to be enabled for EIGRP, meaning that it does not need to be included in one of the EIGRP network commands. However, the interface must be in the up/up state.

Using the criteria previously described, Figure 7-14 shows the default EIGRP router IDs that are determined by the routers' highest active IPv4 address.

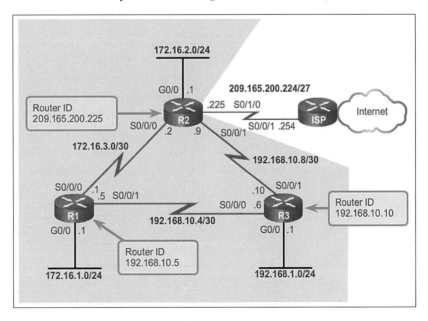

**Figure 7-14**  Topology with Default EIGRP Router IDs

**Note**

The **eigrp router-id** command is used to configure the router ID for EIGRP. Some versions of IOS will accept the command **router-id**, without first specifying **eigrp**. The running config, however, will display **eigrp router-id** regardless of which command is used.

## Configuring the EIGRP Router ID (7.2.1.5)

The **eigrp router-id** command is used to configure the EIGRP router ID and takes precedence over any loopback or physical interface IPv4 addresses. The command syntax is

```
Router(config)# router eigrp autonomous-system
Router(config-router)# eigrp router-id ipv4-address
```

**Note**

The IPv4 address used to indicate the router ID is actually any 32-bit number displayed in dotted-decimal notation.

The router ID can be configured with any IPv4 address with two exceptions: 0.0.0.0 and 255.255.255.255. The router ID should be a unique 32-bit number in the EIGRP routing domain; otherwise, routing inconsistencies can occur.

## Loopback Address Used as the Router ID

Another option to specify the EIGRP router ID is to use an IPv4 loopback address. The advantage of using a loopback interface, instead of the IPv4 address of a physical interface, is that unlike physical interfaces, it cannot fail. There are no actual cables or adjacent devices on which the loopback interface depends for being in the up state. Therefore, using a loopback address for the router ID can provide a more consistent router ID than using an interface address.

If the **eigrp router-id** command is not used and loopback interfaces are configured, EIGRP chooses the highest IPv4 address of any of its loopback interfaces. The following commands are used to enable and configure a loopback interface:

```
Router(config)# interface loopback number
Router(config-if)#  ip address ipv4-address subnet-mask
```

**Note**

The EIGRP router ID is not changed unless the EIGRP process is removed with the **no router eigrp** command or if the router ID is manually configured with the **eigrp router-id** command.

Example 7-4 shows the configuration of the router ID for the routers in Figure 7-14.

**Example 7-4**    Configuring and Verifying the EIGRP Router ID

```
R1(config)# router eigrp 1
R1(config-router)# eigrp router-id 1.1.1.1
R1(config-router)#


R2(config)# router eigrp 1
R2(config-router)# eigrp router-id 2.2.2.2
R2(config-router)#


R3(config)# router eigrp 1
R3(config-router)# eigrp router-id 3.3.3.3
R3(config-router)# end
R3# show ip protocols
*** IP Routing is NSF aware ***
Routing Protocol is "eigrp 1"
<Output omitted>
  EIGRP-IPv4 Protocol for AS(1)
    Metric weight K1=1, K2=0, K3=1, K4=0, K5=0
    NSF-aware route hold timer is 240
    Router-ID: 3.3.3.3
    Topology : 0 (base)
      Active Timer: 3 min
      Distance: internal 90 external 170
<Output omitted>
```

## Verifying the EIGRP Process

Example 7-4 displays the **show ip protocols** output for R3, including its router ID. The **show ip protocols** command displays the parameters and current state of any active routing protocol processes, including both EIGRP and OSPF. The **show ip protocols** command displays different types of output specific to each routing protocol.

## The **network** Command (7.2.1.6)

EIGRP router configuration mode allows for the configuration of the EIGRP routing protocol. Figure 7-12 shows that R1, R2, and R3 all have networks that should be included within a single EIGRP routing domain. To enable EIGRP routing on an interface, use the **network** router configuration mode command and enter the classful network address for each directly connected network.

The **network** command has the same function as in all IGP routing protocols. The **network** command in EIGRP

- Enables any interface on this router that matches the network address in the **network** router configuration mode command to send and receive EIGRP updates

- The network of the interfaces is included in EIGRP routing updates.

The **network** command in EIGRP is as follows:

```
Router(config-router)# network ipv4-network-address
```

The *ipv4-network-address* argument is the classful IPv4 network address for this interface. Figure 7-15 shows the network commands configured for R1.

**Figure 7-15**   EIGRP Network Commands Explained

In the figure, a single classful **network** statement, **network 172.16.0.0**, is used on R1 to include both interfaces in subnets 172.16.1.0/24 and 172.16.3.0/30. Notice that only the classful network address is used.

Example 7-5 shows the **network** command used to enable EIGRP on R2's interfaces for subnets 172.16.1.0/24 and 172.16.2.0/24.

**Example 7-5**   EIGRP Neighbor Adjacency Message

```
R2(config)# router eigrp 1
R2(config-router)# network 172.16.0.0
R2(config-router)#
*Feb 28 17:51:42.543: %DUAL-5-NBRCHANGE: EIGRP-IPv4 1: Neighbor 172.16.3.1
  (Serial0/0/0) is up: new adjacency
R2(config-router)#
```

When EIGRP is configured on R2's S0/0/0 interface, DUAL sends a notification message to the console stating that a neighbor adjacency with another EIGRP router on that interface has been established. This new adjacency happens automatically because both R1 and R2 use the same **eigrp 1** autonomous system number, and both routers now send updates on their interfaces in the 172.16.0.0 network.

By default, the **eigrp log-neighbor-changes** router configuration mode command is enabled. This command is used to

- Display any changes in EIGRP neighbor adjacencies
- Help verify neighbor adjacencies during configuration of EIGRP
- Advise the network administrator when any EIGRP adjacencies have been removed

### The **network** Command and Wildcard Mask (7.2.1.7)

By default, when using the **network** command and an IPv4 network address, such as 172.16.0.0, all interfaces on the router that belong to that classful network address are enabled for EIGRP. However, there can be times when the network administrator does not want to include all interfaces within a network when enabling EIGRP. For example, in Figure 7-16, assume that an administrator wants to enable EIGRP on R2, but only for the subnet 192.168.10.8 255.255.255.252, on the S0/0/1 interface.

**Figure 7-16**   EIGRP for IPv4 Topology

To configure EIGRP to advertise specific subnets only, use the *wildcard-mask* option with the **network** command:

```
Router(config-router)# network network-address [wildcard-mask]
```

Think of a wildcard mask as the inverse of a subnet mask. The inverse of subnet mask 255.255.255.252 is 0.0.0.3. To calculate the inverse of the subnet mask, subtract the subnet mask from 255.255.255.255 as follows:

```
  255.255.255.255
- 255.255.255.252
  ---------------
    0.  0.  0.  3   Wildcard mask
```

Figure 7-17 continues the EIGRP network configuration of R2.

**Figure 7-17**    Network Command with Wildcard Mask

The **network 192.168.10.8 0.0.0.3** command specifically enables EIGRP on the S0/0/1 interface, a member of the 192.168.10.8 255.255.255.252 subnet.

Some IOS versions also let you enter the subnet mask instead of a wildcard mask. Example 7-6 shows an example of configuring the same S0/0/1 interface on R2, but this time using a subnet mask in the **network** command.

**Example 7-6**    Alternative **network** Command Configuration Using a Subnet Mask

```
R2(config)# router eigrp 1
R2(config-router)# network 192.168.10.8 255.255.255.252
R2(config-router)# end
R2# show running-config | section eigrp 1
router eigrp 1
 network 172.16.0.0
 network 192.168.10.8 0.0.0.3
 eigrp router-id 2.2.2.2
R2#
```

However, if the subnet mask is used, the IOS converts the command to the *wild-card-mask* format within the configuration. This is verified in the **show running-config** output in Example 7-6.

Example 7-7 shows the EIGRP configuration for Router R3.

**Example 7-7**   Configuring the **network** Command and Wildcard Mask on R3

```
R3(config)# router eigrp 1
R3(config-router)# network 192.168.1.0
R3(config-router)# network 192.168.10.4 0.0.0.3
*Feb 28 20:47:22.695: %DUAL-5-NBRCHANGE: EIGRP-IPv4 1: Neighbor 192.168.10.5
  (Serial0/0/0) is up: new adjacency
R3(config-router)# network 192.168.10.8 0.0.0.3
*Feb 28 20:47:06.555: %DUAL-5-NBRCHANGE: EIGRP-IPv4 1: Neighbor 192.168.10.9
  (Serial0/0/1) is up: new adjacency
R3(config-router)#
```

## Passive Interface (7.2.1.8)

As soon as a new interface is enabled within the EIGRP network, EIGRP attempts to form a neighbor adjacency with any neighboring routers to send and receive EIGRP updates.

At times it might be necessary, or advantageous, to include a directly connected network in the EIGRP routing update, but not allow any neighbor adjacencies connected to that interface to form. The **passive-interface** command can be used to prevent the neighbor adjacencies. There are two primary reasons for enabling the **passive-interface** command:

- To suppress unnecessary update traffic, such as when an interface is a LAN interface, with no other routers connected

- To increase security controls, such as preventing unknown rogue routing devices from receiving EIGRP updates

Figure 7-18 shows that R1, R2, and R3 do not have EIGRP neighbors on their GigabitEthernet 0/0 interfaces. Yet, each router is still sending out a Hello message every 5 seconds.

The **passive-interface** router configuration mode command disables the transmission and receipt of EIGRP Hello packets on these interfaces.

```
Router(config)# router eigrp as-number
Router(config-router)# passive-interface interface-type interface-number
```

**Figure 7-18** Hello Messages Sent Out LAN Interfaces

Example 7-8 shows the **passive-interface** command configured to suppress Hello packets on the LANs for all three routers.

**Example 7-8** Configuring and Verifying EIGRP Passive Interfaces

```
R1(config)# router eigrp 1
R1(config-router)# passive-interface gigabitethernet 0/0


R3(config)# router eigrp 1
R3(config-router)# passive-interface gigabitethernet 0/0


R2(config)# router eigrp 1
R2(config-router)# passive-interface gigabitethernet 0/0
R2(config-router)# end
R2# show ip protocols
*** IP Routing is NSF aware ***

Routing Protocol is "eigrp 1"
  Outgoing update filter list for all interfaces is not set
  Incoming update filter list for all interfaces is not set
  Default networks flagged in outgoing updates
  Default networks accepted from incoming updates
  Redistributing: static
  EIGRP-IPv4 Protocol for AS(1)
```

```
      Metric weight K1=1, K2=0, K3=1, K4=0, K5=0
      NSF-aware route hold timer is 240
      Router-ID: 2.2.2.2
      Topology : 0 (base)
        Active Timer: 3 min
        Distance: internal 90 external 170
        Maximum path: 4
        Maximum hopcount 100
        Maximum metric variance 1

  Automatic Summarization: disabled
  Maximum path: 4
  Routing for Networks:
    172.16.0.0
    192.168.10.8/30
  Passive Interface(s):
    GigabitEthernet0/0
  Routing Information Sources:
    Gateway         Distance      Last Update
    192.168.10.10         90      02:14:28
    172.16.3.1           90      02:14:28
  Distance: internal 90 external 170

R2#
```

Without a neighbor adjacency, EIGRP cannot exchange routes with a neighbor. Therefore, the **passive-interface** command prevents the exchange of routes on the interface. Although EIGRP does not send or receive routing updates on an interface configured with the **passive-interface** command, it still includes the address of the interface in routing updates sent out of other nonpassive interfaces.

### Note

To configure all interfaces as passive, use the **passive-interface default** command. To disable an interface as passive, use the **no passive-interface** *interface-type interface-number* command.

An example of using the passive interface to increase security controls is when a network must connect to a third-party organization for which the local administrator has no control, such as when connecting to an ISP network. In this case, the local network administrator would need to advertise the interface link through his own network, but would not want the third-party organization to receive or send routing updates to the local routing device, as this is a security risk.

### Verifying the Passive Interface

To verify whether any interface on a router is configured as passive, use the **show ip protocols** privileged EXEC mode command, as shown in Example 7-8. Notice that although R3's GigabitEthernet 0/0 interface is a passive interface, EIGRP still includes the interface's network address of 192.168.1.0 in its routing updates.

## Verifying EIGRP with IPv4 (7.2.2)

This topic discusses the verification commands unique to EIGRP as well as examines EIGRP routes in the routing table.

### Verifying EIGRP: Examining Neighbors (7.2.2.1)

Before EIGRP can send or receive any updates, routers must establish adjacencies with their neighbors. EIGRP routers establish adjacencies with neighbor routers by exchanging EIGRP Hello packets.

As shown in Figure 7-19, use the **show ip eigrp neighbors** command to view the neighbor table and verify that EIGRP has established an adjacency with its neighbors.

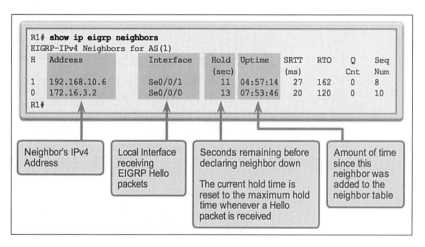

**Figure 7-19   show ip eigrp neighbors Command**

For each router, you should be able to see the IPv4 address of the adjacent router and the interface that this router uses to reach that EIGRP neighbor. Using this topology, each router has two neighbors listed in the neighbor table.

The **show ip eigrp neighbors** command output includes

- **H column:** Lists the neighbors in the order that they were learned.

- **Address:** IPv4 address of the neighbor.

- **Interface:** Local interface on which this Hello packet was received.

- **Hold:** Current hold time. When a Hello packet is received, this value is reset to the maximum hold time for that interface, and then counts down to 0. If 0 is reached, the neighbor is considered down.

- **Uptime:** Amount of time since this neighbor was added to the neighbor table.

- **Smooth Round Trip Timer (SRTT)** and **Retransmission Timeout (RTO):** Used by RTP to manage reliable EIGRP packets.

- **Queue Count:** Should always be 0. If more than 0, EIGRP packets wait to be sent.

- **Sequence Number:** Used to track updates, queries, and reply packets.

The **show ip eigrp neighbors** command is very useful for verifying and trouble-shooting EIGRP. If a neighbor is not listed after adjacencies have been established with a router's neighbors, check the local interface to ensure that it is activated with the **show ip interface brief** command. If the interface is active, try pinging the IPv4 address of the neighbor. If the ping fails, it means that the neighbor interface is down and must be activated. If the ping is successful and EIGRP still does not see the router as a neighbor, examine the following configurations:

- Are both routers configured with the same EIGRP autonomous system number?

- Is the directly connected network included in the EIGRP **network** statements?

## Verifying EIGRP: **show ip protocols** Command (7.2.2.2)

As shown in Figure 7-20, the **show ip protocols** command displays the parameters and other information about the current state of any active IPv4 routing protocol processes configured on the router.

The **show ip protocols** command displays different types of output specific to each routing protocol.

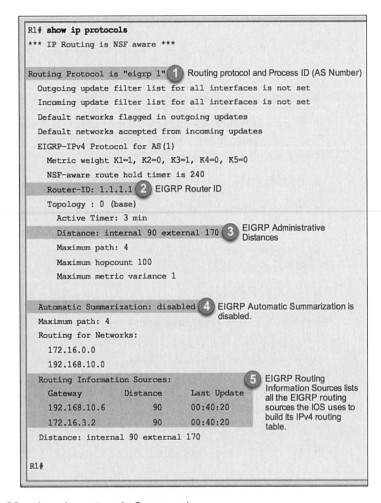

**Figure 7-20   show ip protocols Command**

The output in Figure 7-20 indicates several EIGRP parameters, including

1. EIGRP is an active dynamic routing protocol on R1 configured with the autonomous system number 1.

2. The EIGRP router ID of R1 is 1.1.1.1.

3. The EIGRP administrative distances on R1 are internal AD of 90 and external of 170 (default values).

4. By default, EIGRP does not automatically summarize networks. Subnets are included in the routing updates.

5. The Routing Information Sources are EIGRP neighbor adjacencies that indicate from which routers R1 will receive EIGRP routing updates.

**Note**

Prior to IOS Release 15, EIGRP automatic summarization was enabled by default.

The output from the **show ip protocols** command is useful in debugging routing operations. Information in the Routing Information Sources field can help identify a router suspected of delivering bad routing information. The Routing Information Sources field lists all the EIGRP routing sources that the Cisco IOS Software uses to build its IPv4 routing table. For each source, note the following:

- IPv4 address

- Administrative distance

- Time the last update was received from this source

As shown in Table 7-3, EIGRP has a default AD of 90 for internal routes and 170 for routes imported from an external source, such as default routes.

**Table 7-3**    Default Administrative Distances

| Route Source | Administrative Distance |
| --- | --- |
| Connected | 0 |
| Static | 1 |
| EIGRP summary route | 5 |
| External BGP | 20 |
| Internal EIGRP | 90 |
| IGRP | 100 |
| OSPF | 110 |
| IS-IS | 115 |
| RIP | 120 |
| External EIGRP | 170 |
| Internal BGP | 200 |

When compared to other IGPs, EIGRP is the most preferred by the Cisco IOS, because it has the lowest administrative distance. EIGRP has a third AD value of 5, for summary routes.

## Verifying EIGRP: Examine the IPv4 Routing Table (7.2.2.3)

Another way to verify that EIGRP and other functions of the router are configured properly is to examine the IPv4 routing tables with the **show ip route** command. As with any dynamic routing protocol, the network administrator must verify the information in the routing table to ensure that it is populated as expected, based on configurations entered. For this reason, it is important to have a good understanding of the routing protocol configuration commands, as well as the routing protocol operations and the processes used by the routing protocol to build the IP routing table.

Notice that the outputs used throughout this course are from Cisco IOS Release 15. Prior to IOS Release 15, EIGRP automatic summarization was enabled by default. The state of automatic summarization can make a difference in the information displayed in the IPv4 routing table. If a previous version of the IOS is used, automatic summarization can be disabled using the **no auto-summary** router configuration mode command:

```
Router(config-router)# no auto-summary
```

In Example 7-9, the IPv4 routing table is examined using the **show ip route** command.

**Example 7-9**   IPv4 Routing Tables

```
R1# show ip route
Codes: L - local, C - connected, S - static, R - RIP, M - mobile, B - BGP
       D - EIGRP, EX - EIGRP external, O - OSPF, IA - OSPF inter area
       <Output omitted>


Gateway of last resort is not set


      172.16.0.0/16 is variably subnetted, 5 subnets, 3 masks
C        172.16.1.0/24 is directly connected, GigabitEthernet0/0
L        172.16.1.1/32 is directly connected, GigabitEthernet0/0
D        172.16.2.0/24 [90/2170112] via 172.16.3.2, 00:14:35, Serial0/0/0
C        172.16.3.0/30 is directly connected, Serial0/0/0
L        172.16.3.1/32 is directly connected, Serial0/0/0
D     192.168.1.0/24 [90/2170112] via 192.168.10.6, 00:13:57, Serial0/0/1
      192.168.10.0/24 is variably subnetted, 3 subnets, 2 masks
C        192.168.10.4/30 is directly connected, Serial0/0/1
L        192.168.10.5/32 is directly connected, Serial0/0/1
D        192.168.10.8/30 [90/2681856] via 192.168.10.6, 00:50:42, Serial0/0/1
                         [90/2681856] via 172.16.3.2, 00:50:42, Serial0/0/0
R1#
```

```
R2# show ip route
Codes: L - local, C - connected, S - static, R - RIP, M - mobile, B - BGP
       D - EIGRP, EX - EIGRP external, O - OSPF, IA - OSPF inter area
               <Output omitted>


Gateway of last resort is not set


 172.16.0.0/16 is variably subnetted, 5 subnets, 3 masks
D        172.16.1.0/24 [90/2170112] via 172.16.3.1, 00:11:05, Serial0/0/0
C        172.16.2.0/24 is directly connected, GigabitEthernet0/0
L        172.16.2.1/32 is directly connected, GigabitEthernet0/0
C        172.16.3.0/30 is directly connected, Serial0/0/0
L        172.16.3.2/32 is directly connected, Serial0/0/0
D     192.168.1.0/24 [90/2170112] via 192.168.10.10, 00:15:16, Serial0/0/1
       192.168.10.0/24 is variably subnetted, 3 subnets, 2 masks
D        192.168.10.4/30 [90/2681856] via 192.168.10.10, 00:52:00, Serial0/0/1
                         [90/2681856] via 172.16.3.1, 00:52:00, Serial0/0/0
C        192.168.10.8/30 is directly connected, Serial0/0/1
L        192.168.10.9/32 is directly connected, Serial0/0/1
      209.165.200.0/24 is variably subnetted, 2 subnets, 2 masks
C        209.165.200.224/27 is directly connected, Loopback209
L        209.165.200.225/32 is directly connected, Loopback209
R2#
```

```
R3# show ip route
Codes: L - local, C - connected, S - static, R - RIP, M - mobile, B - BGP
       D - EIGRP, EX - EIGRP external, O - OSPF, IA - OSPF inter area
               <Output omitted>


Gateway of last resort is not set


 172.16.0.0/16 is variably subnetted, 3 subnets, 2 masks
D        172.16.1.0/24 [90/2170112] via 192.168.10.5, 00:12:00, Serial0/0/0
D        172.16.2.0/24 [90/2170112] via 192.168.10.9, 00:16:49, Serial0/0/1
D        172.16.3.0/30 [90/2681856] via 192.168.10.9, 00:52:55, Serial0/0/1
                       [90/2681856] via 192.168.10.5, 00:52:55, Serial0/0/0
       192.168.1.0/24 is variably subnetted, 2 subnets, 2 masks
C        192.168.1.0/24 is directly connected, GigabitEthernet0/0
L        192.168.1.1/32 is directly connected, GigabitEthernet0/0
       192.168.10.0/24 is variably subnetted, 4 subnets, 2 masks
C        192.168.10.4/30 is directly connected, Serial0/0/0
L        192.168.10.6/32 is directly connected, Serial0/0/0
C        192.168.10.8/30 is directly connected, Serial0/0/1
L        192.168.10.10/32 is directly connected, Serial0/0/1
R3#
```

EIGRP routes are denoted in the routing table with a **D**. The letter D is used to represent EIGRP because the protocol is based upon the DUAL algorithm.

The **show ip route** command verifies that routes received by EIGRP neighbors are installed in the IPv4 routing table. The **show ip route** command displays the entire routing table, including remote networks learned dynamically, directly connected, and static routes. For this reason, it is normally the first command used to check for convergence. After routing is correctly configured on all routers, the **show ip route** command reflects that each router has a full routing table, with a route to each network in the topology.

Notice that R1 has installed routes to three IPv4 remote networks in its IPv4 routing table:

- 172.16.2.0/24 network, received from Router R2 on the Serial0/0/0 interface

- 192.168.1.0/24 network, received from Router R2 on the Serial0/0/1 interface

- 192.168.10.8/30 network, received from both R2 on the Serial0/0/0 interface and from R3 on the Serial0/0/1 interface

R1 has two paths to the 192.168.10.8/30 network, because its cost or metric to reach that network is the same or equal using both routers. These are known as equal-cost routes. R1 uses both paths to reach this network, which is known as load balancing. The EIGRP metric is discussed later in this chapter.

For R2 and R3, notice that similar results are displayed, including equal-cost routes.

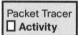

### Packet Tracer Activity 7.2.2.4: Configuring Basic EIGRP with IPv4

In this activity, you will implement basic EIGRP configurations including **network** commands, passive interfaces, and disabling automatic summarization. You will then verify your EIGRP configuration using a variety of **show** commands and testing end-to-end connectivity.

### Lab 7.2.2.5: Configuring Basic EIGRP with IPv4

In this lab, you will complete the following objectives:

- Part 1: Build the Network and Verify Connectivity

- Part 2: Configure EIGRP Routing

- Part 3: Verify EIGRP Routing

- Part 4: Configure Bandwidth and Passive Interfaces

# Operation of EIGRP (7.3)

This section digs deeper into the details of EIGRP operations, including EIGRP convergence, metric calculation, and how DUAL installs and maintains the tables used by EIGRP.

## EIGRP Initial Route Discovery (7.3.1)

Initial route discovery begins with forming a neighbor adjacency and proceeds from there through a series of steps until the topology table is complete.

### EIGRP Neighbor Adjacency (7.3.1.1)

The goal of any dynamic routing protocol is to learn about remote networks from other routers and to reach convergence in the routing domain. Before any EIGRP update packets can be exchanged between routers, EIGRP must first discover its neighbors. EIGRP neighbors are other routers running EIGRP on directly connected networks.

EIGRP uses Hello packets to establish and maintain neighbor adjacencies. For two EIGRP routers to become neighbors, several parameters between the two routers must match. For example, two EIGRP routers must use the same EIGRP metric parameters and both must be configured using the same autonomous system number.

Each EIGRP router maintains a neighbor table, which contains a list of routers on shared links that have an EIGRP adjacency with this router. The neighbor table is used to track the status of these EIGRP neighbors.

Figure 7-21 shows two EIGRP routers exchanging initial EIGRP Hello packets.

When an EIGRP-enabled router receives a Hello packet on an interface, it adds that router to its neighbor table.

1. A new router (R1) comes up on the link and sends an EIGRP Hello packet through all its EIGRP-configured interfaces.

2. Router R2 receives the Hello packet on an EIGRP-enabled interface. R2 replies with an EIGRP update packet that contains all the routes it has in its routing table, except those learned through that interface (split horizon). However, the neighbor adjacency is not established until R2 also sends an EIGRP Hello packet to R1.

3. After both routers have exchanged Hellos, the neighbor adjacency is established. R1 and R2 update their EIGRP neighbor tables, adding the adjacent router as a neighbor.

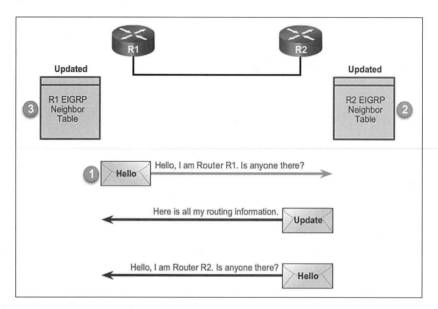

**Figure 7-21**   Discovery Neighbors

## EIGRP Topology Table (7.3.1.2)

EIGRP updates contain networks that are reachable from the router sending the update. As EIGRP updates are exchanged between neighbors, the receiving router adds these entries to its EIGRP topology table.

Each EIGRP router maintains a topology table for each routed protocol configured, such as IPv4 and IPv6. The topology table includes route entries for every destination that the router learns from its directly connected EIGRP neighbors.

Figure 7-22 shows the continuation of the initial route discovery process from the previous page.

It now shows the update of the topology table.

When a router receives an EIGRP routing update, it adds the routing information to its EIGRP topology table and replies with an EIGRP acknowledgment.

1. R1 receives the EIGRP update from neighbor R2 and includes information about the routes that the neighbor is advertising, including the metric to each destination. R1 adds all update entries to its topology table. The topology table includes all destinations advertised by neighboring (adjacent) routers and the cost (metric) to reach each network.

2. EIGRP update packets use reliable delivery; therefore, R1 replies with an EIGRP acknowledgment packet informing R2 that it has received the update.

3. R1 sends an EIGRP update to R2 advertising the routes that it is aware of, except those learned from R2 (split horizon).

4. R2 receives the EIGRP update from neighbor R1 and adds this information to its own topology table.

5. R2 responds to R1's EIGRP update packet with an EIGRP acknowledgment.

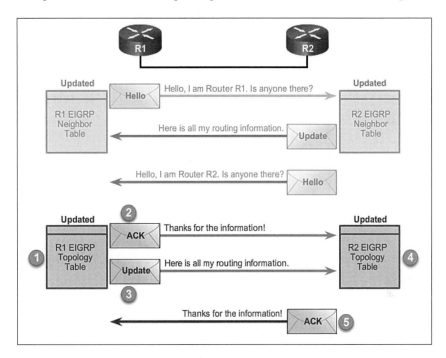

**Figure 7-22**  Exchanging Routing Updates

## EIGRP Convergence (7.3.1.3)

Figure 7-23 illustrates the final steps of the initial route discovery process.

1. After receiving the EIGRP update packets from R2, using the information in the topology table, R1 updates its IP routing table with the best path to each destination, including the metric and the next-hop router.

2. Similar to R1, R2 updates its IP routing table with the best path routes to each network.

At this point, EIGRP on both routers is considered to be in the converged state.

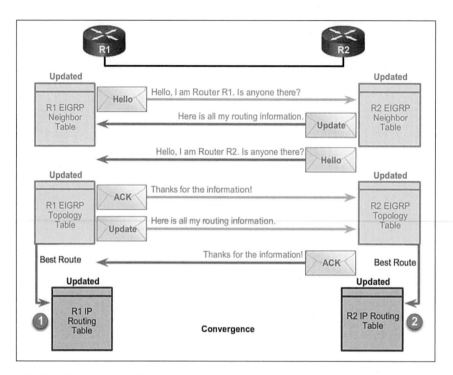

**Figure 7-23**    Updating the IPv4 Routing Table

**Activity 7.3.1.4: Identify the Steps in Establishing EIGRP Neighbor Adjacencies**

Go to the course online to perform this practice activity.

# Metrics (7.3.2)

Although EIGRP can use five different inputs to calculate a metric, it defaults to bandwidth and delay.

## EIGRP Composite Metric (7.3.2.1)

By default, EIGRP uses the following values in its *composite metric* to calculate the preferred path to a network:

- **Bandwidth:** The slowest bandwidth among all the outgoing interfaces, along the path from source to destination.

- **Delay:** The cumulative (sum) of all interface delays along the path (in tens of microseconds).

The following values can be used, but are not recommended, because they typically result in frequent recalculation of the topology table:

- **Reliability:** Represents the worst reliability between the source and destination, which is based on keepalives.

- **Load:** Represents the worst load on a link between the source and destination, which is computed based on the packet rate and the configured bandwidth of the interface.

---

**Note**

Although the MTU is included in the routing table updates, it is not a routing metric used by EIGRP.

---

### The Composite Metric

Figure 7-24 shows the composite metric formula used by EIGRP.

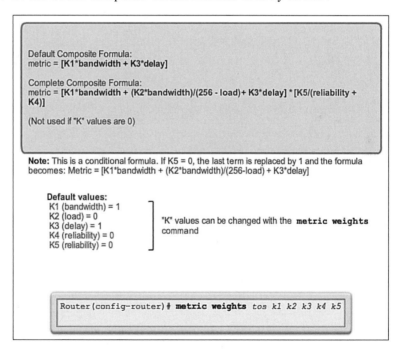

**Figure 7-24**   EIGRP Composite Metric

The formula consists of values K1 to K5, known as EIGRP metric weights. K1 and K3 represent bandwidth and delay, respectively. K2 represents load, and K4 and K5 represent reliability. By default, K1 and K3 are set to 1, and K2, K4, and K5 are set to 0. The result is that only the bandwidth and delay values are used in the computation of the default composite metric. EIGRP for IPv4 and EIGRP for IPv6 use the same formula for the composite metric.

The metric calculation method ($k$ values) and the EIGRP autonomous system number must match between EIGRP neighbors. If they do not match, the routers do not form an adjacency.

The default $k$ values can be changed with the **metric weights** router configuration mode command:

```
Router(config-router)# metric weights tos k1 k2 k3 k4 k5
```

### Note

Modifying the **metric weights** value is generally not recommended and is beyond the scope of this course. However, its relevance is important in establishing neighbor adjacencies. If one router has modified the metric weights and another router has not, an adjacency does not form.

## Verifying the $k$ Values

The **show ip protocols** command is used to verify the $k$ values. The command output for R1 is shown in Example 7-10.

**Example 7-10**   Verifying Metric K Values

```
R1# show ip protocols
*** IP Routing is NSF aware ***

Routing Protocol is "eigrp 1"
  Outgoing update filter list for all interfaces is not set
  Incoming update filter list for all interfaces is not set
  Default networks flagged in outgoing updates
  Default networks accepted from incoming updates
  EIGRP-IPv4 Protocol for AS(1)
    Metric weight K1=1, K2=0, K3=1, K4=0, K5=0
    NSF-aware route hold timer is 240
    Router-ID: 1.1.1.1
<Output omitted>
R1#
```

Notice that the $k$ values on R1 are set to the default.

## Examining Interface Values (7.3.2.2)

The **show interfaces** command displays interface information, including the parameters used to compute the EIGRP metric. Example 7-11 shows the **show interface** command for the Serial 0/0/0 interface on R1.

**Example 7-11**   Verifying Metrics with the **show interface** Command

```
R1# show interface serial 0/0/0
Serial0/0/0 is up, line protocol is up
  Hardware is WIC MBRD Serial
  Internet address is 172.16.3.1/30
  MTU 1500 bytes, BW 1544 Kbit/sec, DLY 20000 usec,
      reliability 255/255, txload 1/255, rxload 1/255
  Encapsulation HDLC, loopback not set
<Output omitted>
R1# show interface gigabitethernet 0/0
GigabitEthernet0/0 is up, line protocol is up
  Hardware is CN Gigabit Ethernet, address is fc99.4775.c3e0 (bia fc99.4775.c3e0)
  Internet address is 172.16.1.1/24
  MTU 1500 bytes, BW 100000 Kbit/sec, DLY 100 usec,
      reliability 255/255, txload 1/255, rxload 1/255
  Encapsulation ARPA, loopback not set
<Output omitted>
R1#
```

- **BW:** Bandwidth of the interface (in kilobits per second).

- **DLY:** Delay of the interface (in microseconds).

- **Reliability:** Reliability of the interface as a fraction of 255 (255/255 is 100% reliability), calculated as an exponential average over five minutes. By default, EIGRP does not include its value in computing its metric.

- **Txload, Rxload:** Transmit and receive load on the interface as a fraction of 255 (255/255 is completely saturated), calculated as an exponential average over five minutes. By default, EIGRP does not include its value in computing its metric.

**Note**

Throughout this course, bandwidth is referenced as kb/s. However, router output displays bandwidth using the Kbit/sec abbreviation. Router output also displays delay as μsec. In this course, delay is referenced as microseconds.

## Bandwidth Metric (7.3.2.3)

The bandwidth metric is a static value used by some routing protocols, such as EIGRP and OSPF, to calculate their routing metric. The bandwidth is displayed in kilobits per second (kb/s). Most serial interfaces use the default bandwidth value of 1544 kb/s or 1,544,000 b/s (1.544 Mb/s). This is the bandwidth of a T1 connection. However, some serial interfaces use a different default bandwidth value. Figure 7-25 shows the topology now with bandwidth values labeled on the serial links.

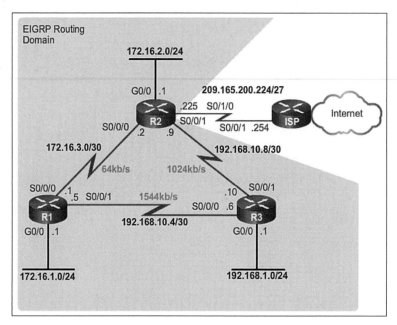

**Figure 7-25** EIGRP for IPv4 Topology with Bandwidth Values

The types of serial interfaces and their associated bandwidths might not necessarily reflect the more common types of connections found in networks today.

Always verify bandwidth with the **show interfaces** command.

The default value of the bandwidth might or might not reflect the actual physical bandwidth of the interface. If the actual bandwidth of the link differs from the default bandwidth value, the bandwidth value should be modified.

## Configuring the Bandwidth Parameter

On most serial links, the bandwidth metric defaults to 1544 kb/s. Because both EIGRP and OSPF use bandwidth in default metric calculations, a correct value for bandwidth is very important to the accuracy of routing information.

Use the following interface configuration mode command to modify the bandwidth metric:

```
Router(config-if)# bandwidth kilobits-bandwidth-value
```

Use the **no bandwidth** command to restore the default value.

In Figure 7-25, the link between R1 and R2 has a bandwidth of 64 kb/s, and the link between R2 and R3 has a bandwidth of 1024 kb/s. Example 7-12 shows the configurations used on all three routers to modify the bandwidth on the appropriate serial interfaces.

**Example 7-12**   Bandwidth Configuration on All Three Routers

```
R1(config)# interface s 0/0/0
R1(config-if)# bandwidth 64

R2(config)# interface s 0/0/0
R2(config-if)# bandwidth 64
R2(config-if)# exit
R2(config)# interface s 0/0/1
R2(config-if)# bandwidth 1024

R3(config)# interface s 0/0/1
R3(config-if)# bandwidth 1024
```

## Verifying the Bandwidth Parameter

Use the **show interface** command to verify the new bandwidth parameters, as shown in Example 7-13 for the link between R1 and R2.

**Example 7-13**   Verifying the Bandwidth Value

```
R1# show interface s 0/0/0
Serial0/0/0 is up, line protocol is up
  Hardware is WIC MBRD Serial
  Internet address is 172.16.3.1/30
  MTU 1500 bytes, BW 64 Kbit/sec, DLY 20000 usec,
     reliability 255/255, txload 1/255, rxload 1/255
<Output omitted>
R1#

R2# show interface s 0/0/0
Serial0/0/0 is up, line protocol is up
  Hardware is WIC MBRD Serial
```

```
   Internet address is 172.16.3.2/30
   MTU 1500 bytes, BW 64 Kbit/sec, DLY 20000 usec,
       reliability 255/255, txload 1/255, rxload 1/255
<Output omitted>
R2#
```

It is important to modify the bandwidth metric on both sides of the link to ensure proper routing in both directions.

Modifying the bandwidth value does not change the actual bandwidth of the link. The **bandwidth** command only modifies the bandwidth metric used by routing protocols, such as EIGRP and OSPF.

## Delay Metric (7.3.2.4)

Delay is the measure of the time it takes for a packet to traverse a route. The delay (DLY) metric is a static value based on the type of link to which the interface is connected and is expressed in microseconds. Delay is not measured dynamically. In other words, the router does not actually track how long packets take to reach the destination. The delay value, much like the bandwidth value, is a default value that can be changed by the network administrator.

When used to determine the EIGRP metric, delay is the cumulative (sum) of all interface delays along the path (measured in tens of microseconds).

Table 7-4 shows the default delay values for various interfaces.

**Table 7-4**    Interface Delay Values

| Media | Delay |
| --- | --- |
| Ethernet | 1000 |
| Fast Ethernet | 100 |
| Gigabit Ethernet | 10 |
| FDDI | 100 |
| T1 (Serial Default) | 20,000 |
| DS0 (64 kbps) | 20,000 |
| 1024 kbps | 20,000 |
| 56 kbps | 20,000 |

Notice that the default value is 20,000 microseconds for serial interfaces and 10 microseconds for Gigabit Ethernet interfaces.

Use the **show interface** command to verify the delay value on an interface, as shown in Example 7-14.

**Example 7-14**   Verifying the Delay Value

```
R1# show interface s 0/0/0
Serial0/0/0 is up, line protocol is up
  Hardware is WIC MBRD Serial
  Internet address is 172.16.3.1/30
  MTU 1500 bytes, BW 64 Kbit/sec, DLY 20000 usec,
     reliability 255/255, txload 1/255, rxload 1/255
<Output omitted>
R1# show interface g 0/0
GigabitEthernet0/0 is up, line protocol is up
  Hardware is CN Gigabit Ethernet, address is fc99.4775.c3e0 (bia fc99.4775.c3e0)
  Internet address is 172.16.1.1/24
  MTU 1500 bytes, BW 1000000 Kbit/sec, DLY 10 usec,
     reliability 255/255, txload 1/255, rxload 1/255
<Output omitted>
R1#
```

Although an interface with various bandwidths can have the same delay value, by default, Cisco recommends not modifying the delay parameter, unless the network administrator has a specific reason to do so.

## How to Calculate the EIGRP Metric (7.3.2.5)

Although EIGRP automatically calculates the routing table metric used to choose the best path, it is important that the network administrator understands how these metrics were determined. Figure 7-26 shows the composite metric used by EIGRP.

Using the default values for K1 and K3, the calculation can be simplified to the slowest bandwidth (or minimum bandwidth), plus the sum of all the delays.

**Figure 7-26**   Default EIGRP Metric

In other words, by examining the bandwidth and delay values for all the outgoing interfaces of the route, we can determine the EIGRP metric as follows:

**Step 1.**   Determine the link with the slowest bandwidth. Use that value to calculate bandwidth (10,000,000/bandwidth).

**Step 2.**   Determine the delay value for each outgoing interface on the way to the destination. Add the delay values and divide by 10 (sum of delay/10).

**Step 3.**   Add the computed values for bandwidth and delay, and multiply the sum by 256 to obtain the EIGRP metric.

The routing table output for R2 shows that the route to 192.168.1.0/24 has an EIGRP metric of 3,012,096.

## Calculating the EIGRP Metric (7.3.2.6)

This example illustrates how EIGRP determines the metric displayed in R2's routing table for the 192.168.1.0/24 network.

### Bandwidth

EIGRP uses the slowest bandwidth in its metric calculation. The slowest bandwidth can be determined by examining each interface between R2 and the destination network 192.168.1.0. The Serial 0/0/1 interface on R2 has a bandwidth of 1024 kb/s.

The GigabitEthernet 0/0 interface on R3 has a bandwidth of 1,000,000 kb/s. Therefore, the slowest bandwidth is 1024 kb/s and is used in the calculation of the metric.

EIGRP divides a reference bandwidth value of 10,000,000 by the interface bandwidth value in kb/s. This results in higher bandwidth values receiving a lower metric and lower bandwidth values receiving a higher metric. 10,000,000 is divided by 1024. If the result is not a whole number, the value is rounded down. In this case, 10,000,000 divided by 1024 equals 9,765.625. The .625 is dropped from this value to yield 9765 for the bandwidth portion of the composite metric, as shown in Figure 7-27.

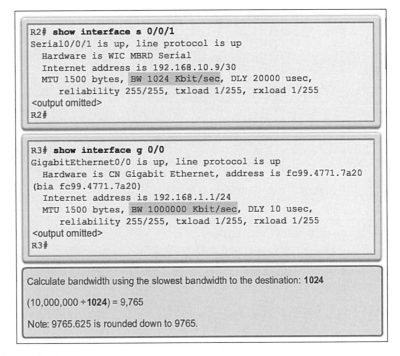

```
R2# show interface s 0/0/1
Serial0/0/1 is up, line protocol is up
  Hardware is WIC MBRD Serial
  Internet address is 192.168.10.9/30
  MTU 1500 bytes, BW 1024 Kbit/sec, DLY 20000 usec,
    reliability 255/255, txload 1/255, rxload 1/255
<output omitted>
R2#
```

```
R3# show interface g 0/0
GigabitEthernet0/0 is up, line protocol is up
  Hardware is CN Gigabit Ethernet, address is fc99.4771.7a20
(bia fc99.4771.7a20)
  Internet address is 192.168.1.1/24
  MTU 1500 bytes, BW 1000000 Kbit/sec, DLY 10 usec,
    reliability 255/255, txload 1/255, rxload 1/255
<output omitted>
R3#
```

Calculate bandwidth using the slowest bandwidth to the destination: **1024**

(10,000,000 ÷ **1024**) = 9,765

Note: 9765.625 is rounded down to 9765.

**Figure 7-27**   Calculating the Bandwidth

## Delay

The same outgoing interfaces are used to determine the delay value, as shown in Figure 7-28.

EIGRP uses the sum of all delays to the destination. The Serial 0/0/1 interface on R2 has a delay of 20,000 microseconds. The Gigabit 0/0 interface on R3 has a delay of 10 microseconds. The sum of these delays is divided by 10. In the example, (20,000+10)/10 results in a value of 2001 for the delay portion of the composite metric.

```
R2# show interface s 0/0/1
Serial0/0/1 is up, line protocol is up
  Hardware is WIC MBRD Serial
  Internet address is 192.168.10.9/30
  MTU 1500 bytes, BW 1024 Kbit/sec, DLY 20000 usec,
    reliability 255/255, txload 1/255, rxload 1/255
<output omitted>
R2#
```

```
R3# show interface g 0/0
GigabitEthernet0/0 is up, line protocol is up
  Hardware is CN Gigabit Ethernet, address is fc99.4771.7a20
(bia fc99.4771.7a20)
  Internet address is 192.168.1.1/24
  MTU 1500 bytes, BW 1000000 Kbit/sec, DLY 10 usec,
    reliability 255/255, txload 1/255, rxload 1/255
<output omitted>
R3#
```

Calculate delay using the sum of all delays to the destination: **20,000 + 10**

**(20,000 + 10)** ÷ 10 = 2001

**Figure 7-28**   Calculating the Delay Values

## Calculate Metric

Use the calculated values for bandwidth and delay in the metric formula. This results in a metric of 3,012,096, as shown in Figure 7-29.

```
R2# show ip route
<output omitted>

D 192.168.1.0/24 [90/3012096] via 192.168.10.10, 00:12:32,
  Serial0/0/1
```

Use the results in the default metric formula:

**(Bandwidth + Delay)** * 256 = **Metric**

**(9765 + 2001)** * 256 = **3,012,096**

**Figure 7-29**   Verifying the EIGRP Metric

This value matches the value shown in the routing table for R2.

Interactive
Graphic

**Activity 7.3.2.7: Calculate the EIGRP Metric**

Go to the course online to perform this practice activity.

# DUAL and the Topology Table (7.3.3)

This topic discusses the terminology unique to EIGRP and DUAL as well as looks, in detail, at the EIGRP topology table.

## DUAL Concepts (7.3.3.1)

EIGRP uses the Diffusing Update Algorithm (DUAL) to provide the best loop-free path and loop-free backup paths.

DUAL uses several terms, which are discussed in more detail throughout this section:

- *Successor*

- *Feasible Distance (FD)*

- *Feasible Successor (FS)*

- *Reported Distance (RD)* or *Advertised Distance (AD)*

- *Feasible Condition* or Feasibility Condition *(FC)*

These terms and concepts are at the center of the loop avoidance mechanism of DUAL.

## Introduction to DUAL (7.3.3.2)

EIGRP uses the convergence algorithm DUAL. Convergence is critical to a network to avoid routing loops.

Routing loops, even temporary ones, can be detrimental to network performance. Distance vector routing protocols, such as RIP, prevent routing loops with hold-down timers and split horizon. Although EIGRP uses both of these techniques, it uses them somewhat differently; the primary way that EIGRP prevents routing loops is with the DUAL algorithm.

The DUAL algorithm is used to obtain loop freedom at every instance throughout a route computation. This allows all routers involved in a topology change to synchronize at the same time. Routers that are not affected by the topology changes are not involved in the recomputation. This method provides EIGRP with faster convergence times than other distance vector routing protocols.

The decision process for all route computations is done by the DUAL *Finite State Machine (FSM)*. An FSM is a workflow model, similar to a flowchart that is comprised of the following:

■ A finite number of stages (states)

■ Transitions between those stages

■ Operations

The DUAL FSM tracks all routes; uses EIGRP metrics to select efficient, loop-free paths; and identifies the routes with the least-cost path to be inserted into the routing table.

Recomputation of the DUAL algorithm can be processor intensive. EIGRP avoids recomputation whenever possible by maintaining a list of backup routes that DUAL has already determined to be loop-free. If the primary route in the routing table fails, the best backup route is immediately added to the routing table.

### Successor and Feasible Distance (7.3.3.3)

Figure 7-30 shows the topology for this topic.

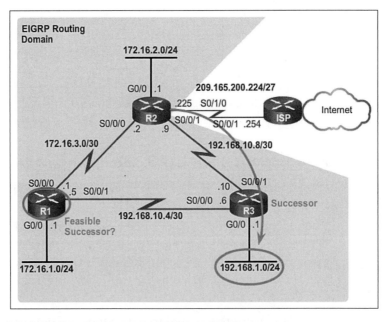

**Figure 7-30** EIGRP for IPv4 Topology: Successor Example

A successor is a neighboring router that is used for packet forwarding and is the least-cost route to the destination network. The IP address of a successor is shown in a routing table entry right after the word *via*.

FD is the lowest calculated metric to reach the destination network. FD is the metric listed in the routing table entry as the second number inside the brackets. As with other routing protocols, this is also known as the metric for the route.

Examining the routing table for R2 in Figure 7-31, notice that EIGRP's best path for the 192.168.1.0/24 network is through Router R3 and that the feasible distance is 3,012,096. This is the metric that was calculated in the previous topic.

**Figure 7-31**   Feasible Distance to the Successor

## Feasible Successors, Feasibility Condition, and Reported Distance (7.3.3.4)

DUAL can converge quickly after a change in the topology because it can use backup paths to other networks without recomputing DUAL. These backup paths are known as Feasible Successors (FS).

An FS is a neighbor that has a loop-free backup path to the same network as the successor, and it satisfies the Feasibility Condition (FC). R2's successor for the 192.168.1.0/24 network is R3, providing the best path or lowest metric to the destination network. Notice in Figure 7-30 that R1 provides an alternative path, but is it an FS? Before R1 can be an FS for R2, R1 must first meet the FC.

The FC is met when a neighbor's Reported Distance (RD) to a network is less than the local router's feasible distance to the same destination network. If the reported distance is less, it represents a loop-free path. The reported distance is simply an EIGRP neighbor's feasible distance to the same destination network. The reported distance is the metric that a router reports to a neighbor about its own cost to that network.

In Figure 7-32, R1's feasible distance to 192.168.1.0/24 is 2,170,112.

- R1 reports to R2 that its FD to 192.168.1.0/24 is 2,170,112.

- From R2's perspective, 2,170,112 is R1's RD.

**Figure 7-32**   Sending the Reported Distance

R2 uses this information to determine whether R1 meets the FC and, therefore, can be an FS.

As shown in Figure 7-33, because the RD of R1 (2,170,112) is less than R2's own FD (3,012,096), R1 meets the FC.

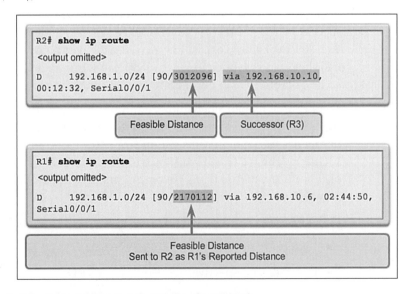

**Figure 7-33**   Does It Meet the Feasibility Condition?

R1 is now an FS for R2 to the 192.168.1.0/24 network.

If there is a failure in R2's path to 192.168.1.0/24 through R3 (successor), R2 immediately installs the path through R1 (FS) in its routing table. R1 becomes the new successor for R2's path to this network, as shown in Figure 7-34.

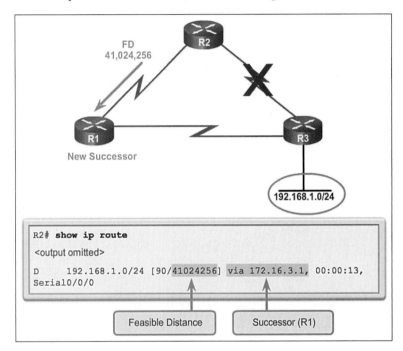

**Figure 7-34**   Using the Feasible Successor

## Topology Table: **show ip eigrp topology** Command (7.3.3.5)

The EIGRP topology table contains all the routes that are known to each EIGRP neighbor. As an EIGRP router learns routes from its neighbors, those routes are installed in its EIGRP topology table.

As shown in Example 7-15, use the **show ip eigrp topology** command to view the topology table.

**Example 7-15**   Topology Table for R2

```
R2# show ip eigrp topology
EIGRP-IPv4 Topology Table for AS(1)/ID(2.2.2.2)
Codes: P - Passive, A - Active, U - Update, Q - Query, R - Reply,
       r - reply Status, s - sia Status
```

```
P 172.16.2.0/24, 1 successors, FD is 2816
        via Connected, GigabitEthernet0/0
P 192.168.10.4/30, 1 successors, FD is 3523840
        via 192.168.10.10 (3523840/2169856), Serial0/0/1
        via 172.16.3.1 (41024000/2169856), Serial0/0/0
P 192.168.1.0/24, 1 successors, FD is 3012096
        via 192.168.10.10 (3012096/2816), Serial0/0/1
        via 172.16.3.1 (41024256/2170112), Serial0/0/0
P 172.16.3.0/30, 1 successors, FD is 40512000
        via Connected, Serial0/0/0
P 172.16.1.0/24, 1 successors, FD is 3524096
        via 192.168.10.10 (3524096/2170112), Serial0/0/1
        via 172.16.3.1 (40512256/2816), Serial0/0/0
P 192.168.10.8/30, 1 successors, FD is 3011840
        via Connected, Serial0/0/1

R2#
```

The topology table lists all successors and FSs that DUAL has calculated to destination networks. Only the successor is installed into the IP routing table.

### Topology Table: **show ip eigrp topology** Command (Cont.) (7.3.3.6)

As shown in Figure 7-35, the first line in the topology table displays the following:

**Figure 7-35**   Examining an Entry in the Topology Table: First Line

- **P:** Route in the passive state. When DUAL is not performing its diffusing computations to determine a path for a network, the route is in a stable mode, known as the passive state. If DUAL recalculates or searches for a new path, the route is in an active state and displays an A. All routes in the topology table should be in the passive state for a stable routing domain.

- **192.168.1.0/24:** Destination network that is also found in the routing table.

- **1 successors:** Displays the number of successors for this network. If there are multiple equal-cost paths to this network, there are multiple successors.

- **FD is 3012096:** FD, the EIGRP metric to reach the destination network. This is the metric displayed in the IP routing table.

As shown in Figure 7-36, the first subentry in the output shows the successor:

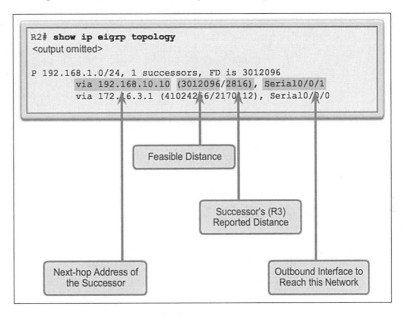

**Figure 7-36**   Examining an Entry in the Topology Table: First Subentry

- **via 192.168.10.10:** Next-hop address of the successor, R3. This address is shown in the routing table.

- **3012096:** FD to 192.168.1.0/24. It is the metric shown in the IP routing table.

- **2816:** RD of the successor and is R3's cost to reach this network.

- **Serial 0/0/1:** Outbound interface used to reach this network, also shown in the routing table.

As shown in Figure 7-37, the second subentry shows the FS, R1 (if there is not a second entry, there are no FSs):

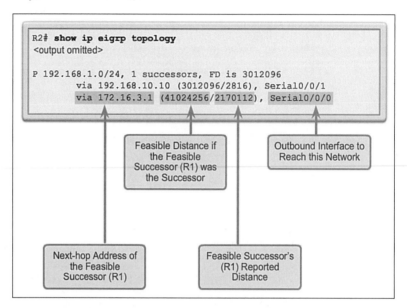

**Figure 7-37**   Examining an Entry in the Topology Table: Second Subentry

- **via 172.16.3.1:** Next-hop address of the FS, R1.

- **41024256:** R2's new FD to 192.168.1.0/24, if R1 became the new successor and would be the new metric displayed in the IP routing table.

- **2170112:** RD of the FS, or R1's metric to reach this network. The RD must be less than the current FD of 3,012,096 to meet the FC.

- **Serial 0/0/0:** This is the outbound interface used to reach FS, if this router becomes the successor.

## Topology Table: No Feasible Successor (7.3.3.7)

To see how DUAL uses successors and FSs, examine the routing table of R1, assuming that the network is converged.

Figure 7-38 displays a partial output from the **show ip route** command on R1.

The route to 192.168.1.0/24 shows that the successor is R3 through 192.168.10.6 with an FD of 2,170,112.

**Figure 7-38**   R1 Routing Table Entry for 192.168.1.0/24

The IP routing table only includes the best path, the successor. To see whether there are any FSs, we must examine the EIGRP topology table. The topology table in Figure 7-39 only shows the successor 192.168.10.6, which is R3. There are no FSs.

**Figure 7-39**   R1 Topology Table Entry for 192.168.1.0/24

By looking at the actual physical topology or network diagram, it is obvious that there is a backup route to 192.168.1.0/24 through R2. R2 is not an FS because it does not meet the FC. Although the topology clearly shows that R2 is a backup route, EIGRP does not have a map of the network topology. EIGRP is a distance vector routing protocol and only knows about remote network information through its neighbors.

DUAL does not store the route through R2 in the topology table. All links can be displayed using the **show ip eigrp topology all-links** command. This command displays links whether they satisfy the FC or not.

As shown in Figure 7-40, the **show ip eigrp topology all-links** command shows all possible paths to a network, including successors, FSs, and even those routes that are not FSs.

**Figure 7-40**   R1 All-Links Topology Table Entry for 192.168.1.0/24

R1's FD to 192.168.1.0/24 is 2,170,112 through the successor R3. For R2 to be considered an FS, it must meet the FC. R2's RD to R1 to reach 192.168.1.0/24 must be less than the R1's current FD. Per the figure, R2's RD is 3,012,096, which is higher than R1's current FD of 2,170,112.

Even though R2 looks like a viable backup path to 192.168.1.0/24, R1 has no idea that the path is not a potential loop back through itself. EIGRP is a distance vector routing protocol, without the ability to see a complete, loop-free topological map of the network. DUAL's method of guaranteeing that a neighbor has a loop-free path is that the neighbor's metric must satisfy the FC. By ensuring that the RD of the neighbor is less than its own FD, the router can assume that this neighboring router is not part of its own advertised route, thus always avoiding the potential for a loop.

R2 can be used as a successor if R3 fails; however, there is a longer delay before adding it to the routing table. Before R2 can be used as a successor, DUAL must do further processing.

**Interactive Graphic**

**Activity 7.3.3.8: Determine the Feasible Successor**

Go to the course online to perform this practice activity.

## DUAL and Convergence (7.3.4)

DUAL is responsible for maintaining the EIGRP topology table and installing routes in the routing table.

## DUAL Finite State Machine (FSM) (7.3.4.1)

The centerpiece of EIGRP is DUAL and its EIGRP route-calculation engine. The actual name of this technology is DUAL Finite State Machine (FSM). This FSM contains all the logic used to calculate and compare routes in an EIGRP network. Figure 7-41 shows a simplified version of the DUAL FSM.

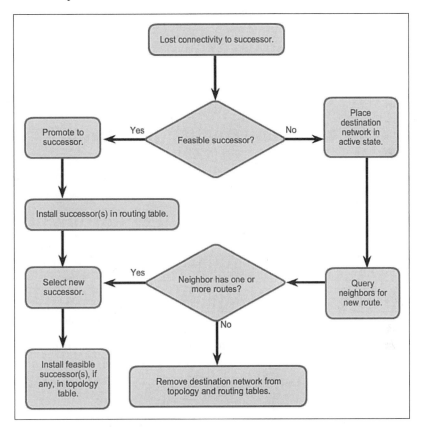

**Figure 7-41**   DUAL Finite State Machine

An FSM is an abstract machine, not a mechanical device with moving parts. FSMs define a set of possible states that something can go through, what events cause those states, and what events result from those states. Designers use FSMs to describe how a device, computer program, or routing algorithm reacts to a set of input events.

FSMs are beyond the scope of this course. However, the concept is used to examine some of the output from EIGRP's FSM using the **debug eigrp fsm** command. Use this command to examine what DUAL does when a route is removed from the routing table.

## DUAL: Feasible Successor (7.3.4.2)

R2 is currently using R3 as the successor to 192.168.1.0/24. In addition, R2 currently lists R1 as an FS, as shown in Figure 7-42. Currently, all links are operational. The red X in the figure indicates a link failure to be simulated later.

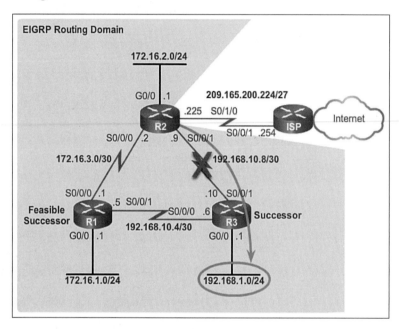

**Figure 7-42**   EIGRP for IPv4 Topology with Simulated Link Failure

The **show ip eigrp topology** output for R2 in Figure 7-43 verifies that R3 is the successor and R1 is the FS for the 192.168.1.0/24 network.

**Figure 7-43**   R2 Topology Table Entry for 192.168.1.0/24

To understand how DUAL can use an FS when the path using the successor is no longer available, a link failure is simulated between R2 and R3. Before simulating the failure, DUAL debugging must be enabled using the **debug eigrp fsm** command on R2, as shown in Example 7-16.

**Example 7-16**   Debugging EIGRP Finite State Machine on R2

```
R2# debug eigrp fsm
EIGRP Finite State Machine debugging is on
R2# conf t
Enter configuration commands, one per line.  End with CNTL/Z.
R2(config)# interface s 0/0/1
R2(config-if)# shutdown
<Output omitted>
EIGRP-IPv4(1):Find FS for dest 192.168.1.0/24. FD is 3012096, RD is 3012096 on tid 0
DUAL: AS(1) Removing dest 172.16.1.0/24, nexthop 192.168.10.10
DUAL: AS(1) RT installed 172.16.1.0/24 via 172.16.3.1
<Output omitted>
R2(config-if)# end
R2# undebug all
```

A link failure is simulated using the **shutdown** command on the Serial 0/0/1 interface on R2. The **debug** output displays the activity generated by DUAL when a link goes down. R2 must inform all EIGRP neighbors of the lost link, as well as update its own routing and topology tables. This example only shows selected **debug** output. In particular, notice that the DUAL FSM searches for and finds an FS for the route in the EIGRP topology table.

The FS R1 now becomes the successor and is installed in the routing table as the new best path to 192.168.1.0/24, as shown in Figure 7-44.

**Figure 7-44**   R2 Routing Table Entry for 192.168.1.0/24

With an FS, this change in the routing table happens almost immediately.

As shown in Figure 7-45, the topology table for R2 now shows R1 as the successor and there are no new FSs.

**Figure 7-45**    R2 Topology Table Entry for 192.168.1.0/24

If the link between R2 and R3 is made active again, R3 returns as the successor and R1 once again becomes the FS.

## DUAL: No Feasible Successor (7.3.4.3)

Occasionally, the path to the successor fails and there are no FSs. In this instance, DUAL does not have a guaranteed loop-free backup path to the network, so the path is not in the topology table as an FS. If there are no FSs in the topology table, DUAL puts the network into the active state. DUAL actively queries its neighbors for a new successor.

R1 is currently using R3 as the successor to 192.168.1.0/24, as shown in Figure 7-46.

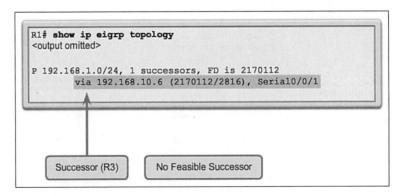

**Figure 7-46**    R1 Topology Table Entry for 192.168.1.0/24

However, R1 does not have R2 listed as an FS, because R2 does not satisfy the FC. To understand how DUAL searches for a new successor when there is no FS, a link failure is simulated between R1 and R3.

Before the link failure is simulated, DUAL debugging is enabled with the **debug eigrp fsm** command on R1, as shown in Example 7-17.

**Example 7-17**    Debugging EIGRP Finite State Machine on R1

```
R1# debug eigrp fsm
EIGRP Finite State Machine debugging is on
R1# conf t
Enter configuration commands, one per line.  End with CNTL/Z.
R1(config)# interface s 0/0/1
R1(config-if)# shutdown
<Output omitted>
EIGRP-IPv4(1): Find FS for dest 192.168.1.0/24. FD is 2170112, RD is 2170112
DUAL: AS(1) Dest 192.168.1.0/24 entering active state for tid 0.
EIGRP-IPv4(1): dest(192.168.1.0/24) active
EIGRP-IPv4(1): rcvreply: 192.168.1.0/24 via 172.16.3.2 metric 41024256/3012096
  EIGRP-IPv4(1): reply count is 1
EIGRP-IPv4(1): Find FS for dest 192.168.1.0/24. FD is 72057594037927935, RD is
  72057594037927935
DUAL: AS(1) Removing dest 192.168.1.0/24, nexthop 192.168.10.6
DUAL: AS(1) RT installed 192.168.1.0/24 via 172.16.3.2
<Output omitted>
R1(config-if)# end
R1# undebug all
```

A link failure is simulated using the **shutdown** command on the Serial 0/0/1 interface on R1.

When the successor is no longer available and there is no feasible successor, DUAL puts the route into an active state. DUAL sends EIGRP queries, asking other routers for a path to the network. Other routers return EIGRP replies, letting the sender of the EIGRP query know whether they have a path to the requested network. If none of the EIGRP replies have a path to this network, the sender of the query does not have a route to this network.

The highlighted **debug** output in Example 7-17 shows the 192.168.1.0/24 network put into the active state and EIGRP queries sent to other neighbors. R2 replies with a path to this network, which becomes the new successor and is installed into the routing table.

If the sender of the EIGRP queries receives EIGRP replies that include a path to the requested network, the preferred path is added as the new successor and added to the routing table. This process takes longer than if DUAL had an FS in its topology table and was able to quickly add the new route to the routing table. In Figure 7-47, notice that R1 has a new route to the 192.168.1.0/24 network. The new EIGRP successor is Router R2.

**Figure 7-47**   R1 Routing Table Entry for 192.168.1.0/24

Figure 7-48 shows that the topology table for R1 now has R2 as the successor with no new FSs.

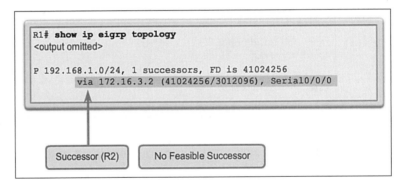

**Figure 7-48**   R1 Topology Table Entry for 192.168.1.0/24

If the link between R1 and R3 is made active again, R3 returns as the successor. However, R2 is still not the FS, because it does not meet the FC.

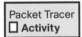

**Packet Tracer Activity 7.3.4.4: Investigating DUAL FSM**

In this activity, you will modify the EIGRP metric formula to cause a change in the topology. This allows you to see how EIGRP reacts when a neighbor goes down because of unforeseen circumstances. You will then use the **debug** command to view topology changes and see how the DUAL Finite State Machine determines successor and feasible successor paths to reconverge the network.

# Configuring EIGRP for IPv6 (7.4)

This section compares EIGRP for IPv4 and IPv6 as well as discusses EIGRP for IPv6 configuration and verification.

## EIGRP for IPv4 Versus IPv6 (7.4.1)

EIGRP for IPv6 is very similar to EIGRP for IPv4, although IPv6 requires some unique considerations.

### EIGRP for IPv6 (7.4.1.1)

Similar to its IPv4 counterpart, EIGRP for IPv6 exchanges routing information to populate the IPv6 routing table with remote prefixes. EIGRP for IPv6 was made available in Cisco IOS Release 12.4(6)T.

**Note**

In IPv6, the network address is referred to as the *prefix* and the subnet mask is called the *prefix length*.

EIGRP for IPv4 runs over the IPv4 network layer, communicating with other EIGRP IPv4 peers, and advertising only IPv4 routes. EIGRP for IPv6 has the same functionality as EIGRP for IPv4 but uses IPv6 as the network layer transport, communicating with EIGRP for IPv6 peers and advertising IPv6 routes.

EIGRP for IPv6 also uses DUAL as the computation engine to guarantee loop-free paths and backup paths throughout the routing domain.

As with all IPv6 routing protocols, EIGRP for IPv6 has separate processes from its IPv4 counterpart. The processes and operations are basically the same as in the IPv4 routing protocol; however, they run independently. EIGRP for IPv4 and EIGRP for IPv6 each have separate EIGRP neighbor tables, EIGRP topology tables, and IP routing tables, as shown in Figure 7-49. EIGRP for IPv6 is a separate protocol-dependent module (PDM).

The EIGRP for IPv6 configuration and verification commands are very similar to those used in EIGRP for IPv4. These commands are described later in this section.

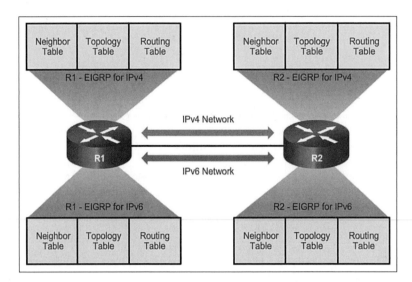

**Figure 7-49**   Comparing EIGRP for IPv4 and EIGRP for IPv6

## Comparing EIGRP for IPv4 and IPv6 (7.4.1.2)

Table 7-5 displays a quick comparison of EIGRP for IPv4 and EIGRP for IPv6.

**Table 7-5**   Comparing EIGRP for IPv4 and IPv6

| Characteristic | EIGRP for IPv4 | EIGRP for IPv6 |
|---|---|---|
| Advertised routes | IPv4 networks | IPv6 prefixes |
| Distance vector | Yes | Yes |
| Convergence technology | DUAL | DUAL |
| Metric | Bandwidth and delay by default, reliability and load are optional | Bandwidth and delay by default, reliability and load are optional |
| Transport protocol | RTP | RTP |
| Update messages | Incremental, partial, and bounded updates | Incremental, partial, and bounded updates |
| Neighbor discovery | Hello packets | Hello packets |
| Source and destination addresses | IPv4 source address and 224.0.0.10 IPv4 multicast destination address | IPv6 link-local source address and FF02::10 IPv6 multicast destination address |
| Authentication | Plain text and MD5 | MD5 |
| Router ID | 32-bit router ID | 32-bit router ID |

The following is a detailed explanation of the similarities and differences in the main features of EIGRP for IPv4 and EIGRP for IPv6:

- **Advertised routes:** EIGRP for IPv4 advertises IPv4 networks. EIGRP for IPv6 advertises IPv6 prefixes.

- **Distance vector:** Both EIGRP for IPv4 and IPv6 are advanced distance vector routing protocols. Both protocols use the same administrative distances.

- **Convergence technology:** EIGRP for IPv4 and IPv6 both use the DUAL algorithm. Both protocols use the same DUAL techniques and processes, including successor, FS, FD, and RD.

- **Metric:** Both EIGRP for IPv4 and IPv6 use bandwidth, delay, reliability, and load for their composite metric. Both routing protocols use the same composite metric and use only bandwidth and delay, by default.

- **Transport protocol:** The Reliable Transport Protocol (RTP) is responsible for guaranteed delivery of EIGRP packets to all neighbors for both protocols, EIGRP for IPv4 and IPv6.

- **Update messages:** Both EIGRP for IPv4 and IPv6 send incremental updates when the state of a destination changes. The terms *partial* and *bounded* are used when referring to updates for both protocols.

- **Neighbor discovery mechanism:** EIGRP for IPv4 and EIGRP for IPv6 use a simple Hello mechanism to learn about neighboring routers and form adjacencies.

- **Source and destination addresses:** EIGRP for IPv4 sends messages to the multicast address 224.0.0.10. These messages use the source IPv4 address of the outbound interface. EIGRP for IPv6 sends its messages to the multicast address FF02::A. EIGRP for IPv6 messages are sourced using the IPv6 link-local address of the exit interface.

- **Authentication:** EIGRP for IPv4 can use either plain text authentication or Message Digest 5 (MD5) authentication. EIGRP for IPv6 uses MD5.

- **Router ID:** Both EIGRP for IPv4 and EIGRP for IPv6 use a 32-bit number for the EIGRP router ID. The 32-bit router ID is represented in dotted-decimal notation and is commonly referred to as an IPv4 address. If the EIGRP for IPv6 router has not been configured with an IPv4 address, the **eigrp router-id** command must be used to configure a 32-bit router ID. The process for determining the router ID is the same for both EIGRP for IPv4 and IPv6.

### IPv6 Link-Local Addresses (7.4.1.3)

Routers running a dynamic routing protocol such as EIGRP exchange messages between neighbors on the same subnet or link. Routers only need to send and receive routing protocol messages with their directly connected neighbors. These messages are always sent from the source IP address of the router that is doing the forwarding.

IPv6 link-local addresses are ideal for this purpose. An IPv6 link-local address enables a device to communicate with other IPv6-enabled devices on the same link and only on that link (subnet). Packets with a source or destination link-local address cannot be routed beyond the link from where the packet originated.

EIGRP for IPv6 messages are sent using

- **Source IPv6 address:** This is the IPv6 link-local address of the exit interface.

- **Destination IPv6 address:** When the packet needs to be sent to a multicast address, it is sent to the IPv6 multicast address FF02::A, the all-EIGRP-routers with link-local scope. If the packet can be sent as a unicast address, it is sent to the link-local address of the neighboring router.

> **Note**
>
> IPv6 link-local addresses are in the FE80::/10 range. The /10 indicates that the first 10 bits are 1111 1110 10xx xxxx, which results in the first hextet having a range of 1111 1110 1000 0000 (FE80) to 1111 1110 1011 1111 (FEBF).

**Interactive Graphic**

**Activity 7.4.1.4: Compare EIGRPv4 and EIGRPv6**

Go to the course online to perform this practice activity.

## Configuring EIGRP for IPv6 (7.4.2)

This topic discusses the commands unique to configuring EIGRP for IPv6.

### EIGRP for IPv6 Network Topology (7.4.2.1)

Figure 7-50 shows the network topology that is used for configuring EIGRP for IPv6.

If the network is running dual-stack, using both IPv4 and IPv6 on all devices, EIGRP for both IPv4 and IPv6 can be configured on all the routers. However, in this section, the focus is solely on EIGRP for IPv6.

Only the IPv6 global unicast addresses have been configured on each router.

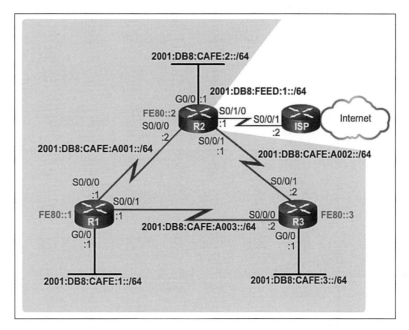

**Figure 7-50**  EIGRP for IPv6 Topology

Example 7-18 displays the starting interface configurations on each router.

**Example 7-18**  IPv6 Interface Configurations

```
R1# show running-config
<Output omitted>
!
interface GigabitEthernet0/0
 ipv6 address 2001:DB8:CAFE:1::1/64
!
interface Serial0/0/0
 ipv6 address 2001:DB8:CAFE:A001::1/64
 clock rate 64000
!
interface Serial0/0/1
 ipv6 address 2001:DB8:CAFE:A003::1/64
```

```
R2# show running-config
<Output omitted>
!
interface GigabitEthernet0/0
 ipv6 address 2001:DB8:CAFE:2::1/64
!
interface Serial0/0/0
```

```
 ipv6 address 2001:DB8:CAFE:A001::2/64
!
interface Serial0/0/1
 ipv6 address 2001:DB8:CAFE:A002::1/64
 clock rate 64000
!
interface Serial0/1/0
 ipv6 address 2001:DB8:FEED:1::1/64
```

```
R3# show running-config
<Output omitted>
!
interface GigabitEthernet0/0
 ipv6 address 2001:DB8:CAFE:3::1/64
!
interface Serial0/0/0
 ipv6 address 2001:DB8:CAFE:A003::2/64
 clock rate 64000
!
interface Serial0/0/1
 ipv6 address 2001:DB8:CAFE:A002::2/64
```

Notice the interface bandwidth values from the previous EIGRP for IPv4 configuration. Because EIGRP for IPv4 and IPv6 use the same metrics, modifying the bandwidth parameters influences both routing protocols.

## Configuring IPv6 Link-Local Addresses (7.4.2.2)

Link-local addresses are automatically created when an IPv6 global unicast address is assigned to the interface. Global unicast addresses are not required on an interface; however, IPv6 link-local addresses are.

Unless configured manually, Cisco routers create the link-local address using the FE80::/10 prefix and the EUI-64 process. EUI-64 involves using the 48-bit Ethernet MAC address, inserting FFFE in the middle and flipping the seventh bit. For serial interfaces, Cisco uses the MAC address of an Ethernet interface. A router with several serial interfaces can assign the same link-local address to each IPv6 interface, because link-local addresses only need to be local on the link.

Link-local addresses created using the EUI-64 format, or in some cases random interface IDs, make it difficult to recognize and remember those addresses. Because IPv6 routing protocols use IPv6 link-local addresses for unicast addressing and next-hop address information in the routing table, it is common practice to make it an easily recognizable address. Configuring the link-local address manually provides the ability to create an address that is recognizable and easier to remember.

Link-local addresses can be configured manually using the same interface configuration mode command used to create IPv6 global unicast addresses, but with different parameters:

```
Router(config-if)# ipv6 address link-local-address link-local
```

A link-local address has a prefix within the range of FE80 to FEBF. When an address begins with this hextet (16-bit segment), the **link-local** keyword must follow the address.

Example 7-19 shows the configuration of a link-local address using the **ipv6 address** interface configuration mode command.

**Example 7-19**    Configuring Link-Local Addresses on R1

```
R1(config)# interface s 0/0/0
R1(config-if)# ipv6 address fe80::1 ?
  link-local  Use link-local address

R1(config-if)# ipv6 address fe80::1 link-local
R1(config-if)# exit
R1(config)# interface s 0/0/1
R1(config-if)# ipv6 address fe80::1 link-local
R1(config-if)# exit
R1(config)# interface g 0/0
R1(config-if)# ipv6 address fe80::1 link-local
R1(config-if)#
```

The link-local address FE80::1 is used to make it easily recognizable as belonging to router R1. The same IPv6 link-local address is configured on all of R1's interfaces. FE80::1 can be configured on each link because it only has to be unique on that link. The configurations for R2 and R3 are similar to R1.

As shown in Figure 7-51, the **show ipv6 interface brief** command is used to verify the IPv6 link-local and global unicast addresses on all interfaces.

**Figure 7-51**   Verifying Link-Local Addresses on R1

## Configuring the EIGRP for IPv6 Routing Process (7.4.2.3)

The **ipv6 unicast-routing** global configuration mode command enables IPv6 routing on the router. This command is required before any IPv6 routing protocol can be configured. This command is not required to configure IPv6 addresses on the interfaces, but it is necessary for the router to be enabled as an IPv6 router.

### EIGRP for IPv6

The following global configuration mode command is used to enter router configuration mode for EIGRP for IPv6:

```
Router(config)# ipv6 router eigrp autonomous-system
```

Similar to EIGRP for IPv4, the *autonomous-system* value must be the same on all routers in the routing domain, as shown in Example 7-20.

**Example 7-20**   Configuring the EIGRP for IPv6 Routing Process

```
#R1(config)# ipv6 router eigrp 2
% IPv6 routing not enabled
R1(config)# ipv6 unicast-routing
R1(config)# ipv6 router eigrp 2
R1(config-rtr)# eigrp router-id 1.0.0.0
R1(config-rtr)# no shutdown

R2(config)# ipv6 unicast-routing
R2(config)# ipv6 router eigrp 2
R2(config-rtr)# eigrp router-id 2.0.0.0
R2(config-rtr)# no shutdown
R2(config-rtr)#
```

```
R3(config)# ipv6 unicast-routing
R3(config)# ipv6 router eigrp 2
R3(config-rtr)# eigrp router-id 3.0.0.0
R3(config-rtr)# no shutdown
R3(config-rtr)#
```

Notice in the example that the EIGRP for IPv6 routing process could not be configured until IPv6 routing was enabled with the **ipv6 unicast-routing** global configuration mode command.

### Router ID

The **eigrp router-id** command is used to configure the router ID. EIGRP for IPv6 uses a 32-bit value for the router ID. To obtain that value, EIGRP for IPv6 uses the same process as EIGRP for IPv4. The **eigrp router-id** command takes precedence over any loopback or physical interface IPv4 addresses. If an EIGRP for IPv6 router does not have any active interfaces with an IPv4 address, the **eigrp router-id** command is required.

The router ID should be a unique 32-bit number in the EIGRP for IP routing domain; otherwise, routing inconsistencies can occur.

**Note**

The **eigrp router-id** command is used to configure the router ID for EIGRP. Some versions of IOS will accept the command **router-id**, without first specifying **eigrp**. The running config, however, will display **eigrp router-id**, regardless of which command is used.

By default, the EIGRP for IPv6 process is in a shutdown state. The **no shutdown** command is required to activate the EIGRP for IPv6 process, as shown in Example 7-20. This command is not required for EIGRP for IPv4. Although EIGRP for IPv6 is enabled, neighbor adjacencies and routing updates cannot be sent and received until EIGRP is activated on the appropriate interfaces.

Both the **no shutdown** command and a router ID are required for the router to form neighbor adjacencies.

### The **ipv6 eigrp** Interface Command (7.4.2.4)

EIGRP for IPv6 uses a different method to enable an interface for EIGRP. Instead of using the **network** router configuration mode command to specify matching interface addresses, EIGRP for IPv6 is configured directly on the interface.

Use the following interface configuration mode command to enable EIGRP for IPv6 on an interface:

```
Router(config-if)# ipv6 eigrp autonomous-system
```

The *autonomous-system* value must be the same as the autonomous system number used to enable the EIGRP routing process. Similar to the **network** command used in EIGRP for IPv4, the **ipv6 eigrp interface** command

- Enables the interface to form adjacencies and send or receive EIGRP for IPv6 updates

- Includes the prefix (network) of this interface in EIGRP for IPv6 routing updates

Example 7-21 shows the configuration to enable EIGRP for IPv6 on the interfaces for all three routers.

**Example 7-21** Enabling EIGRP for IPv6 on the Interfaces

```
R1(config)# interface g0/0
R1(config-if)# ipv6 eigrp 2
R1(config-if)# exit
R1(config)# interface s 0/0/0
R1(config-if)# ipv6 eigrp 2
R1(config-if)# exit
R1(config)# interface s 0/0/1
R1(config-if)# ipv6 eigrp 2
R1(config-if)#

R2(config)# interface g 0/0
R2(config-if)# ipv6 eigrp 2
R2(config-if)# exit
R2(config)# interface s 0/0/0
R2(config-if)# ipv6 eigrp 2
R2(config-if)# exit
%DUAL-5-NBRCHANGE: EIGRP-IPv6 2: Neighbor FE80::1 (Serial0/0/0) is up: new adjacency
R2(config)# interface s 0/0/1
R2(config-if)# ipv6 eigrp 2
R2(config-if)#

R3(config)# interface g 0/0
R3(config-if)# ipv6 eigrp 2
R3(config-if)# exit
R3(config)# interface s 0/0/0
R3(config-if)# ipv6 eigrp 2
R3(config-if)#
```

```
*Mar  4 03:02:00.696: %DUAL-5-NBRCHANGE: EIGRP-IPv6 2: Neighbor FE80::1
  (Serial0/0/0) is up: new adjacency
R3(config-if)# exit
R3(config)# interface s 0/0/1
R3(config-if)# ipv6 eigrp 2
R3(config-if)#
*Mar  4 03:02:17.264: %DUAL-5-NBRCHANGE: EIGRP-IPv6 2: Neighbor FE80::2
  (Serial0/0/1) is up: new adjacency
```

Notice the message following the serial 0/0/0 interface in R2:

```
%DUAL-5-NBRCHANGE: EIGRP-IPv6 2: Neighbor FE80::1 (Serial0/0/0) is up: new adjacency
```

This message indicates that R2 has now formed an EIGRP-IPv6 adjacency with the neighbor at link-local address FE80::1. Because static link-local addresses were configured on all three routers, it is easy to determine that this adjacency is with Router R1 (FE80::1).

## Passive Interface with EIGRP for IPv6

The same **passive-interface** command used for IPv4 is used to configure an interface as passive with EIGRP for IPv6. As shown in Example 7-22, the **show ipv6 protocols** command is used to verify the configuration.

**Example 7-22**    Configuring and Verifying EIGRP for IPv6 Passive Interfaces

```
R1(config)# ipv6 router eigrp 2
R1(config-rtr)# passive-interface gigabitethernet 0/0
R1(config-rtr)# end

R1# show ipv6 protocols

IPv6 Routing Protocol is "eigrp 2"
EIGRP-IPv6 Protocol for AS(2)
<output omitted>

  Interfaces:
    Serial0/0/0
    Serial0/0/1
    GigabitEthernet0/0 (passive)
  Redistribution:
    None
R1#
```

## Verifying EIGRP for IPv6 (7.4.3)

Verifying EIGRP for IPv6 is similar to verifying EIGRP for IPv4. The commands are almost identical. Simply replace the **ip** with **ipv6**.

### Verifying EIGRP for IPv6: Examining Neighbors (7.4.3.1)

Similar to EIGRP for IPv4, before any EIGRP for IPv6 updates can be sent or received, routers must establish adjacencies with their neighbors.

Use the **show ipv6 eigrp neighbors** command to view the neighbor table and verify that EIGRP for IPv6 has established an adjacency with its neighbors. The output shown in Figure 7-52 displays the IPv6 link-local address of the adjacent neighbor and the interface that this router uses to reach that EIGRP neighbor.

**Figure 7-52   show ipv6 eigrp neighbors Command**

Using meaningful link-local addresses makes it easy to recognize the neighbors R2 at FE80::2 and R3 at FE80::3.

The output from the **show ipv6 eigrp neighbors** command includes

- **H column:** Lists the neighbors in the order that they were learned.

- **Address:** IPv6 link-local address of the neighbor.

- **Interface:** Local interface on which this Hello packet was received.

- **Hold:** Current hold time. When a Hello packet is received, this value is reset to the maximum hold time for that interface and then counts down to 0. If 0 is reached, the neighbor is considered down.

- **Uptime:** Amount of time since this neighbor was added to the neighbor table.

- **SRTT** and **RTO:** Used by RTP to manage reliable EIGRP packets.

- **Queue Count:** Should always be 0. If it is more than 0, EIGRP packets are waiting to be sent.

- **Sequence Number:** Used to track updates, queries, and reply packets.

The **show ipv6 eigrp neighbors** command is useful for verifying and troubleshooting EIGRP for IPv6. If an expected neighbor is not listed, ensure that both ends of the link are up/up using the **show ipv6 interface brief** command. The same requirements exist for establishing neighbor adjacencies with EIGRP for IPv6 as they do for IPv4. If both sides of the link have active interfaces, check to see

- Are both routers configured with the same EIGRP autonomous system number?

- Is the interface enabled for EIGRP for IPv6 with the correct autonomous system number?

## Verifying EIGRP for IPv6: **show ipv6 protocols** Command (7.4.3.2)

The **show ipv6 protocols** command displays the parameters and other information about the state of any active IPv6 routing protocol processes currently configured on the router. The **show ipv6 protocols** command displays different types of output specific to each IPv6 routing protocol.

The output in Figure 7-53 is labeled for easy reference.

The labels in Figure 7-53 indicate several EIGRP for IPv6 parameters previously discussed, including

1. EIGRP for IPv6 is an active dynamic routing protocol on R1 configured with the autonomous system number 2.

2. These are the *k* values used to calculate the EIGRP composite metric. K1 and K3 are 1, by default, and K2, K4, and K5 are 0, by default.

3. The EIGRP for IPv6 router ID of R1 is 1.0.0.0.

4. Same as EIGRP for IPv4, EIGRP for IPv6 administrative distances have an internal AD of 90 and an external AD of 170 (default values).

5. The interfaces are enabled for EIGRP for IPv6.

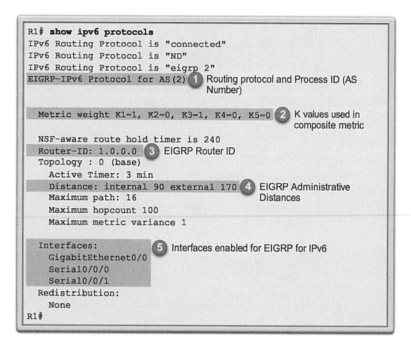

**Figure 7-53  show ipv6 protocols Command**

The output from the **show ipv6 protocols** command is useful in debugging routing operations. The Interfaces section shows on which interfaces EIGRP for IPv6 has been enabled. This is useful in verifying that EIGRP is enabled on all the appropriate interfaces with the correct autonomous system number.

### Verifying EIGRP for IPv6: Examine the IPv6 Routing Table (7.4.3.3)

As with any routing protocol, the goal is to populate the IP routing table with routes to remote networks and the best paths to reaching those networks. As with IPv4, it is important to examine the IPv6 routing table and determine whether it is populated with the correct routes.

The IPv6 routing table is examined using the **show ipv6 route** command. EIGRP for IPv6 routes are denoted in the routing table with a D, similar to its counterpart for IPv4.

Example 7-23 displays the EIGRP for IPv6 routes on all three routers.

**Example 7-23  IPv6 EIGRP Routes**

```
R1# show ipv6 route eigrp
<Output omitted>

D    2001:DB8:CAFE:2::/64 [90/3524096]
```

```
     via FE80::3, Serial0/0/1
D    2001:DB8:CAFE:3::/64 [90/2170112]
     via FE80::3, Serial0/0/1
D    2001:DB8:CAFE:A002::/64 [90/3523840]
     via FE80::3, Serial0/0/1
R1#
```

```
R2# show ipv6 route eigrp
<Output omitted>

D    2001:DB8:CAFE:1::/64 [90/3524096]
     via FE80::3, Serial0/0/1
D    2001:DB8:CAFE:3::/64 [90/3012096]
     via FE80::3, Serial0/0/1
D    2001:DB8:CAFE:A003::/64 [90/3523840]
     via FE80::3, Serial0/0/1
R2#
```

```
R3# show ipv6 route eigrp
<Output omitted>

D    2001:DB8:CAFE:1::/64 [90/2170112]
     via FE80::1, Serial0/0/0
D    2001:DB8:CAFE:2::/64 [90/3012096]
     via FE80::2, Serial0/0/1
D    2001:DB8:CAFE:A001::/64 [90/41024000]
     via FE80::1, Serial0/0/0
     via FE80::2, Serial0/0/1
R3#
```

The output in Example 7-23 shows that R1 has installed three EIGRP routes to remote IPv6 networks in its IPv6 routing table:

- 2001:DB8:CAFE:2::/64 through R3 (FE80::3) using its Serial 0/0/1 interface
- 2001:DB8:CAFE:3::/64 through R3 (FE80::3) using its Serial 0/0/1 interface
- 2001:DB8:CAFE:A002::/64 through R3 (FE80::3) using its Serial 0/0/1 interface

All three routes are using Router R3 as the next-hop router (successor). Notice that the routing table uses the link-local address as the next-hop address. Because each router has had all its interfaces configured with a unique and distinguishable link-local address, it is easy to recognize that the next-hop router through FE80::3 is Router R3. Also, notice that R3 has two equal-cost paths to

2001:DB8:CAFE:A001::/64. One path is through R1 at FE80::1, and the other path is through R2 at FE80::2.

### Packet Tracer Activity 7.4.3.4: Configuring Basic EIGRP with IPv6

In this activity, you will configure the network with EIGRP routing for IPv6. You will also assign router IDs, configure passive interfaces, verify that the network is fully converged, and display routing information using **show** commands.

- EIGRP for IPv6 has the same overall operation and features as EIGRP for IPv4. There are a few major differences between them.

- EIGRP for IPv6 is configured directly on the router interfaces.

- With EIGRP for IPv6, a router ID is required on each router or the routing process does not start.

- The EIGRP for IPv6 routing process uses a shutdown feature.

### Lab 7.4.3.5: Configuring Basic EIGRP for IPv6

In this lab, you will complete the following objectives:

- Part 1: Build the Network and Verify Connectivity

- Part 2: Configure EIGRP for IPv6 Routing

- Part 3: Verify EIGRP for IPv6 Routing

- Part 4: Configure and Verify Passive Interfaces

# Summary (7.5)

**Class Activity 7.5.1.1: Portfolio RIP and EIGRP**

You are preparing a portfolio file for comparison of RIP and EIGRP routing protocols.

Think of a network with three interconnected routers with each router providing a LAN for PCs, printers, and other end devices. The graphic on this page depicts one example of a topology like this.

In this modeling activity scenario, you will be creating, addressing, and configuring a topology, using verification commands, and comparing/contrasting RIP and EIGRP routing protocol outputs.

Complete the PDF reflection questions accompanying this activity. Save your work and be prepared to share your answers with the class. Also save a copy of your work for later use within this course or for portfolio reference.

---

EIGRP (Enhanced Interior Gateway Routing Protocol) is a classless, distance vector routing protocol. EIGRP is an enhancement of another Cisco routing protocol, IGRP (Interior Gateway Routing Protocol), which is now obsolete. EIGRP was initially released in 1992 as a Cisco-proprietary protocol available only on Cisco devices. In 2013, Cisco released a basic functionality of EIGRP as an open standard to the IETF.

EIGRP uses the source code of "D" for DUAL in the routing table. EIGRP has a default administrative distance of 90 for internal routes and 170 for routes imported from an external source, such as default routes.

EIGRP is an advanced distance vector routing protocol that includes features not found in other distance vector routing protocols like RIP. These features include Diffusing Update Algorithm (DUAL), establishing neighbor adjacencies, Reliable Transport Protocol (RTP), partial and bounded updates, and equal and unequal cost load balancing.

EIGRP uses PDMs (Protocol-Dependent Modules), giving it the capability to support different Layer 3 protocols, including IPv4 and IPv6. EIGRP uses RTP (Reliable Transport Protocol) as the transport layer protocol for the delivery of EIGRP packets. EIGRP uses reliable delivery for EIGRP updates, queries, and replies, and uses unreliable delivery for EIGRP Hellos and acknowledgments. Reliable RTP means that an EIGRP acknowledgment must be returned.

Before any EIGRP updates are sent, a router must first discover its neighbors. This is done with EIGRP Hello packets. The Hello and hold-down values do not need to match for two routers to become neighbors. The **show ip eigrp neighbors** command is used to view the neighbor table and verify that EIGRP has established an adjacency with its neighbors.

EIGRP does not send periodic updates like RIP. EIGRP sends partial or bounded updates, which include only the route changes and only to those routers that are affected by the change. The EIGRP composite metric uses bandwidth, delay, reliability, and load to determine the best path. By default, only bandwidth and delay are used.

At the center of EIGRP is DUAL (Diffusing Update Algorithm). The DUAL Finite State Machine is used to determine the best path and potential backup paths to every destination network. The successor is a neighboring router that is used to forward the packet using the least-cost route to the destination network. Feasible distance (FD) is the lowest calculated metric to reach the destination network through the successor. A feasible successor (FS) is a neighbor that has a loop-free backup path to the same network as the successor, and also meets the feasibility condition. The feasibility condition (FC) is met when a neighbor's reported distance (RD) to a network is less than the local router's feasible distance to the same destination network. The reported distance is simply an EIGRP neighbor's feasible distance to the destination network.

EIGRP is configured with the **router eigrp** *autonomous-system* command. The *autonomous-system* value is actually a process ID and must be the same on all routers in the EIGRP routing domain. The **network** command is similar to that used with RIP. The network is the classful network address of the directly connected interfaces on the router. A wildcard mask is an optional parameter that can be used to include only specific interfaces.

## Practice

The following activities provide practice with the topics introduced in this chapter. The Labs and Class Activities are available in the companion *Scaling Networks Lab Manual* (ISBN 978-1-58713-325-1). The Packet Tracer Activities PKA files are found in the online course.

## Class Activities

- Class Activity 7.0.1.2: Classless EIGRP
- Class Activity 7.5.1.1: Portfolio RIP and EIGRP

## Labs

- Lab 7.2.2.5: Configuring Basic EIGRP with IPv4

- Lab 7.4.3.5: Configuring Basic EIGRP for IPv6

## Packet Tracer Activities

- Packet Tracer Activity 7.2.2.4: Configuring Basic EIGRP with IPv4

- Packet Tracer Activity 7.3.4.4: Investigating DUAL FSM

- Packet Tracer Activity 7.4.3.4: Configuring Basic EIGRP with IPv6

# Check Your Understanding Questions

Complete all the review questions listed to test your understanding of the topics and concepts in this chapter. The appendix "Answers to 'Check Your Understanding' Questions" lists the answers.

1. Which of the following protocols can be routed by EIGRP as a consequence of the PDM feature? (Choose two.)

    A. RTP

    B. UDP

    C. IPv4

    D. IPv6

    E. TCP

2. Which IPv4 multicast address does an EIGRP-enabled router use to send query packets?

    A. 224.0.0.5

    B. 224.0.0.9

    C. 224.0.0.12

    D. 224.0.0.10

3. Which protocol number is used to indicate that an EIGRP packet is encapsulated in an IP packet?

    A. 6

    B. 17

    C. 88

    D. 89

4. In the **router eigrp 100** command, what does the value **100** represent?

   A. The router ID

   B. The metric

   C. The autonomous system number

   D. The administrative distance

5. What address and wildcard mask can be used to enable EIGRP for only the subnet 192.168.100.192 255.255.255.192?

   A. 192.168.100.192 0.0.0.7

   B. 192.168.100.192 0.0.0.15

   C. 192.168.100.192 0.0.0.63

   D. 192.168.100.192 0.0.0.127

6. Refer to Example 7-24. A network administrator is verifying the EIGRP configuration. Which conclusion can be drawn?

**Example 7-24**    Command Output for Question 6

```
R1# show ip protocols
Routing Protocol is "eigrp  64515"
  Outgoing update filter list for all interfaces is not set
  Incoming update filter list for all interfaces is not set
  Default networks flagged in outgoing updates
  Default networks accepted from incoming updates
  EIGRP metric weight K1=1, K2=0, K3=1, K4=0, K5=0
  EIGRP maximum hopcount 100
  EIGRP maximum metric variance 1
Redistributing: eigrp 64515
  Automatic network summarization is not in effect
  Maximum path: 4
  Routing for Networks:
     192.168.1.4/30
  Routing Information Sources:
    Gateway          Distance      Last Update
    192.168.1.6      90            6284
  Distance: internal 90 external 170
```

A. There are 90 internal networks and 170 external networks in the routing table.

B. Up to four paths to the same destination with different costs can be included in the routing table.

C. Subnetted networks are included in route updates.

D. Metric weight values have been changed from their default values.

7. Which of the following values are included by default in the calculation of an EIGRP metric? (Choose two.)

A. Hop count

B. Reliability

C. Bandwidth

D. Delay

E. Load

8. Which bandwidth value is used when calculating the EIGRP metric of a route?

A. The fastest bandwidth of all outgoing interfaces between the source and destination

B. The slowest bandwidth of all outgoing interfaces between the source and destination

C. The slowest bandwidth of all interfaces on the router

D. The fastest bandwidth of all interfaces on the router

9. Refer to Example 7-25. What does the value 2816 represent in the output display?

**Example 7-25**    Command Output for Question 9

```
R1# show ip eigrp topology
IP-EIGRP Topology Table for AS 64515

Codes: P - Passive, A - Active, U - Update, Q - Query, R - Reply,
       r - Reply status

P 192.168.1.4/30, 1 successors, FD is 2169856
        via Connected, Serial0/0/1
P 172.16.0.64/26, 1 successors, FD is 2170112
        via 192.168.1.6 (2170112/2816), Serial0/0/1
R1#
```

A. Shortest distance

B. Reported distance

C. Feasible distance

D. Administrative distance

10. Which of the following conditions occurring simultaneously will result in an EIGRP route going into the active state? (Choose two.)

A. The successor is down.

B. The network has been recalculated.

C. One neighbor has not met the feasibility condition.

D. The router is not sending queries.

E. There is no feasible successor.

11. What operational feature is different for EIGRP for IPv6 compared to EIGRP for IPv4?

A. Router ID configuration

B. Neighbor discovery mechanisms

C. The source and destination addresses used within the EIGRP messages

D. DUAL algorithm calculations

12. Which address will EIGRP for IPv6 use as the router ID?

A. The highest link-local address that is configured on any enabled interface

B. The highest IPv6 address that is configured on any enabled interface

C. The highest interface MAC address

D. The highest IPv4 address that is configured on an enabled interface

13. Which destination address is used by EIGRP for IPv6 messages?

A. The 32-bit router ID of the neighbor

B. The all-EIGRP-routers link-local multicast address

C. The IPv6 global unicast address of the neighbor

D. The unique local IPv6 address of the neighbor

**14.** Fill in the blank. What EIGRP packet type is described by the function?

The _____ packet is used to distribute routing information.

The _____ packet is used to form an EIGRP neighbor relationship.

The _____ packet is used by an EIGRP router to request more information.

The _____ packet is used in response to an EIGRP router searching for a network.

The _____ packet is used to confirm reliable delivery of a packet

**15.** What are the default administrative distances for each of the following types of EIGRP route?

Internal _____

External _____

Summary _____

# CHAPTER 8

# EIGRP Advanced Configurations and Troubleshooting

## Objectives

Upon completion of this chapter, you will be able to answer the following questions:

- What are the commands to configure EIGRP automatic summarization?

- What are the commands to configure EIGRP manual summarization?

- What are the commands to configure EIGRP to propagate a default route?

- What are the commands to configure EIGRP interface settings to improve network performance?

- What are the commands to configure EIGRP authentication to secure routing updates?

- What processes and tools are available to troubleshoot an EIGRP network?

- What are the steps to troubleshoot a neighbor adjacency issue in an EIGRP network?

- What are the steps to troubleshoot missing route entries in an EIGRP routing table?

## Key Terms

This chapter uses the following key terms. You can find the definitions in the Glossary.

# Introduction (8.0.1.1)

EIGRP is a versatile routing protocol that can be fine-tuned in many ways. Two of the most important tuning capabilities are the ability to summarize routes and the ability to implement load balancing. Other tuning capabilities include being able to propagate a default, fine-tune timers, and implement authentication between EIGRP neighbors to increase security.

This chapter discusses these additional tuning features and the configuration mode commands to implement these features for both IPv4 and IPv6.

### Class Activity 8.0.1.2: EIGRP — Back to the Future

This chapter teaches you how to maintain your EIGRP networks and to influence them to do what you want them to do. EIGRP concepts from this chapter include

- Auto-summarization
- Load balancing
- Default routes
- Hold-down timers
- Authentication

With a partner, write ten EIGRP review questions based on the previous chapter's curriculum content. Three of the questions must focus on the previous bulleted items. Ideally, Multiple Choice, True/False, or Fill-in-the-Blank question types will be designed. As you design your questions, ensure that you record the curriculum section and page numbers of the supporting content in case you need to refer back for answer verification.

Save your work and then meet with another group, or the entire class, and quiz them using the questions you developed.

# Advanced EIGRP Configurations (8.1)

This section discusses advanced EIGRP configurations, including automatic and manual summarization, default route propagation, fine-tuning EIGRP interfaces, and securing EIGRP routing updates.

# Automatic Summarization (8.1.1)

Prior to IOS Releases 15.0(1)M and 12.2(33), EIGRP defaulted to automatically summarizing networks at the classful boundary. With the new releases, automatic summarization must be configured to enable this behavior.

## Network Topology (8.1.1.1)

Before fine-tuning EIGRP features, start with a basic implementation of EIGRP.

Figure 8-1 shows the network topology for IPv4 used for this chapter.

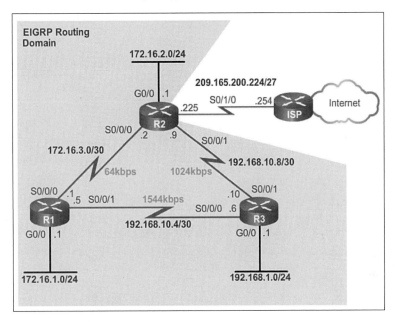

**Figure 8-1**   EIGRP for IPv4 Topology

Examples 8-1, 8-2, and 8-3 show the IPv4 interface configurations and the EIGRP implementations on R1, R2, and R3, respectively.

**Example 8-1**   Starting IPv4 Interface and EIGRP for IPv4 Configuration for R1

```
R1# show running-config
<Output omitted>
version 15.2
!
interface GigabitEthernet0/0
 ip address 172.16.1.1 255.255.255.0
!
interface Serial0/0/0
```

```
 bandwidth 64
 ip address 172.16.3.1 255.255.255.252
 clock rate 64000
!
interface Serial0/0/1
 ip address 192.168.10.5 255.255.255.252
!
router eigrp 1
 network 172.16.0.0
 network 192.168.10.0
 eigrp router-id 1.1.1.1
```

**Example 8-2**   Starting IPv4 Interface and EIGRP for IPv4 Configuration for R2

```
R2# show running-config
<Output omitted>
version 15.2
!
interface GigabitEthernet0/0
 ip address 172.16.2.1 255.255.255.0
!
interface Serial0/0/0
 bandwidth 64
 ip address 172.16.3.2 255.255.255.252
!
interface Serial0/0/1
 bandwidth 1024
 ip address 192.168.10.9 255.255.255.252
 clock rate 64000
!
interface Serial0/1/0
 ip address 209.165.200.225 255.255.255.224
!
router eigrp 1
 network 172.16.0.0
 network 192.168.10.8 0.0.0.3
 eigrp router-id 2.2.2.2
```

**Example 8-3**   Starting IPv4 Interface and EIGRP for IPv4 Configuration for R3

```
R3# show running-config
<Output omitted>
version 15.2
```

```
!
interface GigabitEthernet0/0
 ip address 192.168.1.1 255.255.255.0
!
interface Serial0/0/0
 ip address 192.168.10.6 255.255.255.252
 clock rate 64000
!
interface Serial0/0/1
 bandwidth 1024
 ip address 192.168.10.10 255.255.255.252
!
router eigrp 1
 network 192.168.1.0
 network 192.168.10.4 0.0.0.3
 network 192.168.10.8 0.0.0.3
 eigrp router-id 3.3.3.3
```

The types of serial interfaces and their associated bandwidths might not necessarily reflect the more common types of connections found in networks today. The bandwidths of the serial links used in this topology help explain the calculation of the routing protocol metrics and the process of best path selection.

Notice that the **bandwidth** commands on the serial interfaces were used to modify the default bandwidth of 1544 kb/s.

In this chapter, the ISP router is used as the routing domain's gateway to the Internet. All three routers are running Cisco IOS Release 15.2.

## EIGRP Automatic Summarization (8.1.1.2)

One of the most common tuning methods of EIGRP is enabling and disabling automatic route summarization. *Route summarization* allows a router to group networks together and advertises them as one large group using a single, summarized route. The ability to summarize routes is necessary because of the rapid growth of networks.

A border router is a router that sits at the edge of a network. This router must be able to advertise all the known networks within its route table to a connecting network router or ISP router. This convergence can potentially result in very large route tables. Imagine if a single router had ten different networks and had to advertise all ten route entries to a connecting router. What if that connecting router also had ten networks, and had to advertise all 20 routes to an ISP router? If every enterprise router followed this pattern, the routing table of the ISP router would be huge.

Summarization decreases the number of entries in routing updates and reduces the number of entries in local routing tables. It also reduces bandwidth utilization for routing updates and results in faster routing table lookups.

To limit the number of routing advertisements and the size of routing tables, routing protocols such as EIGRP use *automatic summarization* at classful boundaries. This means that EIGRP recognizes subnets as a single Class A, B, or C network, and creates only one entry in the routing table for the summary route. As a result, all traffic destined for the subnets travels across that one path. Figure 8-2 shows an example of how automatic summarization works.

**Figure 8-2**   Automatic Summarization at a Classful Network Boundary

Routers R1 and R2 are both configured using EIGRP for IPv4 with automatic summarization. R1 has three subnets in its routing table: 172.16.1.0/24, 172.16.2.0/24, and 172.16.3.0/24. In the classful network addressing architecture, these subnets are all considered part of a larger Class B network, 172.16.0.0/16. Because EIGRP on Router R1 is configured for automatic summarization, when it sends its routing update to R2, it summarizes the three /24 subnets as a single network of 172.16.0.0/16, which reduces the number of routing updates sent and the number of entries in R2's IPv4 routing table.

All traffic destined for the three subnets travels across the one path. R2 does not maintain routes to individual subnets, and no subnet information is learned. In an enterprise network, the path chosen to reach the summary route might not be the best choice for the traffic that is trying to reach each individual subnet. The only way that all routers can find the best routes for each individual subnet is for neighbors to send subnet information. In this situation, automatic summarization should be disabled. When automatic summarization is disabled, updates include subnet information.

## Configuring EIGRP Automatic Summarization (8.1.1.3)

EIGRP for IPv4 automatic summarization is disabled by default beginning with Cisco IOS Release 15.0(1)M and 12.2(33). Prior to this, automatic summarization was enabled by default. This meant that EIGRP performed automatic summarization each time the EIGRP topology crossed a border between two different major class networks.

In Example 8-4, the output from the **show ip protocols** command on R1 indicates that EIGRP automatic summarization is disabled.

**Example 8-4**  Verifying That Automatic Summarization Is Disabled

```
R1# show ip protocols
*** IP Routing is NSF aware ***

Routing Protocol is "eigrp 1"
  Outgoing update filter list for all interfaces is not set
  Incoming update filter list for all interfaces is not set
  Default networks flagged in outgoing updates
  Default networks accepted from incoming updates
  EIGRP-IPv4 Protocol for AS(1)
    Metric weight K1=1, K2=0, K3=1, K4=0, K5=0
<Output omitted>

  Automatic Summarization: disabled
  Maximum path: 4
  Routing for Networks:
    172.16.0.0
    192.168.10.0
<Output omitted>
```

This router is running IOS Release 15.2; therefore, EIGRP automatic summarization is disabled by default. Example 8-5 shows the current routing table for R3.

**Example 8-5**  Verifying That Routes Are Not Automatically Summarized

```
R3# show ip route eigrp
<Output omitted>

   172.16.0.0/16 is variably subnetted, 3 subnets, 2 masks
D        172.16.1.0/24 [90/2170112] via 192.168.10.5, 02:21:10, Serial0/0/0
D        172.16.2.0/24 [90/3012096] via 192.168.10.9, 02:21:10, Serial0/0/1
D        172.16.3.0/30 [90/41024000] via 192.168.10.9, 02:21:10, Serial0/0/1
                       [90/41024000] via 192.168.10.5, 02:21:10, Serial0/0/0
R3#
```

Notice that the IPv4 routing table for R3 contains all the networks and subnets within the EIGRP routing domain.

To enable automatic summarization for EIGRP, use the **auto-summary** command in router configuration mode, as shown in Example 8-6, for all three routers in the topology.

**Example 8-6**   Configuring Automatic Summarization

```
R1(config)# router eigrp 1
R1(config-router)# auto-summary
R1(config-router)#
*Mar  9 19:40:19.342: %DUAL-5-NBRCHANGE: EIGRP-IPv4 1: Neighbor 192.168.10.6
  (Serial0/0/1) is resync: summary configured
*Mar  9 19:40:19.342: %DUAL-5-NBRCHANGE: EIGRP-IPv4 1: Neighbor 192.168.10.6
  (Serial0/0/1) is resync: summary up, remove components
*Mar  9 19:41:03.630: %DUAL-5-NBRCHANGE: EIGRP-IPv4 1: Neighbor 192.168.10.6
  (Serial0/0/1) is resync: peer graceful-restart
```

```
R2(config)# router eigrp 1
R2(config-router)# auto-summary
R2(config-router)#
```

```
R3(config)# router eigrp 1
R3(config-router)# auto-summary
R3(config-router)#
```

### Verifying Auto-Summary: **show ip protocols** (8.1.1.4)

Notice in Figure 8-1 that the EIGRP routing domain has three classful networks:

- 172.16.0.0/16 Class B network, consisting of 172.16.1.0/24, 172.16.2.0/24, and 172.16.3.0/30 subnets

- 192.168.10.0/24 Class C network, consisting of the 192.168.10.4/30 and 192.168.10.8/30 subnets

- 192.168.1.0/24 Class C network, which is not subnetted

The output from R1's **show ip protocols** command in Example 8-7 shows that automatic summarization is now enabled.

**Example 8-7**   Verifying That Automatic Summarization Is Enabled

```
R1# show ip protocols
*** IP Routing is NSF aware ***
```

```
Routing Protocol is "eigrp 1"
  Outgoing update filter list for all interfaces is not set
  Incoming update filter list for all interfaces is not set
  Default networks flagged in outgoing updates
  Default networks accepted from incoming updates
  EIGRP-IPv4 Protocol for AS(1)
    Metric weight K1=1, K2=0, K3=1, K4=0, K5=0
<Output omitted>

Automatic Summarization: enabled
    192.168.10.0/24 for Gi0/0, Se0/0/0
      Summarizing 2 components with metric 2169856
    172.16.0.0/16 for Se0/0/1
      Summarizing 3 components with metric 2816
<Output omitted>
```

The output also indicates the networks that are summarized and on which interfaces. Notice that R1 summarizes two networks in its EIGRP routing updates:

- 192.168.10.0/24 sent out the GigabitEthernet 0/0 and Serial 0/0/0 interfaces
- 172.16.0.0/16 sent out the Serial 0/0/1 interface

R1 has the subnets 192.168.10.4/30 and 192.168.10.8/30 in its IPv4 routing table.

As indicated in Figure 8-3, R1 summarizes the 192.168.10.4/30 and 192.168.10.8/30 subnet.

**Figure 8-3**   R1 192.168.10.0/24 Summary

It forwards the summarized address of 192.168.10.0/24 to its neighbors on its Serial 0/0/0 and GigabitEthernet 0/0 interfaces. Because R1 does not have any EIGRP neighbors on its GigabitEthernet 0/0 interface, the summarized routing update is only received by R2.

As indicated in Figure 8-4, R1 also has the 172.16.1.0/24, 172.16.2.0/24, and 172.16.3.0/30 subnets in its IPv4 routing table.

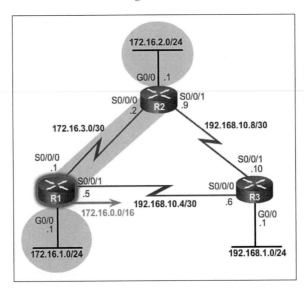

**Figure 8-4**   R1 172.16.0.0/16 Summary

R3 selects R1 as the successor to 172.16.0.0/16 because it has a lower feasible distance. The R3 S0/0/0 interface connecting to R1 uses a default bandwidth of 1544 kb/s. The R3 link to R2 has a higher feasible distance because the R3 S0/0/1 interface has been configured with a lower bandwidth of 1024 kb/s.

Notice that the 172.16.0.0/16 summarized update is not sent out R1's GigabitEthernet 0/0 and Serial 0/0/0 interfaces. This is because these two interfaces are members of the same 172.16.0.0/16 Class B network. The 172.16.1.0/24 nonsummarized routing update is sent by R1 to R2. Summarized updates are only sent out interfaces on different major classful networks.

## Verifying Auto-Summary: Topology Table (8.1.1.5)

In Figure 8-5, Routers R1 and R2 will send R3 a summarized EIGRP routing update of 172.16.0.0/16.

Routing tables for R1 and R2 contain subnets of the 172.16.0.0/16 network; therefore, both routers send the summary advertisement across a different major network to R3.

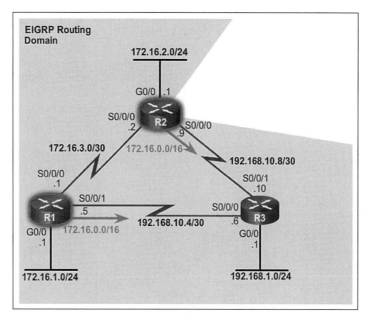

**Figure 8-5**   R3 Sources for 172.16.0.0/16

Example 8-8 shows the output from the **show ip eigrp topology all-links** command used to view R3's complete EIGRP topology table.

**Example 8-8**   Verifying the Summary Route in the Topology Table

```
R3# show ip eigrp topology all-links

P 172.16.0.0/16, 1 successors, FD is 2170112, serno 9
        via 192.168.10.5 (2170112/2816), Serial0/0/0
        via 192.168.10.9 (3012096/2816), Serial0/0/1
<Output omitted>
```

This verifies that R3 has received the 172.16.0.0/16 summary route from both R1 at 192.168.10.5 and R2 at 192.168.10.9. The first entry through 192.168.10.5 is the successor, and the second entry through 192.168.10.9 is the feasible successor. R1 is the successor because its 1544-kb/s link with R3 gives R3 a better EIGRP cost to 172.16.0.0/16 than R2, which is using a slower 1024-kb/s link.

The **all-links** option shows all received updates, whether the route qualifies as a feasible successor (FS) or not. In this instance, R2 does qualify as an FS. R2 is considered an FS because its reported distance (RD) of 2816 is less than the feasible distance (FD) of 2,170,112 through R1.

## Verifying Auto-Summary: Routing Table (8.1.1.6)

Examine the routing table to verify that the summarized route was received. Example 8-9 shows R3's routing table prior to automatic summarization, and then with automatic summarization enabled using the **auto-summary** command.

**Example 8-9** Verifying the Summary Route in the Routing Table

```
!Automatic Summarization Disabled
R3# show ip route eigrp
<Output omitted>

 172.16.0.0/16 is variably subnetted, 3 subnets, 2 masks
D        172.16.1.0/24 [90/2170112] via 192.168.10.5, 02:21:10, Serial0/0/0
D        172.16.2.0/24 [90/3012096] via 192.168.10.9, 02:21:10, Serial0/0/1
D        172.16.3.0/30 [90/41024000] via 192.168.10.9, 02:21:10, Serial0/0/1
                       [90/41024000] via 192.168.10.5, 02:21:10, Serial0/0/0
R3#
!Automatic Summarization Enabled
R3# show ip route eigrp
<Output omitted>

D     172.16.0.0/16 [90/2170112] via 192.168.10.5, 00:12:05, Serial0/0/0
      192.168.10.0/24 is variably subnetted, 5 subnets, 3 masks
D        192.168.10.0/24 is a summary, 00:11:43, Null0
R3#
```

Notice that with automatic summarization enabled, R3's routing table now only contains the single Class B network address 172.16.0.0/16. The successor or next-hop router is R1 through 192.168.10.5.

**Note**

Automatic summarization is only an option with EIGRP for IPv4. Classful addressing does not exist in IPv6; therefore, there is no need for automatic summarization with EIGRP for IPv6.

When enabling automatic summarization, it is also necessary to understand the Null interface. Example 8-10 shows the routing table for R1.

**Example 8-10** Null0 Summary Routes on R1

```
R1# show ip route

    172.16.0.0/16 is variably subnetted, 6 subnets, 4 masks
```

```
D        172.16.0.0/16 is a summary, 00:03:06, Null0
C        172.16.1.0/24 is directly connected, GigabitEthernet0/0
L        172.16.1.1/32 is directly connected, GigabitEthernet0/0
D        172.16.2.0/24 [90/40512256] via 172.16.3.2, 00:02:52, Serial0/0/0
C        172.16.3.0/30 is directly connected, Serial0/0/0
L        172.16.3.1/32 is directly connected, Serial0/0/0
D     192.168.1.0/24 [90/2170112] via 192.168.10.6, 00:02:51, Serial0/0/1
      192.168.10.0/24 is variably subnetted, 4 subnets, 3 masks
D        192.168.10.0/24 is a summary, 00:02:52, Null0
C        192.168.10.4/30 is directly connected, Serial0/0/1
L        192.168.10.5/32 is directly connected, Serial0/0/1
D        192.168.10.8/30 [90/3523840] via 192.168.10.6, 00:02:59, Serial0/0/1
R1#
```

Notice that the two entries highlighted are using an exit interface of *Null0*. EIGRP has automatically included a summary route to Null0 for two classful networks 192.168.10.0/24 and 172.16.0.0/16.

The Null0 interface is a virtual IOS interface that is a route to nowhere, commonly known as "the bit bucket." Packets that match a route with a Null0 exit interface are discarded.

EIGRP for IPv4 automatically includes a Null0 summary route whenever the following conditions exist:

- There is at least one subnet that was learned through EIGRP.
- There are two or more **network** EIGRP router configuration mode commands.
- Automatic summarization is enabled.

The purpose of the Null0 summary route is to prevent routing loops for destinations that are included in the summary, but do not actually exist in the routing table.

### Summary Route (8.1.1.7)

Figure 8-6 illustrates a scenario where a routing loop could occur:

1. R1 has a default route, 0.0.0.0/0, through the ISP router.

2. R1 sends a routing update to R2 containing the default route.

3. R2 installs the default route from R1 in its IPv4 routing table.

4. R2's routing table contains the 172.16.1.0/24, 172.16.2.0/24, and 172.16.3.0/24 subnets in its routing table.

5. R2 sends a summarized update to R1 for the 172.16.0.0/16 network.

6. R1 installs the summarized route for 172.16.0.0/16 through R2.

7. R1 receives a packet for 172.16.4.10. Because R1 has a route for 172.16.0.0/16 through R2, it forwards the packet to R2.

8. R2 receives the packet with the destination address 172.16.4.10 from R1. The packet does not match any specific route, so using the default route in its routing table, R2 forwards the packet back to R1.

9. The packet for 172.16.4.10 is looped between R1 and R2 until the TTL expires and the packet is dropped.

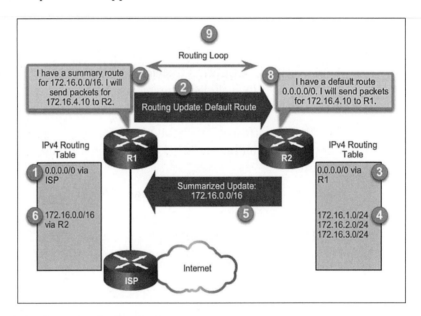

**Figure 8-6**    Example of a Routing Loop

## Summary Route (Cont.) (8.1.1.8)

EIGRP uses the Null0 interface to prevent these types of routing loops. Figure 8-7 illustrates a scenario where a Null0 route prevents the routing loop illustrated in the previous example:

1. R1 has a default route, 0.0.0.0/0, through the ISP router.

2. R1 sends a routing update to R2 containing the default route.

3. R2 installs the default route from R1 in its IPv4 routing table.

4. R2's routing table contains the 172.16.1.0/24, 172.16.2.0/24, and 172.16.3.0/24 subnets in its routing table.

5. R2 installs the 172.16.0.0/16 summary route to Null0 in its routing table.

6. R2 sends a summarized update to R1 for the 172.16.0.0/16 network.

7. R1 installs the summarized route for 172.16.0.0/16 through R2.

8. R1 receives a packet for 172.16.4.10. Because R1 has a route for 172.16.0.0/16 through R2, it forwards the packet to R2.

9. R2 receives the packet with the destination address 172.16.4.10 from R1. The packet does not match any specific subnet of 172.16.0.0 and does match the 172.16.0.0/16 summary route to Null0. Using the Null0 route, the packet is discarded.

**Figure 8-7**  Null0 Route is Used for Loop Prevention

A summary route on R2 for 172.16.0.0/16 to the Null0 interface discards any packets that begin with 172.16.x.x, but do not have a longer match with any of the subnets 172.16.1.0/24, 172.16.2.0/24, or 172.16.3.0/24.

Even if R2 has a default route of 0.0.0.0/0 in its routing table, the Null0 route is a longer match.

**Note**

The Null0 summary route is removed when auto-summary is disabled using the **no auto-summary** router configuration mode command.

**Activity 8.1.1.9: Determine the Classful Summarization**

Go to the course online to perform this practice activity.

Interactive
Graphic

**Interactive
Graphic**

**Activity 8.1.1.10: Determine the Exit Interface for a Given Packet**

Go to the course online to perform this practice activity.

# Manual Summarization (8.1.2)

Sometimes automatic summarization is not the best way to handle route summarization. For example, if the network addressing design is discontiguous, automatic summarization can cause issues. EIGRP provides a way to summarize just those networks that you want to advertise.

## Manual Summary Routes (8.1.2.1)

EIGRP can be configured to summarize routes, whether or not automatic summarization (**auto-summary**) is enabled. Because EIGRP is a classless routing protocol and includes the subnet mask in the routing updates, manual summarization can include supernet routes. Remember, a supernet is an aggregation of multiple major classful network addresses.

In Figure 8-8, two more networks are added to Router R3 using loopback interfaces 192.168.2.0/24 and 192.168.3.0/24. Although the loopback interfaces are virtual interfaces, they are used to represent physical networks for this example.

**Figure 8-8**  EIGRP for IPv4 Topology with Simulated R3 LANs

Example 8-11 shows the commands on R3 to configure the two loopback interfaces and the configuration to enable both interfaces for EIGRP.

**Example 8-11**    Configuring Loopback Interfaces on R3

```
R3(config)# interface loopback 2
R3(config-if)# ip add 192.168.2.1 255.255.255.0
R3(config-if)# exit
R3(config)# interface loopback 3
R3(config-if)# ip add 192.168.2.1 255.255.255.0
R3(config-if)# ip add 192.168.3.1 255.255.255.0
R3(config-if)# exit
R3(config)# router eigrp 1
R3(config-router)# network 192.168.2.0
R3(config-router)# network 192.168.3.0
R3(config-router)#
```

To verify that R3 sent EIGRP update packets to R1 and R2, the routing tables are examined on both routers.

In Example 8-12, only the pertinent routes are shown.

**Example 8-12**    Additional Routes Verified on R1 and R2

```
R1# show ip route
<Output omitted>


D     192.168.1.0/24 [90/2170112] via 192.168.10.6, 00:47:39, Serial0/0/1
D     192.168.2.0/24 [90/2297856] via 192.168.10.6, 00:08:09, Serial0/0/1
D     192.168.3.0/24 [90/2297856] via 192.168.10.6, 00:08:04, Serial0/0/1
R1#


R2# show ip route
<Output omitted>


D     192.168.1.0/24 [90/3012096] via 192.168.10.10, 00:47:58, Serial0/0/1
D     192.168.2.0/24 [90/3139840] via 192.168.10.10, 00:08:28, Serial0/0/1
D     192.168.3.0/24 [90/3139840] via 192.168.10.10, 00:08:23, Serial0/0/1
R2#
```

R1 and R2 show these additional networks in their routing tables: 192.168.2.0/24 and 192.168.3.0/24. Instead of sending three separate networks, R3 can summarize the 192.168.1.0/24, 192.168.2.0/24, and 192.168.3.0/24 networks as a single route.

## Configuring EIGRP Manual Summary Routes (8.1.2.2)

Before configuring an EIGRP manual summary route, it is necessary to calculate what the summary should be.

### Determining the Summary EIGRP Route

Figure 8-9 shows the two manual summary routes that are configured on R3.

**Figure 8-9**  EIGRP for IPv4 Topology: R3 Summary Route

These summary routes are sent out of the Serial 0/0/0 and Serial 0/0/1 interfaces to R3's EIGRP neighbors.

To determine the summary of these three networks, the same method is used to determine summary static routes, as shown in Figure 8-10:

```
192.168.1.0:  11000000 . 10101000 . 000000001 . 00000000
192.168.2.0:  11000000 . 10101000 . 000000010 . 00000000
192.168.3.0:  11000000 . 10101000 . 000000011 . 00000000

          ←——  22 matching bits  ——→

22 matching bits = a /22 or 255.255.252.0 subnet mask
```

**Figure 8-10**  Calculating a Summary Route

**Step 1.**    Write out the networks to be summarized in binary.

**Step 2.**    To find the subnet mask for summarization, start with the far-left bit.

**Step 3.**    Working from left to right, find all the bits that match consecutively.

**Step 4.**    When there is a column of bits that do not match, stop. This is the summary boundary.

**Step 5.**    Count the number of far-left matching bits, which in this example is 22. This number is used to determine the subnet mask for the summarized route: /22 or 255.255.252.0.

**Step 6.**    To find the network address for summarization, copy the matching 22 bits and add all 0 bits to the end to make 32 bits.

The result is the summary network address and mask for 192.168.0.0/22.

## Configure EIGRP Manual Summarization

To establish EIGRP manual summarization on a specific EIGRP interface, use the following interface configuration mode command:

```
Router(config-if)# ip summary-address eigrp as-number network-address subnet-mask
```

Example 8-13 shows the configuration to propagate a manual summary route. Because R3 has two EIGRP neighbors, the EIGRP manual summarization must be configured on both Serial 0/0/0 and Serial 0/0/1.

**Example 8-13**    Configuring a Summary Route

```
R3(config)# interface serial 0/0/0
R3(config-if)# ip summary-address eigrp 1 192.168.0.0 255.255.252.0
R3(config-if)# interface serial 0/0/1
R3(config-if)# ip summary-address eigrp 1 192.168.0.0 255.255.252.0
R3(config-if)#
```

## Verifying Manual Summary Routes (8.1.2.3)

Example 8-14 illustrates that after the summary route is configured, the routing tables of R1 and R2 no longer include the individual 192.168.1.0/24, 192.168.2.0/24, and 192.168.3.0/24 networks.

**Example 8-14** Verifying Summary Route Received on R1 and R2

```
R1# show ip route
<Output omitted>


D    192.168.0.0/22 [90/2170112] via 192.168.10.6, 01:53:19, Serial0/0/1
R1#
```

```
R2# show ip route
<Output omitted>


D    192.168.0.0/22 [90/3012096] via 192.168.10.10, 01:53:33, Serial0/0/1
R2#
```

Instead, they show a single summary route of 192.168.0.0/22. Summary routes reduce the number of total routes in routing tables, which makes the routing table lookup process more efficient. Summary routes also require less bandwidth utilization for the routing updates, because a single route can be sent instead of multiple individual routes.

## EIGRP for IPv6: Manual Summary Routes (8.1.2.4)

While automatic summarization is not available for EIGRP IPv6 networks, it is possible to enable manual summarization for EIGRP IPv6. Figure 8-11 shows an EIGRP IPv6 topology with four loopback addresses configured on R3.

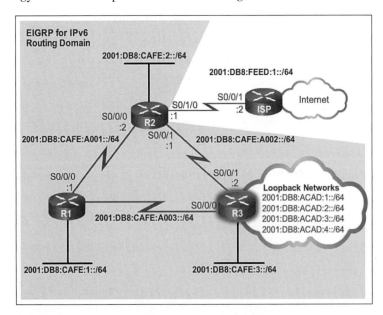

**Figure 8-11** EIGRP for IPv6 Topology with Simulated R3 LANs

These virtual addresses are used to represent physical networks in R3's IPv6 routing table. These networks can be manually summarized in EIGRP for IPv6.

Example 8-15 shows the configuration of the IPv6 loopback addresses on R3.

**Example 8-15**    IPv6 Loopback Configuration on R3

```
R3(config)# interface loopback 11
R3(config-if)# ipv6 address 2001:db8:acad:1::1/64
R3(config-if)# ipv6 eigrp 2
R3(config-if)# exit
R3(config)# interface loopback 12
R3(config-if)# ipv6 address 2001:db8:acad:2::1/64
R3(config-if)# ipv6 eigrp 2
R3(config-if)# exit
R3(config)# interface loopback 13
R3(config-if)# ipv6 address 2001:db8:acad:3::1/64
R3(config-if)# ipv6 eigrp 2
R3(config-if)# exit
R3(config)# interface loopback 14
R3(config-if)# ipv6 address 2001:db8:acad:4::1/64
R3(config-if)# ipv6 eigrp 2
```

Only four loopback addresses are shown in the topology and configured on R3; however, for this example, it is assumed that all 2001:DB8:ACAD::/48 subnets can be reachable through R3.

To configure EIGRP for IPv6 manual summarization on a specific EIGRP interface, use the following interface configuration mode command:

```
Router(config-if)# ipv6 summary-address eigrp as-number prefix/prefix-length
```

Example 8-16 shows the configuration to propagate an EIGRP for IPv6 manual summary route to R1 and R2 for the 2001:DB8:ACAD::/48 prefix.

**Example 8-16**    Configuration and Verification of EIGRP for IPv6 Manual Summary Route

```
R3(config)# interface serial 0/0/0
R3(config-if)# ipv6 summary-address eigrp 2 2001:db8:acad::/48
R3(config-if)# exit
R3(config)# interface serial 0/0/1
R3(config-if)# ipv6 summary-address eigrp 2 2001:db8:acad::/48
R3(config-if)# end
```

```
R3# show ipv6 route
<Output omitted>
D    2001:DB8:ACAD::/48 [5/128256]
        via Null0, directly connected
```

Similar to EIGRP for IPv4, R3 includes a summary route to Null0 as a loop-prevention mechanism.

The reception of the manual summary route can be verified by examining the routing table of the other routers in the routing domain. Example 8-17 shows the 2001:DB8:ACAD::/48 route in the IPv6 routing table of R1.

**Example 8-17** Verification of EIGRP for IPv6 Manual Summary Route

```
R1# show ipv6 route | include 2001:DB8:ACAD:
D    2001:DB8:ACAD::/48 [90/2297856]
R1#
```

**Packet Tracer Activity 8.1.2.5: Configuring EIGRP Manual Summary Routes for IPv4 and IPv6**

In this activity, you will calculate and configure summary routes for the IPv4 and IPv6 networks. EIGRP is already configured; however, you are required to configure IPv4 and IPv6 summary routes on the specified interfaces. EIGRP will replace the current routes with a more specific summary route, thereby reducing the size of the routing tables.

# Default Route Propagation (8.1.3)

This topic discusses the **redistribute static** method of propagating a default route in EIGRP.

## Propagating a Default Static Route (8.1.3.1)

Using a static route to 0.0.0.0/0 as a default route is not routing protocol dependent. The *"quad zero"* static default route can be used with any currently supported routing protocols. The static default route is usually configured on the router that has a connection to a network outside the EIGRP routing domain, for example, to an ISP.

In Figure 8-12, R2 is the gateway router connecting the EIGRP routing domain with the Internet.

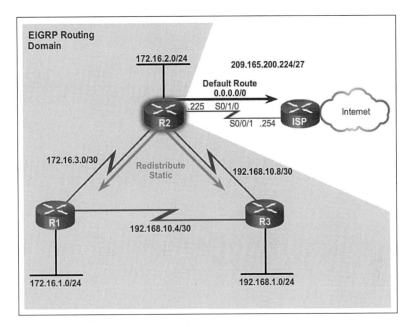

**Figure 8-12**   EIGRP for IPv4 Topology: Default Route Propagation

When the static default route is configured, it is necessary to propagate that route throughout the EIGRP domain. One method of propagating a static default route within the EIGRP routing domain is by using the **redistribute static** command. The **redistribute static** command tells EIGRP to include static routes in its EIGRP updates to other routers. Example 8-18 shows the configuration of the static default route and the **redistribute static** command on Router R2.

**Example 8-18**   R2 Static Default Route Configuration and Propagation

```
R2(config)# ip route 0.0.0.0 0.0.0.0 serial 0/1/0
R2(config)# router eigrp 1
R2(config-router)# redistribute static
```

Example 8-19 verifies that the default route has been received by Router R2 and installed in its IPv4 routing table.

**Example 8-19**   Verifying the Default Route on R2

```
R2# show ip route | include 0.0.0.0
Gateway of last resort is 0.0.0.0 to network 0.0.0.0
S*    0.0.0.0/0 is directly connected, Serial0/1/0
R2#
```

In Example 8-20, the **show ip protocols** command verifies that R2 is redistributing static routes within the EIGRP routing domain.

**Example 8-20**   Verifying Redistribution on R2

```
R2# show ip protocols
*** IP Routing is NSF aware ***

Routing Protocol is "eigrp 1"
  Outgoing update filter list for all interfaces is not set
  Incoming update filter list for all interfaces is not set
  Default networks flagged in outgoing updates
  Default networks accepted from incoming updates
  Redistributing: static
  EIGRP-IPv4 Protocol for AS(1)
<Output omitted>
```

## Verifying the Propagated Default Route (8.1.3.2)

Example 8-21 displays a portion of the IPv4 routing tables for R1 and R3.

**Example 8-21**   Verifying the Default Route on R1 and R3

```
R1# show ip route | include 0.0.0.0
Gateway of last resort is 192.168.10.6 to network 0.0.0.0
D*EX  0.0.0.0/0 [170/3651840] via 192.168.10.6, 00:25:23, Serial0/0/1
R1#

R3# show ip route | include 0.0.0.0
Gateway of last resort is 192.168.10.9 to network 0.0.0.0
D*EX  0.0.0.0/0 [170/3139840] via 192.168.10.9, 00:27:17, Serial0/0/1
R3#
```

In the routing tables for R1 and R3, notice the routing source and administrative distance for the new default route learned using EIGRP. The entry for the EIGRP-learned default route is identified by the following:

- **D:** This route was learned from an EIGRP routing update.

- **\*:** The route is a candidate for a default route.

- **EX:** The route is an external EIGRP route, in this case a static route outside of the EIGRP routing domain.

- **170:** This is the administrative distance of an external EIGRP route.

Notice that R1 selects R3 as the successor to the default route because it has a lower feasible distance. Default routes provide a default path to outside the routing domain and, like summary routes, minimize the number of entries in the routing table.

## EIGRP for IPv6: Default Route (8.1.3.3)

Recall that EIGRP maintains separate tables for IPv4 and IPv6; therefore, an IPv6 default route must be propagated separately, as shown in Figure 8-13.

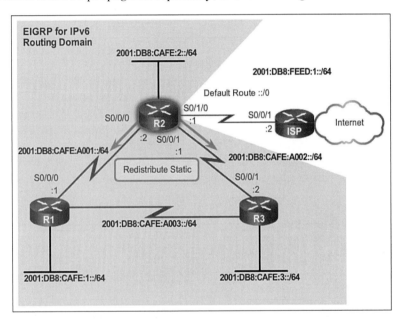

**Figure 8-13**  EIGRP for IPv6 Topology: Default Route Propagation

Similar to EIGRP for IPv4, a default static route is configured on the gateway router (R2), as shown in Example 8-22.

**Example 8-22**  R2 IPv6 Static Default Route Configuration and Propagation

```
R2(config)# ipv6 route ::/0 serial 0/1/0
R2(config)# ipv6 router eigrp 2
R2(config-router)# redistribute static
```

The ::/0 prefix and prefix length are equivalent to the 0.0.0.0 0.0.0.0 address and subnet mask used in IPv4. Both are all-zero addresses with a /0 prefix length.

The IPv6 default static route is redistributed into the EIGRP for IPv6 domain using the same **redistribute static** command used in EIGRP for IPv4.

**Note**

Some IOSs might require that the **redistribute static** command include the EIGRP metric parameters before the static route can be redistributed.

### Verifying Propagation of Default Route

The propagation of the IPv6 static default route can be verified by examining R1's IPv6 routing table using the **show ipv6 route** command, as shown in Example 8-23.

**Example 8-23**   Verifying the Default Route on R1

```
R1# show ipv6 route
IPv6 Routing Table - default - 12 entries
Codes: C - Connected, L - Local, S - Static, U - Per-user Static route
       B - BGP, R - RIP, I1 - ISIS L1, I2 - ISIS L2
       IA - ISIS interarea, IS - ISIS summary, D - EIGRP, EX - EIGRP external
       ND - ND Default, NDp - ND Prefix, DCE - Destination, NDr - Redirect
       O - OSPF Intra, OI - OSPF Inter, OE1 - OSPF ext 1, OE2 - OSPF ext 2
       ON1 - OSPF NSSA ext 1, ON2 - OSPF NSSA ext 2
EX  ::/0 [170/3523840]
     via FE80::3, Serial0/0/1
<output omitted>
```

Notice that the successor or next-hop address is not R2, but R3. This is because R3 provides a better path to R2, at a lower cost metric than R1.

**Packet Tracer Activity 8.1.3.4: Propagating a Default Route in EIGRP for IPv4 and IPv6**

In this activity, you will configure and propagate a default route in EIGRP for IPv4 and IPv6 networks. EIGRP is already configured. However, you are required to configure an IPv4 and an IPv6 default route. Then, you will configure the EIGRP routing process to propagate the default route to downstream EIGRP neighbors. Finally, you will verify the default routes by pinging hosts outside the EIGRP routing domain.

## Fine-Tuning EIGRP Interfaces (8.1.4)

This topic discusses how to configure EIGRP to better utilize the available bandwidth as well as how to customize the timers. Load balancing is also covered.

## EIGRP Bandwidth Utilization (8.1.4.1)

Configuring bandwidth utilization is essentially the same whether configuring EIGRP for IPv4 or EIGRP for IPv6.

### EIGRP Bandwidth for IPv4

By default, EIGRP uses only up to 50 percent of an interface's bandwidth for EIGRP information. This prevents the EIGRP process from overutilizing a link and not allowing enough bandwidth for the routing of normal traffic.

Use the **ip bandwidth-percent eigrp** command to configure the percentage of bandwidth that can be used by EIGRP on an interface:

```
Router(config-if)# ip bandwidth-percent eigrp as-number percent
```

In Figure 8-14, R1 and R2 share a very slow 64-kb/s link.

**Figure 8-14**   EIGRP for IPv4 Topology: Bandwidth

The configuration to limit how much bandwidth EIGRP uses is shown in Example 8-24.

**Example 8-24**   Configuring Bandwidth Utilization with EIGRP for IPv4

```
R1(config)# interface serial 0/0/0
R1(config-if)# ip bandwidth-percent eigrp 1 50
R1(config-if)#

R2(config)# interface serial 0/0/0
R2(config-if)# ip bandwidth-percent eigrp 1 50
```

```
R2(config-if)#
R2(config)# interface serial 0/0/1
R2(config-if)# ip bandwidth-percent eigrp 1 75

R3(config)# interface serial 0/0/1
R3(config-if)# ip bandwidth-percent eigrp 1 75
```

The **ip bandwidth-percent eigrp** command uses the amount of configured bandwidth (or the default bandwidth) when calculating the percent that EIGRP can use. In this example, EIGRP is limited to no more than 40 percent of the link's bandwidth. Therefore, EIGRP never uses more than 32 kb/s of the link's bandwidth for EIGRP packet traffic.

To restore the default value, use the **no** form of this command.

### EIGRP Bandwidth for IPv6

To configure the percentage of bandwidth that can be used by EIGRP for IPv6 on an interface, use the **ipv6 bandwidth-percent eigrp** command in interface configuration mode. To restore the default value, use the **no** form of this command.

```
Router(config-if)# ipv6 bandwidth-percent eigrp as-number percent
```

Example 8-25 shows the configuration of the interfaces between R1 and R2 to limit the bandwidth used by EIGRP for IPv6.

**Example 8-25**   Configuring Bandwidth Utilization with EIGRP for IPv6

```
R1(config)# interface serial 0/0/0
R1(config-if)# ipv6 bandwidth-percent eigrp 2 50
R1(config-if)#

R2(config)# interface serial 0/0/0
R2(config-if)# ipv6 bandwidth-percent eigrp 2 50
R2(config-if)#
```

### Hello and Hold Timers (8.1.4.2)

Like the bandwidth commands, configuring Hello intervals and Hold timers is essentially the same whether configuring EIGRP for IPv4 or EIGRP for IPv6.

### Hello Intervals and Hold Times with EIGRP for IPv4

EIGRP uses a lightweight Hello protocol to establish and monitor the connection status of its neighbor. The Hold time tells the router the maximum time that the router should wait to receive the next Hello before declaring that neighbor as unreachable. The default values are shown in Table 8-1.

**Table 8-1**   Default Hello Intervals and Hold Times for EIGRP

| Bandwidth | Example Link | Default Hello Interval | Default Hold Time |
|---|---|---|---|
| 1.544 Mbps | Multipoint Frame Relay | 60 seconds | 180 seconds |
| Greater than 1.544 Mbps | T1, Ethernet | 5 seconds | 15 seconds |

Hello intervals and Hold times are configurable on a per-interface basis and do not have to match with other EIGRP routers to establish or maintain adjacencies. The command to configure a different Hello interval is

```
Router(config-if)# ip hello-interval eigrp as-number seconds
```

If the Hello interval is changed, ensure that the Hold time value is equal to, or greater than, the Hello interval. Otherwise, neighbor adjacency goes down after the Hold time expires and before the next Hello interval. Use the following command to configure a different Hold time:

```
Router(config-if)# ip hold-time eigrp as-number seconds
```

The *seconds* value for both Hello and Hold time intervals can range from 1 to 65,535.

Example 8-26 shows the configuration of R1 to use a 50-second Hello interval and 150-second Hold time.

**Example 8-26**   Configuring EIGRP for IPv4 Hello and Hold Times

```
R1(config)# interface serial 0/0/0
R1(config-if)# ip hello-interval eigrp 1 60
R1(config-if)# ip hold-time eigrp 1 180

R2(config)# interface serial 0/0/0
R2(config-if)# ip hello-interval eigrp 1 60
R2(config-if)# ip hold-time eigrp 1 180
```

The **no** form can be used on both of these commands to restore the default values.

The Hello interval time and Hold time do not need to match for two routers to form an EIGRP adjacency.

## Hello Intervals and Hold Times with EIGRP for IPv6

EIGRP for IPv6 uses the same Hello interval and Hold times as EIGRP for IPv4. The interface configuration mode commands are similar to those for IPv4:

```
Router(config-if)# ipv6 hello-interval eigrp as-number seconds
Router(config-if)# ipv6 hold-time eigrp as-number seconds
```

Example 8-27 shows the Hello interval and Hold time configurations for R1 and R2 with EIGRP for IPv6.

**Example 8-27**   Configuring EIGRP for IPv6 Hello and Hold Times

```
R1(config)# inter serial 0/0/0
R1(config-if)# ipv6 hello-interval eigrp 2 60
R1(config-if)# ipv6 hold-time eigrp 2 180

R2(config)# inter serial 0/0/0
R2(config-if)# ipv6 hello-interval eigrp 2 60
R2(config-if)# ipv6 hold-time eigrp 2 180
```

## Load-Balancing IPv4 (8.1.4.3)

*Equal-cost load balancing* is the ability of a router to distribute outbound traffic using all interfaces that have the same metric from the destination address. Load balancing uses network segments and bandwidth more efficiently. For IP, Cisco IOS Software applies load balancing using up to four equal-cost paths by default. Figure 8-15 shows the EIGRP for IPv4 network topology.

**Figure 8-15**   EIGRP for IPv4 Topology: Load Balancing

In this topology, R3 has two EIGRP equal-cost routes for the network between R1 and R2, 172.16.3.0/30. One route is through R1 at 192.168.10.4/30, and the other route is through R2 at 192.168.10.8/30.

The **show ip protocols** command can be used to verify the number of equal-cost paths currently configured on the router. The output in Example 8-28 shows that R3 is using the default of four equal-cost paths.

**Example 8-28**   Maximum Paths for R3

```
R3# show ip protocols
*** IP Routing is NSF aware ***

Routing Protocol is "eigrp 1"
  Outgoing update filter list for all interfaces is not set
  Incoming update filter list for all interfaces is not set
  Default networks flagged in outgoing updates
  Default networks accepted from incoming updates
  EIGRP-IPv4 Protocol for AS(1)
    Metric weight K1=1, K2=0, K3=1, K4=0, K5=0
    NSF-aware route hold timer is 240
    Router-ID: 3.3.3.3
    Topology : 0 (base)
      Active Timer: 3 min
      Distance: internal 90 external 170
      Maximum path: 4
      Maximum hopcount 100
      Maximum metric variance 1

  Automatic Summarization: disabled
  Address Summarization:
    192.168.0.0/22 for Se0/0/0, Se0/0/1
      Summarizing 3 components with metric 2816
  Maximum path: 4
<Output omitted>
```

The routing table maintains both routes. Example 8-29 shows that R3 has two EIGRP equal-cost routes for the 172.16.3.0/30 network.

**Example 8-29**   IPv4  Routing Table for R3

```
R3# show ip route eigrp
<Output omitted>

Gateway of last resort is 192.168.10.9 to network 0.0.0.0
```

```
D*EX  0.0.0.0/0 [170/3139840] via 192.168.10.9, 00:14:24, Serial0/0/1
      172.16.0.0/16 is variably subnetted, 3 subnets, 2 masks
D        172.16.1.0/24 [90/2170112] via 192.168.10.5, 00:14:28, Serial0/0/0
D        172.16.2.0/24 [90/3012096] via 192.168.10.9, 00:14:24, Serial0/0/1
D        172.16.3.0/30 [90/41024000] via 192.168.10.9, 00:14:24, Serial0/0/1
                       [90/41024000] via 192.168.10.5, 00:14:24, Serial0/0/0
D     192.168.0.0/22 is a summary, 00:14:40, Null0
R3#
```

One route is through R1 at 192.168.10.5, and the other route is through R2 at 192.168.10.9. Looking at the topology in Figure 8-15, it might seem as if the path through R1 is the better route because there is a 1544-kb/s link between R3 and R1, whereas the link to R2 is only a 1024-kb/s link. However, EIGRP only uses the slowest bandwidth in its composite metric, which is the 64-kb/s link between R1 and R2. Both paths have the same 64-kb/s link as the slowest bandwidth; this results in both paths being equal.

When a packet is process switched, load balancing over equal-cost paths occurs on a per-packet basis. When packets are fast switched, load balancing over equal-cost paths occurs on a per-destination basis. *Cisco Express Forwarding (CEF)* can perform both per-packet and per-destination load balancing.

Cisco IOS, by default, allows load balancing using up to four equal-cost paths; however, this can be modified. Using the **maximum-paths** router configuration mode command, up to 32 equal-cost routes can be kept in the routing table:

```
Router(config-router)# maximum-paths value
```

The *value* argument refers to the number of paths that should be maintained for load balancing. If the value is set to **1**, load balancing is disabled.

## Load-Balancing IPv6 (8.1.4.4)

Figure 8-16 shows the EIGRP for IPv6 network topology. The serial links in the topology have the same bandwidth that is used in the EIGRP for IPv4 topology.

Similar to the previous scenario for IPv4, R3 has two EIGRP equal-cost routes for the network between R1 and R2, 2001:DB8:CAFE:A001::/64. One route is through R1 at FE80::1, and the other route is through R2 at FE80::2.

Example 8-30 shows that the EIGRP metrics are the same in the IPv6 routing table and in the IPv4 routing table for the 2001:DB8:CAFE:A001::/64 and 172.16.3.0/30 networks. This is because the EIGRP composite metric is the same for both EIGRP for IPv6 and for IPv4.

**Figure 8-16**   EIGRP for IPv6 Topology: Load Balancing

**Example 8-30**   IPv6 Routing Table for R3

```
R3# show ipv6 route eigrp
<Output omitted>


EX   ::/0 [170/3011840]
     via FE80::2, Serial0/0/1
D    2001:DB8:ACAD::/48 [5/128256]
     via Null0, directly connected
D    2001:DB8:CAFE:1::/64 [90/2170112]
     via FE80::1, Serial0/0/0
D    2001:DB8:CAFE:2::/64 [90/3012096]
     via FE80::2, Serial0/0/1
D    2001:DB8:CAFE:A001::/64 [90/41024000]
     via FE80::2, Serial0/0/1
     via FE80::1, Serial0/0/0
R3#
```

## Unequal-Cost Load Balancing

EIGRP for IPv4 and IPv6 can also balance traffic across multiple routes that have different metrics. This type of balancing is called *unequal-cost load balancing*. Setting a value using the **variance** command in router configuration mode enables EIGRP to install multiple loop-free routes with unequal cost in a local routing table.

A route learned through EIGRP must meet two criteria to be installed in the local routing table:

- The route must be loop-free, being either a feasible successor or having a reported distance that is less than the total distance.

- The metric of the route must be lower than the metric of the best route (the successor) multiplied by the variance configured on the router.

For example, if the variance is set to 1, only routes with the same metric as the successor are installed in the local routing table. If the variance is set to 2, any EIGRP-learned route with a metric less than 2 times the successor metric will be installed in the local routing table.

To control how traffic is distributed among routes when there are multiple routes for the same destination network that have different costs, use the **traffic-share balanced** command. Traffic is then distributed proportionately to the ratio of the costs.

**Interactive Graphic**

**Activity 8.1.4.5: Determine the EIGRP Fine-Tuning Commands**

Go to the course online to perform this practice activity.

# Secure EIGRP (8.1.5)

Like OSPF, it is essential that EIGRP messages are authenticated so that the receiving router can trust the information.

## Routing Protocol Authentication Overview (8.1.5.1)

Network administrators must be aware that routers are at risk from attack just as much as end-user devices. Anyone with a packet sniffer, such as Wireshark, can read information propagating between routers. In general, routing systems can be attacked through the disruption of peer devices or the falsification of routing information.

Disruption of peers is the less critical of the two attacks because routing protocols heal themselves, making the disruption last only slightly longer than the attack itself.

The falsification of routing information is a more subtle class of attack that targets the information carried within the routing protocol. The consequences of falsifying routing information are as follows:

- Redirect traffic to create routing loops

- Redirect traffic to monitor on an insecure line

- Redirect traffic to discard it

A method to protect routing information on the network is to authenticate routing protocol packets using the Message Digest 5 (MD5) algorithm. MD5 allows the routers to compare signatures that should all be the same, confirming that they are from a credible source.

The three components of such a system include

- Encryption algorithm, which is generally public knowledge

- Key used in the encryption algorithm, which is a secret shared by the routers authenticating their packets

- Contents of the packet itself

Figure 8-17 illustrates MD5 authentication between R1 and R3.

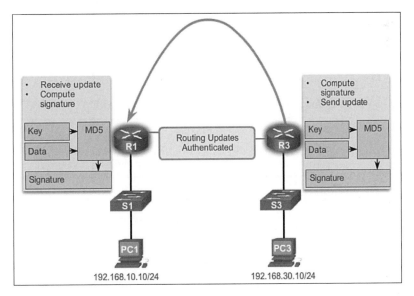

**Figure 8-17**   Authenticating Using MD5

Generally, the originator of the routing information produces a signature using the key and routing data it is about to send as inputs to the encryption algorithm. The router receiving the routing data can then repeat the process using the same key and the same routing data it has received. If the signature the receiver computes is the same as the signature the sender computes, the update is authenticated and considered reliable.

Routing protocols such as RIPv2, EIGRP, OSPF, IS-IS, and BGP all support various forms of MD5 authentication.

## Configuring EIGRP with MD5 Authentication (8.1.5.2)

EIGRP message authentication ensures that routers only accept routing messages from other routers that know the same preshared key. Without authentication configured, if an unauthorized person introduces another router with different or conflicting route information on the network, the routing tables on the legitimate routers can become corrupt and a DoS attack can ensue. Thus, when authentication is added to the EIGRP messages sent between routers, it prevents someone from purposely, or accidentally, adding another router to the network and causing a problem.

EIGRP supports routing protocol authentication using MD5. The configuration of EIGRP message authentication consists of two steps: the creation of a keychain and key, and the configuration of EIGRP authentication to use that keychain and key.

Step 1.   **Create a keychain and key.** Routing authentication requires a *key* on a *keychain* to function. Before authentication can be enabled, create a keychain and at least one key, as shown in Example 8-31, with a detailed explanation to follow.

**Example 8-31**   Step 1: Create a Keychain

```
Router(config)# key chain name-of-chain
Router(config-keychain)# key key-id
Router(config-keychain-key)# key-string key-string-text
```

a.   In global configuration mode, create the keychain. Although multiple keys can be configured, this section focuses on the use of a single key.

```
Router(config)# key chain name-of-chain
```

b.   Specify the key ID. The key ID is the number used to identify an authentication key within a keychain. The range of keys is from 0 to 2,147,483,647. It is recommended that the key number be the same on all routers in the configuration.

```
Router(config-keychain)# key key-id
```

c.   Specify the key string for the key. The key string is similar to a password. Routers exchanging authentication keys must be configured using the same key string.

```
Router(config-keychain-key )# key-string key-string-text
```

Step 2.   **Configure EIGRP authentication using a keychain and key.** Configure EIGRP to perform message authentication with the previously defined key. Complete this configuration on all interfaces enabled for EIGRP, as shown in Example 8-32, with a detailed explanation to follow.

**Example 8-32**    Step 2: Configure EIGRP Authentication Using a Keychain and Key

```
Router(config)# interface type number
Router(config-if)# ip authentication mode eigrp as-number md5
Router(config-if)# ip authentication key-chain eigrp as-number name-of-chain
```

    **a.** In global configuration mode, specify the interface on which to configure EIGRP message authentication.

```
Router(config)# interface type number
```

    **b.** Enable EIGRP message authentication. The **md5** keyword indicates that the MD5 hash is to be used for authentication.

```
Router(config-if)# ip authentication mode eigrp as-number md5
```

    **c.** Specify the keychain that should be used for authentication. The *name-of-chain* argument specifies the keychain that was created in Step 1.

```
Router(config-if)# ip authentication key-chain eigrp as-number
name-of-chain
```

Each key has its own key ID, which is stored locally. The combination of the key ID and the interface associated with the message uniquely identifies the authentication algorithm and MD5 authentication key in use. The keychain and the routing update are processed using the MD5 algorithm to produce a unique signature.

## EIGRP Authentication Example (8.1.5.3)

To authenticate routing updates, all EIGRP-enabled interfaces must be configured to support authentication. Example 8-33 shows the configuration for Router R1 using the **EIGRP_KEY** keychain and the **cisco123** key string.

**Example 8-33**    Configuring EIGRP MD5 Authentication on R1

```
R1(config)# key chain EIGRP_KEY
R1(config-keychain)# key 1
R1(config-keychain-key)# key-string cisco123
R1(config-keychain-key)# exit
R1(config-keychain)# exit
R1(config)# interface serial 0/0/0
R1(config-if)# ip authentication mode eigrp 1 md5
R1(config-if)# ip authentication key-chain eigrp 1 EIGRP_KEY
R1(config-if)# exit
R1(config)# interface serial 0/0/1
R1(config-if)# ip authentication mode eigrp 1 md5
R1(config-if)# ip authentication key-chain eigrp 1 EIGRP_KEY
R1(config-if)# end
R1#
```

After R1 is configured, the other routers receive authenticated routing updates. Adjacencies are lost until the neighbors are configured with routing protocol authentication. Examples 8-34 and 8-35 show similar configurations for R2 and R3.

**Example 8-34**   Configuring EIGRP MD5 Authentication on R2

```
R2(config)# key chain EIGRP_KEY
R2(config-keychain)# key 1
R2(config-keychain-key)# key-string cisco123
R2(config-keychain-key)# exit
R2(config-keychain)# exit
R2(config)# interface serial 0/0/0
R2(config-if)# ip authentication mode eigrp 1 md5
R2(config-if)# ip authentication key-chain eigrp 1 EIGRP_KEY
R2(config-if)# exit
R2(config)# interface serial 0/0/1
R2(config-if)# ip authentication mode eigrp 1 md5
R2(config-if)# ip authentication key-chain eigrp 1 EIGRP_KEY
R2(config-if)# end
```

**Example 8-35**   Configuring EIGRP MD5 Authentication on R3

```
R3(config)# key chain EIGRP_KEY
R3(config-keychain)# key 1
R3(config-keychain-key)# key-string cisco123
R3(config-keychain-key)# exit
R3(config-keychain)# exit
R3(config)# interface serial 0/0/0
R3(config-if)# ip authentication mode eigrp 1 md5
R3(config-if)# ip authentication key-chain eigrp 1 EIGRP_KEY
R3(config-if)# exit
R3(config)# interface serial 0/0/1
R3(config-if)# ip authentication mode eigrp 1 md5
R3(config-if)# ip authentication key-chain eigrp 1 EIGRP_KEY
R3(config-if)# end
```

Notice that the same key string, **cisco123**, is used to authenticate information with R1 and ultimately R3.

## Configuring EIGRP for IPv6 Authentication

The algorithms and the configuration to authenticate EIGRP for IPv6 messages are the same as EIGRP for IPv4. The only difference is that the interface configuration mode commands use **ipv6** instead of **ip**.

```
Router(config-if)# ipv6 authentication mode eigrp as-number md5
Router(config-if)# ipv6 authentication key-chain eigrp as-number name-of-chain
```

Example 8-36 shows the commands to configure EIGRP for IPv6 authentication on Router R1 using the **EIGRP_IPV6_KEY** keychain and the **cisco123** key string. Similar configurations would be entered on R2 and R3.

**Example 8-36**  Configuring EIGRP for IPv6 MD5 Authentication on R1

```
R1(config)# key chain EIGRP_IPV6_KEY
R1(config-keychain)# key 1
R1(config-keychain-key)# key-string cisco123
R1(config-keychain-key)# exit
R1(config-keychain)# exit
R1(config)# interface serial 0/0/0
R1(config-if)# ipv6 authentication mode eigrp 2 md5
R1(config-if)# ipv6 authentication key-chain eigrp 2 EIGRP_IPV6_KEY
R1(config-if)# exit
R1(config)# interface serial 0/0/1
R1(config-if)# ipv6 authentication mode eigrp 2 md5
R1(config-if)# ipv6 authentication key-chain eigrp 2 EIGRP_IPV6_KEY
R1(config-if)#
```

## Verify Authentication (8.1.5.4)

After EIGRP message authentication is configured on one router, any adjacent neighbors that have not yet been configured for authentication are no longer EIGRP neighbors. For example, when R1's Serial 0/0/0 interface was configured for MD5 authentication, but R2 had not yet been configured, the following IOS message appeared on R1:

```
%DUAL-5-NBRCHANGE: EIGRP-IPv4 1: Neighbor 172.16.3.2 (Serial0/0/0) is down:
    authentication mode changed
```

When the adjacent Serial 0/0/0 interface on R2 is configured, the adjacency is reestablished and the following IOS message is displayed on R1:

```
%DUAL-5-NBRCHANGE: EIGRP-IPv4 1: Neighbor 172.16.3.2 (Serial0/0/0) is up: new
    adjacency
```

Similar messages are also displayed on R2.

Adjacencies are only formed when both connecting devices have authentication configured. To verify that the correct EIGRP adjacencies were formed after being configured for authentication, use the **show ip eigrp neighbors** command on each router. Example 8-37 shows that all three routers have reestablished neighbor adjacencies after being configured for EIGRP authentication.

**Example 8-37**    Verify EIGRP MD5 Authentication

```
R1# show ip eigrp neighbors
EIGRP-IPv4 Neighbors for AS(1)
H    Address          Interface    Hold Uptime    SRTT    RTO   Q   Seq
                                   (sec)          (ms)          Cnt Num
1    172.16.3.2       Se0/0/0       140 03:28:12    96   2340   0   23
0    192.168.10.6     Se0/0/1        14 03:28:27    49    294   0   24
R1#


R2# show ip eigrp neighbors
EIGRP-IPv4 Neighbors for AS(1)
H    Address          Interface    Hold Uptime    SRTT    RTO   Q   Seq
                                   (sec)          (ms)          Cnt Num
1    172.16.3.1       Se0/0/0       136 00:22:50 1046   5000   0   32
0    192.168.10.10    Se0/0/1        10 07:51:37   62    372   0   35
R2#


R3# show ip eigrp neighbors
EIGRP-IPv4 Neighbors for AS(1)
H    Address            Interface     Hold Uptime    SRTT    RTO   Q   Seq
                                      (sec)          (ms)          Cnt Num
0    192.168.10.5       Se0/0/0        14 00:21:26 1297   5000   0   33
1    192.168.10.9       Se0/0/1        14 07:51:50   43    258   0   36
R3#
```

To verify the neighbor adjacencies for EIGRP for IPv6, use the **show ipv6 eigrp neighbors** command.

**Lab 8.1.5.5: Configuring Advanced EIGRP for IPv4 Features**

In this lab, you will complete the following objectives:

- Part 1: Build the Network and Configure Basic Device Settings
- Part 2: Configure EIGRP and Verify Connectivity
- Part 3: Configure Summarization for EIGRP
- Part 4: Configure and Propagate a Default Static Route
- Part 5: Fine-Tune EIGRP
- Part 6: Configure EIGRP Authentication

# Troubleshoot EIGRP (8.2)

This section discusses the commands and techniques for troubleshooting EIGRP.

## Components of Troubleshooting EIGRP (8.2.1)

Whether troubleshooting EIGRP for IPv4 or EIGRP for IPv6, there are specific commands available to locate and isolate just about any problem.

### Basic EIGRP Troubleshooting Commands (8.2.1.1)

EIGRP is commonly used in large enterprise networks. Troubleshooting problems related to the exchange of routing information is an essential skill for a network administrator. This is particularly true for administrators who are involved in the implementation and maintenance of large, routed enterprise networks that use EIGRP as the interior gateway protocol (IGP). There are several commands that are useful when troubleshooting an EIGRP network.

The **show ip eigrp neighbors** command verifies that the router recognizes its neighbors. The output in Example 8-38 indicates two successful EIGRP neighbor adjacencies on R1.

**Example 8-38**   R1 EIGRP Neighbor Table

```
R1# show ip eigrp neighbors
EIGRP-IPv4 Neighbors for AS(1)
H    Address          Interface     Hold Uptime    SRTT    RTO   Q   Seq
                                    (sec)          (ms)         Cnt  Num
1    172.16.3.2       Se0/0/0        140 03:28:12    96   2340   0   23
0    192.168.10.6     Se0/0/1         14 03:28:27    49    294   0   24
R1#
```

In Example 8-39, the **show ip route eigrp** command verifies that the router learned the route to a remote network through EIGRP. The output shows that R1 has learned about four remote networks through EIGRP.

**Example 8-39**   R1 IPv4 Routing Table

```
R1# show ip route eigrp

Gateway of last resort is 192.168.10.6 to network 0.0.0.0

D*EX  0.0.0.0/0 [170/3651840] via 192.168.10.6, 05:32:02, Serial0/0/1
        172.16.0.0/16 is variably subnetted, 5 subnets, 3 masks
```

```
D        172.16.2.0/24 [90/3524096] via 192.168.10.6, 05:32:02, Serial0/0/1
D      192.168.0.0/22 [90/2170112] via 192.168.10.6, 05:32:02, Serial0/0/1
       192.168.10.0/24 is variably subnetted, 3 subnets, 2 masks
D        192.168.10.8/30 [90/3523840] via 192.168.10.6, 05:32:02, Serial0/0/1
R1#
```

Example 8-40 shows the output from the **show ip protocols** command.

**Example 8-40**   R1 Routing Protocol Processes

```
R1# show ip protocols
*** IP Routing is NSF aware ***

Routing Protocol is "eigrp 1"
  Outgoing update filter list for all interfaces is not set
  Incoming update filter list for all interfaces is not set
  Default networks flagged in outgoing updates
  Default networks accepted from incoming updates
  EIGRP-IPv4 Protocol for AS(1)
    Metric weight K1=1, K2=0, K3=1, K4=0, K5=0
    NSF-aware route hold timer is 240
    Router-ID: 1.1.1.1
    Topology : 0 (base)
      Active Timer: 3 min
      Distance: internal 90 external 170
      Maximum path: 4
      Maximum hopcount 100
      Maximum metric variance 1

  Automatic Summarization: disabled
  Maximum path: 4
  Routing for Networks:
    172.16.0.0
    192.168.10.0
  Passive Interface(s):
    GigabitEthernet0/0
  Routing Information Sources:
    Gateway         Distance      Last Update
    192.168.10.6          90      05:43:44
    172.16.3.2           90      05:43:44
  Distance: internal 90 external 170

R1#
```

This command verifies that EIGRP displays the currently configured values for various properties of any enabled routing protocols.

## EIGRP for IPv6

Similar commands and troubleshooting criteria also apply to EIGRP for IPv6.

The following are the equivalent commands used with EIGRP for IPv6:

- Router# **show ipv6 eigrp neighbors**

- Router# **show ipv6 route**

- Router# **show ipv6 protocols**

## Components (8.2.1.2)

Figure 8-18 shows a flowchart for diagnosing EIGRP connectivity issues.

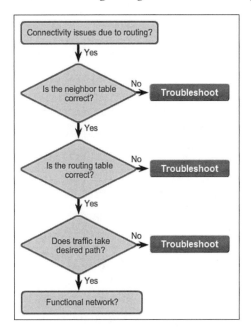

**Figure 8-18**   Diagnosing EIGRP Connectivity Issues

After configuring EIGRP, the first step is to test connectivity to the remote network. If the ping fails, confirm the EIGRP neighbor adjacencies. Neighbor adjacency might not be formed for a number of reasons, including the following:

- The interface between the devices is down.

- The two routers have mismatching EIGRP autonomous system numbers (process IDs).

- Proper interfaces are not enabled for the EIGRP process.

- An interface is configured as passive.

Aside from these issues, there are a number of other, more advanced issues that can cause neighbor adjacencies to not be formed. Two examples are misconfigured EIGRP authentication or mismatched K values, which EIGRP uses to calculate its metric.

If the EIGRP neighbor adjacency is formed between the two routers, but there is still a connection issue, there might be a routing problem. Some issues that can cause a connectivity problem for EIGRP include

- Proper networks are not being advertised on remote routers.

- An incorrectly configured passive interface, or an ACL, is blocking advertisements of remote networks.

- Automatic summarization is causing inconsistent routing in a discontiguous network.

If all the required routes are in the routing table, but the path that traffic takes is not correct, verify the interface bandwidth values.

**Interactive Graphic**

**Activity 8.2.1.3: Identify the Troubleshooting Command**

Go to the course online to perform this practice activity.

# Troubleshoot EIGRP Neighbor Issues (8.2.2)

This topic discusses how to troubleshoot neighbor adjacency issues in EIGRP.

## Layer 3 Connectivity (8.2.2.1)

A prerequisite for a neighbor adjacency to form between two directly connected routers is Layer 3 connectivity. By examining the output of the **show ip interface brief** command, a network administrator can verify that the status and protocol of connecting interfaces are up. A ping from one router to another, directly connected router should confirm IPv4 connectivity between the devices. Example 8-41 displays the **show ip interface brief** command output for R1. R1 shows connectivity to R2, and pings are successful.

**Example 8-41**   Test Connectivity from R1 to R2

```
R1# show ip interface brief
Interface               IP-Address      OK? Method Status              Protocol
GigabitEthernet0/0      172.16.1.1      YES manual up                  up
Serial0/0/0             172.16.3.1      YES manual up                  up
Serial0/0/1             192.168.10.5    YES manual up                  up
R1# ping 172.16.3.2
Type escape sequence to abort.
Sending 5, 100-byte ICMP Echos to 172.16.3.2, timeout is 2 seconds:
!!!!!
Success rate is 100 percent (5/5), round-trip min/avg/max = 28/28/28 ms
R1#
```

If the ping is unsuccessful, check the cabling and verify that the interfaces on connected devices are on a common subnet. A log message that states that EIGRP neighbors are "not on common subnet" indicates that there is an incorrect IPv4 address on one of the two EIGRP neighbor interfaces.

## EIGRP for IPv6

Similar commands and troubleshooting criteria also apply to EIGRP for IPv6.

The equivalent command used with EIGRP for IPv6 is **show ipv6 interface brief**.

## EIGRP Parameters (8.2.2.2)

When troubleshooting an EIGRP network, one of the first things to verify is that all routers that are participating in the EIGRP network are configured with the same autonomous system number. The **router eigrp** *as-number* command starts the EIGRP process and is followed by a number that is the autonomous system number. The value of the *as-number* argument must be the same in all routers that are in the EIGRP routing domain.

In the chapter topology, all routers should be participating in autonomous system number 1. In Example 8-42, the **show ip protocols** command verifies that R1, R2, and R3 all use the same autonomous system number.

**Example 8-42**   Verifying the Autonomous System Number

```
R1# show ip protocols
*** IP Routing is NSF aware ***


Routing Protocol is "eigrp 1"
<Output omitted>
```

```
R2# show ip protocols
*** IP Routing is NSF aware ***

Routing Protocol is "eigrp 1"
<Output omitted>
```

```
R3# show ip protocols
*** IP Routing is NSF aware ***

Routing Protocol is "eigrp 1"
<Output omitted>
```

## EIGRP for IPv6

Similar commands and troubleshooting criteria also apply to EIGRP for IPv6.

The following are the equivalent commands used with EIGRP for IPv6:

- Router(config)# **ipv6 router eigrp** *as-number*
- Router# **show ipv6 protocols**

### Note

At the top of the output, "IP Routing is NSF aware" refers to Nonstop Forwarding (NSF). This capability allows the EIGRP peers of a failing router to retain the routing information that it has advertised, and to continue using this information until the failed router resumes normal operation and is able to exchange routing information. For more information refer to: www.cisco.com/en/US/docs/ios-xml/ios/iproute_eigrp/configuration/15-mt/eigrp-nsf-awa.html.

## EIGRP Interfaces (8.2.2.3)

In addition to verifying the autonomous system number, it is necessary to verify that all interfaces are participating in the EIGRP network. The **network** command that is configured under the EIGRP routing process indicates which router interface participates in EIGRP. This command is applied to the classful network address of the interface or to a subnet when the wildcard mask is included.

In Example 8-43, the **show ip eigrp interfaces** command displays which interfaces are enabled for EIGRP on R1. If connected interfaces are not enabled for EIGRP, neighbors do not form an adjacency.

**Example 8-43**    Verifying EIGRP for IPv4 Interfaces

```
R1# show ip eigrp interfaces
EIGRP-IPv4 Interfaces for AS(1)
                 Xmit Queue   PeerQ        Mean   Pacing Time   Multicast    Pending
Interface  Peers Un/Reliable  Un/Reliable  SRTT   Un/Reliable   Flow Timer   Routes
Gi0/1        0      0/0          0/0          0      0/0            0            0
Se0/0/0      1      0/0          0/0        1295     0/23         6459           0
Se0/0/1      1      0/0          0/0        1044     0/15         5195           0
R1#
```

In Example 8-44, the "Routing for Networks" section of the **show ip protocols** command indicates which networks have been configured; any interfaces in those networks participate in EIGRP.

**Example 8-44**    Verifying EIGRP for IPv4 Networks

```
R1# show ip protocols
*** IP Routing is NSF aware ***

Routing Protocol is "eigrp 1"
<Output omitted>

Routing for Networks:
    172.16.0.0
    192.168.10.0
  Passive Interface(s):
    GigabitEthernet0/0
  Routing Information Sources:
    Gateway         Distance      Last Update
    192.168.10.6          90      00:42:31
    172.16.3.2            90      00:42:31
  Distance: internal 90 external 170

R1#
```

If the network is not present in this section, use **show running-config** to ensure that the proper **network** command was configured.

In Example 8-45, the output from the **show running-config** command confirms that any interfaces with these addresses, or a subnet of these addresses, are enabled for EIGRP.

**Example 8-45**    Verifying the EIGRP for IPv4 Configuration

```
R1# show running-config | section eigrp 1
router eigrp 1
 network 172.16.0.0
 network 192.168.10.0
 passive-interface GigabitEthernet0/0
 eigrp router-id 1.1.1.1
R1#
```

## EIGRP for IPv6

Similar commands and troubleshooting criteria also apply to EIGRP for IPv6.

The following are the equivalent commands used with EIGRP for IPv6:

- Router# **show ipv6 protocols**
- Router# **show ipv6 eigrp interfaces**

**Interactive Graphic**

**Activity 8.2.2.4: Troubleshoot EIGRP Neighbor Issues**

Go to the course online to perform this practice activity.

# Troubleshoot EIGRP Routing Table Issues (8.2.3)

This topic discusses a few of the more common issues encountered when troubleshooting the EIGRP routing table.

## Passive Interface (8.2.3.1)

One reason that route tables might not reflect the correct routes is because of the **passive-interface** command. With EIGRP running on a network, the **passive-interface** command stops both outgoing and incoming routing updates. For this reason, routers do not become neighbors.

To verify whether any interface on a router is configured as passive, use the **show ip protocols** command in privileged EXEC mode. Example 8-46 shows that R2's GigabitEthernet 0/0 interface is configured as a passive interface, because there are no neighbors on that link.

**Example 8-46**   Verifying Passive Interfaces

```
R2# show ip protocols
*** IP Routing is NSF aware ***


Routing Protocol is "eigrp 1"
<Output omitted>


Routing for Networks:
    172.16.0.0
    192.168.10.8/30
Passive Interface(s):
  GigabitEthernet0/0
  Routing Information Sources:
  Gateway           Distance        Last Update
  192.168.10.10           90        00:08:59
  172.16.3.1              90         00:08:59
Distance: internal 90 external 170
R2#
```

In addition to being configured on interfaces that have no neighbors, a passive interface can be enabled on interfaces for security purposes. In Example 8-47, notice that the shading for the EIGRP routing domain is different from previous topologies.

**Example 8-47**   Configuring Network to ISP as a Passive Interface

```
R2(config)# router eigrp 1
R2(config-router)# network 209.165.200.0
R2(config-router)# passive-interface serial 0/1/0
R2(config-router)# end
R2# show ip eigrp neighbors
EIGRP-IPv4 Neighbors for AS(1)
H   Address         Interface       Hold Uptime    SRTT   RTO  Q  Seq
                                    (sec)          (ms)        Cnt Num
1   172.16.3.1      Se0/0/0          175 01:09:18    80  2340  0  16
0   192.168.10.10   Se0/0/1           11 01:09:33 1037  5000  0  17
R2#
```

The 209.165.200.224/27 network is now included in R2's EIGRP updates. However, for security reasons, the network administrator does not want R2 to form an EIGRP neighbor adjacency with the ISP router.

Example 8-48 shows the addition of the 209.165.200.224/27 **network** command on R2. R2 now advertises this network to the other routers in the EIGRP routing domain.

**Example 8-48**   Verifying Network Propagated as an EIGRP Route

```
R1# show ip route | include 209.165.200.224
D       209.165.200.224 [90/3651840] via 192.168.10.6, 00:06:02, Serial0/0/1
R1#
```

The **passive-interface** router configuration mode command is configured on Serial 0/1/0 to prevent R2's EIGRP updates from being sent to the ISP router. The **show ip eigrp neighbors** command on R2 verifies that R2 has not established a neighbor adjacency with ISP.

Example 8-48 shows that R1 has an EIGRP route to the 209.165.200.224/27 network in its IPv4 routing table (R3 will also have an EIGRP route to that network in its IPv4 routing table). However, R2 does not have a neighbor adjacency with the ISP router.

### EIGRP for IPv6

Similar commands and troubleshooting criteria also apply to EIGRP for IPv6.

The following are the equivalent commands used with EIGRP for IPv6:

- Router# **show ipv6 protocols**
- Router(config-rtr)# **passive-interface** *type number*

### Missing Network Statement (8.2.3.2)

Figure 8-19 shows that R1's GigabitEthernet 0/1 interface has now been configured with the 10.10.10.1/24 address and is active.

**Figure 8-19**   Topology for Troubleshooting Missing Network Statement

R1 and R3 still have their neighbor adjacency, but a ping test from the R3 router to R1's G0/1 interface of 10.10.10.1 is unsuccessful. Example 8-49 shows a failed connectivity test from R3 to the destination network of 10.10.10.0/24.

**Example 8-49**    10.10.10.0/24 Unreachable from R3

```
R3# ping 10.10.10.1
Type escape sequence to abort.
Sending 5, 100-byte ICMP Echos to 10.10.10.1, timeout is 2 seconds:
.....
Success rate is 0 percent (0/5)
R3#
```

In Example 8-50, using the **show ip protocols** command on the R1 router shows that the network 10.10.10.0/24 is not advertised to EIGRP neighbors.

**Example 8-50**    Checking for 10.10.10.0/24 R1 Updates

```
R1# show ip protocols | begin Routing for Networks
  Routing for Networks:
    172.16.0.0
    192.168.10.0
  Passive Interface(s):
    GigabitEthernet0/0
  Routing Information Sources:
    Gateway         Distance      Last Update
    192.168.10.6          90      01:34:19
    172.16.3.2            90      01:34:19
  Distance: internal 90 external 170

R1#
```

As shown in Example 8-51, R1's EIGRP process is configured to include the advertisement of the 10.10.10.0/24 network.

**Example 8-51**    Configuring the Missing Network

```
R1(config)# router eigrp 1
R1(config-router)# network 10.0.0.0
```

Example 8-52 shows that there is now a route in R3's routing table for the 10.10.10.0/24 network, and reachability is verified by pinging R1's GigabitEthernet 0/1 interface.

**Example 8-52**  Verifying Network Propagated as an EIGRP Route

```
R3# show ip route | include 10.10.10.0
D        10.10.10.0 [90/2172416] via 192.168.10.5, 00:04:14, Serial0/0/0
R3#
R3# ping 10.10.10.1
Type escape sequence to abort.
Sending 5, 100-byte ICMP Echos to 10.10.10.1, timeout is 2 seconds:
!!!!!
Success rate is 100 percent (5/5), round-trip min/avg/max = 24/27/28 ms
R3#
```

## EIGRP for IPv6

Similar commands and troubleshooting criteria also apply to EIGRP for IPv6.

The following are the equivalent commands used with EIGRP for IPv6:

- Router# **show ipv6 protocols**
- Router# **show ipv6 route**
- Router(config-rtr)# **network** *ipv6-prefix/prefix-length*

**Note**

Another form of missing route can result from the router filtering inbound or outbound routing updates. ACLs provide filtering for different protocols, and these ACLs can affect the exchange of the routing protocol messages that cause routes to be absent from the routing table. The **show ip protocols** command shows whether there are any ACLs that are applied to EIGRP.

## Automatic Summarization (8.2.3.3)

Another issue that can create problems for the network administrator is EIGRP automatic summarization. Figure 8-20 shows a different network topology than what has been used throughout this chapter.

There is no connection between R1 and R3. R1's LAN has the network address 10.10.10.0/24, while R3's LAN is 10.20.20.0/24. The serial connections between both routers and R2 have the same bandwidth of 1024 kb/s.

R1 and R3 have their LAN and serial interfaces enabled for EIGRP, as shown in Example 8-53. Both routers perform EIGRP automatic summarization.

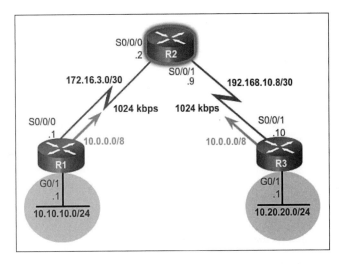

**Figure 8-20**   Topology for Troubleshooting Automatic Summarization

**Example 8-53**   EIGRP Configurations for R1 and R3

```
R1(config)# router eigrp 1
R1(config-router)# network 10.0.0.0
R1(config-router)# network 172.16.0.0
R1(config-router)# auto-summary

R3(config)# router eigrp 1
R3(config-router)# network 10.0.0.0
R3(config-router)# network 192.168.10.0
R3(config-router)# auto-summary
```

EIGRP for IPv4 can be configured to automatically summarize routes at classful boundaries. If there are discontiguous networks, automatic summarization causes inconsistent routing.

In Example 8-54, R2's routing table shows that it does not receive individual routes for the 10.10.10.0/24 and 10.20.20.0/24 subnets. Both R1 and R3 automatically summarized those subnets to the 10.0.0.0/8 classful boundary when sending EIGRP update packets to R2.

**Example 8-54**   Inconsistent Forwarding from R2

```
R2# show ip route
<Output omitted>

     10.0.0.0/8 is subnetted, 1 subnets
```

```
D        10.0.0.0 [90/3014400] via 192.168.10.10, 00:02:06, Serial0/0/1
                  [90/3014400] via 172.16.3.1, 00:02:06, Serial0/0/0
```

The result is that R2 has two equal-cost routes to 10.0.0.0/8 in the routing table, which can result in inaccurate routing and packet loss. Depending upon whether per-packet, per-destination, or CEF load balancing is being used, packets might or might not be forwarded out the proper interface.

In Example 8-55, the **show ip protocols** command verifies that automatic summarization is performed on both R1 and R3.

**Example 8-55**   Verifying Automatic Summarization Status

```
R1# show ip protocols
*** IP Routing is NSF aware ***

Routing Protocol is "eigrp 1"

  Automatic Summarization: enabled
    10.0.0.0/8 for Se0/0/0
      Summarizing 1 component with metric 28160

<Output omitted>

R3# show ip protocols
*** IP Routing is NSF aware ***

Routing Protocol is "eigrp 1"

  Automatic Summarization: enabled
    10.0.0.0/8 for Se0/0/1
      Summarizing 1 component with metric 28160
<Output omitted>
```

Notice that both routers summarize the 10.0.0.0/8 network using the same metric.

The **auto-summary** command is disabled by default in Cisco IOS Software versions of 15 and newer versions of 12.2(33). By default, older software has automatic summarization enabled. To disable automatic summarization, enter the **no auto-summary** command in router EIGRP configuration mode.

To correct this problem, R1 and R3 have automatic summarization disabled, as shown in Example 8-56.

**Example 8-56**   Disabling Automatic Summarization on R1 and R3

```
R1(config)# router eigrp 1
R1(config-router)# no auto-summary

R3(config)# router eigrp 1
R3(config-router)#  no auto-summary
```

After automatic summarization has been disabled on R1 and R3, R2's routing table now indicates that it receives the individual 10.10.10.0/24 and 10.20.20.0/24 subnets from R1 and R3, respectively, as shown in Example 8-57.

**Example 8-57**   All Networks Are Reachable from R2

```
R2# show ip route
<Output omitted>


 10.0.0.0/24 is subnetted, 2 subnets
D        10.10.10.0 [90/3014400] via 172.16.3.1, 00:00:27, Serial0/0/0
D        10.20.20.0 [90/3014400] via 192.168.10.10, 00:00:11, Serial0/0/1
```

Accurate routing and connectivity to both subnets is now restored.

## EIGRP for IPv6

Classful networks do not exist in IPv6; therefore, EIGRP for IPv6 does not support automatic summarization. All summarization must be accomplished using EIGRP manual summary routes.

### Activity 8.2.3.4: Troubleshoot EIGRP Routing Table Issues

Go to the course online to perform this practice activity.

### Packet Tracer Activity 8.2.3.5: Troubleshooting EIGRP for IPv4

In this activity, you will troubleshoot EIGRP neighbor issues. Use **show** commands to identify errors in the network configuration. Then, you will document the errors you discover and implement an appropriate solution. Finally, you will verify that full end-to-end connectivity is restored.

**Lab 8.2.3.6: Troubleshooting Basic EIGRP for IPv4 and IPv6**

In this lab, you will complete the following objectives:

- Part 1: Build the Network and Load Device Configurations
- Part 2: Troubleshoot Layer 3 Connectivity
- Part 3: Troubleshoot EIGRP for IPv4
- Part 4: Troubleshoot EIGRP for IPv6

**Lab 8.2.3.7: Troubleshooting Advanced EIGRP**

In this lab, you will complete the following objectives:

- Part 1: Build the Network and Load Device Configurations
- Part 2: Troubleshoot EIGRP

# Summary (8.3)

**Class Activity 8.3.1.1: Tweaking EIGRP**

The purpose of this activity is to review EIGRP routing protocol fine-tuning concepts.

You will work with a partner to design one EIGRP topology. This topology is the basis for two parts of the activity. The first uses default settings for all configurations and the second incorporates at least three of the following fine-tuning EIGRP options:

- Manual summary route

- Default routes

- Default route propagation

- Hello interval timer settings

Refer to the labs, Packet Tracer activities, and interactive activities to help you as you progress through this modeling activity.

Directions are listed in the PDF file for this activity. Share your completed work with another group. You might want to save a copy of this activity to a portfolio.

---

**Packet Tracer Activity 8.3.1.2: Skills Integration Challenge**

In this activity, you are tasked with implementing EIGRP for IPv4 and IPv6 on two separate networks. Your task includes enabling EIGRP, assigning router IDs, changing the Hello timers, configuring EIGRP summary routes, and limiting EIGRP advertisements.

---

EIGRP is one of the routing protocols commonly used in large enterprise networks. Modifying EIGRP features and troubleshooting problems are two of the most essential skills for a network engineer involved in the implementation and maintenance of large routed enterprise networks that use EIGRP.

Summarization decreases the number of entries in routing updates and reduces the number of entries in local routing tables. It also reduces bandwidth utilization for routing updates and results in faster routing table lookups. EIGRP for IPv4 automatic summarization is disabled by default beginning with Cisco IOS Release 15.0(1) M and 12.2(33). Prior to this, automatic summarization was enabled by default. To enable automatic summarization for EIGRP, use the **auto-summary** command in router configuration mode. Use the **show ip protocols** command to verify the status of automatic summarization. Examine the routing table to verify that automatic summarization is working.

EIGRP automatically includes summary routes to Null0 to prevent routing loops that are included in the summary but do not actually exist in the routing table. The Null0 interface is a virtual IOS interface that is a route to nowhere, commonly known as "the bit bucket." Packets that match a route with a Null0 exit interface are discarded.

To establish EIGRP manual summarization on a specific EIGRP interface, use the following interface configuration mode command:

```
Router(config-if)# ip summary-address eigrp as-number network-address subnet-mask
```

To configure EIGRP for IPv6 manual summarization on a specific EIGRP interface, use the following interface configuration mode command:

```
Router(config-if)# ipv6 summary-address eigrp as-number prefix/prefix-length
```

One method of propagating a default route within the EIGRP routing domain is to use the **redistribute static** command. This command tells EIGRP to include this static route in its EIGRP updates to other routers. The **show ip protocols** command verifies that static routes within the EIGRP routing domain are being redistributed.

Use the **ip bandwidth-percent eigrp** *as-number percent* interface configuration mode command to configure the percentage of bandwidth that can be used by EIGRP on an interface.

To configure the percentage of bandwidth that can be used by EIGRP for IPv6 on an interface, use the **ipv6 bandwidth-percent eigrp** command in interface configuration mode. To restore the default value, use the **no** form of this command.

Hello intervals and Hold times are configurable on a per-interface basis in EIGRP and do not have to match with other EIGRP routers to establish or maintain adjacencies.

For IP in EIGRP, Cisco IOS Software applies load balancing using up to four equal-cost paths by default. With the **maximum-paths** router configuration mode command, up to 32 equal-cost routes can be kept in the routing table.

EIGRP supports routing protocol authentication using MD5. The algorithms and the configuration to authenticate EIGRP for IPv4 messages are the same as EIGRP for IPv6. The only difference is that the interface configuration mode commands use **ip** instead of **ipv6**.

```
Router(config-if)# ipv6 authentication mode eigrp as-number md5
Router(config-if)# ipv6 authentication key-chain eigrp as-number name-of-chain
```

To verify that the correct EIGRP adjacencies were formed after being configured for authentication, use the **show ip eigrp neighbors** command on each router.

The **show ip route** command verifies that the router learned EIGRP routes. The **show ip protocols** command is used to verify that EIGRP displays the currently configured values.

# Practice

The following activities provide practice with the topics introduced in this chapter. The Labs and Class Activities are available in the companion *Scaling Networks Lab Manual* (ISBN 978-1-58713-325-1). The Packet Tracer Activities PKA files are found in the online course.

## Class Activities

- Class Activity 8.0.1.2: EIGRP — Back to the Future
- Class Activity 8.3.1.1: Tweaking EIGRP

## Labs

- Lab 8.1.5.5: Configuring Advanced EIGRP for IPv4 Features
- Lab 8.2.3.6: Troubleshooting Basic EIGRP for IPv4 and IPv6
- Lab 8.2.3.7: Troubleshooting Advanced EIGRP

Packet Tracer
☐ Activity

## Packet Tracer Activities

- Packet Tracer Activity 8.1.2.5: Configuring EIGRP Manual Summary Routes for IPv4 and IPv6
- Packet Tracer Activity 8.1.3.4: Propagating a Default Route in EIGRP for IPv4 and IPv6
- Packet Tracer Activity 8.2.3.5: Troubleshooting EIGRP for IPv4
- Packet Tracer Activity 8.3.1.2: Skills Integration Challenge

# Check Your Understanding Questions

Complete all the review questions listed to test your understanding of the topics and concepts in this chapter. The appendix "Answers to 'Check Your Understanding' Questions" lists the answers.

1. Refer to Example 8-58. Which command was used to generate this output?

**Example 8-58**   Command Output for Question 1

```
Routing Protocol is eigrp 101
  Outgoing update filter list for all interfaces is not set
  Incoming update filter list for all interfaces is not set
  Default networks flagged in outgoing updates
  Default networks accepted from incoming updates
  EIGRP-IPv4 Protocol for AS(101)
    Metric weight K1=1, K2=0, K3=1, K4=0, K5=0
<output omitted>
Automatic Summarization: enabled
    192.168.1.0/24 for GigabitEthernet0/0, Serial0/0/0
      Summarizing 2 components with metric 2169856
    172.20.0.0/16 for Serial0/1/0
      Summarizing 3 components with metric 2816
```

   A. show ip protocols

   B. show ip eigrp topology all-links

   C. show ip eigrp traffic

   D. show ip eigrp neighbors

2. What is the purpose of the EIGRP Null0 summary route?

   A. To prevent routing loops for destination networks that do not actually exist but are included in a summary route

   B. To ensure that all traffic destined for individual subnets uses one single best path

   C. To reduce bandwidth consumption for traffic that is leaving the network

   D. To enhance security by hiding all internal networks that are included in a summary route

3. Refer to Example 8-59. EIGRP has been configured on all routers in the network. What is the reason for the route in the last line of the routing table to be marked as **D EX**?

**Example 8-59** Command Output for Question 3

```
R1# show ip route
<output omitted>
Gateway of last resort is not set

   192.168 10.0/24 is variably subnetted, 3 subnets, 2 masks
D    192.168.10.0/24 is a summary, 00:04:22, Null0
C    192.168.10.4/30 is directly connected, Serial0/0/1
D    192.168.10.8/30 [90/21024000] via 172.16.3.2, 00:04:22, Serial0/0/0
   172.16.0.0/26 is variably subnetted, 3 subnets, 3 masks
D    172.16.0.0/16 is a summary, 00:04:22, Null0
C    172.16.1.0/24 is directly connected, FastEthernet0/0
C    172.16.3.0/30 is directly connected, Serial0/0/0
D    192.168.1.0/24 [90/20514560] via 192.168.10.6, 00:04:23, Serial0/0/1
D EX 192.168.2.0/24 [170/20524560] via 172.16.3.2, 00:04:23, Serial0/0/0
```

A. The route is configured as a static route on Router R1.

B. The route is learned from another routing protocol or from outside the EIGRP network.

C. The route is in the "Active" state and will be removed from the routing table in 4 minutes and 23 seconds.

D. The route is a feasible successor to the destination 192.168.2.0/24 network.

4. A network administrator is analyzing the differences between an EIGRP hold timer and EIGRP Hello interval. What statement is valid about EIGRP Hello and hold timers?

A. EIGRP hold timers specify the minimum time that the router should wait to send the next Hello.

B. EIGRP Hello intervals and hold timers must match between EIGRP neighbors to form an EIGRP adjacency.

C. EIGRP Hello timers specify the maximum time that the router should wait to receive the next Hello.

D. EIGRP Hello intervals should be less than or equal to EIGRP hold timers.

5. When would the network administrator use the **ip bandwidth-percent eigrp** *as-number percent* command?

   A. When the connection is serial instead of Ethernet

   B. When the link is always busy

   C. When the connection is on a shared medium

   D. When there is a low-bandwidth connection

6. Refer to Figure 8-21 and Example 8-60. Routers R1 and R2 were configured with EIGRP message authentication, but the routers cannot exchange EIGRP messages. Which of the following problems are causing the EIGRP authentication failure between R1 and R2 in this configuration? (Choose two.)

**Figure 8-21** Topology for Question 6

**Example 8-60** Configuration Commands for Question 6

```
R1(config)# key chain eigrp_key
R1(config-keychain)# key 0
R1(config-keychain-key)# key-string cisco_123
R1(config-keychain-key)# exit
R1(config-keychain)# exit
R1(config)# interface serial 0/0/0
R1(config-if)# ip authentication mode eigrp 0 md5
R1(config-if)# ip authentication key-chain eigrp 0 eigrp_key

R2(config)# key chain eigrp_key
R2(config-keychain)# key 0
R2(config-keychain-key)# key-string cisco-123
R2(config-keychain-key)# exit
R2(config-if)# exit
R2(config)# interface serial 0/0/1
R2(config-if)# ip authentication mode eigrp 0 md5
R2(config-if)# ip authentication key-chain eigrp 0 eigrp_key
```

    A.  The keychain name must be in uppercase.

    B.  The EIGRP message authentication is being configured on the wrong interface on R2.

    C.  At least two keys had to be created for each keychain.

    D.  The routers have a different value for the key-string.

    E.  The key ID is invalid, because its value has to be in the range of 1 to 2147483647.

**7.** Which of the following statements describe EIGRP authentication? (Choose two.)

    A.  EIGRP authentication uses a preshared key.

    B.  EIGRP authentication uses varying levels of WEP to encrypt data exchanged between routers.

    C.  EIGRP authentication can be configured on one router and updates from this router are protected, whereas a neighbor router can be without the authentication configuration and its updates are unprotected.

    D.  EIGRP authentication uses the MD5 algorithm.

    E.  EIGRP authentication requires that both routers have the same keychain name.

**8.** Refer to Example 8-61. While verifying EIGRP on a router, a network technician issued a command that produced the output that is shown in the exhibit. Which command did the technician use?

**Example 8-61**   Command Output for Question 8

```
IP-EIGRP interfaces for process 1

                        Xmit Queue   Mean    Pacing Time  Multicast      Pending
Interfaces    Peers    Un/Reliable   SRRT    Un/Reliable  Flow Timer     Routes
Se0/0/0       1          0/0         1236       0/10         0              0
Se0/0/1       1          0/0         1236       0/10         0              0
```

    A.  **show ip eigrp neighbors detail**

    B.  **show ip eigrp interfaces**

    C.  **show ip protocols**

    D.  **show ip eigrp topology**

    E.  **show ip interfaces brief**

9. What is a disadvantage of using EIGRP automatic summarization?

A. It increases the number of routes in the routing table.

B. It increases the size of routing updates.

C. It prevents convergence of the routing table.

D. It creates inconsistent routing when the network has discontiguous networks.

10. Fill in the blank. Router R1 has three Fast Ethernet interfaces directly connected to LANs with network addresses 192.168.10.0/27, 192.168.10.32/27, and 192.168.10.64/27. To configure EIGRP manual summarization on a serial interface that will be sent to the EIGRP neighbor of R1, the **ip summary-address eigrp 100** _____ command has to be issued within interface configuration mode.

11. Fill in the blank. An IPv6 default route is represented by _____ .

# CHAPTER 9

# IOS Images and Licensing

## Objectives

Upon completion of this chapter, you will be able to answer the following questions:

- What are the IOS image-naming conventions implemented by Cisco?

- How do you manage Cisco IOS system image files to support network requirements in small- to medium-sized business networks?

- What is the licensing process for Cisco IOS Software in a small- to medium-sized business network?

- What are the commands used to install a Cisco IOS Software image license?

## Key Terms

This chapter uses the following key terms. You can find the definitions in the Glossary.

# Introduction (9.0.1.1)

Cisco IOS (originally Internetwork Operating System) is software used on most Cisco routers and switches. IOS is a package of routing, switching, security, and other internetworking technologies integrated into a single multitasking operating system.

The Cisco IOS portfolio supports a broad range of technologies and features. Customers choose an IOS based on a set of protocols and features supported by a particular image. Understanding the Cisco portfolio of feature sets is helpful in selecting the proper IOS to meet the needs of an organization.

Cisco made significant changes in the packaging and licensing of its IOS when transitioning from IOS Release 12.4 to 15.0. This chapter explains the naming conventions and packaging of IOS Release 12.4 and 15. Beginning with IOS Release 15, Cisco also implemented a new packaging format and licensing process for IOS. This chapter discusses the process of obtaining, installing, and managing Cisco IOS Release 15 software licenses.

**Note**

The release of IOS after 12.4 is 15.0. There is no IOS Software Release 13 or 14.

**Class Activity 9.0.1.2: IOS Detection**

Your school or university has just received a donation of Cisco routers and switches. You transport them from your shipping and receiving department to your Cisco networking lab and start sorting them into switch and router groups.

Refer to the accompanying PDF for directions on how to proceed with this modeling activity. Save your work and share the data you found with another group or the entire class.

# Managing IOS System Files (9.1)

This section discusses the naming convention used to identify the various Cisco IOS images as well as the methods for how to back up and restore or upgrade an IOS image.

## Naming Conventions (9.1.1)

Cisco uses a very precise naming convention that helps the network administrator determine, at a glance, the platform, feature set, and release version of an IOS image.

### Cisco IOS Software Release Families and Trains (9.1.1.1)

Cisco IOS Software has evolved from a single platform operating system for routing to a sophisticated operating system that supports a large array of features and technologies such as VoIP, NetFlow, and IPsec. To better meet the requirements of the different market segments, the software is organized into *software release families* and *software trains*.

A software release family is comprised of multiple IOS Software release versions that

- Share a code base

- Apply to related hardware platforms

- Overlap in support coverage (as one OS comes to end of life, another OS is introduced and supported)

Examples of IOS Software releases, within a software release family, include Releases 12.3, 12.4, 15.0, and 15.1.

Along with each software release, there are new versions of the software created to implement bug fixes and new features. IOS refers to these versions as trains.

A Cisco IOS train is used to deliver releases with a common code base to a specific set of platforms and features. A train can contain several releases, each release being a snapshot of the code base of the train at the moment of the release. Because different software release families can apply to different platforms or market segments, several trains can be current at any point in time.

This chapter examines the trains of both IOS Release 12.4 and 15.

### Cisco IOS Release 12.4 Mainline and T Trains (9.1.1.2)

Figure 9-1 shows the migration from IOS Software Release 12.3 to 12.4. Within a software release family, there can be two or more closely related and active trains. For example, the Cisco IOS Software Release 12.4 family has two trains, the 12.4 mainline and the 12.4T trains.

The Cisco IOS Software Release 12.4 train is considered the *mainline train*. The mainline train receives mostly software (bug) fixes, with the goal of increasing software quality. The mainline train releases are also designated as Maintenance Deployment (MD) releases.

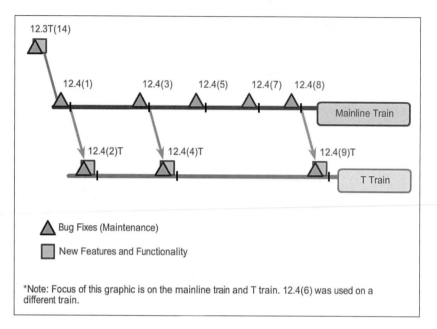

**Figure 9-1**   Cisco IOS Software Release 12.4 Family

A mainline train is always associated with a *technology train* (T train). A T train, such as 12.4T, receives the same software bug fixes as the mainline train. The T train also receives new software and hardware support features. Releases in the Cisco IOS Software Release 12.4T train are considered Early Deployment (ED) releases.

There can be other trains, depending on the software release family. For example, another train available is the service provider train (S train). An S train will contain specific features designed to meet service provider requirements.

All child trains of the mainline train (T, S, and so on) typically contain an uppercase letter designating the train type.

Mainline train = 12.4

T train = 12.4T (12.4 + new software and hardware support features)

Up to and including the Cisco IOS Software Release 12.4 family, the mainline and T trains were separated. In other words, from the mainline train, a T train would branch out and become a separate code base that received new features and hardware support. Eventually, a new mainline train would evolve from an established T train and the cycle would start again. This use of multiple trains was changed with Cisco IOS Software Release 15.

Figure 9-1 illustrates the relationships between the release of the Cisco IOS Software Release 12.4 mainline train and the 12.4T train.

## Cisco IOS Release 12.4 Mainline and T Numbering (9.1.1.3)

The IOS release numbering convention is used to identify the release of the IOS Software, including any bug fixes and new software features. An example of the numbering scheme is shown in Figure 9-2 for both the mainline and T trains:

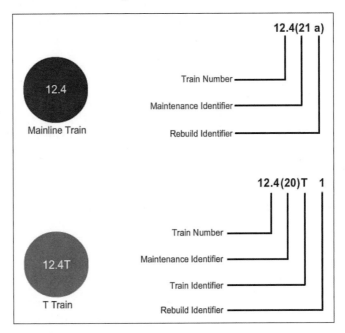

**Figure 9-2**   Cisco IOS Software Mainline and T Trains Numbering

- The software release numbering scheme for a mainline train is comprised of a train number, a maintenance identifier, and a rebuild identifier. For example, the Cisco IOS Software Release 12.4(21a) is a mainline train. The release for a T train is comprised of a train number, a maintenance identifier, a train identifier, and a rebuild identifier. For example, Cisco IOS Software Release 12.4(20)T1 belongs to the Cisco IOS Software Release 12.4T train.

- Each maintenance identifier of Cisco IOS Software Release 12.4 mainline, such as 12.4(7), includes additional software and maintenance fixes. This change is indicated with the number within the parentheses. Each maintenance release of Cisco IOS Software Release 12.4T, such as 12.4(20)T, includes these same software fixes, along with additional software features and hardware support.

- Cisco uses rebuilds of an individual release to integrate fixes for significant issues. This reduces the possible impact on customers that have already deployed and certified an individual release. A rebuild typically includes fixes to a limited number of software defects, which are known as *caveats*. It is indicated by a lowercase letter inside the parentheses of mainline trains, or by a final number in other trains. For example, Cisco IOS Software Release 12.4(21) received a few caveat fixes, and the resulting rebuild was named 12.4(21a). Similarly, 12.4(15)T8 is the eighth rebuild of 12.4(15)T. Each new rebuild increments the rebuild identifier and delivers additional software fixes on an accelerated schedule, prior to the next planned individual release. The criteria for making changes in a rebuild are strict.

A single set of individual release numbers is used for all Cisco IOS Software Release 12.4 trains. Cisco IOS Software Maintenance Release 12.4 and Cisco IOS Software Release 12.4T use a pool of individual release numbers that are shared across the entire Cisco IOS Software Release 12.4 family. Cisco IOS Software Release 12.4(6) T was followed by 12.4(7)T and 12.4(8)T. This permits the administrator to track changes introduced in the code.

**Note**

Any caveat that is fixed in a T train release should be implemented in the next mainline release.

## Cisco IOS Release 12.4 System Image Packaging (9.1.1.4)

Prior to Cisco IOS Software Release 15.0, Cisco IOS Software packaging consisted of eight packages for Cisco routers, as shown in Figure 9-3. This packaging scheme was introduced with the Cisco IOS Software Release 12.3 mainline train and was later used in other trains. The image packaging consists of eight IOS images, three of which are considered premium packages.

The five nonpremium packages are

- **IP Base:** IP Base is the entry-level Cisco IOS Software image.

- **IP Voice:** Converged voice and data, VoIP, VoFR, and IP Telephony.

- **Advanced Security:** Security and VPN features including Cisco IOS Firewall, IDS/IPS, IPsec, 3DES, and VPN.

- **SP (Service Provider) Services:** Adds SSH/SSL, ATM, VoATM, and MPLS to IP Voice.

- **Enterprise Base:** Enterprise protocols: AppleTalk, IPX, and IBM support.

**Note**

Starting with the Cisco IOS Software Release 12.4 family, SSH is available in all images.

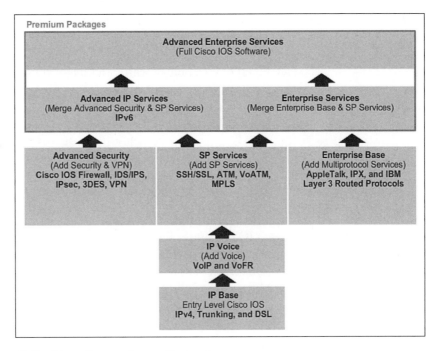

**Figure 9-3**   Cisco System Image Packaging

Three other premium packages offer additional IOS Software feature combinations that address more complex network requirements. All features merge in the Advanced Enterprise Services package. This package integrates support for all routing protocols with Voice, Security, and VPN capabilities:

- **Advanced Enterprise Services:** Full Cisco IOS Software features

- **Enterprise Services:** Enterprise Base and Service Provider Services

- **Advanced IP Services:** Advanced Security, Service Provider Services, and support for IPv6

---

**Note**

The Cisco Feature Navigator is a tool used to find the right Cisco operating system depending on the features and technologies needed.

---

## Cisco IOS Release 15.0 M and T Trains (9.1.1.5)

Following the Cisco IOS Release 12.4(24)T, the next release of Cisco IOS Software was 15.0.

IOS Release 15.0 provides several enhancements to the operating system including

- New feature and hardware support

- Broadened feature consistency with other major IOS releases

- More predictable new feature release and rebuild schedules

- Proactive individual release support policies

- Simplified release numbering

- Clearer software deployment and migration guidelines

As shown in Figure 9-4, Cisco IOS Release 15.0 uses a different release model from the traditional separate mainline and T trains of 12.4. Instead of diverging into separate trains, Cisco IOS Software Release 15 mainline and T will have *extended maintenance releases* (EM releases) and *standard maintenance releases* (T releases). With the new IOS release model, Cisco IOS Release 15 mainline releases are referred to as M trains.

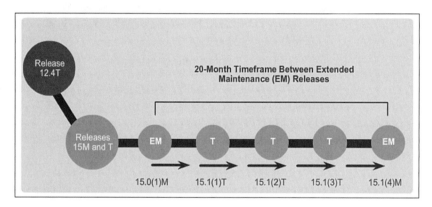

**Figure 9-4**   Cisco IOS Software Release 15 Family

Beginning with Release 15.0, new releases in the form of a T train are available approximately two to three times per year. EM releases are available approximately every 16 to 20 months. T releases enable faster Cisco feature delivery before the next EM release becomes available.

An EM release incorporates the features and hardware support of all the previous T releases. This makes newer EM releases available that contain the full functionality of the train at the time of release.

In summary, the benefits of the new Cisco IOS release model include

- Feature inheritance from Cisco IOS Software Releases 12.4T and 12.4 mainline.

- New feature releases approximately two to three times a year, delivered sequentially from a single train.

- EM releases approximately every 16 to 20 months that include new features.

- T releases for the very latest features and hardware support before the next EM release becomes available on Cisco.com.

- Maintenance rebuilds of M and T releases contain bug fixes only.

### Cisco IOS Release 15 Train Numbering (9.1.1.6)

The release numbering convention for IOS Release 15 identifies the specific IOS release, including bug fixes and new software features, similar to previous IOS release families. Figure 9-5 shows examples of this convention for both the EM release and T release.

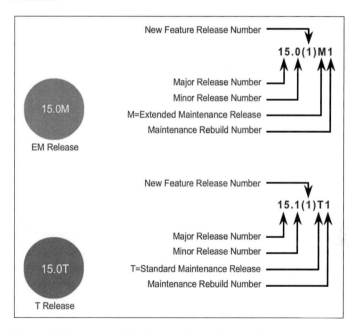

**Figure 9-5**   Cisco IOS Release 15 Software Train Numbering

### Extended Maintenance Release

The EM release is ideal for long-term maintenance, enabling customers to qualify, deploy, and remain on the release for an extended period. The mainline train incorporates features delivered in previous releases plus incremental new feature enhancements and hardware support.

The first maintenance rebuild (for bug fixes only, not new features or new hardware support) of Release 15.0(1)M is numbered 15.0(1)M1. Subsequent maintenance releases are defined by an increment of the maintenance rebuild number (that is, M2, M3, and so on).

## Standard Maintenance Release

The T release is used for short deployment releases that are ideal for the latest new features and hardware support before the next EM release becomes available. The T release provides regular bug fix maintenance rebuilds, plus critical fix support for network-affecting bugs such as Product Security Incident Report Team (PSIRT) issues.

The first planned 15 T new feature release is numbered Release 15.1(1)T. The first maintenance rebuild (for bug fixes only, not new features or new hardware support) of Release 15.1(1)T will be numbered Release 15.1(1)T1. Subsequent releases are defined by an increment of the maintenance rebuild number (that is, T2, T3, and so on).

## IOS Release 15 System Image Packaging (9.1.1.7)

Cisco Integrated Services Routers Generation Two (ISR G2) 1900, 2900, and 3900 Series support services on demand through the use of software licensing. The Services on Demand process enables customers to realize operational savings through ease of software ordering and management. When an order is placed for a new ISR G2 platform, the router is shipped with a single universal Cisco IOS Software image and a license is used to enable the specific feature set packages, as shown in Figure 9-6.

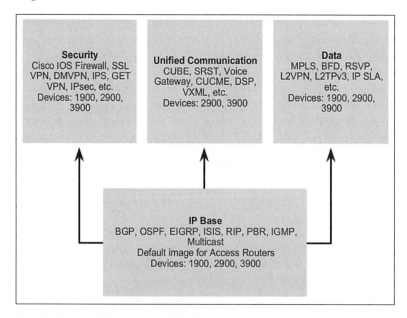

**Figure 9-6**   IOS Packaging Model for ISR G2 Routers

There are two types of universal images supported in ISR G2:

- **Universal images with the "universalk9" designation in the image name:** This universal image offers all the Cisco IOS Software features, including strong payload cryptography features such as IPsec VPN, SSL VPN, and Secure Unified Communications.

- **Universal images with the "universalk9_npe" designation in the image name:** The strong enforcement of encryption capabilities provided by Cisco Software Activation satisfies requirements for the export of encryption capabilities. However, some countries have import requirements that require that the platform does not support any strong cryptography functionality, such as payload cryptography. To satisfy the import requirements of those countries, the npe universal image does not support any strong payload encryption.

With the ISR G2 devices, IOS image selection has been made easier because all features are included within the universal image. Features are activated through licensing. Each device ships with a universal image. The technology packages IP Base, Data, UC (Unified Communications), and SEC (Security) are enabled in the universal image using Cisco Software Activation licensing keys. Each licensing key is unique to a particular device and is obtained from Cisco by providing the product ID and serial number of the router and a *Product Activation Key (PAK)*. The PAK is provided by Cisco at the time of software purchase. The IP Base is installed by default.

Table 9-1 shows the suggested migration for the next-generation ISRs from the IOS Release 12 (IOS Reformation Packaging) to IOS Release 15 (Simplified Packaging).

**Table 9-1**   Suggested Transition from IOS Release 12 to 15

| Reformation Packaging | Suggested Transition to Simplified Packaging |
| --- | --- |
| IP Base | IP Base |
| IP Voice | Unified Communications |
| Enterprise Base | Data |
| Enterprise Services | Data + Unified Communications |
| SP Services | Data + Unified Communications (for feature parity and Enterprise features) |
| Advanced Security | Security |
| Advanced IP Services | Security + Unified Communications + Data (for feature parity and Enterprise features) |
| Advanced Enterprise Services | Security + Unified Communications + Data |

## IOS Image Filenames (9.1.1.8)

When selecting or upgrading a Cisco IOS router, it is important to choose the proper IOS image with the correct feature set and version. The Cisco IOS image file is based on a special naming convention. The name for the Cisco IOS image file contains multiple parts, each with a specific meaning. It is important to understand this naming convention when upgrading and selecting Cisco IOS Software.

As shown in Example 9-1, the **show flash** command displays the files stored in flash memory, including the system image files.

**Example 9-1**   Displaying the Cisco IOS Image

```
R1# show flash0:
-# - --length-- -----date/time------ path

<Output omitted>

8    68831808    Apr 2 2013 21:29:58 +00:00 c1900-universalk9-mz.SPA.152-4.M3.bin

182394880 bytes available (74092544 bytes used)

R1#
```

An example of an IOS Release 12.4 software image name is shown in Figure 9-7.

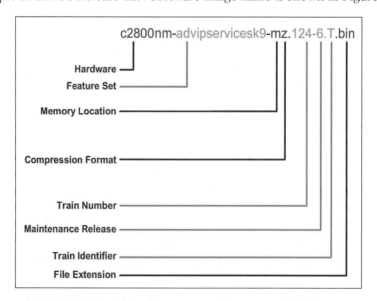

**Figure 9-7**   Example of a Cisco IOS Release 12.4 Software Image Name

- **Image Name (c2800nm):** Identifies the platform on which the image runs. In this example, the platform is a Cisco 2800 router with a network module.

- **advipservicesk9:** Specifies the feature set. In this example, advipservicesk9 refers to the advanced IP services feature set, which includes both the Advanced Security and Service Provider packages, along with IPv6.

- **mz:** Indicates where the image runs and whether the file is compressed. In this example, mz indicates that the file runs from RAM and is compressed.

- **124-6.T:** The filename format for image 12.4(6)T. This is the train number, maintenance release number, and train identifier.

- **bin:** The file extension. This extension indicates that this file is a binary executable file.

Figure 9-8 illustrates the different parts of an IOS Release 15 system image file on an ISR G2 device:

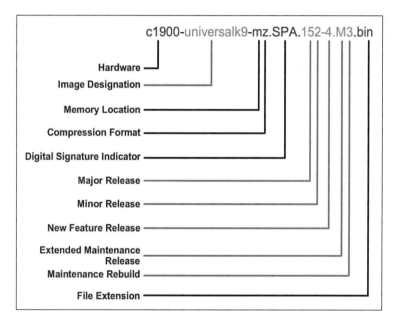

**Figure 9-8**   Example of a Cisco IOS Release 15.2 Software Image Name

- **Image Name (c1900):** Identifies the platform on which the image runs. In this example, the platform is a Cisco 1900 router.

- **universalk9:** Specifies the image designation. The two designations for an ISR G2 are universalk9 and universalk9_npe. Universalk9_npe does not contain strong encryption and is meant for countries with encryption restrictions. Features are controlled by licensing and can be divided into four technology packages. These are IP Base, Security, Unified Communications, and Data.

- **mz:** Indicates where the image runs and whether the file is compressed. In this example, mz indicates that the file runs from RAM and is compressed.

- **SPA:** Designates that the file is digitally signed by Cisco.

- **152-4.M3:** Specifies the filename format for the image 15.2(4)M3. This is the version of IOS, which includes the major release, minor release, maintenance release, and maintenance rebuild numbers. The M indicates that this is an extended maintenance release.

- **bin:** The file extension. This extension indicates that this file is a binary executable file.

The most common designation for memory location and compression format is mz. The first letter indicates the location where the image is executed on the router. The locations can include

- **f:** Flash

- **m:** RAM

- **r:** ROM

- **l:** Relocatable

The compression format can be either z for zip or x for mzip. Zipping is a method Cisco uses to compress some run-from-RAM images that is effective in reducing the size of the image. It is self-unzipping, so when the image is loaded into RAM for execution, the first action is to unzip.

**Note**

The Cisco IOS Software naming conventions, field meaning, image content, and other details are subject to change.

## Memory Requirements

On most Cisco routers, including the integrated services routers, the IOS is stored in compact flash as a compressed image and loaded into DRAM during boot-up. The Cisco IOS Software Release 15.0 images available for the Cisco 1900 and 2900 ISR require 256 MB of flash and 512 MB of RAM. The 3900 ISR requires 256 MB of flash and 1 GB of RAM. This does not include additional management tools such as Cisco Configuration Professional (Cisco CP). For complete details, refer to the product data sheet for the specific router.

**Packet Tracer Activity 9.1.1.9: Decode IOS Image Names**

As a network technician, it is important that you are familiar with the IOS image-naming convention so that you can, at a glance, determine important information about operating systems currently running on a device. In this scenario, Company A has merged with Company B. Company A has inherited network equipment from Company B. You have been assigned to document the features for the IOS images on these devices.

# Managing Cisco IOS Images (9.1.2)

Backing up, restoring, and upgrading IOS images can be done in a number of ways. This topic looks specifically at using a TFTP server to manage Cisco IOS images.

## TFTP Servers as a Backup Location (9.1.2.1)

As a network grows, Cisco IOS Software images and configuration files can be stored on a central TFTP server. This helps to control the number of IOS images and the revisions to those IOS images, as well as the configuration files that must be maintained.

Production internetworks usually span wide areas and contain multiple routers. For any network, it is good practice to keep a backup copy of the Cisco IOS Software image in case the system image in the router becomes corrupted or accidentally erased.

Widely distributed routers need a source or backup location for Cisco IOS Software images. Using a network TFTP server allows image and configuration uploads and downloads over the network. The network TFTP server can be another router, a workstation, or a host system.

## Creating a Cisco IOS Image Backup (9.1.2.2)

To maintain network operations with minimum downtime, it is necessary to have procedures in place for backing up Cisco IOS images. This allows the network administrator to quickly copy an image back to a router in case of a corrupted or erased image.

In Figure 9-9, the network administrator wants to create a backup of the current image file on the router (c1900-universalk9-mz.SPA.152-4.M3.bin) to the TFTP server at 172.16.1.100.

**Figure 9-9**   Copying a Cisco IOS to a TFTP Server

To create a backup of the Cisco IOS image to a TFTP server, perform the following three steps:

**Step 1.**    Ensure that there is access to the network TFTP server. Ping the TFTP server to test connectivity, as shown in Example 9-2.

**Example 9-2**   Verify Connectivity to the TFTP Server

```
R1# ping 172.16.1.100
Type escape sequence to abort.
Sending 5, 100-byte ICMP Echos to 172.16.1.100, timeout is 2 seconds:
!!!!!
Success rate is 100 percent (5/5), round-trip min/avg/max = 56/56/56 ms
R1# show flash0:
-# - --length-- -----date/time------ path
8   68831808   Apr 2 2013 21:29:58   +00:00 c1900-universalk9-mz.SPA.152-4.M3.bin
<Output omitted>
```

**Step 2.**    Verify that the TFTP server has sufficient disk space to accommodate the Cisco IOS Software image. Use the **show flash0:** command on the router to determine the size of the Cisco IOS image file. The file in the example is 68,831,808 bytes long.

**Step 3.**    Copy the image to the TFTP server using the **copy** *source-url destination-url* command, as shown in Example 9-3.

**Example 9-3**   Copy the IOS Image to the TFTP Server

```
R1# copy flash0: tftp:
Source filename []? c1900-universalk9-mz.SPA.152-4.M3.bin
Address or name of remote host []? 172.16.1.100
Destination filename []? c1900-universalk9-mz.SPA.152-4.M3.bin
!!!!!!!!!!!!!!!!!!!!
<output omitted>
68831808 bytes copied in 363.468 secs (269058 bytes/sec)
```

After issuing the command using the specified source and destination URLs, the user is prompted for the source filename, IP address of the remote host, and destination filename. The transfer will then begin.

## Copying a Cisco IOS Image (9.1.2.3)

Cisco consistently releases new Cisco IOS Software versions to resolve caveats and provide new features. This example uses IPv6 for the transfer to show that TFTP can also be used across IPv6 networks.

Figure 9-10 illustrates copying a Cisco IOS Software image from a TFTP server.

**Figure 9-10**   Copying a Cisco IOS Image from a TFTP Server

A new image file (c1900-universalk9-mz.SPA.152-4.M3.bin) will be copied from the TFTP server at 2001:DB8:CAFE:100::99 to the router. Follow these steps to upgrade the software on the Cisco router:

**Step 1.**   Select a Cisco IOS image file that meets the requirements in terms of platform, features, and software. Download the file from Cisco.com and transfer it to the TFTP server.

**Step 2.**   Verify connectivity to the TFTP server. Ping the TFTP server from the router. The output in Example 9-4 shows that the TFTP server is accessible from the router.

**Example 9-4**   Verify Connectivity to the TFTP Server

```
R1# ping 2001:DB8:CAFE:100::99
Type escape sequence to abort.
Sending 5, 100-byte ICMP Echos to 2001:DB8:CAFE:100::99, timeout is 2 seconds:
!!!!!
Success rate is 100 percent (5/5),
round-trip min/avg/max = 56/56/56 ms
```

Success rate is 100 percent (5/5), and round-trip min/avg/
max = 56/56/56 ms.

**Step 3.**   Ensure that there is sufficient flash space on the router that is being
upgraded. The amount of free flash space can be verified using the **show
flash0:** command. Compare the free flash space with the new image file
size. The **show flash0:** command in Example 9-5 is used to verify free
flash size. Free flash space in the example is 182,394,880 bytes.

**Example 9-5**   Verify the Image Size

```
R1# show flash0:
-# - --length-- -----date/time------ path
<Output omitted>


182394880 bytes available (74092544 bytes used)
```

**Step 4.**   Copy the IOS image file from the TFTP server to the router using the
**copy** command shown in Example 9-6. After issuing this command with
the specified source and destination URLs, the user will be prompted for
the IP address of the remote host, source filename, and destination filename. The transfer of the file will begin.

**Example 9-6**   Copy the IOS Image from the TFTP Server

```
R1# copy tftp: flash0:
Address or name of remote host []? 2001:DB8:CAFE:100::99
Source filename []? c1900-universalk9-mz.SPA.152-4.M3.bin
Destination filename []? c1900-universalk9-mz.SPA.152-4.M3.bin
Accessing tftp://2001:DB8:CAFE:100::99/c1900-universalk9-mz.SPA.152-4.M3.bin...
Loading c1900-universalk9-mz.SPA.152-4.M3.bin from 2001:DB8:CAFE:100::99 (via
GigabitEthernet0/0): !!!!!!!!!!!!!!!!!!!!!
<Output omitted>
[OK - 68831808 bytes]
68831808 bytes copied in 368.128 secs (265652 bytes/sec)
```

## Boot System (9.1.2.4)

To upgrade to the copied IOS image after that image is saved in the router's flash
memory, configure the router to load the new image during bootup using the **boot
system** command. Save the configuration. Reload the router to boot the router with
new image. After the router has booted, to verify that the new image has loaded, use
the **show version** command.

During startup, the bootstrap code parses the startup configuration file in NVRAM for the **boot system** commands that specify the name and location of the Cisco IOS Software image to load. Several **boot system** commands can be entered in sequence to provide a fault-tolerant boot plan.

The **boot system** command is a global configuration command that allows the user to specify the source for the Cisco IOS Software image to load. Some of the syntax options available include

- Specify the flash device as the source of the Cisco IOS image.

  ```
  Router(config)# boot system flash0://c1900-universalk9-mz.SPA.152-4.M3.bin
  ```

- Specify the TFTP server as the source of the Cisco IOS image, with ROMMON as backup.

  ```
  Router(config)# boot system tftp://c1900-universalk9-mz.SPA.152-4.M3.bin
  Router(config)# boot system rom
  ```

If there are no **boot system** commands in the configuration, the router defaults to loading the first valid Cisco IOS image in flash memory and running it.

As shown in Example 9-7, the **show version** command can be used to verify the software image file.

**Example 9-7**    Verifying the New Image

```
R1# show version
Cisco IOS Software, C1900 Software (C1900-UNIVERSALK9-M), Version 15.2(4)M3, RELEASE
  SOFTWARE (fc2)
Technical Support: http://www.cisco.com/techsupport
Copyright (c) 1986-2013 by Cisco Systems, Inc.
Compiled Tue 26-Feb-13 02:11 by prod_rel_team


ROM: System Bootstrap, Version 15.0(1r)M15, RELEASE SOFTWARE (fc1)


R1 uptime is 1 hour, 2 minutes
System returned to ROM by power-on
System image file is "flash0:c1900-universalk9-mz.SPA.152-4.M3.bin"
```

**Packet Tracer Activity 9.1.2.5: Using a TFTP Server to Upgrade a Cisco IOS Image**

A TFTP server can help manage the storage of IOS images and revisions to IOS images. For any network, it is good practice to keep a backup copy of the Cisco IOS Software image in case the system image in the router becomes corrupted or accidentally erased. A TFTP server can also be used to store new upgrades to the IOS and then deployed throughout the network where it is needed. In this activity, you will upgrade the IOS images on Cisco devices by using a TFTP server. You will also back up an IOS image with the use of a TFTP server.

Video

**Video Demonstration 9.1.2.6: Managing Cisco IOS Images**

Go to the course online to view this video.

# IOS Licensing (9.2)

This section discusses the significant changes at Cisco to the packaging and licensing of its IOS, including obtaining, installing, and managing Cisco IOS Release 15 software licenses.

## Software Licensing (9.2.1)

This topic explains the new Cisco licensing process and how to obtain and install a license.

### Licensing Overview (9.2.1.1)

Beginning with Cisco IOS Software Release 15.0, Cisco modified the process to enable new technologies within the IOS feature sets. Cisco IOS Software Release 15.0 incorporates cross-platform feature sets to simplify the image selection process. It does this by providing similar functions across platform boundaries. Each device ships with the same universal image. *Technology packages* are enabled in the universal image through Cisco Software Activation licensing keys. The Cisco IOS Software Activation feature allows the user to enable licensed features and register licenses. The Cisco IOS Software Activation feature is a collection of processes and components used to activate Cisco IOS Software feature sets by obtaining and validating Cisco software licenses.

Figure 9-11 shows the technology packages that are available:

■ **IP Base:** Offers features found in IP Base IOS image on ISR 1900, 2900, and 3900 + Flexible NetFlow + IPv6 parity for IPv4 features present in IP Base. Some of the key features are AAA, BGP, OSPF, EIGRP, IS-IS, RIP, PBR, IGMP, Multicast, DHCP, HSRP, GLBP, NHRP, HTTP, HQF, QoS, ACL, NBAR, GRE, CDP, ARP, NTP, PPP, PPPoA, PPPoE, RADIUS, TACACS, SCTP, SMDS,

SNMP, STP, VLAN, DTP, IGMP, Snooping, SPAN, WCCP, ISDN, ADSL over ISDN, NAT-Basic X.25, RSVP, NTP, Flexible Netflow, and so on.

- **Data:** Data features found in SP Services and Enterprise Services IOS image on ISR 1900, 2900, and 3900; for example, MPLS, BFD, RSVP, L2VPN, L2TPv3, Layer 2 Local Switching, Mobile IP, Multicast Authentication, FHRP-GLBP, IP SLAs, PfR, DECnet, ALPS, RSRB, BIP, DLSw+, FRAS, Token Ring, ISL, IPX, STUN, SNTP, SDLC, QLLC, and so on.

- **Unified Communications (UC):** Offers the UC features found in IPVoice IOS image on ISR 1900, 2900, and 3900; for example, TDM/PSTN Gateway, Video Gateway [H320/324], Voice Conferencing, Codec Transcoding, RSVP Agent (voice), FAX T.37/38, CAC/QOS, Hoot-n-Holler, and so on.

- **Security (SEC):** Offers the security features found in Advanced Security IOS image on ISR 1900, 2900, and 3900; for example, IKE v1 / IPsec / PKI, IPsec/ GRE, Easy VPN w/ DVTI, DMVPN, Static VTI, Firewall, Network Foundation Protection, GETVPN, and so on.

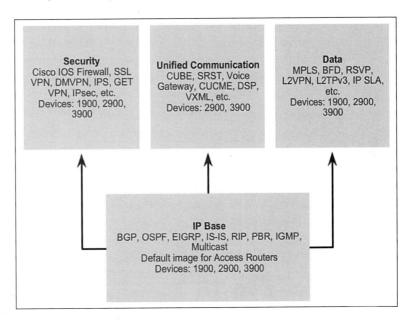

**Figure 9-11**   IOS Packaging Model for ISR G2 Routers

**Note**

The IP Base license is a prerequisite for installing the Data, Security, and Unified Communications licenses. For earlier router platforms that can support Cisco IOS Software Release 15.0, a universal image is not available. It is necessary to download a separate image that contains the desired features.

## Technology Package Licenses

Technology package licenses are supported on Cisco ISR G2 platforms (Cisco 1900, 2900, and 3900 Series routers). The Cisco IOS universal image contains all packages and features in one image. Each package is a grouping of technology-specific features. Multiple technology package licenses can be activated on the Cisco 1900, 2900, and 3900 Series ISR platforms.

> **Note**
>
> Use the **show license feature** command to view the technology package licenses and feature licenses that are supported on the router.

## Licensing Process (9.2.1.2)

When a new router is shipped, it comes preinstalled with the software image and the corresponding permanent licenses for the customer-specified packages and features.

The router also comes with the evaluation license, known as a temporary license, for most packages and features supported on the specified router. This allows customers to try a new software package or feature by activating a specific evaluation license. If customers want to permanently activate a software package or feature on the router, they must get a new software license.

Figure 9-12 shows the three steps to permanently activate a new software package or feature on the router.

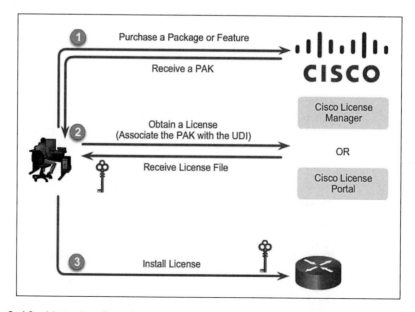

**Figure 9-12**　Licensing Overview

## Step 1. Purchase the Software Package or Feature to Install (9.2.1.3)

The first step is to purchase the software package or feature needed. This can be the IP Base license for a specific software release or adding a package to IP Base, such as Security.

Software Claim Certificates are used for licenses that require software activation. The claim certificate provides the Product Activation Key (PAK) for the license and important information regarding the Cisco End User License Agreement (EULA). In most instances, Cisco or the Cisco channel partner will have already activated the licenses ordered at the time of purchase and no Software Claim Certificate is provided.

In either instance, customers receive a PAK with their purchase. The PAK serves as a receipt and is used to obtain a license. A PAK is an 11-digit alphanumeric key created by Cisco manufacturing. It defines the Feature Set associated with the PAK. A PAK is not tied to a specific device until the license is created. A PAK can be purchased that generates any specified number of licenses. As shown in Figure 9-13, a separate license is required for each package, IP Base, Data, UC, and SEC.

**Figure 9-13**   Purchasing a License for a Feature

## Step 2. Obtain a License (9.2.1.4)

The next step is to obtain the license, which is actually a license file. A license file, also known as a Software Activation License, is obtained using one of the following options:

- **Cisco License Manager (CLM):** This is a free software application available at www.cisco.com/go/clm. Cisco License Manager is a standalone application from Cisco that helps network administrators rapidly deploy multiple Cisco software licenses across their networks. Cisco License Manager can discover network devices, view their license information, and acquire and deploy licenses from

Cisco. The application provides a GUI that simplifies installation and helps automate license acquisition, as well as perform multiple licensing tasks from a central location. CLM is free of charge and can be downloaded from Cisco.com.

■ **Cisco License Registration Portal:** This is the web-based portal for getting and
registering individual software licenses, available at www.cisco.com/go/license.

Both of these processes require a PAK number and a *Unique Device
Identifier (UDI)*.

The PAK is received during purchase.

The UDI is a combination of the Product ID (PID), the Serial Number (SN), and the
hardware version. The SN is an 11-digit number that uniquely identifies a device. The
PID identifies the type of device. Only the PID and SN are used for license creation.
This UDI can be displayed using the **show license udi** command shown in Example
9-8. This information is also available on a pull-out label tray found on the device.

**Example 9-8**    Displaying the UDI

```
R1# show license udi
Device#      PID          SN      UDI

- - - - - - - - - - - - - - - - - - - - - - - - - - - - - - - - - - - - - - - - - - - - - - - - - - -

*0           CISCO1941/K9         FTX1636848Z      CISCO1941/K9:FTX1636848Z
R1#
```

Figure 9-14 shows an example of the pull-out label on a Cisco 1941 router.

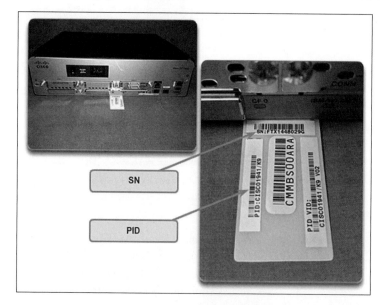

**Figure 9-14**    Locating the UDI (PID/SN) on a Pull-Out Label

After entering the appropriate information, the customer receives an email containing the license information to install the license file. The license file is an XML text file with a .lic extension.

## Step 3. Install the License (9.2.1.5)

After the license has been purchased, the customer receives a license file, which is an XML text file with a .lic extension. Installing a permanent license requires two steps:

**Step 1.** Use the **license install** *stored-location-url* privileged EXEC mode command to install a license file.

**Step 2.** Reload the router using the privileged EXEC command **reload**. A reload is not required if an evaluation license is active.

Example 9-9 shows the configuration for installing the permanent license for the Security package on the router.

**Example 9-9**   Permanent License Installation

```
R1# license install flash0:seck9-C1900-SPE150_K9-FHH12250057.xml
Installing licenses from "seck9-c1900-SPE150_K9-FHH12250057.xml"
Installing...Feature:seck9...Successful:Supported
1/1 licenses were successfully installed
0/1 licenses were existing licenses
0/1 licenses were failed to install
R1#
*Jul 7 17:24:57.391: %LICENSE-6-INSTALL: Feature seck9 1.0 was installed in this
device.
UDI=1900-SPE150/K9:FHH12250057; StoreIndex=15:Primary License Storage
*Jul 7 17:24:57.615: %IOS_LICENSE_IMAGE_APPLICATION-6-LICENSE_LEVEL: Module
name = c1900
Next reboot level = seck9 and License = seck9
R1# reload
```

**Note**

Unified Communications is not supported on 1941 routers.

A permanent license is a license that never expires. After a permanent license is installed on a router, it is good for that particular feature set for the life of the router, even across IOS versions. For example, when a UC, SEC, or Data license is installed on a router, the subsequent features for that license are activated even if the router is upgraded to a new IOS release. A permanent license is the most common license type used when a feature set is purchased for a device.

**Note**

Cisco manufacturing preinstalls the appropriate permanent license on the ordered device for the purchased feature set. No customer interaction with the Cisco IOS Software Activation processes is required to enable that license on new hardware.

## License Verification and Management (9.2.2)

This topic discusses the process of license verification as well as how to activate, back up, and uninstall a license.

### License Verification (9.2.2.1)

After a new license has been installed, the router must be rebooted using the **reload** command. As shown in Example 9-10, the **show version** command is used after the router is reloaded to verify that the license has been installed.

**Example 9-10**   Verifying the Permanent License

```
R1# show version
<Outout omitted>
License Info:
License UDI:
-------------------------------------------------
Device#     PID                    SN
-------------------------------------------------
*0          CISCO1941/K9      FTX1636848Z
Technology Package License Information for Module:'c1900'
-------------------------------------------------------------
Technology     Technology-package          Technology-package
               Current     Type            Next reboot
-------------------------------------------------------------
ipbase         ipbasek9     Permanent      ipbasek9
security       seck9        Permanent      seck9
uc             None         None           None
data           None         None           None
```

The **show license** command in Example 9-11 is used to display additional information about Cisco IOS Software licenses.

**Example 9-11**   Verifying the License Details

```
R1# show license
Index 1 Feature: ipbasek9
    Period left: Life time
    License Type: Permanent
    License State: Active, In Use
    License Count: Non-Counted
    License Priority: Medium
Index 2 Feature: securityk9
    Period left: Life time
    License Type: Permanent
    License State: Active, In Use
    License Count: Non-Counted
    License Priority: Medium
Index 3 Feature: datak9
    Period left: Not Activated
    Period Used: 0  minute  0  second
    License Type: EvalRightToUse
    License State: Not in Use, EULA not accepted
    License Count: Non-Counted
    License Priority: None
<Output omitted>
```

This command displays license information used to help with troubleshooting
issues related to Cisco IOS Software licenses. This command displays all the licenses
installed in the system. In this example, both the IP Base and Security licenses have
been installed. This command also displays the features that are available, but not
licensed to execute, such as the Data feature set. Output is grouped according to
how the features are stored in license storage.

The following is a brief description of the output:

- **Feature:** Name of the feature.

- **License Type:** Type of license, such as Permanent or Evaluation.

- **License State:** Status of the license, such as Active or In Use.

- **License Count:** Number of licenses available and in use, if counted. If
  noncounted is indicated, the license is unrestricted.

- **License Priority:** Priority of the license, such as high or low.

> **Note**
>
> Refer to the Cisco IOS Release 15 command reference guide for complete details on the information displayed in the **show license** command.

### Activate an Evaluation Right-To-Use License (9.2.2.2)

The Evaluation license process has gone through three revisions on the ISR G2 devices. The latest revisions, starting with Cisco IOS Releases 15.0(1)M6, 15.1(1) T4, 15.1(2)T4, 15.1(3)T2, and 15.1(4)M Evaluation licenses, are replaced with Evaluation Right-To-Use (RTU) licenses after 60 days. An Evaluation license is good for a 60-day evaluation period. After the 60 days, this license automatically transitions into an RTU license. These licenses are available on the honor system and require the customer's acceptance of the EULA. The EULA is automatically applied to all Cisco IOS Software licenses.

The **license accept end user agreement** global configuration mode command is used to configure a one-time acceptance of the EULA for all Cisco IOS Software packages and features. After the command is issued and the EULA accepted, the EULA is automatically applied to all Cisco IOS Software licenses and the user is not prompted to accept the EULA during license installation.

Example 9-12 shows how to configure a one-time acceptance of the EULA with the **license accept end user agreement** command and activate an Evaluation RTU license with the **license boot module** *module-name* **technology-package** *package-name* command.

**Example 9-12**   Installing an Evaluation License

```
R1(config)# license accept end user agreement
R1(config)# license boot module c1900 technology-package datak9
% use 'write' command to make license boot config take effect on next boot
R1(config)#
*Apr 25 23:15:01.874: %IOS_LICENSE_IMAGE_APPLICATION-6-LICENSE_LEVEL: Module name =
  c1900 Next reboot level = datak9 and License = datak9
*Apr 25 23:15:02.502: %LICENSE-6-EULA_ACCEPTED: EULA for feature datak9 1.0 has been
  accepted. UDI=CISCO1941/K9:FTX1636848Z; StoreIndex=1:Built-In License Storage
R1(config)#
```

Use the **?** in place of the arguments to determine which module names and supported software packages are available on the router. Technology package names for Cisco ISR G2 platforms are

- **ipbasek9:** IP Base technology package
- **securityk9:** Security technology package

- **datak9:** Data technology package

- **uck9:** Unified Communications package (not available on 1900 series)

---

**Note**

A reload using the **reload** command is required to activate the software package.

---

Evaluation licenses are temporary and are used to evaluate a feature set on new hardware. Temporary licenses are limited to a specific usage period (for example, 60 days).

Reload the router after a license is successfully installed using the **reload** command. The **show license** command in Example 9-13 verifies that the license has been installed.

**Example 9-13**    Verifying an Installed Evaluation License

```
R1# show license
Index 1 Feature: ipbasek9
    Period left: Life time
    License Type: Permanent
    License State: Active, In Use
    License Count: Non-Counted
    License Priority: Medium
Index 2 Feature: securityk9
    Period left: Life time
    License Type: Permanent
    License State: Active, In Use
    License Count: Non-Counted
    License Priority: Medium
Index 3 Feature: datak9
    Period left: 8  weeks 4   days
    Period Used: 0  minute  0   second
    License Type: EvalRightToUse
    License State: Active, Not in Use, EULA accepted
    License Count: Non-Counted
    License Priority: Low<Outout omitted>
```

## Back Up the License (9.2.2.3)

As shown in Example 9-14, the **license save** command is used to copy all licenses in a device and store them in a format required by the specified storage location. Saved licenses are restored by using the **license install** command.

The command to back up a copy of the licenses on a device is

```
Router# license save file-sys://lic-location
```

Use the **show flash0:** command to verify that the licenses have been saved.

**Example 9-14**    Backing Up the License

```
R1# license save flash0:all_licenses.lic
license lines saved ..... to flash0:all_licenses.lic

R1# show flash0:
-# - --length-- -----date/time------ path
<Outout omitted>
8     68831808 Apr 2 2013 21:29:58 +00:00 c1900-universalk9-mz.SPA.152-4.M3.bin
9         1153 Apr 26 2013 02:24:30 +00:00 all_licenses.lic

182390784 bytes available (74096640 bytes used)
```

The license storage location can be a directory or a URL that points to a file system. Use the **?** command to see the storage locations supported by a device.

## Uninstall the License (9.2.2.4)

To clear an active permanent license from the Cisco 1900 Series, 2900 Series, and 3900 Series routers, perform the following steps:

**Step 1.**    Disable the technology package.

- Disable the active license with this command:

  ```
  Router(config)# license boot module module-name technology-package
  package-name disable
  ```

- Reload the router using the **reload** command. A reload is required to make the software package inactive.

**Step 2.**    Clear the license.

- Clear the technology package license from license storage:

  ```
  Router# license clear feature-name
  ```

- Clear the **license boot module** *module-name* **technology-package** *package-name* **disable** command used for disabling the active license:

  ```
  Router(config)# no license boot module module-name technology-package
  package-name disable
  ```

> **Note**
>
> Some licenses, such as built-in licenses, cannot be cleared. Only licenses that have been added by using the **license install** command are removed. Evaluation licenses are not removed.

Example 9-15 shows an example of clearing an active license.

**Example 9-15**   Clearing an Active and Permanent License

```
!Step 1. Disable the Technology Package
R1(config)# license boot module c1900 technology-package seck9 disable
R1(config)# exit
R1# reload
!Step 2. Clear the License
R1# license clear seck9
R1# configure terminal
R1(config)# no license boot module c1900 technology-package seck9 disable
R1(config)# exit
R1# reload
```

**Video**

**Video Demonstration 9.2.2.5: Working with IOS Release 15 Image Licenses**

Go to the course online to view this video.

# Summary (9.3)

### Class Activity 9.3.1.1: Powerful Protocols

At the end of this course, you are asked to complete two Capstone Projects, where you will create, configure, and verify two network topologies using the two main routing protocols taught in this course, EIGRP and OSPF.

To make things easier, you decide to create a chart of configuration and verification commands to use for these two design projects. To help devise the protocol charts, ask another student in the class to help you.

Refer to the PDF for this chapter for directions on how to create a design for this modeling project. When complete, share your work with another group or with the class. You might also want to save the files created for this project in a network portfolio for future reference.

### Packet Tracer Activity 9.3.1.2: EIGRP Capstone Project

In this Capstone Project activity, you will demonstrate your ability to

- Design, configure, verify, and secure EIGRP, IPv4, or IPv6 on a network

- Design a VLSM addressing scheme for the devices connected to the LANs

- Present your design using network documentation from your Capstone Project network

### Packet Tracer Activity 9.3.1.3: OSPF Capstone Project

In this Capstone Project activity, you will demonstrate your ability to

- Configure basic OSPFv2 to enable internetwork communications in a small- to medium-sized IPv4 business network

- Implement advanced OSPF features to enhance operation in a small- to medium-sized business network

- Implement multiarea OSPF for IPv4 to enable internetwork communications in a small- to medium-sized business network

- Configure basic OSPFv3 to enable internetwork communications in a small- to medium-sized IPv6 business network

Packet Tracer
☐ Activity

**Packet Tracer Activity 9.3.1.4: Skills Integration Challenge**

As a network technician familiar with IPv4 addressing, routing, and network security, you are now ready to apply your knowledge and skills to a network infrastructure. Your task is to finish designing the VLSM IPv4 addressing scheme, implement multi-area OSPF, and secure access to the VTY lines using access control lists.

---

Examples of Cisco IOS Software releases include 12.3, 12.4, 15.0, and 15.1. Along with each software release, there are new versions of the software used to implement bug fixes and new features.

Cisco IOS Software Release 12.4 incorporates new software features and hardware support that was introduced in the Cisco IOS Software Release 12.3T train and additional software fixes. Mainline releases (also called maintenance releases) contain no uppercase letter in their release designation and inherit new Cisco IOS Software functionality and hardware from lower-numbered T releases. Prior to and including Release 12.4, the mainline "M" train received bug fixes only. The technology "T" train includes fixes as well as new features and platforms. The Release 12.4T train provides Cisco IOS Software functionality and hardware adoption that introduces new technology, functionality, and hardware advances that are not available in the Cisco IOS Software Release 12.4 mainline train.

In the Cisco IOS Software Release 15.0 family, a new strategy is in place. The Cisco IOS Release 15.0 family does not diverge into separate M and T trains but into M and T releases in the same train. For example, the first release in the Cisco IOS Software Release 15.0 family is 15.0(1)M, where M indicates that it is an extended maintenance release. An extended maintenance release is ideal for long-term maintenance. Not all releases in the Cisco IOS Software Release 15.0 family will be extended maintenance releases; there will also be standard maintenance releases that receive the latest features and hardware support. The standard maintenance releases will have an uppercase T in their designation.

When selecting or upgrading a Cisco IOS router, it is important to choose the proper IOS image with the correct feature set and version. The Cisco IOS image file is based on a special naming convention. The name for the Cisco IOS image file contains multiple parts, each with a specific meaning. Example: c1900-universalk9-mz. SPA.152-4.M3.bin.

Commands are available for upgrading and verification of flash. The **show flash** command displays the files stored in flash memory, including the system image files. This command can also be used to verify free flash size. The **boot system** command is a global configuration command that allows the user to specify the source for the Cisco IOS.

Using a network TFTP server allows image and configuration uploads and downloads over the network. The network TFTP server can be another router, a workstation, or a host system.

Beginning with Cisco IOS Software Release 15.0, Cisco modified the process to enable new technologies within the IOS feature sets. Each device ships with the same universal image. Technology packages such as IP Base, Data, UC, and SEC are enabled in the universal image through Cisco software activation licensing keys. Each licensing key is unique to a particular device and is obtained from Cisco by providing the product ID and serial number of the router and a Product Activation Key (PAK).

License activation is not necessary for factory-ordered preconfigured licenses prior to use. IP Base comes shipped as a permanent license on all ISR-G2 devices. The other three technology packages—Data, Security, and Unified Communications—come with an Evaluation license as the default, but a permanent license can be purchased.

A permanent license is a license that never expires. For example, after a UC (Unified Communications), Security, or Data license is installed on a router, the subsequent features for that license will be activated, even if the router is upgraded to a new IOS release.

## Installing a License

The prerequisites for installing a license are as follows:

- Obtain the necessary PAK, which is an 11-digit ID that can be delivered by mail or electronically.

- Obtain a valid Cisco username/password.

- Retrieve the serial number and PID with the **show license udi** command or from the router label tray.

The **show version** command is used after the router is reloaded to verify that the license has been installed.

The **show license** command is used to display additional information about Cisco IOS Software licenses.

The **license accept end user agreement** global configuration command is used to configure a one-time acceptance of the EULA for all Cisco IOS Software packages and features.

Use the Cisco.com website to research other benefits and information on IOS Release 15.

# Practice

The following activities provide practice with the topics introduced in this chapter. The Labs and Class Activities are available in the companion *Scaling Networks Lab Manual* (ISBN 978-1-58713-325-1). The Packet Tracer Activities PKA files are found in the online course.

## Class Activities

- Class Activity 9.0.1.2: IOS Detection
- Class Activity 9.3.1.1: Powerful Protocols

## Packet Tracer Activities

- Packet Tracer Activity 9.1.1.9: Decode IOS Image Names
- Packet Tracer Activity 9.1.2.5: Using a TFTP Server to Upgrade a Cisco IOS Image
- Packet Tracer Activity 9.3.1.2: EIGRP Capstone Project
- Packet Tracer Activity 9.3.1.3: OSPF Capstone Project
- Packet Tracer Activity 9.3.1.4: Skills Integration Challenge

# Check Your Understanding Questions

Complete all the review questions listed to test your understanding of the topics and concepts in this chapter. The appendix "Answers to 'Check Your Understanding' Questions" lists the answers.

1. What is a characteristic of the Cisco IOS Software Release 12.4 mainline train?

   A. It is updated with software fixes as these are developed.

   B. It is updated with software fixes every 20 months.

   C. It is updated with new features when these are developed.

   D. It is updated with new features every 20 months.

**2.** Which Cisco IOS release followed Release 12.4?

A. 12.5

B. 13

C. 14

D. 15

**3.** If a router had the appropriate hardware, which Cisco IOS version should an administrator install to ensure that the router receives the latest technologies?

A. 12.2

B. 12.4T

C. 12.2(28)

D. 12.4(15)T1

E. 12.4(21a)

**4.** Which Cisco Release 12.4 IOS image package offers the most feature sets?

A. Advanced IP Services

B. Advanced Enterprise Services

C. securityk9

D. Unified Communications k9

E. Advanced Security

**5.** Which command would a network engineer use to restore the IOS image **c1900-universalk9-mz.SPA.152-4.M3.bin** to a router?

A. **copy tftp: flash0:**

B. **copy flash0: tftp:**

C. **copy c1900-universalk9-mz.SPA.152-4.M3.bin tftp:**

D. **copy flash0: c1900-universalk9-mz.SPA.152-4.M3.bin**

**6.** Which Cisco IOS Release 15.0 technology package contains the IPsec framework components required to support the ISR G2 platforms?

A. Data

B. Security

C. Unified Communications

D. IP Base

**7.** Refer to Example 9-16. Based on the exhibited information, which technology package or packages can be used by a network engineer for a production router?

**Example 9-16**   Exhibit for Question 7

```
R1# show license all
License Store: Primary License Storage
StoreIndex: 0    Feature: ipbasek9                      Version: 1.0
        License Type: Permanent
        License State: Active, In Use
        License Count: Non-Counted
        License Priority: Medium


License Store: Evaluation License Storage
StoreIndex: 0    Feature: securityk9                     Version: 1.0
        License Type: Evaluation
        License State: Inactive
            Evaluation total period: 208 weeks 2 days
            Evaluation period left: 208 weeks 2 days
        License Count: Non-Counted
        License Priority: None
StoreIndex: 1    Feature: datak9                         Version: 1.0
        License Type:
        License State: Inactive
            Evaluation total period: 208 weeks 2 days
            Evaluation period left: 208 weeks 2 days
        License Count: Non-Counted
        License Priority: None
```

A.  Only ipbasek9 and securityk9

B.  ipbasek9, securityk9, and datak9

C.  Only ipbasek9

D.  Only securityk9 and datak9

8. A network administrator is asked to provide the UDI to obtain a license for the Data technology package for the IOS Release 15.0 on a Cisco 1900 router. What is a UDI?

   A. A combination of the PAK number and the serial number

   B. A combination of the serial number and the MAC address of Gi0/0

   C. A combination of the product ID and the PAK number

   D. A combination of the product ID, the serial number, and the hardware version

9. Which Cisco IOS Release 15 package would be needed to implement voice over IP in a building where documents important to national defense are stored?

   A. data9

   B. uck9

   C. ipbasek9

   D. securityk9

10. A network engineer purchases, installs, and activates a license key on a Cisco 2911 ISR G2 router. What is the next step in the installation process?

    A. Reload the router.

    B. Register the license with Cisco.

    C. Back up the IOS to a TFTP server.

    D. Back up the license key stored in flash memory.

# Answers to the "Check Your Understanding" Questions

## Chapter 1

1. Correct answers: C, E. Explanation: All modern enterprise networks are expected to support critical applications, converged network traffic, and diverse business needs and provide centralized administrative control. Users expect enterprise networks to be up 99.999 percent of the time (not 90 percent). Support for limited growth is not a usual network design criterion.

2. Correct answers: B, C. Explanation: Using duplicate equipment and using redundant paths are two methods to help prevent network disruptions. The use of VLANs would not affect network availability. Changing the routing protocol could actually reduce availability during convergence. Loops, which are created by the provision of redundant paths, are managed by protocols without removing devices.

3. Correct answer: C. Explanation: VLANs create several groups of users that use a single physical link. Trunk ports are single physical links. Subinterfaces allow one physical link to be used to create several logical links. EtherChannel provides the ability to combine multiple physical links into a single logical link.

4. Correct answer: D. Explanation: EtherChannel allows more data to be moved at the access layer but does not provide network expansion. Redundancy is used to provide failover solutions but does not focus on network expansion. Routing protocols are not used to provide network expansion at the access layer. Wireless connectivity provides network access to a large number of users at the access layer.

5. Correct answer: B. Explanation: A switch operating at full wire speed is capable of generating the cumulative amount of each port on the switch. A 48-port gigabit switch could generate 48 x 1 Gb/s = 48 Gb/s of data. Forwarding rates are determined based on the capabilities of each switch, but are not limited to 24 Gb/s.

6. Correct answer: B. Explanation: Service provider routers provide end-to-end scalable solutions. Customers do not remotely access or connect directly to a service provider router. Network edge routers provide customer interactivity, personalization, and mobility. Wherever customers can access an Internet connection, they can access their content. Branch routers provide simple network configuration and management while maintaining highly available networks.

Modular routers are used to provide greater flexibility in which interfaces are used during network design and installation.

7. Correct answer: A. Explanation: Out-of-band device management is used for initial configuration or when a network connection is unavailable. Configuration that uses out-of-band management requires a direct connection to a console or AUX port and a terminal emulation client.

8. port density. Explanation: Port density is the number of ports on a switch.

9. broadcast. Explanation: Routers effectively stop broadcast traffic between logical IPv4 networks.

10. access

   distribution

   core

   Explanation: Each layer of the hierarchical design model performs important functions. In general, the access layer is where end users connect, the distribution layer is responsible for routing between networks, and the core layer provides high-speed access to remote networks.

# Chapter 2

1. Correct answer: B. Explanation: Redundancy attempts to remove any single point of failure in a network by using multiple physically cabled paths between switches in the network.

2. Correct answers: A, D. Explanation: During a broadcast storm, switches will forward broadcast traffic through every interface except the original ingress interface. New traffic arriving at the switch will be discarded by a switch in a broadcast storm because the switch will be unable to process the new traffic. During a broadcast storm, switches do not automatically adjust duplex settings. However, communication will often fail between end devices because of the heavy processing demands that are created by the broadcast traffic. Constant changes to the MAC address table during a broadcast storm can prevent a switch from forwarding frames.

3. Correct answer: D. Explanation: After a Cisco switch boots, it will send out BPDUs containing its individual BID and the root ID for the network. By default, the initial root ID at bootup will be the ID of that individual switch. After a root bridge is elected, port states and paths are chosen.

4. Correct answer: A. Explanation: After the election of a root bridge has occurred, each switch will have to determine the best path to the root bridge from its location. The path is determined by summing the individual port costs along the path from each switch port to the root bridge.

5. Correct answer: C. Explanation: Ports in the blocking state are nondesignated ports and do not participate in frame forwarding. Ports in the listening state can participate in BPDU frame forwarding according to received BPDU frames, but do not forward data frames. Ports in the forwarding state forward data frames and send and receive BPDU frames. Ports in the disabled state are administratively disabled.

6. Correct answer: D, E. Explanation: A port that is configured with PortFast will immediately transition from the blocking to the forwarding state. PortFast should only be configured on switch ports that support end devices, so no BPDUs should ever be received through a port that is configured with PortFast. Configuring a port with PortFast supports DHCP because PortFast will speed up the transition from blocking to forwarding. Without PortFast, an end device might begin to issue DHCP requests before the port has transitioned to the forwarding state.

7. Correct answer: A, D, E. Explanation: The Rapid PVST+ port states are discarding, learning, and forwarding. Listening is an STP and PVST+ port state. Trunking is not a type of STP port state.

8. Correct answer: B. Explanation: Of all the commands that are listed, only the correct option, **show spanning-tree**, displays STP root bridge information. The **show running-config** and **show startup-config** commands will show the STP configurations, but will not list the root bridge.

9. Correct answer: C. Explanation: The first step that should be taken when there is a spanning tree failure in a Layer 2 network is to remove all redundant links in the failed segment of the network. This will eliminate the loops in the topology, allowing for a normalization of the traffic and CPU loads. The next step would be to investigate the failure of STP on the redundant links and fix these issues prior to restoring the links.

10. Correct answer: C, D. Explanation: In order for a set of routers to present the illusion of being a single router, they must share both an IP address and a MAC address. A static route, BID, or host name does not have to be shared in this context.

11. Correct answer: B, D. Explanation: The first hop redundancy protocols HSRP and GLBP are Cisco proprietary and will not function in a multivendor environment.

12. STP

   Rapid PVST+

   MSTP

13. The standby router stops receiving hello messages from the forwarding router.

   The standby router assumes the role of the forwarding router.

   The new forwarding router assumes the IP and MAC address of the virtual router.

# Chapter 3

1. Correct answer: A. Explanation: EtherChannel relies on existing switch ports, so there is no need to upgrade the links. Configuration tasks are done on the EtherChannel interface, rather than individual ports. STP operates on EtherChannel in the same manner as it does on other links.

2. Correct answers: D, E, F. Explanation: Most configuration tasks can be done on the EtherChannel interface, rather than on individual ports. Existing ports can be used, eliminating the need to upgrade ports to faster speeds. Spanning Tree Protocol runs on EtherChannel links in the same manner as it does on regular links, but it does not recalculate when an individual link within the channel goes down. EtherChannel also supports load balancing.

3. Correct answer: C. Explanation: Fast Ethernet and Gigabit Ethernet interfaces cannot be combined into a single EtherChannel interface. The interfaces must all be of the same type. EtherChannel links can be configured on Layer 2 and Layer 3 switches.

4. Correct answer: C. Explanation: An EtherChannel will be formed through PAgP when both switches are in on mode or when one of them is in auto or desirable mode and the other is in desirable mode.

5. Correct answer: C. Explanation: The **channel-group mode active** command enables LACP unconditionally, and the **channel-group mode passive** command enables LACP only if the port receives an LACP packet from another device. The **channel-group mode desirable** command enables PAgP unconditionally, and the **channel-group mode auto** command enables PAgP only if the port receives a PAgP packet from another device.

6. Correct answers: C, D. Explanation: Port Aggregation Protocol and Link Aggregation Control Protocol are used to implement EtherChannel. Spanning Tree and Rapid Spanning Tree Protocol are used to prevent switching loops. Cisco

Discovery Protocol is Cisco proprietary and is used to discover information about adjacent Cisco devices such as model number and IP address.

7. Correct answer: E. Explanation: All ports in an EtherChannel bundle must either be trunk ports or be access ports in the same VLAN. If VLAN pruning is enabled on the trunk, the allowed VLANs must be the same on both sides of the EtherChannel.

8. Correct answer: B. Explanation: Two protocols can be used to send negotiation frames that are used to try to establish an EtherChannel link: PAgP and LACP. PAgP is Cisco proprietary, and LACP adheres to the industry standard.

9. Correct answers: A, B, E. Explanation: There are some EtherChannel modes that can be different and an EtherChannel will form, such as auto/desirable and active/passive. A port that is currently in the spanning tree blocking mode or has been configured for PortFast can still be used to form an EtherChannel.

10. **show etherchannel summary**. Explanation: When several port channel interfaces are configured on the same device, use the **show etherchannel summary** command to display a single line of information per port channel.

# Chapter 4

1. Correct answer: B. Explanation: 900 MHz is an FCC wireless technology that was used before the development of the 802.11 standards. 900-MHz devices have a larger coverage range than the higher frequencies have and do not require line of sight between devices. 802.11b/g/n/ad devices all operate at 2.4 GHz. 802.11a/n/ac/ad devices operate at 5 GHz, and 802.11ad devices operate at 60 GHz.

2. Correct answer: A. Explanation: Yagi antennas are a type of directional radio antenna that can be used for long-distance Wi-Fi networking. They are typically used to extend the range of outdoor hotspots in a specific direction, owing to their high gain. Omnidirectional Wi-Fi antennas are also referred to as a "rubber duck" design and provide 360-degree coverage.

3. Correct answer: B. Explanation: An ESS consists of two or more BSSs that are interconnected by a wired DS. Bluetooth is an example of ad hoc mode.

4. Correct answer: D. Explanation: Beacon frames are broadcast periodically by the AP to advertise its wireless networks to potential clients. Probing, association, and authentication frames are only sent when a client is associating to the AP.

5. Correct answer: A. Explanation: Management frames include probes, association frames, and authentication frames and are used to facilitate connectivity between a client and an access point.

6. Correct answer: B. Explanation: The mixed setting can slow communication. When all the clients that are connecting to the router are using 802.11n, they all enjoy the better data rates that are provided. If 802.11g clients associate with the AP, all the faster clients that are contending for the channel have to wait for 802.11g clients to clear the channel before those faster clients can transmit.

7. Correct answers: C, D. Explanation: Some recommendations are

   - Position APs vertically near the ceiling in the center of each coverage area, if possible.

   - Position APs in locations where users are expected to be. For example, conference rooms are typically a better location for APs than a hallway.

   - Always consult the specifications for the AP when planning for coverage areas.

   - A BSA represents the coverage area that is provided by a single channel. An ESS should have a 10 to 15 percent overlap in coverage area between BSAs in an ESS. With a 15 percent overlap between BSAs, an SSID, and nonoverlapping channels (that is, one cell on channel 1 and the other on channel 6), roaming capability can be created.

8. Correct answer: D. Explanation: Denial of service attacks can be the result of improperly configured devices which can disable the WLAN. Accidental interference from devices such as microwave ovens and cordless phones can impact both the security and performance of a WLAN. Man-in-the-middle attacks can allow an attacker to intercept data. Rogue access points can allow unauthorized users to access the wireless network.

9. Correct answer: C. Explanation: WPA2 is the Wi-Fi Alliance version of 802.11i, the industry standard for authentication. Neither WEP nor WPA possess the level of authentication provided by WPA2. AES aligns with WPA2 as an encryption standard, and is stronger than TKIP or RC4. PSK refers to preshared passwords, an authentication method that can be used by either WPA or WPA2. EAP is intended for use with enterprise networks that use a RADIUS server.

10. Correct answer: A. Explanation: Bottom-up troubleshooting begins with the physical layer. Cables and power would be a logical place to begin the process. ICMP (ping) is a network layer utility. Channel settings are part of the client software. Firmware is the operating system software used by the AP.

11. ad. Explanation: 802.11ad is the fastest standard to date. It supports backward compatibility with all the previous standards.

12. man-in-the-middle. Explanation: A man-in-the-middle attack involves the deployment of a rogue AP in a given network. User traffic is now sent to the

rogue AP, which in turn captures the data and forwards it to the legitimate AP. Return traffic from the legitimate AP is sent to the rogue AP, captured, and then forwarded to the unsuspecting client. The attacker can steal the password and personal information of the user, gain network access, and compromise the system of the user.

13. WiMAX

    Wi-Fi

    Satellite broadband

    Bluetooth

# Chapter 5

1. Correct answer: B. Explanation: Priority is one way to influence the DR/BDR election process. It will override the router with the highest router ID. However to force an election, either the OSPF process needs to be cleared or all routers need to be rebooted.

2. Correct answer: B. Explanation: The router with the highest priority is elected as the designated router (DR). Because both R1 and R2 have the same priority (20), the router ID must be used as the tie-breaker. R2 has the higher router ID (2.2.2.2), so it is elected as the DR.

3. Correct answer: D. Explanation: OSPFv3 is used for IPv6 routing. When the default route is redistributed, neighboring routers will display the route source as OE2 in their IPv6 routing tables. The **show ip route** command is used to display the IPv4 routing table. The **default-information originate** command is used in the source OSPFv3 router to initiate the static route redistribution. EIGRP uses the **redistribute static** command.

4. Correct answer: B. Explanation: The R1(config-if)# **ip ospf message-digest-key 1 md5 CISCO-123** command enables MD5 authentication for a given interface on a router that is running OSPFv2. The CISCO-123 portion is the password.

5. Correct answers: B, D, F. Explanation: For a pair of routers that are running OSPFv2 to form an adjacency, the following parameters must match: subnet mask, network type, Hello and Dead timers, a corresponding network command, and the authentication information.

6. Correct answer: D. Explanation: The routers need to be in the same subnet to form an adjacency. The routing processes can be different on each router. The router IDs must be different for routers that participate in the same routing domain. The interfaces are not passive.

7. Correct answer: D. Explanation: None

8. Correct answer: B. Explanation: The reference bandwidth must be the same on all routers in the domain. An informational message is displayed on the console and alerts the user to this.

9. **default-information originate.** Explanation: The **redistribute static** command will redistribute all static routes.

10. **show ipv6 route ospf.** Explanation: Add the keyword **ospf** to see only the routes learned through OSPF.

11. 10. Explanation: The process ID is found on the third line of the output, where it states, "IPv6 Routing Protocol is ospf 10."

12. Init

   Two-Way

   Exchange

   Explanation: The Down state indicates that the router is down. No hellos are sent. The ExStart state indicates negotiation of a master/slave relationship and DBD packet sequence number. The Loading state indicates that additional LSRs and LSUs are sent and that the SPF algorithm is calculated. The Full state indicates that the routers in the domain have converged.

# Chapter 6

1. Correct answers: A, B. Explanation: Because of the number of neighbor adjacencies, SPF calculations, and resources, Cisco recommends no more than 50 routers per area.

2. Correct answer: B. Explanation: An internal router has all interfaces in the same area. The Area Border Router and the Autonomous System Boundary Router have interfaces in more than one area. Edge router is not an OSPF router type.

3. Correct answers: B, E. Explanation: OSPF routers within the same area will have the same link-state databases. Without route summarization, OSPF routers can have large routing tables. There is no automatic summarization of routes with OSPF. OSPF does require many CPU cycles to calculate the shortest path by using the SPF algorithm. DUAL is not used with OSPF.

4. Correct answer: B. Explanation: Routers first calculate the best path to destinations within their own area, then to other areas within the internetwork, and then to destinations external to the network.

5. Correct answer: D. Explanation: Converged networks are able to communicate within or outside the autonomous system.

6. Correct answer: B. Explanation: Routes in a multiarea OSPF IPv4 routing table are labeled with an O if they are intra-area, internal routes; with O*E1 or O*E2 if they are external routes; and with O IA if they are interarea routes. O IA routes have been learned by the ABR from external LSAs. The ABR then floods them into the area.

7. Correct answer: E. Explanation: An O routing table entry indicates a route, from within the same area, that was learned through OSPF updates. An O IA route is a route from another OSPF area. An O*E2 or O*E1 route is an external route, such as one redistributed from RIP, EIGRP, or a static route, that was redistributed into the OSPF process. An S entry is for a static route. A C entry represents a directly connected network.

8. Correct answer: D. Explanation: Different from OSPFv2, OSPFv3 does not specify networks to be advertised under the router configuration mode. OSPFv3 enables a network to be in OSPFv3 with the **ipv6 ospf** *process-id* **area** *area-id* command under the interface configuration mode.

9. Correct answer: C. Explanation: R1 is joining two areas, area 0 and area 1, so it is an ABR. The OSPF process number could be any number, and it does not indicate how many OSPF processes are running. Because 192.168.10.0 0.0.0.7 means a prefix length of /29, there are eight total but six valid addresses for hosts. Therefore, area 0 could have up to six routers. R1 is advertising two separate noncontiguous networks from area 1.

10. Correct answer: B. Explanation: The summary routes for the six networks would be 192.168.0.0/22 and 192.168.4.0/23. One LSA is needed to advertise each summary route.

11. Correct answer: B, D. Explanation: Route summarization only happens at the area boundaries, which includes the boundary of the AS. Internal routers, by definition, are not on a boundary. A boundary router is a generic term that does not apply to a specific OSPF router type.

12. 4

5

2

1

3

Explanation: OSPF uses link-state advertisement messages (LSAs) to build the LSDB and maintain routing tables. OSPF routers use LSA types 1 to 5 to describe the networks to which they are directly connected or networks that they learned from other routers. These networks can be located in other areas or can also be from non-OSPF networks. Some LSAs are used to identify an ASBR. While most LSAs will be flooded across multiple areas, some LSAs are flooded only within the area where they originated.

# Chapter 7

1. Correct answers: C, D. Explanation: Protocol-dependent modules (PDM) allow EIGRP to route for various Layer 3 protocol packets. TCP and UDP are Layer 4 protocols, and RTP is used by EIGRP to guarantee delivery of packets.

2. Correct answer: D. Explanation: 224.0.0.10 is the reserved IPv4 multicast address that is used by EIGRP.

3. Correct answer: C. Explanation: In an IPv4 packet header, the Protocol field number, and in an IPv6 packet header, the Next Header number, indicates which protocol is used in the encapsulated PDU. For both IPv4 and IPv6, 6 is TCP, 17 is UDP, 88 is EIGRP, and 89 is OSPF.

4. Correct answer: C. Explanation: For the **router eigrp** command, the number that follows represents the autonomous system to which the EIGRP process belongs. All routers within the EIGRP routing domain must use this same autonomous system number.

5. Correct answer: C. Explanation: The wildcard mask is essentially the inverse of the subnet mask. Calculate the wildcard mask by subtracting the subnet mask from 255.255.255.255. In this example, the subnet mask 255.255.255.192 is subtracted from 255.255.255.255, which leaves a wildcard mask of 0.0.0.63.

6. Correct answer: C. Explanation: The entry "Automatic network summarization is not in effect" indicates that the **no auto-summary** command is entered, which means that subnetted networks (from a major network) are included in route updates. The metric values keep the default values. The numbers 90 and 170 indicate the administrative distances. The routing table can contain up to four equal-cost paths to a destination network because the maximum metric variance parameter is 1.

7. Correct answers: C, D. Explanation: By default, only bandwidth and delay are used in the calculation of an EIGRP metric. This is done by setting K1 and K3 to 1, while K2, K4, and K5 are set to 0, by default.

8. Correct answer: B. Explanation: The bandwidth factor that is used to calculate the composite metric of the EIGRP is defined as the slowest bandwidth of all outgoing interfaces between the source and destination.

9. Correct answer: B. Explanation: The value 2816 in (2170112/2816) is the "reported distance," the metric of the neighbor router (192.168.1.6) to reach the destination network. The value 2170112 is the feasible metric cost to reach the destination network.

10. Correct answers: A, E. Explanation: If a successor is no longer available, and there is no feasible successor, an EIGRP route will be put into the active state while the router actively searches for a new path to the destination.

11. Correct answer: C. Explanation: Most of the EIGRP operational features are the same for IPv6 as they are for IPv4. Both use the same DUAL algorithm calculations, metric values, neighbor discovery mechanisms, and 32-bit router ID. What is not the same between the protocols are the source and destination addresses used for EIGRP messages.

12. Correct answer: D. Explanation: EIGRP for IPv6 uses the same router ID as EIGRP for IPv4 uses. The 32-bit number can be configured with the **router-id** command or automatically assigned from the highest IPv4 address on an enabled interface.

13. Correct answer: B. Explanation: EIGRP for IPv6 uses the all-EIGRP-routers link-local multicast address as the destination address for EIGRP messages.

14. update

    hello

    query

    reply

    acknowledgment

    Explanation: EIGRP update packets are used to propagate routing information to other routers. EIGRP hello packets are used to form and maintain neighbor relationships between EIGRP-enabled routers. EIGRP acknowledgment packets are used when reliable delivery is used and a confirmation needs to be returned. EIGRP reply packets are used in response to a query packet, which searches for a route to a specific destination network.

15. 90

    170

    5

    Explanation: EIGRP uses different administrative distances for each type of source for the routing information. The default values used for summary, internal, and external routes are 5, 90, and 170, respectively.

# Chapter 8

1. Correct answer: A. Explanation: The **show ip protocols** command is used to verify which routing protocol is configured, the AS number, and whether automatic summarization is enabled.

2. Correct answer: A. Explanation: The Null0 interface represents a route to nowhere. Using a route to the Null0 interface prevents routing loops for any destination networks present in the summary route that do not actually exist.

3. Correct answer: B. Explanation: In an EIGRP routing table, code **D** indicates that the route was learned from an EIGRP routing update. Code **EX** indicates that the route is an external EIGRP route; that is, a route outside of the EIGRP routing domain.

4. Correct answer: D. Explanation: EIGRP Hello intervals should be less than or equal to EIGRP hold timers. A Hello should be received before the hold timer has expired. When the EIGRP hold timer has expired, the neighbor adjacency will go down. EIGRP Hello intervals and hold timers do not have to match for two routers to form an EIGRP adjacency.

5. Correct answer: D. Explanation: By default, EIGRP will use only up to 50 percent of an interface's bandwidth for EIGRP information. This prevents the EIGRP process from overutilizing a link and not allowing enough bandwidth for the routing of normal traffic. However, if a connection is in low bandwidth, the up to 50 percent bandwidth might not be able to keep up the EIGRP information exchange. The **ip bandwidth-percent eigrp** command can be used to configure the percentage of bandwidth that can be used by EIGRP on an interface in such a scenario.

6. Correct answers: B, D. Explanation: The errors in the configuration are that the key-string has a different value in each router. The key-string in R1 is cisco_123, while in R2, it is cisco-123. Also, on router R2, the EIGRP authentication commands were issued on the incorrect interface, as serial 0/0/1 is unused. The key ID is a valid number. Its range is from 0 to 2147483647. The keychain name can be in lowercase or uppercase, but the same case must be used on each router. A single key can be created for each keychain.

7. Correct answers: A, D. Explanation: EIGRP message authentication ensures that routers only accept routing messages from other connected routers that know the same preshared key. EIGRP supports routing protocol authentication using MD5.

8. Correct answer: B. Explanation: The output in the exhibit is the result of using the **show ip eigrp interfaces** command.

9. Correct answer: D. Explanation: When an organization has discontiguous networks, automatic summarization can cause inconsistent routing. Automatic summarization does not prevent convergence of the routing table nor does it increase the size of routing updates.

10. 192.168.10.0 255.255.255.128. Explanation: Steps to calculate a summary route:

    1. Count the number of matching bits converting the networks to be summarized in binary:

       192.168.10.0   11000000.10101000.00001010.00000000

       192.168.10.32 11000000.10101000.00001010.00100000

       192.168.10.64 11000000.10101000.00001010.01000000

       ===> 25 matching bits: a /25 subnet prefix or 255.255.255.128 subnet mask

    2. Copy the matching bits, 25 in this case, and add all 0 bits to the end to make 32 bits to find the network address for summarization: 192.168.10.0/25 or 192.168.10.0 255.255.255.128.

11. ::/0. Explanation: The IPv6 address ::/0 is similar to IPv4 address 0.0.0.0 0.0.0.0 (or 0.0.0.0/0).

# Chapter 9

1. Correct answer: A. Explanation: When new feature updates are developed, these are applied to the T train of Cisco IOS Software Release 12.4. The Cisco IOS Software Release 15 family has a 16- to 20-month timeline between extended maintenance releases.

2. Correct answer: D. Explanation: The IOS release after 12.4 is 15.0. There is no IOS Software Release 12.5, 13, or 14.

3. Correct answer: E. Explanation: Even though a "T" on the end of an IOS version means the latest technologies are included as part of the version, any future releases with numbers higher than that include the latest technologies that were released in the "T" version.

4. Correct answer: B. Explanation: The two options of Unified Communications k9 and securityk9 are Cisco IOS Release 15 technology packages. Advanced Enterprise Services contains the full Cisco IOS set of features. Advanced IP Services contains advanced security, service provider services, and support for IPv6. Advanced Security has VPN and firewall features enabled including support for IPsec.

5. Correct answer: A. Explanation: The command syntax to restore an IOS image is **copy** *source destination*, where, in this case, *source* is a TFTP server and *destination* is the router flash memory. The image name (source filename) is entered at a new prompt after the initial **copy** command is issued, not as a parameter of the **copy** command.

6. Correct answer: B. Explanation: In IOS Release 15.0 universal images that support Cisco ISR G2 platforms, the technology package Security offers the security features found in the IPsec framework, such as IKE v1 / IPsec / PKI, IPsec/GRE, and so on.

7. Correct answer: C. Explanation: A production router is a router that is in use on a permanent basis. Only the ipbasek9 license is active.

8. Correct answer: D. Explanation: Beginning with IOS Release 15.0, Cisco modified the process of package licensing. To obtain a license for a technology package, the Unique Device Identifier is required along with the Product Activation Key (PAK). The UDI is a combination of the product ID (PID), the serial number (SN), and the hardware version (VID).

9. Correct answer: B. Explanation: The uck9 package is for Cisco Unified Communications, which includes support for voice over IP and video.

10. Correct answer: A. Explanation: The installation steps are as follows:

    1. Purchase the license key.

    2. Use the **license accept end user agreement** command to accept the EULA.

    3. Use the **license boot module** command to activate the license.

    4. Reload the router.

    5. Use the **show license all** command to verify the installation.

**2.4 GHz (UHF)**   Part of the ultra-high frequency of the ITU radio frequency range allocated to IEEE 802.11b, 802.11g, 802.11n, and 802.11ad.

**5 GHz (SHF)**   Part of the super-high frequency of the ITU radio frequency range allocated to IEEE 802.11a, 802.11n, 802.11ac, and 802.11ad.

**60 GHz (EHF)**   Part of the highest radio band (extremely high frequency) allocated to IEEE 802.11ad.

**802.11**   A standard that defines how radio frequency in the ISM frequency bands is used for the physical layer and the MAC sublayer of wireless links.

**802.11a**   The IEEE standard for wireless LANs using the U-NII spectrum, OFDM encoding, at speeds of up to 54 Mbps.

**802.11ac**   The IEEE standard for wireless LANs operating in the 5-GHz frequency band and provides data rates ranging from 450 Mb/s to 1.3 Gb/s (1300 Mb/s).

**802.11ad**   The IEEE standard, also known as "WiGig" and set for release in 2014, that operates at 2 GHz, 5 GHz, and 60 GHz, with theoretical speeds of up to 7 Gbps.

**802.11b**   The IEEE standard for wireless LANs using the ISM spectrum, DSSS encoding, and speeds of up to 11 Mbps.

**802.11g**   The IEEE standard for wireless LANs using the ISM spectrum, OFDM or DSSS encoding, and speeds of up to 54 Mbps.

**802.11n**   The IEEE standard for wireless LANs using the ISM spectrum, OFDM encoding, and multiple antennas for single-stream speeds up to 150 Mbps.

# A

**access layer**   The access layer in the three-layer hierarchical network model that describes the portion of the network where devices connect to the network and includes controls for allowing devices to communicate on the network.

**Acknowledgment packet**   Used to acknowledge the receipt of an EIGRP message that was sent using reliable delivery.

**ad hoc mode**   A WLAN topology, also called independent basic service set, where mobile clients connect directly without an intermediate access point. Referred to as IBSS by the IEEE.

**Advanced Encryption Standard (AES)**
The National Institute of Standards and Technology (NIST) adopted AES to replace the existing DES encryption in cryptographic devices. AES provides stronger security than DES and is computationally more efficient than 3DES. AES offers three different key lengths: 128-, 192-, and 256-bit keys.

**Advertised Distance (AD)** See *Reported Distance (RD)*.

**alternate and backup port** A switch port in an RSTP topology that offers an alternate path toward the root bridge. An alternate port assumes a discarding state in a stable, active topology. An alternate port will be present on nondesignated bridges and will make a transition to a designated port if the current path fails.

**application-specific integrated circuit (ASIC)** A development process for implementing integrated circuit designs that are specific to the intended application, as opposed to designs for general-purpose use. For example, ASIC is used in Cisco Express Forwarding to route packets at a higher speed than an individual CPU could support.

**Area Border Router (ABR)** In OSPF, this connects one or more nonbackbone areas to the backbone.

**Automatic summarization** A routing protocol feature in which a router that connects to more than one classful network advertises summarized routes for each entire classful network when sending updates out interfaces connected to other classful networks.

**autonomous system boundary router (ASBR)** In OSPF, a router that exchanges routes between OSPF and another routing domain through route redistribution. Routes are injected into OSPF from an ASBR. An ASBR communicates the OSPF routes into another routing domain. The ASBR runs OSPF and another routing protocol.

# B

**Backbone area** In OSPFv2 and OSPFv3, the special area in a multiarea design with all non-backbone areas needing to connect to the backbone area, area 0.

**Backbone router** In OSPF, a router that is configured to participate in area 0 or the backbone area. A backbone router can also be an ABR or ASBR.

**Backup Designated Router (BDR)** In OSPF, a backup to the designated router (DR) in case the DR fails.

**Basic Service Area (BSA)** The area of radio frequency coverage provided by an access point. This area is also referred to as a microcell.

**Basic Service Set (BSS)** A WLAN infrastructure mode whereby mobile clients use a single access point for connectivity to each other or to wired network resources.

**Basic Service Set Identifier (BSSID)** The MAC address of the access point serving the BSS.

**beacon** A wireless LAN packet that signals the availability and presence of the wireless device. Beacon packets are sent by access points and base stations; however, client radio cards send beacons when operating in computer-to-computer (ad hoc) mode.

**blocking state** A port is in the blocking state if it is a nondesignated port and does not participate in frame forwarding. The port continues to process received BPDU frames to determine the location and root ID of the root bridge and what port role the switch port should assume in the final active STP topology.

**Bluetooth** Originally an IEEE 802.15 WPAN standard that uses a device-pairing process to communicate over distances up to 0.05 mile (100m).

**Border Gateway Protocol (BGP)** An exterior gateway routing protocol used by ISPs to propagate routing information.

**bounded updates** Updates that are bounded to those very routers that need the updated information instead of sending updates to all routers.

**BPDU Guard** A Cisco switch feature that listens for incoming STP BPDU messages, disabling the interface if any are received. The goal is to prevent loops when a switch connects to a port expected to only have a host connected to it.

**branch router** A router platform that optimizes branch services while delivering an optimal application experience across branch and WAN infrastructures.

**bridge ID** An 8-byte identifier for bridges and switches used by STP and RSTP. It is comprised of a 2-byte priority field followed by a 6-byte System ID field that is usually filled with a MAC address.

**bridge priority** A customizable value that can be used to influence which switch becomes the root bridge.

**bridge protocol data unit (BPDU)** A frame used by Spanning Tree Protocol to communicate key information about the avoidance of Layer 2 loops in the network topology.

**Broadcast multiaccess** A type of network configuration where multiple routers are interconnected over an Ethernet network.

**broadcast storm** A condition where broadcasts are flooded endlessly, often due to a looping at Layer 2 (bridge loop).

# C

**Carrier Sense Multiple Access with Collision Avoidance (CSMA/CA)** A media access method that requires WLAN devices to sense the medium for energy levels and wait until the medium is free before sending.

**caveat** A software defect that is fixed in an IOS rebuild of an individual release.

**Cellular broadband** Consists of various corporate, national, and international organizations using service provider cellular access to provide mobile broadband network connectivity.

**Cisco Enterprise Architecture** Divides the network into functional components while still maintaining the core, distribution, and access layers of the three-layer model.

**Cisco Express Forwarding (CEF)** A Cisco-proprietary protocol that allows high-speed packet switching in ASICs, rather than using a CPU. CEF offers "wire speed" routing of packets and load balancing.

**Cisco IOS (Cisco Internetwork Operating System)** Cisco operating system software that provides the majority of a router's or switch's features, with the hardware providing the remaining features.

**classless** A concept in IPv4 addressing that defines a subnetted IP address as having two parts: a prefix (or subnet) and a host.

**cluster**   The ability to integrate multiple devices to act as one device to simplify management and configuration.

**Common Spanning Tree (CST)**   The original IEEE 802.1D standard assumes one spanning tree instance for the entire bridged network, regardless of the number of VLANs.

**composite metric**   EIGRP's metric that combines, by default, bandwidth and delay.

**core layer**   The backbone of a switched LAN. All traffic to and from peripheral networks must pass through the core layer. It includes high-speed switching devices that can handle relatively large amounts of traffic.

# D

**default port cost**   The spanning-tree port cost is a measure assigned on a per-link basis in a switched LAN. It is determined by the link bandwidth, with a higher bandwidth giving a lower port cost.

**designated port**   In spanning tree, a nonroot switch port that is permitted to forward traffic on the network. For a trunk link connecting two switches, one end connects to the designated bridge through the designated port. One and only one end of every trunk link in a switched LAN (with spanning tree enabled) connects to a designated port. The selection of designated ports is the last step in the spanning-tree algorithm.

**Designated Router (DR)**   An OSPF router that generates LSAs for a multiaccess network and has other special responsibilities in running OSPF. Each multiaccess OSPF network that has at least two attached routers has a designated router that is elected by the OSPF Hello protocol. The designated router enables a reduction in the number of adjacencies required on a multiaccess network, which in turn reduces the amount of routing protocol traffic and the size of the topological database.

**Diffusing Update Algorithm (DUAL)**   A convergence algorithm used in Enhanced IGRP that provides loop-free operation at every instant throughout a route computation. Allows routers involved in a topology change to synchronize at the same time, while not involving routers that are unaffected by the change.

**Directional Wi-Fi Antenna**   Focuses the radio signal in a given direction to enhance the signal to and from the AP in the direction that the antenna is pointing, providing a stronger signal strength in one direction and less signal strength in all other directions.

**Direct-sequence spread spectrum (DSSS)**   Designed to spread a signal over a larger frequency band, making it more resistant to interference. With DSSS, the signal is multiplied by a "crafted noise" known as a spreading code.

**disabled port**   A port that is administratively shut down.

**disabled state**   A switch port is in the spanning-tree disabled state if it is administratively shut down. A disabled port does not function in the spanning-tree process.

**distance vector routing protocol**   A type of routing protocol where a router's routing table is based on hop-by-hop metrics and is only aware of the topology from a viewpoint of its directly connected neighbors. EIGRP and RIP are examples of distance vector routing protocols.

**Distributed Coordination Function (DCF)**
A collision avoidance mechanism in which a wireless client transmits only if the channel is clear. All transmissions are acknowledged. Therefore, if a wireless client does not receive an acknowledgment, it assumes that a collision occurred and retries after a random waiting interval.

**distribution layer**   In the three-layer hierarchical network design model, the distribution layer is the layer that invokes policy and routing control. Typically, VLANs are defined at this layer.

**DROTHER**   A router in an OSPF multiaccess network that is neither the DR nor the BDR.

# E

**edge port**   An RSTP edge port is a switch port that is never intended to be connected to another switch device. It immediately transitions to the forwarding state when enabled. Edge ports are conceptually similar to PortFast-enabled ports in the Cisco implementation of IEEE 802.1D.

**Enhanced Interior Gateway Routing Protocol (EIGRP)**   An advanced version of IGRP developed by Cisco. Provides superior convergence properties and operating efficiency, and combines the advantages of link-state protocols with those of distance vector protocols.

**Enterprise Campus**   In the Cisco Enterprise Architecture, this module consists of the entire campus infrastructure, to include the access, distribution, and core layers.

**Enterprise Edge**   In the Cisco Enterprise Architecture, this module consists of the Internet, VPN, and WAN modules connecting the enterprise with the service provider's network.

**enterprise network**   A large and diverse network connecting most major points in a company or other organization. Differs from a WAN in that it is privately owned and maintained.

**equal-cost load balancing**   When a router utilizes multiple paths with the same administrative distance and cost to a destination.

**EtherChannel**   A feature in which up to eight parallel Ethernet segments between the same two devices, each using the same speed, can be combined to act as a single link for forwarding and Spanning Tree Protocol logic.

**extended maintenance release**   A Cisco IOS release that incorporates the features and hardware support of all the previous T releases.

**Extended Service Area (ESA)**   The coverage area of an ESS.

**Extended Service Set (ESS)**   A WLAN infrastructure mode whereby two or more basic service sets are connected by a common distribution system. An ESS generally includes a common SSID to allow roaming from access point to access point without requiring client configuration.

**extended system ID**   Constitutes 12 bits of the 8-byte BID and contains the ID of the VLAN with which an STP BPDU is associated. The presence of the extended system ID results in bridge priority values incrementing in multiples of 4096.

# F

**failure domain**   An area of a network that is impacted when a critical device or network service experiences problems.

**Feasible Condition (FC)**   If the receiving router has a Feasible Distance to a particular network and it receives an update from a neighbor with a lower advertised distance (reported distance) to that network, there is a feasibility condition. Used in EIGRP routing.

**Feasible Distance (FD)**   The metric of a network advertised by the connected neighbor plus the cost of reaching that neighbor. The path with the lowest metric is added to the routing table and is called FD or Feasible Distance. Used in EIGRP routing.

**Feasible Successor (FS)**   A next-hop router that leads to a certain destination network. The Feasible Successor can be thought of as a backup next hop if the primary next hop (successor) goes down. Used in EIGRP routing.

**Finite State Machine (FSM)**   A workflow model for an algorithm that has a finite number of stages.

**First Hop Redundancy Protocols (FHRP)** A class of protocols that includes HSRP, VRRP, and GLBP, which allows multiple redundant routers on the same subnet to act as a single default router (first-hop router).

**fixed configuration**   A device with a set number of interfaces.

**forwarding rates**   Define the processing capabilities of a switch by rating how much data the switch can process per second.

**forwarding state**   An STP port in the forwarding state is considered part of the active topology and forwards data frames as well as sending and receiving BPDU frames.

**frequency-hopping spread spectrum (FHSS)** Like DSSS, this relies on spread-spectrum methods to communicate, but transmits radio signals by rapidly switching among many frequency channels.

# G

**Gateway Load Balancing Protocol (GLBP)** A Cisco-proprietary protocol that provides both redundancy and load balancing of data. This is through the use of multiple routers. Routers present a shared GLBP address that end stations use as a default gateway.

# H

**Hello packet**   A packet used by OSPF and EIGRP routers to discover, establish, and maintain neighbor relationships.

**hierarchical network**   A design methodology for building networks in three layers including access, distribution, and core.

**Hot Standby Router Protocol (HSRP)** A Cisco-proprietary protocol that allows two (or more) routers to share the duties of being the default router on a subnet, with an active/ standby model, with one router acting as the default router and the other sitting by waiting to take over that role if the first router fails.

# I

**ICMP Router Discovery Protocol (IRDP)**
A legacy FHRP solution that allows IPv4 hosts to locate routers that provide IPv4 connectivity to other (nonlocal) IP networks.

**IEEE 802.11i/WPA2**    The industry standard for securing wireless networks. The Wi-Fi Alliance version is called WPA2. Both use AES for encryption.

**IEEE 802.1D-2004**    Refers to the original version of the Spanning Tree Protocol specification. See *Spanning Tree Protocol*.

**IEEE 802.1w (RSTP)**    The IEEE standard for an enhanced version of STP, called Rapid STP, which speeds convergence.

**in-band management**    To monitor and make configuration changes to a network device over a network connection using Telnet, SSH, or HTTP access.

**infrastructure mode**    Wireless clients interconnect through a wireless router or AP, such as in WLANs. APs connect to the network infrastructure using the wired distribution system (DS), such as Ethernet.

**internal router**    An OSPF router that has all of its interfaces in the same area. All internal routers in an area have identical LSDBs.

**International Telecommunication Union - Radiocommunication Sector (ITU-R)**    One of the three sectors (divisions or units) of the International Telecommunication Union (ITU), and is responsible for radio communication.

**Internet Assigned Numbers Authority (IANA)**    An organization operated under the auspices of the ISOC as part of the IAB. The IANA delegates authority for IP address space allocation and domain-name assignment to the NIC and other organizations. The IANA also maintains a database of assigned protocol identifiers used in the TCP/IP stack, including autonomous system numbers.

# K

**key**    A secret used in the MD5 encryption algorithm and shared between routers to authenticate packets.

**keychain**    A configuration method that allows the use of multiple keys for the same keychain.

# L

**LACP active**    In this state, the port initiates negotiations with other ports by sending LACP packets.

**LACP passive**    In this state, the port responds to the LACP packets that it receives, but does not initiate LACP packet negotiation.

**learning state**    The IEEE 802.1D learning state is seen in both a stable active topology and during topology synchronization changes. During the learning state, a port accepts data frames to populate the MAC address table in an effort to limit flooding of unknown unicast frames.

**Lightweight AP**    An AP that communicates with a WLAN controller using the Lightweight Access Control Point Protocol (LWAPP).

**link aggregation**    A method of implementing multiple links between equipment to increase bandwidth.

**Link Aggregation Control Protocol (LACP)**    An industry-standard protocol that aids in the automatic creation of EtherChannel links.

**link-state routing protocol**    A routing protocol classification where each router has a topology database based on an SPF tree through the network, with knowledge of all nodes. OSPF and IS-IS are examples of link-state routing protocols.

**listening state**    The IEEE 802.1D listening state is seen in both a stable active topology and during topology synchronization changes. In the listening state, the port cannot send or receive data frames; however, the port is allowed to receive and send BPDUs.

**load balancing**    The capability of a networking device to distribute traffic over some of its network ports on the path to the destination. Load balancing increases the utilization of network segments, thus increasing effective network bandwidth.

**LSA Type 1**    Sent by all routers to advertise their directly connected OSPF-enabled links and forward their network information to OSPF neighbors.

**LSA Type 2**    Only used by the DR in multiaccess and nonbroadcast multiaccess (NBMA) networks to give other routers information about multiaccess networks within the same area. Contains the router ID and IP address of the DR, along with the router ID of all other routers on the multiaccess segment.

**LSA Type 3**    Used by an ABR to advertise networks from other areas.

**LSA Type 4**    Generated by an ABR only when an ASBR exists within an area. Identifies the ASBR and provides a route to it.

**LSA Type 5**    Originated by the ASBR and describes routes to networks outside the OSPF autonomous system.

# M

**mainline train**    A release of the Cisco IOS that receives mostly software (bug) fixes with the goal of increasing software quality. A mainline train is always associated with a technology train.

**man-in-the-middle attack**    Carried out by an attacker who positions himself between two legitimate hosts. The attacker might allow the normal transactions between hosts to occur, and only periodically manipulate the conversation between the two.

**MD5 authentication**    An algorithm used for message authentication. MD5 verifies the integrity of the communication, authenticates the origin, and checks for timeliness.

**MIMO**    Multiple-input and multiple-output antenna. Used in IEEE 802.11n wireless devices, splits a high-data-rate stream into multiple lower-rate streams and broadcasts them simultaneously over the available radios and antennas. This allows for a theoretical maximum data rate of 248 Mbps.

**modular configuration** A device that uses a module design that allows for upgrading the device with different or possibly newer interface configurations.

**Multiarea OSPF** A method for scaling an OSPF implementation. As an OSPF network is expanded, other, nonbackbone areas can be created.

**multilayer switch** Characterized by its ability to build a routing table, support a few routing protocols, and forward IP packets at a rate close to that of Layer 2 forwarding.

**Multiple Spanning Tree Protocol (MSTP)** MSTP, introduced as IEEE 802.1s, is an evolution of IEEE 802.1D STP and IEEE 802.1w (RSTP). MSTP enables multiple VLANs to be mapped to the same spanning-tree instance, reducing the number of instances needed to support a large number of VLANs.

# N

**network edge router** Delivers high-performance, highly secure, and reliable services that unite campus, data center, and branch networks.

**Nonbroadcast multiaccess (NBMA)** A characterization of a type of Layer 2 network in which more than two devices connect to the network, but the network does not allow broadcast frames to be sent to all devices on the network.

**Null0** A virtual IOS interface that is a route to nowhere, commonly known as "the bit bucket." Packets that match a route with a Null0 exit interface are discarded.

# O

**Omnidirectional Wi-Fi Antenna** Uses basic dipole antennas that provide 360-degree coverage and are ideal in open office areas, hallways, conference rooms, and outside areas.

**Open Shortest Path First (OSPF)** A scalable, link-state routing protocol used by many networks inside companies.

**orthogonal frequency-division multiplexing (OFDM)** A frequency modulation technique used with IEEE 802.11g and IEEE 802.11a in which a single channel utilizes multiple subchannels on adjacent frequencies.

**OSPF Hello and Dead intervals** Timers in OSPF used to maintain neighbor adjacency. By default, if an OSPF router does not hear from its neighbor after four Hello intervals, the neighbor is considered down (dead). Configured Hello and Dead intervals must match between neighbors.

**out-of-band management** Used for initial configuration of a device or when network access is unavailable. Requires direct connection to the console or AUX port and terminal emulation software.

# P

**PAgP auto** Places an interface in a passive negotiating state in which the interface responds to the PAgP packets that it receives, but does not initiate PAgP negotiation.

**PAgP desirable** Places an interface in an active negotiating state in which the interface initiates negotiations with other interfaces by sending PAgP packets.

**partial updates** An update only includes information about the route changes, such as a new link or a link becoming unavailable.

**point-to-multipoint** Multiple devices interconnected in a hub-and-spoke topology over an NBMA network.

**point-to-point** Two devices interconnected over a common link. No other devices are on the link.

**Port Aggregation Protocol (PAgP)** A Cisco-proprietary protocol that aids in the automatic creation of EtherChannel links.

**port density** The number of interfaces supported on a switch.

**PortFast** A switch STP feature in which a port is placed in an STP forwarding state as soon as the interface comes up, bypassing the listening and learning states. This feature is meant for ports connected to end-user devices.

**Power over Ethernet (PoE)** Allows the switch to deliver power to a device over the existing Ethernet cabling. This feature can be used by IP phones and some wireless access points.

**Product Activation Key (PAK)** The number assigned by Cisco, during the IOS licensing process, that gives a Cisco customer the right to enable an IOS feature set on one of that customer's routers of a particular model series (chosen at the time the PAK was purchased).

**protocol-dependent module (PDM)** A component that depends on a certain routed protocol. For example, protocol-dependent modules in EIGRP allow it to work with various routed protocols. PDMs allow EIGRP to keep a topology table for each routed protocol such as IP, IPX RIP, AppleTalk Routing Table Maintenance Protocol (RTMP), and IGRP.

**PVST+** A Cisco enhancement of STP that provides a separate 802.1D spanning-tree instance for each VLAN configured in the network.

# Q

**quad zero** A common phrase used to describe the dotted-decimal address 0.0.0.0 used in default routing.

**Query packet** In EIGRP, used to request specific information from a neighbor router.

# R

**Rapid PVST+** A Cisco-proprietary implementation of RSTP.

**Rapid Spanning Tree Protocol (RSTP)** An IEEE 802.1w standard that defines an improved version of STP that converges much more quickly and consistently than STP (802.1d).

**redundancy** The duplication of devices, services, or connections so that, in the event of a failure, the redundant devices, services, or connections can perform the work of those that failed.

**regional Internet registry (RIR)** The generic term for one of five current organizations responsible for assigning the public, globally unique IPv4 and IPv6 address space.

**reliability**    In terms of design, the ability of a network to be up most of the time. Sometimes referred to as 99.999, or "five nines" reliability.

**Reliable Transport Protocol (RTP)**    Unique to EIGRP and provides delivery of EIGRP packets to neighbors. EIGRP does not use TCP.

**Reply packet**    In EIGRP, used to respond to a query.

**Reported Distance (RD)**    The total metric along a path to a destination network as advertised by an upstream neighbor in EIGRP.

**root bridge**    The root of a spanning-tree topology. A root bridge exchanges topology information with other bridges in a spanning-tree topology to notify all other bridges in the network when topology changes are required. This prevents loops and provides a measure of defense against link failure.

**root port**    The unique port on a nonroot bridge that has the lowest path cost to the root bridge. Every nonroot bridge in an STP topology must elect a root port. The root port on a switch is used for communication between the switch and the root bridge.

**route redistribution**    The process of injecting a route from one route source into the routing process of another route source.

**route summarization**    The process of aggregating multiple routes into one routing advertisement to reduce the size of routing tables.

# S

**satellite broadband**    An Internet access method using a directional satellite dish that is aligned with a specific geostationary Earth orbit (GEO) satellite. It is usually more expensive and requires a clear line of sight.

**Server Farm and Data Center Module**    In the Cisco Enterprise Architecture, this module provides high-speed connectivity and protection for servers. It is critical to provide security, redundancy, and fault tolerance.

**Service Provider Edge**    In the Cisco Enterprise Architecture, this module provides Internet, Public Switched Telephone Network (PSTN), and WAN services.

**service provider router**    Responsible for differentiating the service portfolio and increasing revenues by delivering end-to-end scalable solutions and subscriber-aware services.

**service set identifier (SSID)**    A code attached to all packets on a wireless network to identify each packet as part of that network. The code is a case-sensitive text string that consists of a maximum of 32 alphanumeric characters. All wireless devices attempting to communicate with each other must share the same SSID. Apart from identifying each packet, the SSID also serves to uniquely identify a group of wireless network devices used in a given service set.

**Services Module**    In the Cisco Enterprise Architecture, this module provides access to all services, such as IP telephony services, wireless controller services, and unified services.

shared link   In LAN environments, a port operating in half-duplex mode because the switch is connected to a hub that attaches to multiple devices.

Single-Area OSPF   An OSPF configuration that only uses one area, the backbone area 0.

single-homed   An Internet access design in which the organization only has one connection to a service provider.

software release families   Comprised of multiple IOS Software release versions that share a code base, apply to related hardware platforms, and overlap in support coverage with the next OS version.

software trains   Used to deliver releases with a common code base to a specific set of platforms and features.

Spanning Tree Protocol (STP)   A protocol defined by IEEE standard 802.1D. Allows switches and bridges to create a redundant LAN, with the protocol dynamically causing some ports to block traffic so that the bridge/switch forwarding logic will not cause frames to loop indefinitely around the LAN.

SSID   See *service set identifier*.

SSID cloaking   A code attached to all packets on a wireless network to identify each packet as part of that network. The code is a case-sensitive text string that consists of a maximum of 32 alphanumeric characters. All wireless devices attempting to communicate with each other must share the same SSID. Apart from identifying each packet, the SSID also serves to uniquely identify a group of wireless network devices used in a given service set.

stackable configuration   Devices that are capable of being connected to other like devices to provide higher port density.

standard maintenance release   A T release. See *technology train*.

Successor   The path to a destination. The successor is chosen using DUAL from all the known paths or feasible successors to the end destination. Used in EIGRP.

# T

technology train   Also called a T train. A release of the Cisco IOS that receives the same software bug fixes as the mainline train. Also receives new software and hardware support features.

Temporal Key Integrity Protocol (TKIP)   Also referred to as Temporary Key Integrity Protocol, TKIP was designed by the IEEE 802.11i task group and the Wi-Fi Alliance as a solution to replace WEP without requiring the replacement of legacy hardware. This was necessary because the breaking of WEP had left Wi-Fi networks without viable link-layer security, and a solution was required for already deployed hardware. The Wi-Fi Alliance endorsed TKIP under the name Wi-Fi Protected Access (WPA). The IEEE also endorsed TKIP.

time to live (TTL)   The field in an IP header that indicates how long a packet is considered valid. Each routing device that an IP packet passes through decrements the TTL by 1.

type, length, value (TLV)   The data portion of the EIGRP packet. All TLVs begin with a 16-bit Type field and a 16-bit Length field. Different

TLV values exist according to the routed protocol. There is, however, a general TLV that describes generic EIGRP parameters such as Sequence (used by Cisco Reliable Multicast) and EIGRP software version.

# U

unequal-cost load balancing   Load balancing that uses multiple paths to the same destination that have different costs or metrics. EIGRP uses unequal-cost load balancing with the **variance** command.

unique device identifier (UID)   Required to obtain a Cisco license, the UID is a combination of the Product ID (PID), the Serial Number (SN), and the hardware version.

Update packet   An EIGRP packet used to convey routing information to neighbors about known destinations.

# V

virtual links   A special OSPF network used to interconnect distant OSPF areas to the backbone area.

Virtual Router Redundancy Protocol (VRRP)   A TCP/IP RFC protocol that allows two (or more) routers to share the duties of being the default router on a subnet, with an active/standby model, with one router acting as the default router and the other sitting by waiting to take over that role if the first router fails.

# W

Wi-Fi (wireless fidelity)   An IEEE 802.11 WLAN standard commonly deployed to provide network access to home and corporate users, to include data, voice, and video traffic to distances up to 300m (0.18 mile).

Wi-Fi Alliance   The Wi-Fi Alliance owns the trademark to Wi-Fi. The Wi-Fi Alliance is a global, nonprofit, industry trade association devoted to promoting the growth and acceptance of wireless technology.

Wi-Fi Protected Access (WPA)   A class of systems to secure wireless LANs. It was created in response to several serious weaknesses researchers had found in the previous system, Wired Equivalent Privacy (WEP). WPA implements the majority of the IEEE 802.11i standard and was intended as an intermediate measure to take the place of WEP while IEEE 802.11i was prepared. WPA is specifically designed to also work with pre-WPA wireless network interface cards (through firmware upgrades), but not necessarily with first-generation wireless access points. WPA2 implements the full standard and supports AES encryption (WPA does not support AES).

WiMAX (Worldwide Interoperability for Microwave Access)   An IEEE 802.16 WWAN standard that provides wireless broadband access of up to 30 miles (50 km). WiMAX is an alternative to cable and DSL broadband connections. Mobility was added to WiMAX in 2005 and can now be used by service providers to provide cellular broadband.

wire speed   The data rate that an Ethernet port on a switch is capable of attaining.

**Wired Equivalent Privacy (WEP)**    An algorithm to secure IEEE 802.11 wireless networks. Wireless networks broadcast messages using radio frequencies and are more susceptible to eavesdropping than wired networks. WEP, introduced in 1999, was intended to provide confidentiality comparable to that of a traditional wired network.

**wireless access point (AP)**    A device that connects wireless communication devices to form a wireless network, analogous to a hub connecting wired devices to form a LAN. The AP usually connects to a wired network and can relay data between wireless devices and wired devices. Several APs can link together to form a larger network that allows roaming.

**Wireless LAN (WLAN)**    A LAN with access points, together with the devices supporting them and supported by them.

**Wireless Personal-Area Network (WPAN)**    Operates in the range of a few feet. Bluetooth or Wi-Fi Direct-enabled devices are used in WPANs.

**Wireless Wide-Area Network (WWAN)**    Operates in the range of miles such as a metropolitan area, cellular hierarchy, or even on intercity links through microwave relays.

# Y

**Yagi antenna**    Type of directional radio antenna that can be used for long-distance Wi-Fi networking. These antennas are typically used to extend the range of outdoor hotspots in a specific direction, or to reach an outbuilding.

# P

## Q-R

## X-Y-Z

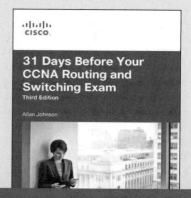